The
Heyday
of Sail

The Heyday of Sail

The Merchant Sailing
Ship 1650–1830

Editor: Robert Gardiner
Consultant Editor: Dr Philip Bosscher

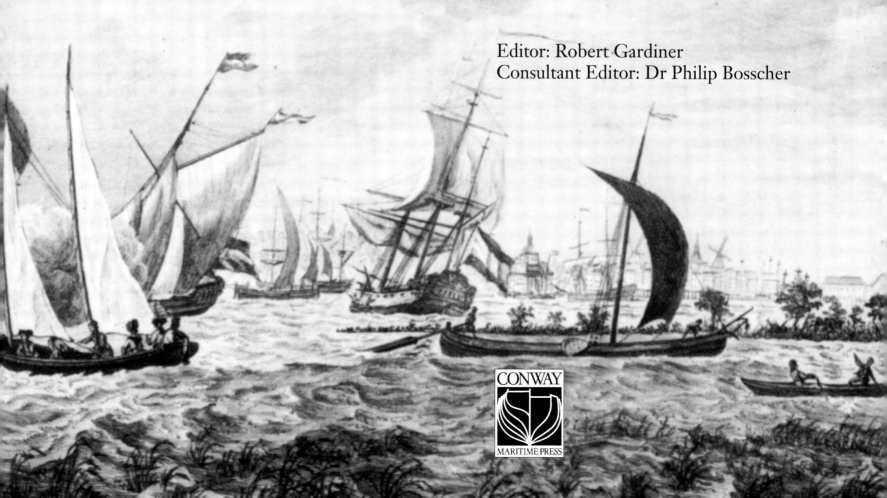

CONWAY
MARITIME PRESS

Series Consultant Dr Basil Greenhill
CB, CMG, FSA, FRHistS

Series Editor Robert Gardiner

Consultant Editor Dr Philip Bosscher

Contributors Dr Philip Bosscher
Carl Olof Cederlund
Henk Dessens
Dr Christopher French
A J Hoving
Dr A H J Prins
Dr P C van Royen

Frontispiece: Rotterdam seen from thr river Maas in 1780, engraving by Matthias de Sallieth after Dirk de Jong. Although past its economic zenith by this date, the Netherlands still depended heavily on shipborne trade, and her ports continued to see a plethora of ship types. From left to right the ships types are: a hoeker, *the Rotterdam-Katendrecht ferry (with a horse-drawn carriage on deck), a three-masted galliot, with a* paviljoenjacht *beyond, and various small craft in the foreground.* (Rijksmuseum, Amsterdam)

© 1995 Brassey's (UK) Ltd

First published in Great Britain 1995 by
Conway Maritime Press, an imprint of Brassey's (UK) Ltd
33 John Street, London WC1N 2AT

British Library Cataloguing-in Publication Data
The Heyday of Sail: The Merchant Sailing Ship 1650–1830
(Conway's History of the Ship Series)
  I. Bosscher, Philip II. Gardiner, Robert
  III. Series
  623.8

ISBN 0 85177 562 4

Typesetting, design and page make-up by Tony Hart
Printed and bound by the The Bath Press, Bath

Contents

Preface

THIS TITLE is the penultimate in an ambitious programme of twelve volumes intended to provide the first detailed and comprehensive account of a technology that has shaped human history. It has been conceived as a basic reference work, the essential first stop for anyone seeking information on any aspect of the subject, so it is more concerned to be complete than to be original. However, the series takes full account of all the latest research and in certain areas is publishing entirely new material. In the matter of interpretation care has been taken to avoid the old myths and to present only the most widely accepted modern viewpoints.

To tell a coherent story, in a more readable form than is usual with encyclopaedias, each volume takes the form of independent chapters, all by recognised authorities in the field. Most chapters are devoted to the ships themselves, but others deal with topics like 'Shipping Economics and Trade' that are more generally applicable, giving added depth to the reader's understanding of developments. Some degree of generalisation is inevitable when tackling a subject of this breadth, but wherever possible the specific details of ships and their characteristics have been included. With a few historically unavoidable exceptions, the series is confined to seagoing vessels; to have included boats would have increased the scope of an already massive task.

The history of the ship is not a romanticised story of epic battles and heroic voyages but equally it is not simply a matter of technological advances. Ships were built to carry out particular tasks and their design was as much influenced by the experience of that employment—the lessons or war, or the conditions of trade, for example—as purely technical innovation. Throughout this series an attempt has been made to keep this clearly in view, to describe the *what* and *when* of developments without losing sight of the *why*.

The series is aimed at those with some knowledge of, and interest in, ships and the sea. It would have been impossible to make a contribution of any value to the subject if it had been pitched at the level of the complete novice, so while there is an extensive glossary, for example, it assumes an understanding of the most basic nautical terms. Similarly, the bibliography avoids very general works and concentrates on those which will broaden or deepen the reader's understanding beyond the level of the *History of the Ship*. The intention is not to inform genuine experts in their particular area of expertise, but to provide them with the best available single-volume summaries of less familiar fields.

Each volume is chronological in approach, with the periods covered getting shorter as the march of technology quickens, but organised around a dominant theme—represented by the title of the book—that sums up the period in question. In this way each book is fully self-sufficient, although when completed the twelve titles will link up to form a coherent history, chronicling the progress of ship design from its earliest recorded forms to the present day.

This volume has proved one of the most difficult to assemble, partly because of the vast range and variety of merchant ship types to be found at sea between 1650 and 1830, but primarily because only a fraction of them have been the subject of serious study. The economic importance of some types, like the Dutch flute, has been recognised, but often it is the large—and very atypical—vessels like East Indiamen that have received most scholarly attention. Given the fragmented and small-scale nature of shipowning for most of our period, it is inevitable that organisations like the great trading companies, with their extensive and well preserved archives, should be the primary target of academic research. However, the sum of these problems is that it is still very difficult to get much sense of coherent develop-

ment within merchant ship design—there are simply too many variations, influenced by too many local conditions.

We have responded to this difficulty by concentrating not on ship types as such but on geographical areas. Had we but world enough and time, additional chapters could have covered other parts of the globe—the absence of anything on Indian Ocean and Far Eastern traditions is a particular regret—but, at the risk of seeming Euro-centric, we feel justified in emphasising those economies that dominated the period. In 1650 the chief trading nation was the Netherlands; by 1830 it was Great Britain, and much of this book is concerned with that shift in power. Furthermore, it was usually through trade that the rest of the world first came to experience European influence, and whatever the rights and wrongs of imperialism it is difficult to play down its impact.

Despite the focus on the leading European maritime nations, the northern and southern peripheries have not been ignored. Both the Baltic and the Mediterranean experience conditions that are individual enough to have produced very distinctive ship designs, and two lengthy chapters are devoted to the most important of these local types.

Other departures from the overall pattern of the series are the inclusion of a survey of European inland vessels and a brief look at pleasure craft. Both might be regarded as excluded by the 'seagoing ships only' criterion, but the riverine vessels are mostly sailing types (rather than towed barges), while early pleasure craft are usually large enough to be seagoing. In any case, both are significant aspects of non-naval shipping and deserve some reference within the series; and because they are not covered elsewhere, both chapters exceed the 1650 to 1830 parameters of this volume.

Robert Gardiner
Series Editor

Introduction

WHEN I WAS teaching naval history in the Royal Netherlands Naval Academy at Den Helder I always devoted particular attention to the development of shipbuilding and naval armament during the last three centuries. When I introduced that subject I used to say that if a seaman from Admiral De Ruyter's *De Zeven Provincien* was transferred by a time machine, for instance, to Admiral Nelson's *Victory* he would not need

much time to become conversant with the construction, rigging and armament of the latter vessel. More or less the same thing can be said about merchant sailing ships during the period covered in this book. An important witness for the truth of the statement just made is Dr Alan McGowan. In his admirable short survey of the development of sailing ships during 'the century before steam' he uses the word 'gradual' remarkably often when describing changing trends in shipbuilding and rigging.[1] Yet, this still implies that there were changes in shipbuilding and rigging practice. Some of the most important should be mentioned here. About 1703 the steering wheel began to be

adopted (like so many innovations which date from the period covered in this book it was first tried in a warship). The triangular headsail, or jib, made its appearance towards the end of the seventeenth century. Not long after the first

A significant factor in the dominance of seventeenth-century Dutch merchant shipping was the fluit *or* flyboat, *a capacious but economical carrier. Its origins go back to before 1650 but it continued to be developed for a hundred years or more. One advantage was that the same basic hull form and rig could be applied to vessels of different sizes, as demonstrated by the two* fluits *in this painting by Abraham Matthys. However, broader-sterned ship types like the cat, or the* bootship *shown on the right of this picture, built on the success of the* fluyt *in the following centuries. (Private Collection)*

1. See Alan McGowan, *The Century before Steam. The Development of the Sailing Ship1700-1820* (London 1980), fourth volume of 'The Ship' series of ten short books published under the auspices of the National Maritime Museum.

Developed in response to the special shoal conditions on the coast of the Netherlands, the 'camel' was a primitive floating dock designed to lift deep-sea ships over the shallows and mudflats at the entrance to Dutch harbours and waterways, especially Amsterdam. The camel consisted of two parts, the insides of which were approximately shaped to the outsides of the ship's hull. Both parts were flooded down, lashed to the ship, and when the water was pumped out of the camel, the complete ensemble floated up to a draught that allowed it to be towed over the shallows. The process was reversed to allow the ship to sail on. This engraving dates from 1705.

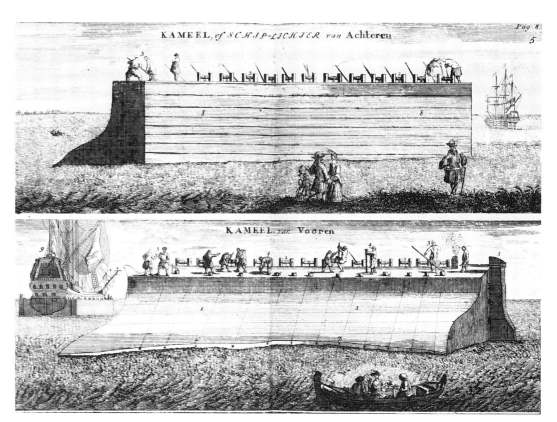

cats were built; a derivation of the *fluyt* or flyboat, the type was particularly suitable for the timber trade. Towards the end of the Napoleonic Wars the British naval constructor Sir Robert Seppings (1767-1840) perfected a new method of diagonally braced hull construction which made it possible to build wooden ships much longer than had been practicable before.

Much was done to provide naval architecture with a more solid theoretical foundation. In this connection at least two names should be mentioned. The first is that of Nicolaes Witsen, burgomaster of Amsterdam (1641-1717). His *Aeloude en Hedendaegsche Scheepsbouw en Bestier* ('Ancient and Present-day Shipbuilding and Government') was first published in 1671, followed by a second edition in 1690. Witsen was a *savant* with a profound interest in, and deep knowledge of, his subject. He definitely was not a naval architect or shipbuilder. This circumstance naturally has a bearing on the usefulness of his book–the first comprehensive treatise on the art of shipbuilding ever published in the Netherlands–as a practical guide to the shipwright's buisness. It is not easy to follow, and one of the contributors to this volume did good work when he recently 'opened up' Witsen's work and demonstrated how it could be used as a builder's manual. The other name that should be mentioned here is that of Fredrik Henrik af Chapman (1721-1808).[2] This Swede of English extraction (his father was a Yorkshireman) was very much a practical shipbuilder: he ended his professional career as Chief Constructor to the Swedish Royal Navy. He made his mark as the author of important books on shipbuilding, among which *Architectura Navalis Mercatoria*, first published in 1768, perhaps holds pride of place, but also as one of the first shipbuilders, if not the first one, who ever used a tank for the testing of ship models.

Such achievements should not obscure the fact that the development of naval architecture and shipbuilding, at least in so far it affected merchant ships, was of a basically gradual nature. However, there were developments in other fields which profoundly influenced the employment of these ships and were by no means always gradual. A summary of the most important of these follows.

Political changes had a great impact on the patterns of maritime trade. England and the Netherlands acquired vast overseas empires, but both subsequently lost important parts of them. The United States of America gained their independence in a war which lasted from 1775 to 1783. The Netherlands lost nearly their entire overseas empire, to Britain, during the American War of Independence and the Napoleonic Wars. However, they regained most of it after the fall of Napoleon and both Britain and the Netherlands remained colonial powers until long after the period covered in this book. France had to surrender most of its original colonial empire (but not the West Indian possesions which were perhaps the most valuable according to the standards of the time) at the end of the Seven Years' War, in 1763. Spain lost most of its Latin American possessions–although not, for the time being, Puerto Rico and Cuba, nor the Philippines–when their 'Creole' populations rebelled after the fall of Napoleon. Portugal lost its most important colony when the Regent of Brazil, a scion of the Portuguese Royal House, let himself be persuaded to proclaim that country's independence in 1822. Portugal retained the remainder of its overseas possessions, but this was in fact no more than a string of factories with in most cases an undeveloped and often unexplored hinterland. Russian forces took the fortress of Azov in 1696 and so opened up access to the Black Sea. In 1702-1703 the army of Czar Peter the Great took the Swedish fortresses of Nöteborg and Nyenschants, so Russia regaining direct access to the Baltic. Soon after, the Czar started building a new capital at the mouth of the river Neva, the present St Petersburg. During the subsequent decades Russia, with much assistance from foreign–chiefly Netherlands and British–experts, developed into a naval, if not a maritime,[3] power of the first rank. It soon started to build up an impressive record in the field of maritime exploration. In this connection the name of Vitus Bering (1681-1741), a Dane by birth, should be mentioned. He discovered the strait named after him, and Alaska (which remained Russian until 1867).

In the eighteenth century several other countries engaged to some degree in explo-

---

2. This choice of two names is, of course, arbitrary and determined by my personal background. Had that been different it would perhaps have included the French naval architect Antoine Groignard (1727-1798) or Jorge Juan who in the middle of the eighteenth century designed the dockyards of Cartagena and Ferrol.

3. The development of its merchant navy was certainly not comparable to that of its fighting fleet and the country remained basically 'continental' in orientation.

ration of the Pacific – and so made possible the extension of maritime trade. However, this vast ocean only became something of a *mare liberum* in the course of the following century. This was mainly due to the restrictions the Spanish authorities imposed upon ships of other nations (a reminder how much the patterns of trade were influenced by the monopolistic and mercantilist ideas prevalent in Europe from the seventeenth century to about 1850).[4] Jacob Roggeveen (1659-1729), a native of the Dutch city of Middelburg in Zeeland, discovered Easter Island in 1721-1722, part of the Tuamotu Archipelago and the Samoa Islands. Captain Cook (1728-1779) led the three voyages of exploration between 1768 and 1779 which made him deservedly famous. After the Seven Years' War there was a 'veritable rush of English and French voyages of discovery',[5] including Louis Antoine de Bougainville (1729-1811) crossing the Pacific on his famous circumnavigation of the globe. The last great voyages of exploration in the Pacific were led by his countryman Jules Dumont d'Urville (1790-1842), but the Pacific expedition undertaken in 1789-1794 under the leadership of Alexandro Malaspina (1754-1810), an Italian serving in the Spanish navy, deserves to be better known than it is.[6]

During the second half of the eighteenth century the art of navigation made such progress that these voyages of exploration, like any sea voyage, became considerably less hazardous than before. John Harrison (1693-1776) succeeded in designing and constructing a chronometer of such accuracy and reliability that it could be used to calculate a ship's longitude at sea (Captain Cook took a copy of Harrison's fourth 'time-keeper' with him on his second expedition). It was also in Britain that, in 1757, the sextant was developed as an instrument for measuring horizontal and vertical angles at sea. This could also be used to calculate a ship's longitude with a considerable degree of exactness, so disasters like the foundering of Sir Cloudisley Shovell's fleet on the Scillies (1707) could be avoided in the future.

The introduction of the chronometer and the sextant are only two examples of technological innovations which had a great impact on the practice of seafaring. One comes across others when exploring the history of what I would like to call maritime infrastructure: waterways, harbours and the like. In the seventeenth century the first 'mud-mills' were constructed in the Netherlands for the dredging of shallow waterways.[7] Richard Trevithick (1771-1833) constructed one of the first bucket

dredgers in 1806. Improved building techniques made it possible to construct larger graving docks (the first known example was built at Portsmouth in 1495) and to build wet docks (principally for the loading and unloading of ships). At the end of the seventeenth century Edward Dummer supervised the building of the first stepped stone dry docks at Portsmouth and Plymouth. The Port of London got its first two wet docks, at Blackwall and Rotherhithe, in the seventeenth century. The development of Liverpool's dock system started in the eighteenth century. Altogether between 1753 and 1830 some 370 acres of wet docks were provided in England. Not only in Britain, but also in other parts of the world many ports acquired larger and improved facilities during the period covered in this book. To give just one example: between 1655 and 1695 five seaports in the Netherlands devoted substantial sums to the extension or improvement of their harbours. Towards the end of the period just mentioned the 'camel' was developed to lift ships over the mudflats near the entrance to Amsterdam roadstead.[8]

Improved building techniques also made possible an engineering feat like the rebuilding, in 1759, of Eddystone lighthouse, to the design of John Smeaton (1724-1792).[9] Smeaton also devoted his engineering skill to the construction of canals, which was such an important activity in Britain during the initial stages of what we usually call *the* Industrial Revolution.[10] The beginning of what has been called the 'canal revolution' in Britain can be dated to 1742.[11] Before that, France had experienced its heroic period of canal building, when for example the Briare Canal, linking the Loire and the Seine, was constructed (1642). It was followed by an even more spectacular feat of engineering: the Canal du Midi, from Toulouse to Etang de Thau near Agde, with no less than 65 locks (completed in 1681). In the Netherlands the great age of canal building was during the reign of the 'King-Merchant' William I (1813-1840). The Groot Noordhollandsch Kanaal ('Great North Holland Canal') linking Amsterdam with the North Sea (it reaches the open sea at the Texel), was perhaps the greatest engineering work of the age. Its designer was Jan Blanken (1755-1838). A man of many parts, like the leading British engineers of his time, his achievements bear comparison with theirs.[12]

A branch of science the development of which has been of particular importance to seafaring folk is medicine. It is impossible to pay adequate attention here to the saga of naval (or maritime) medicine during the period covered

in this book. Yet the name of James Lind (1716-1794) should be mentioned because of his ultimately successful efforts to combat scurvy.

I would like to end this brief survey by pointing out that in 1807 the British Parliament took an important step towards ending the African slave trade[13] and that during the first half of the nineteenth century piracy in the Mediterranean practically came to an end.[14]

So, if the period 1650-1830 may not have been a time of spectacular advances in the art of building merchant sailing ships, there were many developments which had great impact on the maritime world. Therefore there is ample reason to regard it as a period in maritime history characterised by many and momentous changes.

Dr Philip Bosscher

---

4. Perhaps one can say that this period started with the adoption of the 1651 Navigation Acts in England and ended with their replacement by more liberal laws in 1853-1854.

5. A Carré, 'Eighteenth century French voyages of exploration', in *Starving Sailors. The influence of nutrition on naval and maritime history* (Greenwich 1981), p78.

6. The only account in English of this expedition which I am acquainted with is by Julian de Zulueta and Lola Higueras, 'Health and navigation in the South Seas: the Spanish Experience' on pp85-99 of the publication mentioned in the preceding footnote, the Proceedings of a conference organised by the National Maritime Museum in April 1980.

7. Several pictures and models exist of this engine. It was equipped with 'scooping-boards' instead of buckets. Motive power was supplied by horses harnessed to an horizontal treadmill.

8. As a lifting device the camel was the predecessor of the floating dock which was, as far as I know, a nineteenth century invention.

9. Smeaton's lighthouse survived *in situ* until 1882 when it was moved to Plymouth Hoe where it still stands.

10. Compare my remarks on p134 of this book.

11. See Neil Cossons, 'Rivers and Canals' in *The BP Book of Industrial Archeology* (Newton Abbot 1975), p343.

12. His work is discussed extensively in the essays accompanying a catalogue of an exhibition about him in the Rijksmuseum, Amsterdam: J Bardet and others, *De Physique Existentie dezes Lands. Jan Blanken, Inspecteur-Generaal van de Waterstaat (1755-1838)* (Beetsterzwaag 1987).

13. The Abolition Act of 1807 enacted that no slaver could clear from a British port after 1 May 1807, and that no slave could be landed in a British possession after 1 March 1808. It marked the beginning of a process which put an end to a trade which in the minds of some people had the, undeserved, reputation of being a 'nursery of seamen' and brought death on the Middle Passage or a hardly happier fate to the millions worked to death after their delivery to 'the silver mine or the plantation'. It may be said to have formally ended in 1888 when slavery was abolished in Brazil.

14. Privateering was formally outlawed in April 1856, when the Declaration of Paris, concerning points of maritime law, was adopted by several nations.

1

Merchant Shipping of the British Empire

IN THE TWO centuries following the Restoration in 1660, Britain's economic and imperial position was revolutionised, propelling her from being just one of a number of influential seaborne empires into the world's most powerful industrial nation. Many forces underpinned this advance towards economic and imperial power, and historians have highlighted the wide variety of factors–economic, social, political, and cultural–in explaining Britain's rise to (and subsequent decline from) international supremacy. The expansion of commercial and maritime activity throughout these two centuries must be at the heart of such explanations, highlighting the impact of trade, ports, merchants, and shipping. For example, the growth of Britain's overseas trade helped to widen markets for her industrial products and to ensure a ready supply of essential foodstuffs and raw materials, whilst profits generated by overseas trade could provide a valuable source of finance for future economic development. Similarly, the expansion of port towns such as London, Liverpool, Bristol, Whitehaven, Newcastle and Sunderland stimulated economic activity both in their regions and nationally. In turn the merchant community were instrumental in establishing what Jacob Price has called 'an infrastructure of great utility to the entire economy in the ensuing era of rapid industrialisation' consisting of:

> commercial and financial institutions, including banks, clearing houses, insurance companies, Lloyd's exchange, and the stock exchange . . . commercial practices and law, commercial education . . . human capital and good will created by the worldwide experience of hundreds, even thousands, of firms.[1]

Illustrations of ordinary merchantmen of the mid seventeenth century are rare, and the ships themselves are difficult to tell apart from warships. The use of this etching by Wenceslaus Hollar on the title page of Ussher's Annales *of 1654 suggests a merchant ship, but the complete tier of guns is equally apparent.*

At the centre of this commercial expansion was one of the major industries of the seventeenth, eighteenth and nineteenth centuries– the shipping industry. Shipping was the lifeblood of the British maritime empire, and her diversifying trading network based on the major ports and lubricated by the increasingly sophisticated merchant community, cannot be fully understood without reference to the shipping industry. A large and adaptable shipping industry at this time was essential for opening up trade routes, for protecting those trade routes, for establishing and then protecting a colonial empire, and for supplying both ships and men during periods of war. It is no exaggeration, therefore, to argue that the British shipping industry between 1650 and 1830, in all its rich diversity, was a major element in Britain's growing world influence.

Both merchant and naval vessels were important sectors of the industry, but it is with merchant shipping engaged in both overseas and coasting trade with which this chapter is concerned. Areas for analysis must include such areas as fluctuations within the shipping industry over time; vessel types and characteristics including size, crew levels and armament requirements; productivity changes within the industry; the cargoes carried; places of build; places of ownership; and organisational changes in the infrastructure within which merchant shipping operated. Significant developments took place in all of these areas, but in examining them it is necessary to emphasise the

1. J M Price, 'What did merchants do? Reflections on British overseas trade, 1660-1790', *Journal of Economic History* XLIX (1989), pp283-4.

Historians are greatly indebted to the great Dutch maritime artists Willem van de Velde, father and son, for an astonishing range of reliable and detailed depictions of late seventeenth-century ships. They are naturally most concerned with warships and large Indiamen, but they occasionally sketched small craft as well. This ship rigged merchantman represents an alternative to the fluit *tradition in its square stern and relatively modest tumblehome. It is catalogued as Dutch but might as easily be English.* (National Maritime Museum)

tremendous variety of vessels within the merchant fleet–from the small 20 ton or less coasters plying their trade from port to port, to the East Indiamen of 600 tons or more embarking on two-year-long trading voyages between London and the East.

Nor can merchant shipping be looked at in isolation. Shipping activity cannot be divorced from the trade goods being carried, the ports which ships entered or cleared, and the decisions taken by ship owners, merchants, and ship masters. Trade, ports, and owners/merchants/masters, therefore, must feature as crucial elements in the history of merchant shipping. As a result, during the years being examined, 'the shipping industry' embraced a multitude of activities offering employment to thousands of people. In the early eighteenth

century, for example, it was estimated that one quarter of the London labour force depended on the Port of London and its various trades for their employment.

On a wider scale, the context of the period being studied must also be taken into account when analysing such an important industry. Between 1650 and 1830 three overriding influences affected the shipping industry: the frequent outbreak of war; the gathering pace of the industrial revolution; and the state's commercial policy. War, for example, not only had a major impact on many facets of merchant shipping in the seventeenth and eighteenth centuries, but the size and adaptability of the merchant fleet, in turn, was an important influence on the outcome of the wars Britain engaged in at this time. Coasting vessels, for example, were widely regarded as a readily available source of seamen to be used during times of war, and their large number may help to explain Britain's many naval successes throughout this period.[2] Similarly, the quickening of economic development–especially from the 1780s onwards–was inextricably linked with the expansion of Britain's overseas trade[3] which inevitably had repercussions for the shipping industry. Both war and economic growth altered the forces of supply and demand operating within the shipping industry, and must be emphasised in any discussion of mer-

chant shipping during these two centuries.

Commercial policy, thirdly, was dominated by principles of mercantilism which aimed to protect the home country's trade and shipping against European rivals. In the seventeenth and eighteenth centuries it was stressed by statesmen and political commentators that a healthy shipping industry was essential to the country's commercial and military strength. Consequently, merchant shipping was the subject of a great deal of contemporary analysis and debate, resulting in much protective legislation. The fisheries, for example, were encouraged as crucial to the country's sea power,[4] whilst the Navigation Acts of the seventeenth century were designed to protect British trade and shipping from the incursions of the more efficient and competitive Dutch. The efficiency of Dutch shipping, according to Violet Barbour, was the result of 'cheap but seaworthy

Another anonymous small merchant ship sketched by van de Velde. Many of the details are instructive: a pair of suction pumps abreast the main mast; a bundle of sweeps (long oars) lashed to the quarter; and a light armament of three guns a side–one on the forecastle, one on the quarterdeck and one further aft. (National Maritime Museum)

2. This point is argued strongly in D E Robinson, 'Secret of British power in the age of sail: Admiralty records of the coasting fleet', *American Neptune* 48 (1988), pp5-21.

3. For a survey of the debate over 'the relationship between the expansion of external trade and empire and the nature and growth of the domestic economy' see Pat Hudson, *The Industrial Revolution* (London 1992), pp181-199.

4. One contemporary who emphasised the importance of the fisheries to sea power and detailed the actions taken by the Dutch, French and Spanish to increase their fisheries was Malachy Postlethwayte in his *Great Britain's Commercial Interest Explained and Improved* (2nd ed, London 1759), Vol II, Dissertation XXVI, pp274-304.

An anonymous painting of the East India company's yard at Deptford about 1660; in the early years the company both built and refitted its ships here. Apart from the striped HEIC ensign there is virtually nothing to distinguish the ships from warships. (National Maritime Museum)

construction, good burthen with convenience of stowage suited to the cargo, simplicity of rigging so that a small crew would suffice, a low wage for seamen, cheap victualling.'[5] Such economies (for example, shipbuilding costs *and* freight rates were between one-third and one-half higher in Britain than in Holland) were especially associated with the famous Dutch flyboat (*fluitschip*) defined in William Falconer's eighteenth-century marine dictionary as 'a large flat-bottom'd Dutch vessel, whose burthen is generally from four to six hundred tons. It is distinguished by a stern remarkably high, resembling a Gothic turret, and by very broad buttocks below.'[6] It was the carrying activities of these Dutch vessels in the seventeenth century which the British Navigation Acts were designed to curtail, whilst at the same time excluding European rivals from the rapidly expanding colonial trades.

A van de Velde sketch of an English cat of about 1670. Although rapidly executed, it shows well the rounded stern surmounted by a narrow taffrail that were characteristics of the type. The small ports in the lower deck may indicate that the ship has been converted for naval service as a fireship. (National Maritime Museum)

The Navigation Acts of the second half of the seventeenth century, therefore, stipulated that: (a) British and colonial trade had to be undertaken in British or colonial vessels; (b) at least three-quarters of the crew of these vessels had to be British; (c) certain enumerated commodities such as tobacco and sugar must be shipped to Britain first from where they could be re-exported. Clearly such legislation was aimed at stimulating the British merchant marine and was largely successful in pursuing this aim. For example, Thomas Irving, the

Inspector-General of Imports and Exports between 1786 and 1799, and one of the most perceptive observers of Britain's commercial

5. V Barbour, 'Dutch and English merchant shipping in the seventeenth century', *Economic History Review* 2 (1929-30), p273.

6. William Falconer, *An Universal Dictionary of the Marine* (2nd ed, London 1771). For a further description of the flyboat see Barbour, 'Dutch and English merchant shipping', p280; and a detailed discussion of its origins in 'The History of the Ship' *Cogs, Caravels and Galleons*, Chapter 7, pp115-130

position, wrote in a letter to Prime Minister William Pitt of 'that wise system of policy contained in our navigation laws by which this country has been gradually raised to its present exalted state of Naval power and commercial wealth.'[7] The Navigation Acts were not finally repealed until 1849.

Despite this contemporary concern with the shipping industry, the registration of all British vessels over 15 tons did not become compulsory until the Registration Act of 1786,[8] with the result that until the end of the eighteenth century there is a shortage of comprehensive statistics covering such areas as places of ship building and ports of ship ownership. Aggregate data on entrances and/or clearances at specific ports is also rather patchy. This does not mean, however, that the historian of merchant shipping before 1786 is short of suitable source material. For example, there is a wealth of data on size, crew, armament levels, cargoes, place of build/registration etc of thousands of vessels to be found in Admiralty records listing all vessels taking out a Mediterranean Pass for protection against the Barbary pirates; or all vessels contributing their Seamen's Sixpences towards the upkeep of Greenwich Hospital; and in the Colonial Office Naval Office Shipping Lists, recording all vessels entering or clearing colonial ports.[9] By combining data from these sources with both the patchy aggregate data available before the end of the eighteenth century and the more comprehensive data available after the 1780s, maritime historians have recently begun to construct a fairly comprehensive picture of the British shipping industry after 1650. A major aspect of this work has been a number of port or regional studies, and of individual types of merchant ships which have extended and built on the pioneering analysis of the English shipping industry produced by Ralph Davis in the 1960s.[10] As a result, there is now available an increasing amount of relevant material which has been utilised in this discussion of British merchant shipping between 1650 and 1830.

7. Public Record Office (hereafter PRO) Customs 17/20, ff1-2.

8. 26 Geo.III, c.60. On the complicated evolution of ship registry in Britain see the three articles by R C Jarvis: 'Ship registry to 1707', *Maritime History* 1 (1971), pp29-45; 'Ship registry–1707-86', *Maritime History* 2 (1972), pp151-167; 'Ship registry–1786', *Maritime History* 4 (1974), pp12-30.

9. For exactly what is recorded in these groups of records, and for a listing of further available sources, see K Morgan, *Bristol and the Atlantic Trade in the Eighteenth Century* (Cambridge 1993), pp225-231.

10. R Davis, *The Rise of the English Shipping Industry in the 17th and 18th Centuries* (London 1962; reprinted Newton Abbot 1972).

A.

D.

B.

C.

First-hand accounts of life in the merchant service in the seventeenth century are very rare, the best known being Edward Barlow's journal covering his seagoing experiences from seaman to acting Master in the years between 1659 and 1703. The manuscript journal is enlivened by a series of naive but convincing sketches executed by Barlow himself, showing many details of the merchant ships of the period.

A.
Rone [or Rouen] Factor *of about 85 tons and 4 guns, newly built at Ipswich in 1677. The ship was a pink and the characteristic pinched-in stern is clearly visible; the gunports are abaft the main chains.*

B.
Guannaboe, *a Flemish-built West Indiaman of about 350 tons in which Barlow shipped in 1677-78. Note that the ship is almost as heavily decorated as a contemporary warship. The ship carried 20 guns, two a side on the forecastle and the rest aft in two tiers on what appears to be the main deck and in the 'gunroom' below.*

C.
Cadiz Merchant, *a 280-ton Newcastle-built ship of 24 guns, in which Barlow made a voyage to the West Indies in 1680-81. The layout of guns, with a lower battery that did not extend much further forward than the main mast was typical of the period; indeed, naval Fifth Rates of the time had much the same arrangement, although the upper deck battery was complete.*

D.
The East Indiaman Septer *in which Barlow undertook a round trip to the East Indies in 1695-98. Note the loading ports amidships, the half-battery aft, and the furled staysails between the masts.*

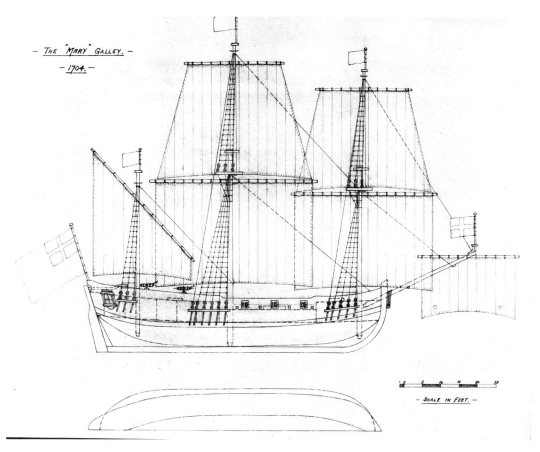

THE "MARY" GALLEY.
— 1704. —

SCALE IN FEET.

A reconstruction of Thomas Bowery's East India 'interloper' [unlicensed trader] as reconstructed by Laird Clowes from Bowery's papers. The ship was a mere 141 tons and was built in 1704 by Richard Wells of Rotherhithe on the Thames. (The Science Museum)

Table 1/1   Size of the Merchant Fleet, 1686-1830 (000 Tons)

Year	Size	Year	Size
1686	340	1788	1279
1702	323	1799	1551
1751-55	454	1803	1986
1760	434	1810	2211
1763	496	1815	2448
1764-69	551	1820	2439
1770-75	587	1825	2329
1786	752	1830	2201

Sources: R Davis, *The Rise of the English Shipping Industry*, p27; A P Usher, 'The growth of English Shipping 1572-1922', *Quarterly Journal of Economics* XLII (1927-28), p467.

Note: D E Robinson (see reference in footnote 2) has suggested that Ralph Davis's figure for 1775 is too low on the grounds that he underestimated the size of the coasting fleet by over 500,000 tons! However, Davis's figures refer to *English* tonnage and Robinson's revision to *British* tonnage, so the later has not been incorporated into Table 1/1. To do so would mean that the figures given are not comparable over time. The best discussion of the available shipping statistics, including the many problems involved in their use, is in Appendix A of Davis's book.

The historical context

The period as a whole saw a substantial increase in the size of the merchant fleet as indicated in Table 1/1. Size, whether of the merchant fleet as a whole or of individual vessels, was recorded in terms of tons, but there were significant changes in how a ship's tonnage was arrived at during the period being studied. Before 1786, most recorded tonnage figures were 'registered tonnage' which 'denotes a vessel's legal tonnage, the tonnage at which a vessel was initially registered and which appeared . . . in all official records relating to that vessel'.[11]

This registered tonnage was normally based on a vessel's carrying capacity and was consistently lower than a vessel's 'measured tonnage' which was obtained by means of a given formula and was used in the building, buying and selling of vessels. In 1695 this formula was set as:

$$\text{tonnage} = \frac{\text{length x breadth x 1/2 breadth}}{94}$$

changed in 1773 to:

$$\text{tonnage} = \frac{(\text{length} - 3/5 \text{ breadth}) \text{ x breadth x 1/2 breadth}}{94}$$

11. J J McCusker, 'The tonnage of ships engaged in British colonial trade during the eighteenth century', in P Uselding (ed), *Research in Economic History* VI (1981), p75.

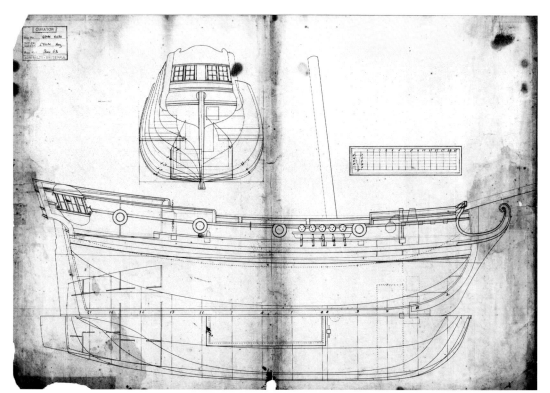

CURATOR

Early draughts of merchant ships from commercial yards are almost non-existent, but the Admiralty either hired, purchased or built mercantile vessels for its own purposes and often produced plans. This hoy for use in one of the Royal Dockyards is probably the Lyon *of 108 tons, built at Deptford in 1709. Among the interesting features on the sheer plan is a wheel just forward of the break of the poop; wheel steering at this period and on so small a craft must be unusual, but given the low headroom of the cabin tiller steering would have been difficult.* (National Maritime Museum)

Two views of an English mercantile 'brigantine' by one T or F Boon dated 1725. The main course and topsail are lugsails, which would normally lead the rig to be described as a bilander, but later examples of this latter rig have square main topsails; there are also examples of vessels from about the middle of the century with gaff-headed fore-and-aft sails on the main–much closer to the later meaning of the term brigantine. (National Maritime Museum)

Such under-recording of registered tonnages was encouraged by ship owners and ship masters in order to lessen port and lighthouse dues based on tonnages, but in 1786 it was stipulated that the tonnage recorded in all ships' registers (registered tonnage) had to be obtained by means of the 1773 formula (measured tonnage), so that the two types of shipping tonnage were now the same. Since post-1786 measured tonnages have been estimated at being 34 per cent greater than pre-1786 registered tonnages, 'when measured tonnage became compulsory in 1786 . . . the overall tonnage of the British merchant fleet increased by about one-third of its previous figure.'[12] These complications indicate that care must be taken when looking at shipping tonnages either in aggregate or of individual vessels – over this period, especially when comparing tonnages pre- and post-1786. For example, a comparison of tonnage 'belonging' to Scottish ports immediately before the 1786 Act with the tonnage registered at Scottish ports after the Act indicated a 38.6 per cent increase 'which is quite out of keeping with any earlier or later shifts in tonnage.'[13]

Despite these variations in the recording of tonnages, it is clear that the overall size of the merchant marine increased significantly between the end of the seventeenth century and the 1830s, a five- or six-fold increase being a reasonable estimate. This, however, was not a linear process and several periods of growth and stagnation can be identified. For example, Ralph Davis has demonstrated that the size of the merchant fleet expanded rapidly between 1660 and 1689, only to be followed by a long period of stagnation when 'the size of the English merchant fleet stood still for over twenty years during the wars of William III and Anne, and made only limited progress during the ensuing twenty-five years of peace'.[14] From the middle of the eighteenth century, however, the shipping industry was given fresh and sustained impetus by the demand for more vessels generated by expanding overseas trade (especially colonial trade) and by the Napoleonic Wars. As Ronald Hope has argued: '. . . a great new expansion of the British merchant fleet

began in the middle of the eighteenth century'.[15] This expansion lasted until the end of the Napoleonic Wars with the exception of the depressed years induced by the suspension of Anglo-American trade during the American War of Independence, which had a particularly harmful impact on Scottish shipping because of the collapse of the tobacco trade. In 1815 once again depression struck the merchant shipping and shipbuilding industries since demand for shipping dropped rapidly at a time when the supply of merchant ships, no longer needed for the war effort, was increasing. This depression in shipping activity was to last for the next two decades.

The most obvious causes of these fluctuations in the size of the merchant fleet were – as indicated above – war, economic progress, and state policy. The policy of mercantilism, for example, provided a protective framework within which the shipping industry, under normal conditions, could expand. Similarly, the quickening pace of economic progress – of which the increase in overseas trade was a major aspect – increased the demand for more and larger merchant vessels in which to carry goods such as sugar, tea, tobacco, timber, naval stores etc. However, the impact of the third factor, war, was far less clear-cut, leading one recent analysis to conclude of the eighteenth century that the '. . . impact of war on . . . shipbuilding and shipping was altogether more ambiguous'.[16] This ambiguity was neatly summed up by Thomas Irving (the Inspector-General of Imports and Exports) in his letter to

William Pitt in 1799 in which he points out that:

it appears that the increase of our shipping in the course of last year (1798) over the year preceding amounted to nearly 50,000 tons . . . we are chiefly to attribute the increase of our shipping to the great number of new vessels which were built in the last and two preceding years. However considerable that increase has been it has certainly by no means kept pace with the increase of our commerce.

12. C J French, 'Eighteenth-century shipping tonnage measurements', *Journal of Economic History* XXXIII (1973), p437. In his report to William Pitt, 12 December 1791, Thomas Irving (then Inspector-General of Imports and Exports) estimated measured tonnage as being 50 per cent greater than registered tonnage, but from the text of this report it is clear that Irving had not taken into account the change in the formula for measuring tonnage introduced in 1773 (PRO Customs 17/12, f1). There is a growing literature on the problems of shipping tonnage measurements before 1830 which is discussed in the articles by French and McCusker already cited and in S Ville, 'The problem of shipping tonnage measurement in the English shipping industry, 1780-1830', *International Journal of Maritime History* I (1989), pp65-83. McCusker and Ville also examine a third type of shipping tonnage–cargo tonnage–which was even larger than either of the two types of shipping tonnage mentioned in this discussion.

13. G Jackson, 'Scottish shipping, 1775-1805', in P L Cottrell and D H Aldcroft (eds), *Shipping, Trade and Commerce: Essays in Memory of Ralph Davis* (Leicester 1981), p127.

14. Davis, *Shipping Industry*, p22.

15. R Hope, *A New History of Shipping* (London 1990), p220.

16. J Brewer, *The Sinews of Power: War, Money and the English State, 1688-1783* (New York 1989), p197.

In our colonial and East India trade and in all the other branches which are confined to British bottoms, we find the merchants complaining of the great inconveniences they labour under from the scarcity of shipping and high prices of freight.[17]

On the one hand, therefore, war had a favourable impact on shipbuilding, increasing the demand for all types of vessels–especially for ships of the line–and this demand was met partly by civilian British shipyards. For example, between 1742 and 1744 merchant builders were contracted to construct fourteen 50-gun ships, with four of these contracts going to Thames yards, and the remainder to country yards. The latter included John Barnard's Harwich shipyard which built the *Harwich* (976

Charles Brooking's portrait of a snow in two positions. Brooking was active in the 1740s and 1750s, and the main difference at this period between a snow and a brig was that the former had a separate trysail mast or horse from which was set a loose-footed fore-and-aft main sail that was sheeted home inside the taffrail, whereas the brig had a larger boomed sail set direct from the main; this is why the snow's main mast is so far forward. Note also that this snow set a square main sail from what in a brig would be the crossjack yard. (National Maritime Museum)

tons), *Colchester* (976 tons), and *Lichfield* (979 tons). Similarly, of the 181 ships of the line and frigates launched between 1783 and 1804, 126 were built in private yards; whilst Bayley's of Ipswich built 31 warships between 1804 and 1814.[18] Demand for general shipping also increased with the navy's need for transport services during wartime. During the French wars at the end of the eighteenth century, for example, it has been estimated that such activities accounted for 10 per cent of mercantile marine operations, providing many shipowners with regular employment for their vessels.[19]

On the other hand, war could have an adverse impact on shipping activity by diverting shipping away from its normal trading functions. With the exception of East Indiamen, however, the practice of using merchantmen as warships was less prevalent in the eighteenth than the seventeenth century. Thus it has been argued that by about '. . . 1715, the divorce between ships of war and commerce was quite complete . . . merchantmen were hired only to serve as bomb vessels, fireships, small cruisers and transports. The chief exception to this was in the case of the great East Indiamen, which were built and owned practically like small ships of the line and were often utilised for purposes of war.'[20]

In addition, since war–certainly until the Seven Years War–disrupted overseas trade this in turn disrupted shipping, either through reduced demand for cargo space or through the need to operate a convoy system. The convoy system was necessary in order to protect British shipping against enemy action–especially from enemy privateers–but, for example, proved inadequate during the War of the Spanish Succession, when widespread captures were made by French privateers. Although the operation of the convoy system gained in efficiency during the course of the eighteenth century (fewer vessels were lost during the Seven Years War than during previous wars, for example), the most obvious impact of war on shipping activity was still seen in the losses inflicted on

17. PRO Customs 17/20, f1.

18. Details from J E Barnard, 'John Barnard the younger, shipbuilder of Ipswich and Harwich 1705-1784', *The Mariner's Mirror* 78 (1992), p164; R Stewart-Brown, *Liverpool Ships in the Eighteenth Century* (Liverpool 1932), p72; and D Macgregor, *Merchant Sailing Ships 1815-1850* (London 1984), p40.

19. S Ville, *English Shipowning During the Industrial Revolution: Michael Henley and Son, London Shipowners, 1770-1830* (Manchester 1987), p12.

20. R G Albion, *Forests and Seapower: The Timber Problem of the Royal Navy, 1652-1862*, (Cambridge, Mass 1926), pp76-77.

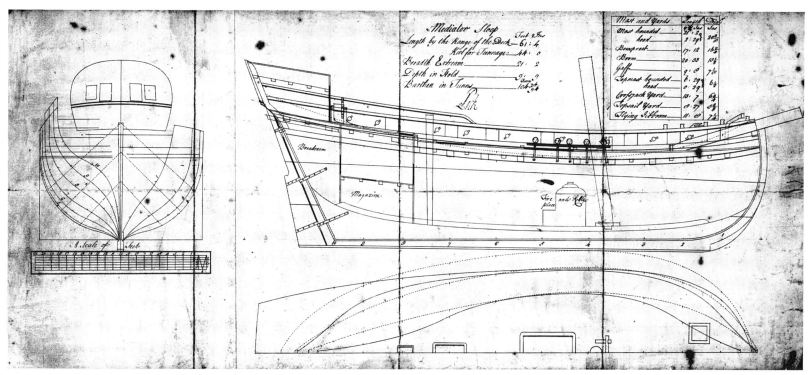

The Virginia-built merchant sloop Mediator *purchased by the Royal Navy in 1745. Judging by other evidence, she is probably typical of the small coasting vessels of the Chesapeake Bay area. She measured 104 tons, and despite the dumpy proportions has sharp lines. The list of spars includes a gaff and boom for the main sail, and square topsail yard and crossjack, plus a jibboom, so the rig must have been similar to that of an English cutter. (National Maritime Museum)*

the merchant marine by enemy action. It has been estimated that 3250 merchant ships were captured during the War of the Spanish Succession; 3238 ships during the War of the Austrian Succession; and 3386 during the American War of Independence, with this trend being interrupted during the Seven Years War when 'very few merchant vessels were lost and no fewer than 1165 French merchant ships were taken as prizes'.[21]

21. Brewer, *Sinews of Power*, p198. For a comprehensive study of the convoy system see P Crowhurst, *The Defence of British Trade, 1689-1815* (Folkestone 1977).

The English fishing fleet off Shetland about 1750. The large ship rigged vessels are probably the fishery protection squadron (there are a number of Dutch vessels on the left of the picture), but the small craft show a variety of rigs. There are a couple of cutters, but the majority of the fishing boats have a ketch's main and mizzen, with a large square main sail and a small triangular fore-and-aft sail on the mizzen, this latter being the steadying sail. There is also at least one small two-masted vessel with a rig like the late seventeenth-century naval sloop – a single square fore sail, and square main and main topsail, without any apparent fore-and-aft canvas. (National Maritime Museum)

A copy of the draught for a 'British buss' for use by the Society of the Free British Fishery, dated 1752. The plan view clearly shows the double-ended hull form with straight sides; the body plan is also wall-sided, and in general the hull is very boxy for maximum capacity. (National Maritime Museum)

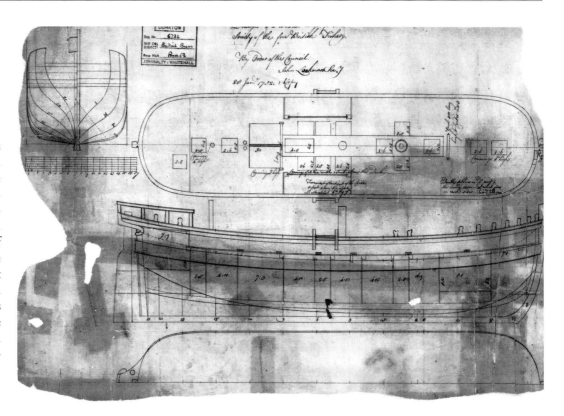

The capture of foreign merchant ships helped to compensate for these losses inflicted on the British merchant fleet, and during the wars between 1702 and 1783 it has been estimated that 6625 foreign prizes were condemned to naval vessels and to privateers. Although it was possible that the availability of a large number of prize vessels could reduce the demand for British built ships, in general it seems that privateering activity—which accounted for 3065 of the condemnations noted above—was of considerable benefit to the shipping industry and its related activities. According to the most recent historian of privateering:

Thus privateering represented an alternative wartime investment opportunity for merchants and shipowners, stimulating activity in the marine-based industries of a port and providing employment for men and resources. This peculiar trade assumed an added significance when the economy of a port was depressed by the adverse conditions of war. At times commerce

was disrupted to such a degree by enemy naval and privateering activity and the fluctuating market conditions of wartime that the fitting out of private men-of-war was one of the few viable investment opportunities available to a port's merchant community.'[22]

Having established the context within which British merchant shipping developed after 1650, emphasising the point that the shipping industry cannot be analysed in isolation from this context, it is now necessary to examine in a little more detail various aspects of British merchant shipping focusing on such interconnected aspects as shipping activity in the major ports; vessel type and characteristics; technolo-

gy and productivity; and organisation of the shipping industry.

The ports and shipping activity

For much of the period 1650-1830, the port of London dominated Britain's commercial and maritime expansion, and was, therefore, the major centre of shipbuilding and shipping

22. D J Starkey, 'The economic and military significance of British privateering, 1702-83', *Journal of Transport History* 9 (1988), p54. The numbers of prizes condemned in the Admiralty Court in London are given in Table 2, p56 of this article. The fullest analysis of privateering is to be found in D J Starkey, *British Privateering Enterprise in the Eighteenth Century* (Exeter 1990).

Around the coasts of Britain many of the small coasters were rigged as cutters, as depicted in this Brooking painting. This is a relatively small example, with no topsail and only one headsail set, but others often carried far more canvas, including square topsails. However, their speed and the relatively large crews needed to handle such voluminous sail areas tended to give the bigger cutters a raffish reputation, and in particular a close association with smuggling. (National Maritime Museum)

activity. Whether measured in terms of tonnage entering or clearing the port, or of tonnage belonging to the port, or of tonnage built in the port, London's domination over the outports was clear. But the noticeable stirrings of provincial economic growth from the mid-eighteenth century onwards, based on demographic expansion and developments in such crucial industries as textiles, coal and iron, stimulated trade and shipping activity in the outports at the expense of London's previous dominant position.[23] London's relative position was being challenged by the expansion of both overseas and coastal trade based on the outports, and the subsequent growth of merchant shipping using such ports as Glasgow, Liverpool, Bristol, Hull, and Newcastle; and by the growth of shipbuilding in the ports of the east coast, especially Scarborough, Whitby, Newcastle and Sunderland. Indeed, Professor Davis has argued that as early as 1700, London was already passed its peak relative position and there is evidence of the slow relative decline of the country's major port. However, this should not be exaggerated since shipping activity centred on London continued to expand significantly throughout the eighteenth and early nineteenth centuries with the result that by the end of the period being discussed London was still the major port in the country in terms of ship ownership and tonnage entrances and clearances. Only in shipbuilding had London been overtaken by another port (Sunderland) by 1830, and this did not happen until the early nineteenth century.

A Danish draught of the 499-ton Indiaman Warwick *of 1750. The seventeenth-century layout of a few guns on the lower deck aft persists—in what naturally came to be called the gunroom—but although not shown on this plan, there was usually a loading port further forward as well; this was particularly useful in getting the ballast on board. (Rigsarkivet, Copenhagen)*

For example, in terms of tonnage owned in individual ports, in 1686 44 per cent of all English-owned tonnage was owned in London, declining to 28 per cent in 1752, 25 per cent in 1765, and 24 per cent on the eve of the American Revolution in 1775. But despite this relative decline, London still owned three times as much tonnage (315,300 tons) as its closest rival, Newcastle, in 1788 when the proportion of English shipping owned in London had risen back to 30 per cent. The major centres of ship ownership after London and Newcastle at this time were Liverpool, Sunderland, Whitehaven, Hull, Whitby, Bristol and Yarmouth. The only Scottish port owning a comparable amount of shipping as these English ports at this time was Glasgow which, with 40,000 tons, owned a greater tonnage than Yarmouth or Bristol, but less than the others. The other main shipowning centres in Scotland as the eighteenth century ended were Aberdeen, Leith, Bo'ness and Dundee.[24] With the exception of the decline of Bristol as a shipowning port, this position had changed very little by the early 1830s when 25 per cent of UK (not just English) shipping was still owned at London constituting a total of 562,839 tons, followed by Newcastle (220,784 tons); Liverpool (166,028 tons); Sunderland (129,082 tons); Whitehaven (69,013 tons); and Hull (68,892 tons).[25]

In terms of ownership, therefore, London maintained a healthy, if slightly declining, lead over all other ports throughout the period from 1650 to 1830. The relative decline of shipbuilding at London, however, was more noticeable. The demand for large (500 tons plus) East Indiamen—which only the Thames shipyards were capable of supplying for much of the period—and the larger (200-350 tons) vessels employed in the Atlantic trades, ensured the

relative prosperity of shipbuilding on the Thames for much of the eighteenth century. But, increasingly, the centre of the shipbuilding industry was shifting away from the old centres such as London and East Anglia towards the northeast ports of Scarborough, Whitby, Newcastle and Sunderland. The reasons for this, according to Alan McGowan, were that 'the yards of East Anglia were unwilling to supply the type of hull that had become economically vital to the bulk cargo trades in coal, timber and flax' despite the fact that the large number of flyboats captured during the Dutch Wars in the second half of the seventeenth century had given the East Anglian yards a model on which to build. As a result, shipbuilding became centred on the ports of the northeast where a larger (250-300 tons) version of the flyboat was developed.[26]

It is difficult to be more precise about shipbuilding activity before the late eighteenth century since records which did include place

23. London's domination of overseas trade is discussed in C J French, ' "crowded with traders and a great commerce": London's domination of English overseas trade, 1700-1775', *London Journal* 17 (1992), pp27-35.

24. The percentages in this paragraph have been calculated from the absolute tonnages of ownership in London and the outports given in Davis, *Shipping Industry*, p27; whilst the ranking of tonnage ownership (with the actual tonnages) can be found in the same reference p35. For more details of shipownership at London, Newcastle, Sunderland, Liverpool and Hull, 1785-1800, see S Ville, 'Shipping in the port of Newcastle', *Journal of Transport History* 9 (1988), Table 1, p63. The Scottish data is from Jackson, 'Scottish shipping', Table 19, p134.

25. The tonnage data for the early 1830s are taken from S Ville, 'Rise to pre-eminence: the development and growth of the Sunderland shipbuilding industry, 1800-1850', *International Journal of Maritime History* 1 (1989), Table 4, p80.

26. A McGowan, *The Ship : The Century Before Steam* (London 1980), pp25-26.

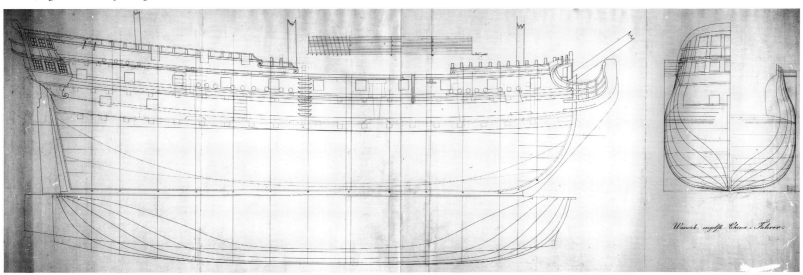

Warwich insgelst China Faherer

of build information usually categorised vessels simply in terms of 'British-built'; 'plantation-built'; or 'foreign prize made free'. However, in the last quarter of the eighteenth century ship-building details become more plentiful, especially following the 1786 Registry Act, and this allows a more detailed picture of shipbuilding activity to be presented. For example, in his analysis of shipbuilding sites in *Lloyd's Register* of 1776, J A Goldenberg has shown that 40 per cent of the total English tonnage was built in the northeast; 19 per cent on the Thames; 14 per cent in the northwest; 14 per cent on the south coast; 10 per cent in East Anglia; and 3 per cent in Wales. This analysis has also indicated that for Great Britain as a whole, 49.6 per cent of total tonnage in the *Register* was British-built; 31.9 per cent was built in British America; and 18.5 per cent foreign-built.[27] For the rest of the eighteenth century London still

A pictorial deck and longitudinal section of the East Indiaman Falmouth *of 1752. Down to the lower deck the ship follows naval practice in such details as the siting of the galley and the capstans, but the hold lacks the many platforms and store rooms that would be found on a warship.* (National Maritime Museum)

accounted for about 20 per cent of total tonnage built in English ports –as the following tonnage figures indicate–whilst a further 34,776 tons of shipping were built in Scottish yards between 1787 and 1789.[28]

Period	Built in London	Built in England	Percentage in London
1787-89	33,813	187,702	18
1796-98	49,420	220,696	22

The increasingly dominant position of the northeast as a shipbuilding region by the end of the eighteenth century has also been highlighted by Rupert Jarvis whose analysis of London's foreign-going shipping in the mid-1780s has shown that 25 per cent of this shipping was built on the east coast, with only 20 per cent being built in the Thames.[29] Similarly, 79 per cent of Newcastle tonnage registered between 1786 and 1800 was built in the northeast, whilst overall during these years the average tonnage built per year at the major shipbuilding ports was:

London   : 8979 tons
Newcastle   : 7065 tons
Whitby   : 5130 tons
Sunderland : 4804 tons
Liverpool   : 3318 tons[30]

The position achieved by Newcastle as one of the country's leading shipbuilding ports was

27. J A Goldenberg, 'An analysis of shipbuilding sites in *Lloyd's Register* of 1776', *The Mariner's Mirror* LIX (1973), pp419-435. It should be noted that '*Lloyd's Register*, however, did not include merchant ships which were uninsured or covered by the mutual insurance clubs which predominated in the north-east'. See Ville, 'Rise to pre-eminence: the development and growth of the Sunderland shipbuilding industry, 1800-50', p67.

28. Calculated from PRO Customs 17/12, f3 for 1787-89; and Customs 17/18, ff4-5, Customs 17/19, ff3-4, and Customs 17/20, ff3-4 for 1796-98. Scottish data from Jackson, 'Scottish shipping', Table 17, p128.

29. This 25 per cent included all east coast ports, not just those in the north. The remainder were built as follows: ¹⁄₂₀th on the south coast; ¹⁄₁₀th on the west coast; 'a negligible quantity' in Scotland and Ireland; ¹⁄₅th in North America; and the remainder had been taken as prize. See R C Jarvis, 'Eighteenth-century London shipping', in A E J Hollaender and W Kellaway (eds), *Studies in London History* (London 1969), p408.

30. Ville, 'Shipping in the port of Newcastle', p65.

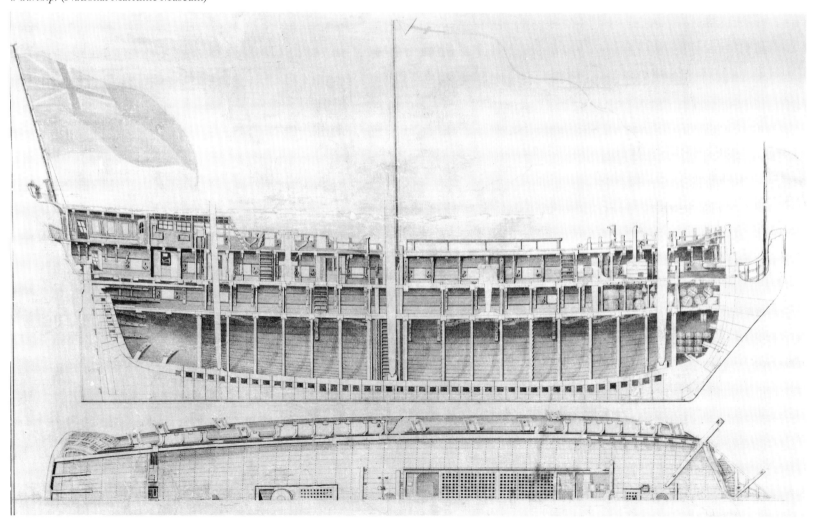

A medium class (499-ton) East Indiaman, the True Briton, *built by Wells at Rotherhithe, an experienced builder of Indiamen. The ship made four round voyages between 1760 and 1769. The painstaking detail of this watercolour makes it a useful adjunct to the plan of the* Warwick, *a slightly earlier ship of the same class.* (National Maritime Museum)

based on her reputation for producing large, well-designed craft ideally suited to carry bulky cargoes such as coal and timber, yet able to switch into other trades or transport services should market conditions change–as they did frequently during the French wars. During the first three decades of the nineteenth century, the northeast strengthened its position as the country's leading shipbuilding area largely because, during this time, 'Sunderland became England's premier shipbuilding centre'.[31] Her shipyards were producing quality vessels at competitive costs not only for the traditional coal trade of the northeast but also for the East Indian and Australian trades which required much larger ships. As a result, by 1832

Sunderland was responsible for 27 per cent of the UK's shipbuilding output and was far and away the leading English shipbuilding port.

A similar picture of the shifting relative position between London and the outports, but coupled with London's continuing lead over all other centres of shipping activity, can be seen from the available data on merchant shipping entering and clearing individual ports. As far as overseas trade was concerned, it was inevitable that as the centre of trade in, for example, sugar, tobacco and slaves increasingly switched from London to ports such as Bristol, Glasgow and Liverpool, that shipping activity at these ports would increase. At the same time, the gradual loss of power by the London-based monopolistic trading companies also allowed more of the country's overseas trade to flow through the outports. As a result, although during the course of the eighteenth century it has been estimated that the total tonnage entering and clearing the port of London increased four-fold,[32] for many of the outports

this increase was even greater. Between 1710 and 1760 total tonnage entering and clearing Liverpool, for example, increased from 27,000 tons to 100,000 tons (a four-fold increase in only 50 years), increasing to a massive 709,000 tons by 1805, which, even allowing for the impact of the change in the method of recording tonnages introduced in 1786, constituted a growth in shipping activity far greater than that experienced by London over the same period.[33]

The overall growth of entrances and clearances in overseas trade during the course of the

31. Ville, 'Rise to pre-eminence: the development and growth of the Sunderland shipbuilding industry, 1800-50', p65. Table 1 pp66-67 and Table 2, p70, provide the evidence for this statement.

32. Jarvis, 'Eighteenth-century London shipping', p406.

33. The 1710 and 1760 tonnages are from Hope, *New History of Shipping*, p222; whilst the 1805 figure has been calculated from the table produced in C Northcote Parkinson (ed), *The Trade Winds: A Study of British Overseas Trading During the French Wars 1793-1815* (London 1948), p63.

The Gallant *of Bristol, a 200-ton Jamaica trader that took out a Letter of Marque (a licence to act as a privateer) in November 1762. Unlike the privateer proper, whose sole purpose was to cruise against enemy shipping in the hope of profit, a Letter of Marque ship carried on normal trading activities with permission to capture enemy ships if the opportunity arose. Accordingly, the* Gallant, *in company with another Bristol ship, the* Hector, *took the French* Amphion *and carried her into St Kitts.*(National Maritime Museum)

eighteenth century is given in Table 1/2, which also highlights the relative position of merchant shipping activity at London *vis-à-vis* the rest of the country. Although London's relative position did decline in the face of greater competition from the provincial ports (more so in the case of entrances than clearances), nonetheless by the end of the century the capital's port still accounted for one-third of all shipping tonnage in overseas trade entering and clearing English ports.

The port of London was also the major centre of coasting activity. Thousands of coasting vessels entered and cleared the port each year since internally 'the chief trade of most places was with London, whose voracious appetite for food and fuel was the supreme influence on the prosperity of many provincial ports and a most important encouragement to the production of agricultural surpluses or coal in their hinterlands.'[34] Nonetheless, as with overseas trade, so with the coasting trade: the outports experienced faster *growth* than London during the period under discussion. In the pre-railway age, coastal routes were the main channels for the exchange of goods (either those produced in Britain or those imported from abroad) and as the pace of economic change accelerated during the eighteenth and early nineteenth centuries, coastal shipping also expanded rapidly in order to facilitate the movement of goods around the country—embracing not only the seventy-four

officially designated English ports, but also the other 500 or so places which were accessible by water. Similarly, Scotland had twenty-eight 'legal' ports and for much of the eighteenth century coasters accounted for about 75 per cent of total shipping activity in Scottish ports.[35]

Measuring the extent of tonnage engaged in coastal trade is notoriously difficult, but a recent comprehensive survey of coastal shipping estimated that 'tonnage engaged in this trade rose from 92,929 in 1709 to 154,640 in 1760' and then increased at least four-fold between 1760 and 1830.[36] The main centres of activity after London were again concentrated

on the east coast–Newcastle, Sunderland, Scarborough, Whitby, Great Yarmouth and Hull–and undoubtedly the major coasting trade was the movement of coal from the northeast to London, rising from 750,975 tons of coal in 1779 to 2,019,080 tons of coal in 1829.[37] This trade necessitated a substantial fleet of relatively large colliers, which, on average, completed eight or nine voyages a year. In 1795 4395 colliers (including repeat voyages) arrived in London, rising to about 7000 vessels twenty years later, and the average size of vessel's in Newcastle's (the main source of London's coal) coastal trade in 1785 has

34. G Jackson, 'The ports', in D H Aldcroft and M J Freeman (eds), *Transport in the Industrial Revolution* (Manchester 1983), p180.

35. A map of the English ports is given in Jackson, 'The ports', p179. Scottish coasting activity is discussed in Jackson, 'Scottish shipping', p122.

36. J Armstrong and P S Bagwell, 'Coastal shipping', in Aldcroft and Freeman (eds), *Transport in the Industrial Revolution*, pp143-147. This reference spells out the difficulties of interpreting coastal shipping tonnages.

37. Armstrong and Bagwell, 'The coasting trade', p154.

38. *British Parliamentary Papers* (hereafter *BPP*) XLVII, Reports XVII, HC No 129 (1795-96), p202 for the number of colliers in 1795; MacGregor, *Merchant Sailing Ships 1815-1850*, p49 for the later number; and Ville, 'Shipping in the port of Newcastle', p73 for the 1785 average tonnage figure.

Table 1/2:   Entrances and Clearances in the Eighteenth Century

Year	Entrances		Clearances	
	London (000 tons)	Total	London (000 tons)	Total
1702	157		96 (30%)	318
1718-19	199 (54%)	366	128 (29%)	445
1751	234 (49%)	480	174 (25%)	694
1765	341 (49%)	693	212 (28%)	758
1772	382 (49%)	780	247 (28%)	888
1790-91	575 (39%)	1481	375 (26%)	1445

Sources: 1702, 1751, 1790-91 : *British Parliamentary Papers* XLVII, Reports XVII, HC No 129 (1796), Appendix G; 1718-19 : PRO CO 390/5 ff73 & 75; 1765 and 1772 : BM Add Mss 11256.

been estimated at 231 tons.[38] This was far larger than vessels in any other branch of Britain's coasting trade.

In general, coastal vessels differed from overseas vessels in several respects–in particular, of course, (with the noted exception of the northeast colliers) they were much smaller. Vessels engaged in Scotland's coasting trade in the 1770s, for example, averaged only 43 tons, compared with an average of 80 tons for vessels engaged in Scotland's overseas trade.[39] They could also operate with very small crews. Thus between June 1731 and June 1732 three of the 122 coasting vessels leaving Chichester (two of 15 tons and one of only 8 tons) operated with just the master and a boy, whilst the other 119 coasters operated with crews of just 2.8 men per vessel.[40] In addition, they could load and unload quickly; and they could make several trips a year. In fact, coastal shipping became so

A draught of the brig Industry, *taken off at Deptford in December 1765. At 221 tons the vessel is of a moderate size for the period, but the low freeboard, flat sheer and lack of bulwarks would seem to suggest a coastal rather than a deep-water employment, although vessels of this size regularly crossed the Atlantic.* (National Maritime Museum)

active during the early years of the industrial revolution that Basil Greenhill has argued that 'the nineteenth century became the great era of the coasting sailing vessel.' And the characteristics of the coasting fleet began to change. Thus:

Fore and aft rigged vessels, at first schooners and later barquentines and ketches as well, largely replaced the old complex square-rigged ships. They cost far less to equip when they were built, and less to sail and maintain afterwards. They needed smaller crews, they were usually more seaworthy and, with the development of better hull forms, easier to handle and faster than their predecessors.[41]

Unfortunately, the massive expansion in coastal trade associated with the early years of the industrial revolution contributed significantly to the overcrowding and confusion experienced by all of the major ports as they struggled to cope with more and more shipping using their facilities. For example, in his evidence to the committee set up to look at the best way of increasing the accommodation of the port of London in the 1790s, William Vaughan, a merchant, argued that:

Without entering into details, I beg to state, that the colliers and coasting traders form the greatest proportion of shipping and tonnage of the Port of London; and that the evils of the river have arisen more from this cause, than from the extent of the shipping and tonnage employed in our foreign trade.[42]

As a result, by the early nineteenth century, not only London but also ports such as Bristol, Liverpool, Hull and Grimsby had initiated major dock building or improvement schemes to enable them to handle the increase taking place in both overseas and coastal shipping.[43] In at least one case, however (that of Liverpool) dock expansion was at the expense of the ship-

39. Jackson, 'Scottish shipping', p123.

40. T S Willan, *The English Coasting Trade 1600-1750*, (Manchester 1938), pp16-17.

41. B Greenhill and L Willis, *The Coastal Trade* (London 1975). This book provides notes and very clear drawings of forty-five different craft employed in Britain's coastal waters.

42. *BPP* XLVII, Reports XVII, HC No 129 (1795-96), p202.

43. For details of these schemes see Jackson, 'The ports', pp194-208.

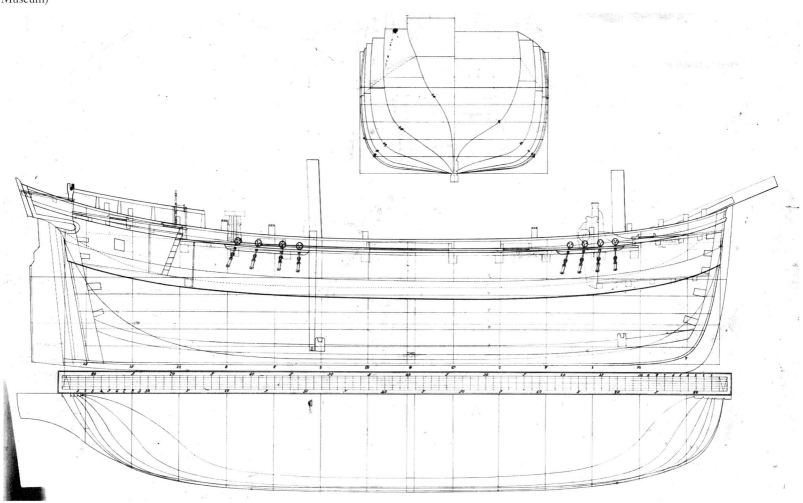

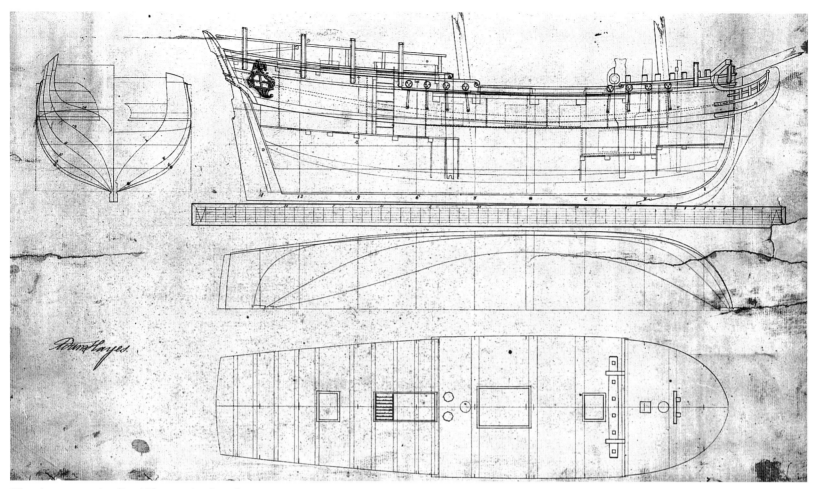

The schooner came into Royal Navy service through purchase in North America, being used to try to enforce English laws and regulations that were unpopular and widely evaded. The 52-ton Sultana *was the smallest of these, and the survey reported her to have been built at Boston in the autumn of 1767. Not as extreme in hull form as the later pilot-boat model and the so-called Baltimore clippers, the ship is nevertheless quite sharp in her lines. She did not carry carriage guns so the Navy has probably made fewer alterations to the vessel than to some of the other schooners purchased during the same period.* (National Maritime Museum)

building industry, since the occupation by the new docks of more and more of the river front pushed its shipyards out of business.[44]

Characteristics of the merchant fleet before 1830

The various aspects of British merchant shipping so far discussed–ports of ownership, places of construction and entrances and clearances–have largely been concerned with merchant shipping in aggregate terms. Behind these aggregates were the many thousands of ships which plied there trades either over short distances between individual British ports or with nearby Irish or European ports; or over

longer distance trade routes into the Baltic Sea, the Atlantic Ocean or the East Indies. These various routes and the differing types of commodities being traded largely determined the characteristics and features of the merchant craft involved. The profile of the merchant fleet, however, was also influenced by certain broader trends such as the advance of technology and the search for productivity gains; and the growing safety of sea travel, periodically interrupted by the outbreak of war. As a result, the period 1650 to 1830 witnessed significant developments in the characteristics of the British merchant marine.[45]

The most obvious of these developments was the tendency for the average size of vessels to increase. Increasing size was particularly noticeable after the middle of the eighteenth century when the expansion of colonial trade required relatively large vessels fitted out to carry colonial produce such as sugar and tobacco. This demand for larger ships was reinforced by the rapid increase in trade associated with the industrial revolution from the 1780s onwards, and by the frequent outbreak of war throughout the period which provided every incentive to the building of large vessels which could carry more guns and a larger crew

without sacrificing too much cargo space. The demands of the Napoleonic Wars, in particular, had a positive impact on size. Size, therefore, was largely determined by a vessel's normal trading area coupled with the special requirements of protecting trade and shipping during periods of war.

Throughout the seventeenth century, it has been argued that the average size of English shipping was small due to the fact that ships 'of 100 tons or less could be built economically with a minimum of imported supplies; larger ships, whose construction leaned more heavily on such supplies, could be afforded only by the privileged or by the monopolised trades.'[46] Trade with the East Indies fell into this latter category, and the ships engaged in such trade were many times larger than the craft employed in all other trades. For example, in 1681

44. Stewart-Brown, *Liverpool Ships*, p60.

45. The analysis of shipping characteristics is an expanding area of study, and readers are particularly recommended to W E Minchinton, 'Characteristics of British slaving vessels, 1698-1775', *Journal of Interdisciplinary History* XX (1989), pp53-81; and Morgan, *Bristol and the Atlantic Trade*, Chapter 2.

46. Barbour, 'Dutch and English merchant shipping', p270.

the East India Company owned an estimated thirty-five vessels whose size varied between 100 and 775 tons, whilst between 1682 and 1689 sixteen East Indiamen were built and their sizes varied from 900 tons to 1300 tons.[47] It is likely that during the first half of the eighteenth century there was a reduction in the size of vessels trading with the East, but it is impossible to calculate the average size of East Indiamen because of the practice on the part of the Company of chartering only 499 tons of vessels larger than this. As a result, in certain records a large number of vessels trading with the East have a recorded tonnage of 499 tons when in fact the vessels were probably much larger than this.[48] The English East India Company, unlike its Dutch counterpart, preferred this practice of hiring shipping rather than building or buying the vessels it needed. But, in order to ensure that ships of sufficient size would be built for the Company to hire, it had to guarantee the owners of such vessels regular employment. The result, as Walter Minchinton has recently demonstrated, was:

a rigid system of formal saleable rights, which included the right of the owners to have their ship employed in strict rotation with others of the same standing. This meant that although the voyage itself rarely lasted more than two

A draught of the West Indiaman Hydra *of 1776, at 446 tons a moderately large vessel for this trade. The hull form is capacious, with fairly full ends, but there is some deadrise. Very little internal detail is recorded, but the run of the decks is apparent, with a low 'tween deck below the upper deck, with separate forecastle and quarterdeck above; these latter do not seem to have been connected by gangways either side of the waist as was contemporary practice in warships. (National Maritime Museum)*

years, the four voyages which a ship usually made in the service of the East India Company before it was considered unfit for long tropical voyages could be spread over some fourteen years or so.[49]

Despite this complication in determining their size, East Indiamen were still far larger than any other type of merchant vessel, and there is little doubt that the average size of East Indiamen began to increase again in the second half of the eighteenth century to cater for the increasing volume of trade and the continuing need to carry armaments and large crews over lengthy voyages. For example, between 1778 and 1781, of the six East Indiamen with Jewish owners which took out Letters of Marque, five of them were in excess of 700 tons, including the 750-ton *York* owned by Moses Franks and four others, and the 800-ton *Calcutta* owned by Raphael Franco and two others. Similarly, in 1787 the Company employed the *Ceres*, *Boddam* and *Nottingham* to trade with China and all were in excess of 1000 tons, whilst the *Marquis of Cornwallis* (1360 tons) was built for the East India trade in 1804.[50]

The average size of other merchant vessels was far less than that of the East Indiamen, and varied from trade to trade being influenced by such factors as length of voyages involved, the navigational problems of such voyages, and the types of commodities being carried. For example, wine ships tended to be small (less than 100 tons), although the average size of vessels clearing English ports for Portugal did increase from 75 tons in 1715-17 to 117 tons by the early 1770s.[51] Vessels trading with nearby European ports in such countries as Holland, France and Ireland were even smaller than this, because the nature of the trades involved – shut-

tling from port to port and carrying a whole variety of goods in small quantities – did not require large vessels. Trading expeditions to northern Europe, on the other hand, required much larger merchant craft due to the type of commodities – principally timber, iron, and naval stores – imported into English ports, and the high possibility of heavy weather in the Sound, the Baltic and the North Sea. Typically, the maximum size of vessels in the Baltic trade increased from 300-350 tons to 400-500 tons after the mid-eighteenth century.

Similarly, sugar and tobacco vessels grew in size during the course of the seventeenth and eighteenth centuries, especially as the rapid expansion of the sugar and tobacco trades, and improvements in the organisation of those trades, reduced the fear of under-utilisation of available cargo space. Larger vessels, therefore, became more profitable. Before the middle of the eighteenth century, the largest merchantmen in the Atlantic trades were between 150 and 200 tons, and many were less than 50 tons. By the early nineteenth century, however, the average tonnage of the 326 ships which left London for the West Indies was 324 tons,

47. E Keble Chatterton, *The Old East Indiamen* (London 1914; reprinted 1970), pp123-124.

48. The practice of chartering 499 tons in ships larger than this is discussed in Davis, *Shipping Industry*, p262, n1. An example of this type of recording is given in M Woolf, 'Eighteenth-century London Jewish shipowners', *Jewish Historical Society of England* XXIV (1974), pp201-4.

49. W E Minchinton, 'Corporate ship operation from the late sixteenth to the late eighteenth century', *International Journal of Maritime History* II (1990), pp133-4.

50. Details from Woolf, 'Eighteenth-century London Jewish shipowners', pp203-4; Minchinton, 'Corporate ship operation', p145; and Hope, *New History of Shipping*, p258.

51. H E S Fisher, *The Portugal Trade* (London 1971), p88.

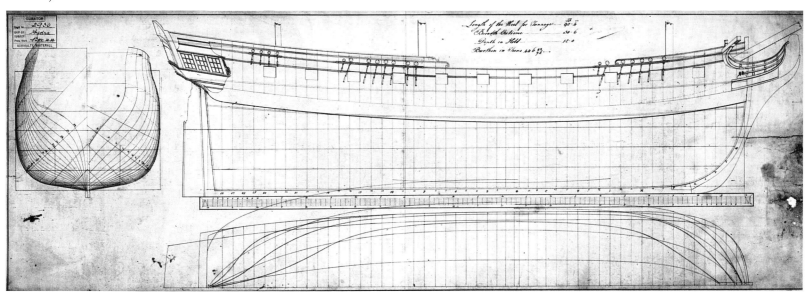

whilst that of the 188 ships dispatched from the outports for the same destination was 277 tons.[52]

This West Indian example of the differing size between London and outport merchant craft was typical of the merchant fleet as a whole. In general, those ships which were built and/or owned in London, were larger than those which were built and/or owned in the outports, although this began to change with the rise of shipbuilding in the northeast. At the end of the seventeenth century, as illustration, London owned about 70 vessels of 350 tons or more, rising to 150 by 1775 and 200 by 1788. London, of course, had a near monopoly of the building and ownership of the East Indiamen, and the majority of the largest West Indiamen were also built and owned in London. In comparison, only six ships over 350 tons were owned in the outports as the eighteenth century opened, although their numbers did begin to increase with the expansion of the timber, sugar and tobacco trades involving Glasgow, Bristol, Liverpool and the east coast ports. After the middle of the eighteenth century, for example, large ships (300-400 tons)

An interesting ensemble of ships of the American War period depicted in this Francis Holman painting of a British privateer brig with her merchant prizes, 1778. The prizes are a brig and a schooner forward and astern of the brig, and may be another example of the common convention of showing ships in two or more positions; on the other hand the schooner to the left has topmasts and square topsails while that to the right does not. (National Maritime Museum)

for the Baltic trade were being built at ports such as Whitby, Scarborough and Newcastle. In 1788, therefore, the outports owned 110 ships of 360 tons or more, with half of them owned at ports on the northeast coast.[53]

Not all of the larger ships in the merchant fleet were built in Britain, and there were alternative sources of shipping available to the merchant community. A notable characteristic of merchant shipping at this time, therefore, was the increasing importance of prize and colonial-built ships in the profile of the merchant fleet. During and immediately after each war, for example, the number of foreign prizes employed in Britain's overseas trade increased, and very often such vessels were larger than either English- or colonial-built vessels. For example, the 350-ton *Harmony* was a French prize which sailed from London for Jamaica in February 1760, whilst the huge 800-ton *Earl Temple*, sailing from London for the East Indies in the same month, was also captured from the French.[54] Large prize vessels were particularly numerous in the tobacco trade, with those trading between London and Virginia averaging 253 tons in the years immediately after the Seven Years War.[55] The largest was the 305-ton *Justitia* of London, a French prize made free on 5 July 1757, which entered Virginia in December 1764 carrying European goods and left for London the following June with 545 hogsheads of tobacco.[56]

War could also increase the purchase and use of colonial-built vessels in the merchant fleet. For much of the eighteenth century there was a

degree of prejudice against colonial-built vessels within the shipping community. Thus it was claimed that 'New England ships for sale are not substantial or well-built, or so durable as the British; partly arising from the timber not being so lasting and partly from its not being so well seasoned.'[57] As a result the oak used in New England shipbuilding was likely to rot after only five or six years. One consequence of this was that the average age of British-built vessels in the merchant fleet was roughly twice that of colonial-built vessels. During the many years of war, however, with the navy requiring more of the shipping built in Britain, it was logical for merchants to turn towards colonial-built shipping. Elias Bland and partners, for example, had their ship the *Tetsworth* built in Philadelphia, so that it would not be claimed by the navy as a warship.[58]

Thus it has been argued that it was during the major wars between 1689 and 1763 that

52. Northcote Parkinson (ed), *The Trade Winds*, p182.

53. Statistics in this paragraph from Davis, *Shipping Industry*, p79.

54. PRO Adm 7/90.

55. Calculated from PRO CO 5/1449-1450. Vessels built in Britain or the colonies and trading between London and Virginia at this time averaged 214 tons and 150 tons respectively.

56. PRO CO 5/1449, ff64 and 85.

57. John Holroyd, Lord Sheffield, *Observations on the Commerce of the American States* (London 1784), p84.

58. H E Gillingham, 'Some colonial ships built in Philadelphia', *Pennsylvania Magazine of History and Biography* LVI (1932), p170.

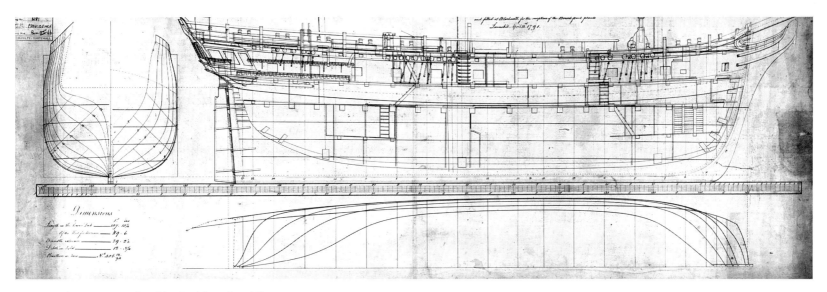

The Providence *was purchased by the Admiralty while building in 1791, and fitted out for Bligh's second attempt (after the* Bounty *mutiny) to bring back a cargo of breadfruit from the South Seas. Therefore, although the hull form of this 406-ton vessel may be regarded as typical, the topside detail and many of the fittings are not (notably the two-level racks for the plant-pots in the great cabin). However, the low 'tween deck is probably an original feature.* (National Maritime Museum)

sales of colonial-built vessels in Britain increased, owing to such factors as the increasing expense of importing naval stores into Britain; losses to the enemy; and the increased demand by the navy for shipbuilding and repair facilities. Although this demand usually fell off after each war, a large number of American-built vessels would still be in use; and after the Seven Years War this fall-off did not occur because a 'demand had been generated for certain types of ships of medium size' with the result that 'by the eve of the Revolution London and the west coast ports of England were full of English-owned, American-built brigs and snows.'[59]

It can be seen from the evidence presented above that increasing size within the merchant fleet was largely a characteristic of the years after the middle of the eighteenth century, and was most noticeable in those vessels which were already relatively large and were engaged in long distance trades. Such evidence, however, should not obscure the fact that until the early decades of the nineteenth century, the majority of merchant ships were still less than 200 tons. These variations in size were also associated with variations in rig. Until the end of the eighteenth century, merchant ships were classified according to hull form, with the main merchant ship hulls being frigate, bark, flute, pink, cat, and hagboat;[60] but, as Davis points out, ships began to be classified by rig from the late eigh-

teenth century onwards. In descending order of size (with the number of masts in brackets) these classifications were: ship (3); bark (3); snow (2); brig (2); schooner (2); and sloop (1). As the size of merchant ships began to increase, 'the tonnage at which vessels were rigged with three masts rose sharply' so that by the end of the eighteenth century, nearly all vessels over 200 tons were three-masted, with the largest (above 350 tons) classified as 'ship rigged'. Vessels in the middle size range (200-350 tons) increasingly became classified as 'bark rigged', distinguished from ship rigged as follows:

A vessel square-rigged on all three masts became a ship and a vessel rigged with no square sail on the mizzen became known as a bark, perhaps transferred to barque by nineteenth-century Romanticism in Britain, although North American usage continued with the earlier spelling.

Vessels of less than 200 tons, finally, which were still in the majority, were two-masted and most of them were classified as brigs or snows.[61] For example, of the 1353 vessels registered for the first time at Newcastle between 1786 and 1800, 768 were either brigs (average tonnage 177) or snows (average tonnage 204), followed by 33 ships (average tonnage 290), 115 barks (average tonnage 263), 92 sloops (average tonnage 54), and 14 schooners (average tonnage 64).[62]

In this example of Newcastle shipping, the schooner rig was the least numerous. This situation, however, was about to change dramatically. Indeed, Alan McGowan has argued 'that the schooner represents one of the two major developments in sailing rig since the appearance of the three-masted ship in the fifteenth century.'[63] In 1776, only 0.4 per cent of British-

built vessels in *Lloyd's Register* were schooners, with the majority of vessels being square-rigged, either brigs (47.1 per cent) or fully rigged ships (25.6 per cent). However, because of their speed and cheaper cost of operation, the popularity of schooners increased rapidly in the first half of the nineteenth century, especially from the 1820s onwards. As a result, by 1831 15.8 per cent of vessels listed in *Lloyd's Register* of that year were classified as schooners, with the ports of South Devon being the most active in their construction.[64]

These inter-connected characteristics of size, type of hull, and type of rig because they could influence a vessel's carrying capacity, the size of its crew and its speed, were important

59. R Davis, 'Untapped sources and research opportunities in the field of maritime history from the beginning to about 1815', in *Untapped Sources and Research Opportunities in the Field of American Maritime History: A Symposium* (Mystic Seaport, Connecticut 1966), pp11-26.

60. These hull types are discussed in D MacGregor, *Merchant Sailing Ships 1775-1815: Their Design and Construction* (Watford 1980), especially pp19-36.

61. This discussion of rig is based on Davis, *Shipping Industry*, pp78-79; and McGowan, *The Ship*, pp29-30, with the two quotes taken from the latter reference. For 'simplified profiles' of the types of vessels mentioned in this paragraph see the descriptions from Falconer's *Universal Dictionary of the Marine* reproduced in Minchinton, 'Characteristics of British slaving vessels, 1698-1775', pp77-81. These profiles are accompanied by useful diagrams. The definitive study of eighteenth-century rigging is K H Marquardt, *Eighteenth-century Rigs and Rigging* (London 1992).

62. Ville, 'Shipping at the port of Newcastle', Table 3, p64.

63. McGowan, *The Ship*, p38.

64. The details in this paragraph are from D Starkey, 'Schooner development in Britain', in 'History of the Ship', *Sail's Last Century* (London 1993), especially pp135-137. On the growing popularity of the schooner after 1820 also see the table on shipbuilding, 1791-1850, in Macgregor, *Merchant Sailing Ships 1815-1850*; and B Greenhill, *The Merchant Schooners* (London 1988), p9.

elements in determining the efficiency, and therefore the profitability, of merchant shipping activity. The level of capital invested into a trading voyage – covering such things as the cost of the vessel itself, the crew, protection in the form of guns, and goods to be traded – was relatively high. Returns on this investment would depend on such factors as the amount of cargo a vessel could carry relative to its size; the length of time taken completing a trading voyage; the size of crew needed to operate the vessel; and the number of crew and guns required to provide protection against enemy action or pirate activity. Clearly, size, hull and rig were crucial to these problems, helping to determine how much cargo a ship could carry; the optimum size of crew needed; and the speed of sailing. Greater efficiency was achieved in each of these areas during the eighteenth and early nineteenth centuries. In addition, the growing safety of the seas reduced not only the

costs of protection but also of marine insurance. Greater efficiency plus lower costs meant productivity gains and higher profits on investment in shipping activity. These were the result, however, not only of improvements in shipping technology and in the safety of sea travel, but also of the growing availability of information covering all important aspects of maritime activity.

Advances in shipping technology before 1830 were less significant and obvious than those which were to occur during the 'age of iron and steam' after 1830. As a result maritime historians have tended to play down the role played by technology when explaining productivity and efficiency gains in the shipping industry before the early nineteenth century. For example, Douglass North has demonstrated that in the two centuries after 1650 productivity in the shipping industry rose significantly, but he claims that this was due to

'a decline in piracy and an improvement in economic organisation' rather than technological improvements.[65] Nonetheless, technology must be considered because of its impact, in particular, on speed and on a merchant vessel's crew size. There is no doubt that in proportion to tonnage, the size of crew declined during the eighteenth century as shown in Table 1/3.

To some extent, this was hardly surprising because as the average size of vessels increased, the increase in crew size would not need to be proportionate, and the tons per man ratio would therefore go up. However, other factors were also at work to increase the ratio of tons to men. For example, Dr McGowan has argued that 'if technical innovation caused the increase in tons per man it was surely in the adoption of the wheel for steering and the increasing awareness of the value of the fore-and-aft sail on large vessels' early in the eighteenth century.[66] Improvements in rig design were, therefore, fundamental to technical advance in the shipping industry because, according to Russell Menard, they involved 'the breakup of total sail area into smaller units and an increase in the number of sails. The result was ships with an improved capacity for sailing close to the wind that could be handled by smaller

65. D C North, 'Sources of productivity change in ocean shipping, 1600-1850', *Journal of Political Economy* 76 (1968), p953.

66. McGowan, *The Ship*, p31. On the advantages of the fore-and-aft sail over the square sail see p36 of this reference.

Table 1/3:   Tons Per Man Ratios on Vessels Trading Between London and Various Areas, 1726-1772

Year	Northwest Europe	North Europe	Southern Europe	British Islands	East Indies	Greenland	West Indies	Southern Am. Cols	Northern Am. Cols	Total
1726	8.9	17.7	9.1	–	4.8	7.7	9.3	10.8	10.1	11.2
1732	9.0	18.1	10.2	9.0	4.3	9.1	9.1	11.5	9.5	11.2
1742	14.5	15.3	8.5	9.3	4.1	9.6	10.3	11.0	9.6	10.6
1752	11.7	19.7	11.4	9.8	4.7	7.7	11.4	12.3	10.0	12.0
1760	13.0	17.9	9.7	10.7	4.7	7.4	11.2	13.7	13.1	11.1
1772	13.5	19.3	10.1	11.4	5.1	7.4	14.7	14.6	13.9	12.6

Sources : Calculated from PRO Adm 68/194,196,197,199,200,202 (known as Seamen's Sixpences); and PRO Adm 7/78,83,87,88,90,96,98 (known as Mediterranean Passes).

Note : All figures for 1726, for northern Europe, for northwest Europe, for the British islands, and for Greenland are calculated from entrances into London only. All other figures are based on entrances and clearances at the port of London.

crews while making faster, safer voyages.'[67] Douglass North, on the other hand, underplaying the role of technology as indicated above, has argued that the decline in crew levels was the result of the diffusion of design techniques introduced in the Dutch flyboats, which, shaped like an oblong box, provided high stowage relative to their nominal tonnage. Such ships 'were designed more for carrying cargo, had less requirements of manning for protection than they had in earlier centuries. *But these changes did not represent fundamental technical change.*'[68]

Despite this difference in interpreting the role of technology, it does seem that technology did play a part in the growing efficiency of British merchant shipping between 1650 and 1830. But, as can be seen in Table 1/3, the ten-

For large parts of the eighteenth century merchant ships were exposed – above and beyond the usual perils of the sea and the uncertainties of commerce – to the additional risks of war. Britain, with the world's largest merchant fleet, was particularly vulnerable to the guerre de course, *and replied by instituting convoys, a system which eventually became compulsory. This late eighteenth-century illustration shows the West Indiaman* Lady Juliana, *which has sprung her main mast, under tow by a British frigate in an attempt to keep up with the rest of the convoy. It is obviously an important convoy because the escort includes a line of battle ship (on the* Lady Juliana's *starboard beam).* (National Maritime Museum)

dency towards fewer men per ton was counteracted during the war years in the table (1742 and 1760) when larger crews would be needed for protection. And there were exceptions to the general trend towards fewer men per ton. For example, ships engaged in the specialist Greenland fishing trade and trade with the East Indies needed to maintain large crews throughout the eighteenth century – estimated at 45 men per vessel in the London/Greenland trade; and just under 100 men per vessel in the London/East India trade. East Indiamen had to carry large crews because of the incidence of piracy in the Indian Ocean, coupled with the lack of naval protection in the area which also necessitated a large number of guns. The safety – or otherwise – of particular trading areas, therefore, also had a bearing on the size of crew and the number of guns carried by a merchantman, and this may have been just as important as technology in influencing the level of efficiency (and also profitability) within the shipping industry.

Indeed, the two may well have been linked, for it has been argued that 'the rate of technological diffusion in shipping, 1675-1775, was primarily a function of changes in the incidence of piracy, privateering and similar hazards.'[69] With the exception of the war years of the period, in the two centuries after 1650 the safety of maritime activity improved considerably, helping to bring about not only a reduc-

tion in crew levels, as already indicated, but also in the cost of protection. Protection basically meant guns and there is no doubt that during the years being examined there was a significant change in the maritime environment, from a situation where many merchantmen carried guns as a matter of routine, to one where the majority of merchantmen carried no guns at all. In general, the number of guns carried by a vessel was primarily conditioned by the possibility of attack from enemy shipping, although the growth of marine insurance meant that some vessels did not carry the number of guns they should have done. Consequently, as the seas grew in safety the number of guns carried by merchant ships declined significantly.

However, there were exceptions to this trend. Throughout the whole of the period from the 1670s to the late eighteenth century,

67. R Menard, 'Transport costs and long-range trade, 1300-1800: was there a European "transport revolution" in the early modern era?', in J D Tracey (ed), *The Political Economy of Merchant Empires: State Power and World Trade 1350-1750* (Cambridge 1991), p262.

68. D C North, 'The role of transportation in the economic development of North America', *Les Grandes Voies Maritimes dans le Monde XVe-XIXe Siècles* (Paris 1965), p219. The last sentence has been italicised by the present writer to emphasise the point that some historians minimise the role of technology at this time.

69. G M Walton, 'Obstacles to technical diffusion in ocean shipping, 1675-1775', *Explorations in Economic History* VIII (1971), p125.

for example, it was stipulated that East Indiamen had to carry between 24 and 28 guns;[70] and since Caribbean waters remained less safe than elsewhere, sugar traders were more heavily armed than others. It is also true that the frequent outbreak of war tended to interrupt this trend towards lower armament levels. But from the details recorded in the various shipping lists compiled in the eighteenth and early nineteenth centuries, it is also clear that because of improvements in the convoy system–the Convoy Act of 1798 which stipulated that, with one or two exceptions such as East Indiamen, all vessels trading overseas had to sail in convoy–and the growing strength of the British navy, merchantmen carried far fewer guns in the wars after the middle of the eighteenth century than they did in the wars before that date.

Improvements in information and organisation

The overall impact of technology and growing maritime security on the characteristics of the merchant fleet discussed above–size, rig, and crew and armament levels–helped to bring about lower costs and higher productivity within the merchant shipping industry. However, these physical changes were not the only influences on costs and productivity–and, in turn, on profitability. The availability and diffusion of information on many aspects of maritime activity, and organisational improvements within the commercial sector of the economy were also important factors in increasing the productivity of merchant shipping. At one level, as overseas trade expanded and many of the functions associated with such trade became more complex, ship masters needed more commercial and legal information in order to do their jobs effectively. *Lloyd's List*, for example, first published in 1734, made information on such things as weather conditions and the movement of shipping more widely available. Mungo Murray's *A Treatise on Shipbuilding and Navigation* appeared in the middle of the eighteenth century and contained sections on the theory of shipbuilding and navigation, geography, sea charts and latitudes etc.[71] Similarly, as Robin Craig has pointed

out, commercial information was increasingly provided by publications such as J Goodfellow's *The Universal Dictionary* (1778), subtitled *Or Complete Pocket-Assistance for Merchants, Masters of Ships, Mates and all Persons Concerned in Ships or Shipping of goods*; and D Steel's *The Ship-Masters' Assistant and Owners' Manual* (1788). 'This diffusion of knowledge and practical experience', argues Craig, 'was undoubtedly important in stimulating skill and efficiency' with the result 'that general standards of behaviour and commercial competence were improved by the widespread dissemination of information likely to render the deployment of shipping more rational.'[72]

One indication of this growing 'rationality' was the improvement in the organisation of many overseas trades. All those involved with merchant shipping–owners, masters, and charterers, and themselves taking advantage of the wider availability of maritime and commercial information – became increasingly aware of the financial benefits from improved organisation, and from studying the needs of particular trades. As a result, after 1650, as British merchants spread their trading network to all points of the globe, improved organisation and

better information became both a cause and effect of that expansion. Many vessels in the sugar, tobacco, or timber trades, for example, were adapted to maximise their carrying capacity of those goods; the timing of voyages was calculated in order to maximise the opportunities for buying or selling goods and to minimise the time spent in port; whilst constant traders operating over the same trading route for many years and building up contacts and expertise in that trade became a major feature of Britain's maritime activity. For example, in the middle decades of the eighteenth century the majority of vessels engaged in Bristol's, Glasgow's and London's transatlantic trades undertook regular direct voyages between either Bristol,

70. Minchinton, 'Corporate ship operation', p146.

71. Mungo Murray, *A Treatise on Shipbuilding and Navigation* (London 1765).

72. R Craig, 'Printed guides for master mariners as a source of productivity change in shipping, 1750-1914', *Journal of Transport History*, 3rd series, 3 (1982), pp23-35. The examples and quote are from pp24-25. The importance of better information is also discussed in S Ville, 'The growth of specialisation in English shipowning, 1750-1850', *Economic History Review* XLVI (1993), pp713-715.

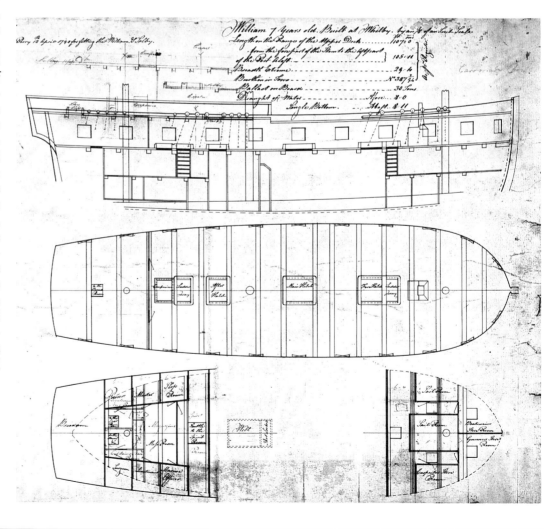

An Admiralty fitting out plan for the William, *purchsed in 1798 as an armed vessel (rated as a sloop), but converted into a storeship in 1800. Built at Whitby about 1791, the vessel was probably one of the innumerable East Coast colliers. Most of the platforms and cabins below the main deck would be naval additions. (National Maritime Museum)*

Robert Salmon's painting of the 'brig' Ariel *is dated 1811 (the separate main trysail mast and the square canvas on the crossjack would probably make this a 'snow' to the seaman of the time). By this period the merchant brig has become flat-sheered, is probably flush-decked, and solid bulwarks run fore and aft.* (National Maritime Museum)

Glasgow or London, the colonies and back again, with a subsequent decline in multilateral voyages.[73] Thus the *New Hatley*, built and registered in London in 1740, completed four round trips in four years (1749-52) between London and Virginia, whilst the *James Dawkins*, built and registered in London in 1761, also completed four round trips in four years (1762-65) between London and Jamaica. Ships in the Clyde tobacco fleet performed even better. The *Cochrane*, for example, completed eighteen round trips in twelve years, and overall this fleet experienced 'a steady improvement in transport utilisation, in the number of voyages per ship, in the reduction of turn-round times' and therefore 'a reduction in the overall cost of transport.'[74]

Regular and direct shipping routes also allowed ship masters to gain experience and expertise in, among other things, the naviga-tional requirements and geographical peculiar-ities and hazards of individual areas, and the organisation of different trades. Decisions taken by a ship's master could be crucial to the success or otherwise of a trading voyage. As a result, the London shipowners Michael Henley and Son, for example, took great care when appointing masters to their vessels, and would normally first appoint a master to the coasting trade in order to judge suitability for promo-tion to overseas voyages.[75]

Not only was the movement of merchant shipping becoming better organised as a result of improved information and experience, but so too was the shipping industry as a whole. The important research of Simon Ville–especially into the operation of the London shipowners Michael Henley and Son–has demonstrated that as overseas trade began to expand from the 1780s onwards, and as the French Wars created an even greater demand for shipping, the whole infrastructure within which merchant shipping operated became more sophisticated. Ship ownership, for example, typically fragmented for much of the seventeenth and eighteenth centuries by the system of investors buying a number of '64th' shares in a vessel, from the late eighteenth century became increasingly specialist and professional. The system whereby a ship would have a large number of owners, generally including the merchants using that vessel, gave way to a system of con-centrated ownership and to the separation between shipowner and merchant.[76]

Other specialist activities growing in impor-tance from the end of the eighteenth century onwards, also contributed to this organisation-al revolution. These included the shipping agent, employed to organise 'the loading and discharge of cargoes' and to provide informa-tion on local economic conditions; the ship

73. Morgan, *Bristol and the Atlantic Trade*, Chapter 3, and R Dell, 'The operational record of the Clyde tobacco fleet, 1747-1775', *Scottish Economic and Social History* 2 (1982), Table 1, p5.

74. Dell, 'Operational record of the Clyde tobacco fleet', pp6 and 15. The voyages of the *New Hatley* and *James Dawkins* are detailed in C J French, 'Productivity in the Atlantic shipping industry: a quantitative study', *Journal of Interdisciplinary History* XVII (1987), pp617 and 619.

75. On the role of the master see Morgan, *Bristol in the Atlantic Trade*, pp82-3; and Ville, *English Shipowning During the Industrial Revolution*, p151.

76. Discussed in more detail in Ville, *English Shipowning During the Industrial Revolution*, especially pp2-5.

broker, whose prime function was to secure freight; and the marine insurer. Insurance in the eighteenth century was monopolised by Lloyd's underwriters, the London Assurance Company and the Royal Exchange Company, and it was not until the 1820s that competition for these companies began to emerge. As a result, mutual insurance clubs sprang up–especially in the northeast–as an alternative method of organising maritime insurance.[77]

Conclusion

By 1830, at the end of this survey, Britain was well on the way to becoming the world's first industrial nation. The merchant shipping industry, as a crucial factor in commercial and maritime expansion in the seventeenth and eighteenth centuries, had played an important role in this development and this role was to continue, of course, throughout the nineteenth century. But this element of continuity was also being influenced by change within the shipping industry. This chapter has traced some of the main changes taking place within the merchant shipping industry between 1650 and 1830, and the influences under which the industry operated. One of these influences was the onset of the industrial revolution and, as part of the whole industrialising process, by the end of the period surveyed here important changes were taking place in construction techniques and methods of propulsion employed by the shipping industry. However, although the period covered in

this chapter was clearly an age of 'wood and sail', it was not suddenly overtaken by an age of 'iron and steam'. Certainly, by 1830 the first steamships were in operation with 298 steamships being registered in that year, and iron was being used in vessel construction. But it would be another 30 years before wood was replaced by iron as the major material used in shipbuilding, and even longer before steam replaced sail on the major trade routes. As Basil Greenhill has argued: 'the sailing vessel's

goodbye was going to be very long drawn out',[78] and in 1830 both wood and sail had a continuing and crucial role to play in Britain's merchant shipping industry.

Christopher French

77. All of these ares are discussed in Ville, 'The growth of specialisation in English shipowning', pp715-718.

78. B Greenhill in his introduction to *Sail's Last Century*, p16.

British Empire: Typical Vessels 1650-1830

Name	Description	Built	Launched	Tonnage	Dimensions (Feet) (Metres)	Remarks
AMITY	Ship	Purchased by Navy 1650		375	90.00 x 28.00 x 12.00 27.43 x 8.53 x 3.66	Classified as Fourth Rate; sold 1667
GILES	Ketch	Purchased by Navy 1661		48	37.00 x 15.50 x 6.00 11.28 x 4.72 x 1.83	Sold 1667
SAMUEL OF STROOD	Hoy (single mast)	Purchased by Navy 1667		58	40.00 x 16.50 x 8.16 12.19 x 5.03 x 2.49	Returned to owner 1668
FRIEZLAND	'Flyboat', ship rig	Captured from Dutch 1672		227	84.50 x 22.50 x 10.50 25.76 x 6.86 x 3.20	Given to Africa Co 1672
SUCCESS	Ship	England	1675	534	102.00 x 31.37 x 31.09 x 9.56 x	Surveyed by Navy
MARY GALLEY	Ship	Richard Wells, Rotherhithe	1704	141	63.00 x 21.50 x 9.75 19.20 x 6.55 x 2.97	East India 'interloper'; captured by French 1707
MARTHA	Ship	Thames	1723	172	68.20 x 21.81 x *4.70 20.79 x 6.65 x 1.43	Surveyed by Navy Board as possible transport 1739
ELEANOR	Ship	New England	1731	192	63.70 x 29.31 x 11.50 19.42 x 8.93 x 3.51	Surveyed by Navy Board as possible fireship 1739
ST ANN	Packet schooner	America	1736	36	46.75 x 11.83 x 6.85 14.25 x 3.61 x 2.09	Sold to Portugal; plan obtained by Chapman in the 1750s
CHANCE	Sloop, square stern	Aberdeen	1746	63	56.75 x 16.83 x 9.41 17.30 x 5.13 x 2.87	
TETSWORTH	Ship, hagboat stern	Philadelphia	1747-48	200	74.00 x 25.00 x 12.00 22.56 x 7.62 x 3.66	Built for Elias Bland & Co, London; captured by Spanish 1748
FALMOUTH	Ship	Blackwall	1752	668	108.75 x 34.00 x 33.15 x 10.36 x	East Indiaman; wrecked in 1766 on sixth voyage
TAVISTOCK	Brig, pink stern	Shoreham	1759	75	57.50 x 18.00 x 10.75 17.53 x 5.49 x 3.28	
FRIENDSHIP	Brig, square stern	Boston	1763	88	61.50 x 19.00 x *3.83 18.75 x 5.79 x 1.17	
TRIO	Ship, square stern	Thames	1771	302	104.50 x 27.91 x *5.5 31.85 x 8.51 x 1.68	
SWALLOW	Snow, square stern	New York	1774	153	84.00 x 21.25 x *6.16 25.60 x 6.48 x 1.88	
EXETER	Ship	Hilhouse, Bristol	1776	267	95.00 x 26.00 x 11.16 28.96 x 7.92 x 3.40	West Indiaman
SUCCESS	Sloop, round stern	Deal	1778	31	38.00 x 14.83 x 6.33 11.58 x 4.52 x 1.93	Coaster
SEA FLOWER	Schooner, square stern	Nova Scotia	1783	87	62.50 x 18.66 x 8.50 19.05 x 5.69 x 2.59	
CAESTUS	Snow, square stern	Stockton	1787	168	78.00 x 23.16 x 15.91 23.77 x 7.06 x 4.85	
BURGESS	Ketch, round stern	Limehouse	1791	106	58.50 x 21.33 x 9.33 17.83 x 6.50 x 2.84	Coaster
ORION	Brig, square stern	Sunderland	1797	221	83.83 x 25.58 x 15.00 25.55 x 7.80 x 4.57	
ALNWICK CASTLE	Ship, square stern	Blackwall	1801	1257	133.95 x 42.00 x 17.00 40.83 x 12.80 x 5.18	East Indiaman of the largest class
BRITANNIA	Smack, square stern	Rochester	1810	75	57.16 x 17.91 x 10.75 17.42 x 5.46 x 3.28	Coaster
MAGDALEN	Brig, square stern	Lower Canada	1811	180	80.00 x 23.66 x 13.58 24.38 x 7.21 x 4.14	
CHATHAM	Lighter, one mast, round stern	Gillingham	1814	29	36.00 x 14.75 x 4.75 10.97 x 4.50 x 1.45	Coaster
ASIA	Ship, square stern	Alexander Hall, Aberdeen	1818	532	118.50 x 32.41 x 15.16 36.12 x 9.88 x 4.62	
GLASGOW	Schooner	T Morton, Leith	1826	155	72.00 x 22.33 x 13.50 21.95 x 6.81 x 4.11	

* = Height between decks

2

Seagoing Ships of The Netherlands

THIS CHAPTER deals with Dutch mercantile naval architecture in the period between the last decade of the sixteenth century, and the end of the eighteenth century. The golden era of the Dutch empire starts with the great voyages of exploration shortly before the beginning of the seventeenth century and ends with the bankruptcy of the Dutch East India Company (VOC) in the year 1795. Before this period the Dutch carried on much European trade, especially with the Iberian, Scandinavian and Baltic countries, so there was already a basis long before the age of Dutch worldwide glory begun. The end of the period is marked by the collapse of the Dutch economy under the French regime, partly as a result of the British economic and military action during the French wars of 1793-1815.

Naval architecture

It is often claimed that, instead of limiting themselves to transporting Spanish and Portuguese colonial goods, salt and wine from the Iberian peninsula to the rest of Europe as they had done for many years, Dutch merchants decided to send their own ships to the East Indies because the Spanish themselves began taking Dutch merchant vessels in Iberian harbours as prizes in times of political stress. In those days Holland was part of the Spanish empire, against which enormous power it had been fighting a war of independence since 1568. Although this war lasted for eighty years, until 1648, Dutch power was felt all over the

world, particularly in the first decades of the seventeenth century. It may be that the hostilities between the Dutch and Iberians promoted the enlargement of the Dutch trading area, or possibly this was merely the next step in the ever growing enterprise of the Dutch cities; but the fact is that, once the need for vessels to make trips around the world was felt, they were there. It is of little use to speculate about the origin of the large ships used in the first *Schipreizen* (voyages), but they were all built under strong inspiration of southern European ship types. However, they were not simple copies. The square tuck stern, for instance, is a southern European feature that was used in Holland for about 150 years, but the construction was very different from the Iberian example: during the reconstruction of the Basque Red Bay vessel,[1] it became clear that its tuck was built on the ground, plank first, and erected in one piece, together with the stern, barely reinforced by transoms or other frame elements. The Dutch square tuck, however, was a rigid construction of a heavy dovetailed frame, which was only planked in at a later stage of construction. From this example it can be inferred that the Dutch must have been open to new ideas from abroad, but that they modified them for their own requirements. This makes it very difficult to determine how they developed the three-masted ships with which they conquered the world, but as stated above, once the time was ripe, they were already in existence, and were to change very little for about two centuries.

Methods of construction

Literature about shipbuilding in Holland begins with Nicolaes Witsen, a Lord Mayor of Amsterdam who wrote a major book on the subject in 1671.[2] This is not only the first book in which can be found all the dimensions necessary to reconstruct a typical Dutch armed trader, the *pinas*, but it also gives an account of the method by which ships were actually built in those days. Furthermore, the work contains

a massive store of general remarks, theories and building contracts, all dating from the period from about 1630 up to 1670. Study of the book also provides an almost full understanding of earlier building contracts, so that the relevant period can be extended back to the late sixteenth century. Taken with archaeological finds and some pictorial material, this allows the modern reader insight into some aspects of shipbuilding in the early days.

Shipbuilding is a traditional trade and from ship remains found while draining the Zuiderzee it is absolutely clear that the method Witsen described had been used in the area for centuries. It resembles, and is undoubtedly derived from, the way the Scandinavians built their early seagoing vessels: *ie* shell-first.[3] However, unlike its predecessors such as cogs and hulks, the Dutch seventeenth-century product was not clinker-built, but carvel in construction. The transition to flush-planked

Nicolaes Witsen, author of the first book on Dutch shipbuilding. The portrait claims to show him aged thirty-seven, but comes from a book that was printed in 1671 when Witsen was only thirty years old, so the portrait must have been inserted later.

1. Robert Grenier, *Red Bay Project*, Canadian Conservation Institute (in press).

2. Nicolaes Witsen, *Aeloude en Hedendaegsche Scheeps-bouw en Bestier* (Amsterdam 1671).

3. R Reinders, 'Cog finds in the IJsselmeerpolders', *Flevobericht* 248 (1985).

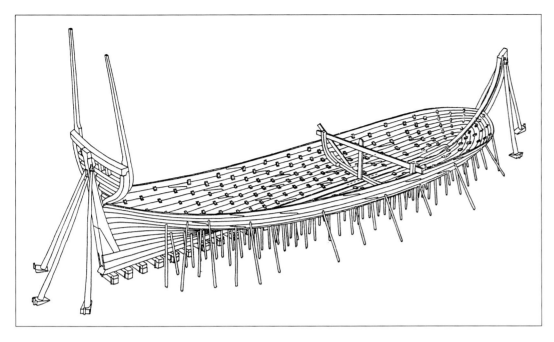

An early stage in the construction of a ship built in the way Witsen described: a shell is formed of the planking of the floor and bilges, one frame former is fitted and the whole construction is supported by small shores underneath. (Drawing by Anton van de Heuvel)

hulls probably took place in the last quarter of the sixteenth century, driven by the ever growing dimensions of the ships needed for an expanding worldwide trade. From archaeological finds it is obvious that the step from clinker to carvel was neither easy nor simple. Not many shipwrecks from the period 1570–1610 have been found, but they all seem to have one typical feature: double exterior planking.[4] One theory has it that the shipwrights put a second layer of planks over the original one to ensure watertightness. No known Dutch shipwreck from after 1610 exhibits this special feature, except the *Batavia* (1626), remains of which have been recovered from the coast of Australia where the ship was wrecked as a result of bad navigation and discipline problems. The tuck of the *Batavia* has a double layer of planks, sealing the butts of the tuck planking and the ship's sides.[5] This is probably one of the last survivors of the Dutch flush double planking period, and proof of the theory that the double planking was meant to keep the ship relatively watertight.

Once the step from clinker to carvel construction had been made, developments came very quickly. The method was perfected within a few years and the products of Dutch shipbuilding began to appear all over Europe before the first quarter of the seventeenth century was out. In Sweden Dutch shipwrights built large warships like the unfortunate *Wasa*; Colbert introduced Dutch ships in France as prototypes for the French fleet; and the same thing happened a little later when Frederick William, the Great Elector, invited a Dutch shipbuilder to build the Brandenburg fleet after Dutch models. The achievements of Dutch

shipbuilders may have been impressive, but the speed with which ships were built was even more amazing. Witsen's *pinas* (of 134 Amsterdam feet) was built in less than four months by twenty or twenty-two men. Therefore, with these cheap but solid and well-designed ships, Holland was ready for the commercial conquest of the world.

However this would never have been possible without the East and the West India Companies. Though the history of these two organisations does not fall within the scope of this chapter, they have to be mentioned: the miles of archival material left by the Dutch East India Company alone is an endless source of detailed instructions about building, rigging, fitting and sailing of ships in those days.[6]

Witsen's method

This method of building seagoing ships is in fact a combination of shell-first and frame-first construction. After laying the keel and erecting the stem and stern timbers the hull bottom was constructed. The planks were temporarily fastened edge to edge with clamps and supported by small shores underneath. The shell-shape was obtained by pinching the ends of the planks in the vertical against stem and sternpost, with the bottom remaining flat amidships. At one-third of the length (between the outside of stem and stern) one floor was placed with a knee on each side, a so-called 'sitter', bolted to the floor. The bilges were then planked up to one-third of the height of the waterline in the same way as for the ship's bottom, the shape of the bilge being determined by the sitters. The shipwright filled the resulting hollow with frame parts. Curved grown futtocks and floors

were fitted, with as little shaping as necessary. Even when applied to ship-model building, this method of filling in the frames makes for rapid completion with a minimum of wasted timber. This was followed by the fixing of a temporary batten–the so-called *scheerstrook*–to a few *oplangen*, which were the upper sections of the frames that shaped the topsides. They were practically all of the same shape and so making drawings or using moulds, the usual characteristics of frame-first shipbuilding, was not necessary. This ends the shell-first phase of the process.

Once the *scheerstrook* was in the right position, the rest of the vertical futtocks could be filled in, the ceiling could be laid, and deck beams, dovetailed into heavy clamps, made the construction as rigid as possible. With the keelson and the inner planking in place the topside of the hull could be shaped. Toptimbers (*stutten*) were lowered into the gaps between the vertical futtocks and the planking, thus forming a reinforcing overlap at gundeck height. The shape of the upperworks was determined with the aid of battens, after which the missing frame parts could be formed. With the rest of the deck beams in place and the remaining unplanked area from the top of the bilge up to the gundeck filled in, the ship was launched to free the yard for the next hull–all achieved within a few months. The ship was finished afloat, so that the hull, supported naturally in water, was not subject to the stresses of a ship launched with its heavy structure complete.

The whole process was speeded up by the fact that the shipyards received their wood in sawn condition, thanks to the sawmill industry in the Zaan area, north of Amsterdam and later, after 1630, in Amsterdam itself. The city of

4. Th J Maarleveld, 'Archaeology and early modern merchant ships. Building sequence and consequences. An introductory review', in A Carmiggelt (ed), *Rotterdam Papers* VII (Rotterdam 1992).

5. J Green, *The loss of the VOC retourschip BATAVIA, Western Australia 1629. An excavation report and catalogue of artefacts*, BAR Int Series 489 (Oxford 1989).

6. J R Bruyn, F S Gaastra and I Schöffer, *Dutch-Asiatic Shipping in the Seventeenth and Eighteenth Century*, Rijks Geschiedkundige Publicatien, Grote serie nr 165, 166, 167 (The Hague 1987); H Den Heijer, *De Geschiedenis van de WIC* (Zutphen 1994); H W Keweloh, *Auf den Spuren der Flösser* (Stuttgart 1988).

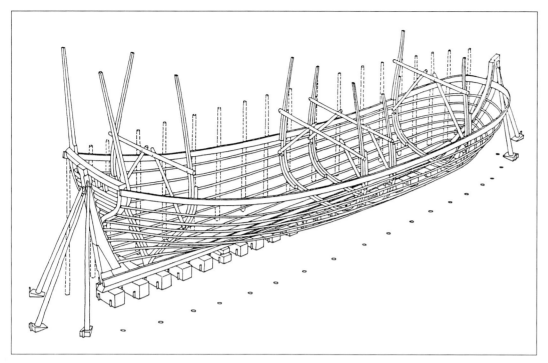

A stage in the construction of a ship built in the way Van Yk described. Ribbands have been attached to four initial frames. The broad top-ribband is called the 'scheerstrook'. (Drawing by Anton van de Heuvel)

Dordrecht was another centre of shipbuilding materials. Enormous rafts of hundreds of metres of timber were floated down the river Rhine, carrying hundreds of men who shipped the load to Dordrecht, where the rafts were broken up and the wood distributed all over Holland.

Van Yk's method

There is another remarkable description of the process of shipbuilding in seventeenth-century Dutch literature. Cornelis van Yk was a shipwright in Delfshaven (near Rotterdam), who published a book on the subject in 1697.[7] Strange as it may seem, he gives a completely different method from Witsen's, in spite of the fact that Amsterdam and Rotterdam are no more than 80 kilometres apart. Van Yk's description is identical to Witsen's up to the first bottom plank, the garboard strake. This plank together with the keel then served as the basis for two identical frames, placed at some distance. The *scheerstrook* was connected to poles driven in to the ground to define the outline of the ship. Then a third almost identical frame was placed on the butt of keel and stem. Using a simple calculation an after frame was deduced from the shape of the forward frame and placed exactly at the same distance from the stern as the forward frame was from the stem. This enabled the shipwright to determine the lines of the stern, and the trim aft, needed to steer satisfactorily. The shipwright

then shaped the hull by using ribbands, temporary battens, which also served as a support for the frame parts that were to be put in subsequently. After the keelson and ceiling were fitted, the deck beams, attached in the same way as in Witsen's method, supplied the necessary rigidity. Finally the ship was planked and launched, again to be finished in the water.

This method is in essence completely different from the one Witsen described. There is no evidence that Van Yk's method was developed from Witsen's, and it seems much more rational to suppose that the Rotterdam method, which was used in Zealand and Flanders as well, was originally an adaptation of the method the Spanish introduced in the sixteenth century in the southern part of the country, where their political grip was much stronger than in the north. In his book Van Yk prints a building contract for a 172ft ship of 1629 (page 157), which gives the Rotterdam method a respectable age and leaves little scope for the theory of related ancestry.

Similarities and differences

Different as they may appear, there are many similarities between the two methods, the most important being the fact that in neither were plans or drawings necessary to build the ship. For both methods contract specifications were used, in which the dimensions of every part of the ship were laid down, usually based on an existing successful ship; these were not only legal documents, but also provided the shipbuilder with sufficient data to replicate the desired prototype.

It is obvious that in those days nobody was too much troubled about the underwater shape of the hull: that was something determined by the eye of the master. However, there were some factors that were believed to be important in the process of shaping the ship. Dutch shipwrights built no standard vessels. The customer ordered a ship for a specific purpose (the timber or corn trade, whaling, privateering, war, etc) and the shipwright translated these wishes into the shape of the ship. In order to achieve his aim, he considered the following items:

1. The ratio between the dimensions. A normal ship had one-fourth of its length as its beam, and one-tenth as its depth in hold. Fast ships were narrower and more shallow, warships were usually a little wider.

2. The length of the keel. Early in the seventeenth century keels were shorter than later on. A long keel was known to resist drifting to leeward when close-hauled.

3. The rake of the stem and stern. This of course was related to the length of the keel. The more the ends raked, the faster the ship was thought to be, but the less it could carry. Extreme raking stems usually cost two expensive naturally-curved, 'grown', trees. When trees of these dimensions became hard to come by, the keel was lengthened and the stem raked less. This, incidentally, improved the ship's performance a great deal. Filling pieces be-

The main frame of a 'jacht', reconstructed by the author from a contract in Witsen's book. The floor is 7 feet wide and the deadrise 10 inches (v = feet, d = inches); the top of the bilge is 9½ feet wide and 4 feet high; and the height of the 'scheerstrook', coinciding with the lower deck is 10½ feet wide and 8½ feet high. The lower deck has a height of 5½ feet.

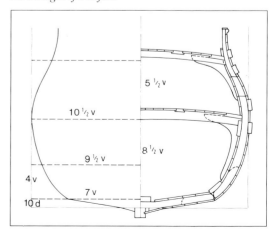

7. C Van Yk, *De Nederlandsche Scheeps-bouw-konst Open Gestelt* (Amsterdam 1697).

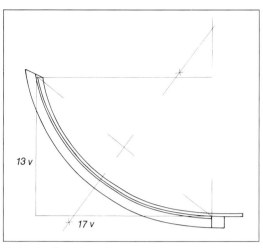

Example of a strongly raking stem (v = feet, d= inches). For fast ships like 'jachts' the stem had more forward projection than height. Reconstruction by the author.

tween stem and keel still allowed the shipwright to make a hull shape that moved over the water, instead of cutting through it. Merchantmen, which needed a large carrying capacity and little speed, showed hardly any rake in stems and sterns, in complete contrast to frigates and *jachts*, which did.

4. The deadrise. This was the amount, seen in cross-section, by which the bottom rose from the keel to the bilge. (The longitudinal rising lines were never mentioned in the contract, but were left to the experience of the

Construction of sternpost and sternframe. Height of the stern: 13¹/₂ feet, rake 3 feet, The transom is 12 feet wide and 10 inches in depth; the fashion pieces meet the sternpost at a height of 7 feet. Note the flat structure below the transom, which was fitted together with dovetails and bolted afterwards. Reconstruction by the author.

builder.) Fast ships were given relatively steep deadrise, whereas merchantmen were practically flat-floored–not that this rising of the bottom was ever dramatic: the shallow nature of Dutch harbours rarely permitted more than a few inches, or a foot at the very most.

5. The width of the floors. The wider the bottom, the more capacious the ship, and the more it could carry.

6. The length of the transom. The transom, together with the fashion-pieces, formed the basis of the flat tuck: the wider it was, the greater the internal volume, and hence carrying capacity of the ship, would be. In the course of the seventeenth century the length of the transom grew from less than two-thirds to three-quarters of the ship's beam.

7. The rising of the decks and wales. For warships it was important to have a relatively flat deck, so that the gun carriages had a stable platform. Merchant ships employed more sheer, as it was one of the ways to prevent hogging.

8. The degree of tumblehome in the topsides. Warships' upperworks were straighter, whereas those of merchantmen were pinched in, to make boarding more difficult, and to reduce duties (like the Danish Sound dues) based on breadth on deck.

9. The rigidity of the hull. Warships were elaborately supplied with riders and other reinforcements to withstand the destructive effects of firing their own guns, while *jachts* were lightly built.

10. The dimensions of the masts and spars. The shipbuilder could choose between relatively low masts and wide yards or tall masts and narrow yards.

There were other ways by which the shipwright could change a design to meet the customer's demands, but those listed above are the most important.

These factors are itemised in building contracts of both northern and southern shipbuilders, and the results of the different styles of building could only be seen under water, where the turn of the bilge was much more angled for the northern ship and rather rounder for the southern one. This was the effect of the planking tongues, that prevented the planks from tipping up in an early stage of construction, when they were pressed together by a system of levers and chains called the *hel*. The planking tongues produced a flat bottom, while the southern shipwright avoided this by almost freely determining the shape of his frames. It should be mentioned, however, that in northern ships with a lot of deadrise, the angle is sometimes very hard to see.

Both methods are similar in the way the dimensions were arrived at by the use of formulae. For instance, the thickness of the stem is one inch for every 10 feet length of the ship. Although the formulae in the two methods often reveal detail differences, the outcome is usually very much the same, so that ships of the two areas in the end did not differ much. They were both products of the same traditional approach to shipbuilding, though the methods may have differed. No draughted design, a flexible application of traditional rules, and a fast and cheap method of building, are the main characteristics of both ways of shipbuilding.

The planking 'tongue' that was used in Witsen's days to help shaping the ship's bottom. (from Witsen's Aeloude en Hedendaegse Scheepsbouw en Bestier *of 1671).*

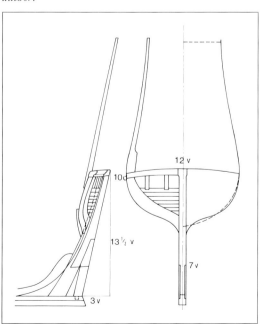

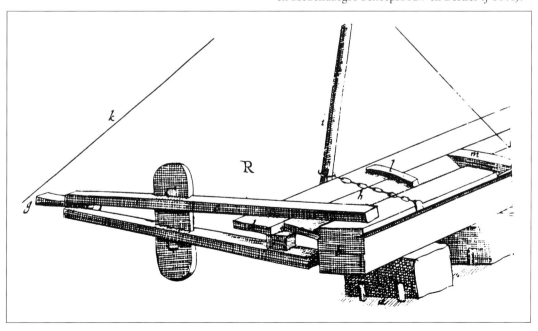

Eighteenth-century developments

After the successful innovations of the first few decades of the seventeenth century a relative decline set in, largely the result of continuing improvements in the British and French shipbuilding industries. Of course there were developments in Dutch design, in both hull and rig, but the methods remained basically the same. However, outside the Netherlands more and more shipwrights worked out their designs on paper, with the result that innovations could be introduced much more easily. Thus the very success of Dutch methods became obstructive by discouraging improvements that were adopted without too much difficulty by foreign competitors.

Naturally, these developments were noticed by a number of influential Dutchmen, including Admiral Schrijver (1687-1768) of the Admiralty of Amsterdam (each of the main provinces of the Netherlands had its own autonomous naval administration). He and others were critical of traditional shipbuilding methods, and their lobbying led to the introduction of three British shipwrights at the Amsterdam Admiralty shipyard, Thomas Davis, Charles Bentham and John May in 1727.[8] It is hard to estimate the impact of their influence. A few innovations were carried through, such as the round tuck stern, but a

The VOC shipyard in Vlissingen (Flushing), Zealand in 1779. This is one of the rare pictures that give details of eighteenth-century construction methods. (Zeeuws Museum, Middelburg)

very different hull shape could hardly be expected given the limitations of shallow Dutch harbours. Tests in which British and Dutch designs were compared never showed any clear superiority of one over the other: in some weathers the British performed better and under other conditions the Dutch.

The appointment of British shipwrights in important positions caused quite a stir in Holland. Dutch shipwrights were deeply insulted and when Schrijver had a translation made of the French works of Duhamel du Monceau[9] in 1757 to show them how to do their job, the limit was reached. In the same year the Rotterdam Admiralty's master shipbuilder, Leendert van Zwijndrecht, wrote a book on draughting in ship design;[10] his brother Pieter did the same in a manuscript;[11] and the master shipwright of the Zealand chamber of the East India Company, Udemans, wrote down his ideas on the subject[12] – all intended to demonstrate that Dutch masters were not inferior to British and French 'modernists'. The survival of these manuscripts gives the historian some idea of eighteenth-century Dutch construction methods.

However, whereas in the seventeenth century two authors (Witsen and Van Yk) wrote about the actual practice in seventeenth-century yards, there is nothing on the subject in eighteenth-century Dutch literature. Van Zwijndrecht and Udeman do supply some clues as to what must have been eighteenth-century building practice: they reveal that it was only necessary to draught nine, ten or twelve frames.

These 'station frames' were erected on the keel, after which ribbands were used to indicate the shape of the hull. 'Filling frames' were placed between the station frames, their profile being determined by the ribbands.

This is obviously a further development of the method Van Yk wrote about in 1697. He suggested a method of determining the aftermost of the four initial frames, which may or may not have needed a little bit of paperwork (although some simple arithmetic would have achieved the same result). Van Zwijndrecht streamlined this method and indicated that Dutch shipbuilding techniques could very well compete with the British, but basically his ideas were no real improvement in comparison with Van Yk's method. Ship design was still based on the application of traditional formulae and though the art of draughting was probably

8. J R Bruyn, 'Engelse Scheepsbouwers op de Amsterdamse Admiraliteitswerf in de 18de eeuw – enkele aspecten', *Mededelingen van de Nederlandse Vereniging voor Zeegeschiedenis* (September 1990).

9. Duhamel du Monceau, *Grondbeginselen van de Scheepsbouw of Werkdadige Verhandeling van de Scheepstimmerkunst* (Amsterdam 1757).

10. L Van Zwijndrecht, *Verhandeling van de Hollandschen Scheepsbouw, raakende de verschillende Charters de Oorlogschepen* (with an additional part by C de Ruiter, *Verhandeling van 't bouwen van Koopvaardyschepen*) (The Hague 1757).

11. P Van Zwijndrecht, 'De Groote Nederlandsche Scheeps – Bouw op een Proportionaale Reegel voor Gestelt', manuscript 1757.

12. W Udemans Jr, *Verhandeling van den Nederlandschen Scheepsbouw* (Middelburg 1757).

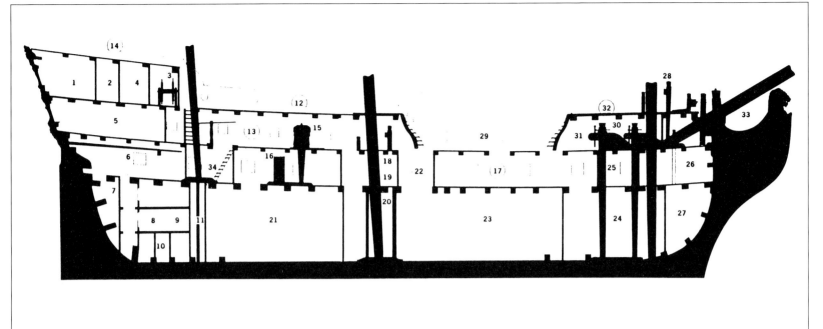

1. *Captain's cabin*
2. *Captain's bedplace*
3. *Officers' cabins*
4. *Surgeon's cabin*
5. *Great cabin*
6. *Gunroom* (constabelskamer)
7. *Store room*
8. *Cartridge lockers*
9. *Bread- and sailrooms*
10. *Powder room*
11. *Pump and pump well*
12. *Quarterdeck*
13. *Upper deck*
14. *Poop*
15. *Capstan*
16. *Ventilator*
17. *Gundeck (berthing for crew)*
18. *Galley (and quarters for cook and assistants)*
19. *Steward's room (and quarters for steward and assistants)*
20. *Well (shot lockers)*
21. *After hold (water and provisions)*
22. *Main hatch*
23. *Main hold (cargo)*
24. *Cable tier*
25. *Cordage store*
26. *Store room*
27. *Manger*
28. *Bitts*
29. *Waist*
30. *Forecastle (berthing for crew)*
31. *Anchor bitts*
32. *Forecastle deck*
33. *Beakhead (heads for crew)*
34. *Sailroom*
(Drawing by A F Hoekstra)

Longitudinal section of an East Indiaman of about 1750.

mastered by the Van Zwijndrechts and Udemans, they still had no idea of displacement, metacentre, etc, as described by Bouger in France.

Witsen's method, on the other hand, did not evolve at all, although it is safe to state that the shell-first method was used in less prominent shipyards in the northern part of Holland up to the very end of wooden shipbuilding. In Frisia it even survived to the present day for small traditional inshore vessels like *boeiers* and *tjotters*.

Apart from construction, the appearance of the ship itself also changed over the period of 200 years. It received a wider transom and a round tuck, lost most of the sheer to both wales and decks, and was built with heavier framing in which the openings characteristic of seventeenth-century designs were filled in with extra futtocks. The beakhead shrank gradually from one-fifth of the ship's length at the beginning of the seventeenth century to one-eighth at the end, and was eventually reduced to an almost rudimentary ornament in the last decades of the eighteenth century.

Van Yk mentions an event in 1661 which caused a change in the internal arrangements of merchantmen: the Dutch East India Company had bought a warship from the Admiralty and had loaded it as usual. In the English Channel however the crew noticed that there was a lot of water in the hold and as they could not find what caused the leak they decided to return to Holland for the required attention. It turned out that because the ship was so deeply laden and the weather was so bad the crew had not yet detached the anchors from the cables, allowing water to come in via the hawse holes and had leaked between frames, planks and ceiling into the hold. (In warships the anchor cables were stowed in the hold, to keep the gundeck free for guns.) The shipwright decided to move the cable tier up to the forward gundeck, lengthening the stem, and closing the bow so that the forecastle deck ended at the stem; the bitts were moved into the forecastle, the original hawse holes closed off, and removed with the beakhead to one deck higher. Thus the water could no longer reach the open hawse holes. An extra advantage of this arrangement was that the hold was free for

merchandise. It worked out so well, Van Yk says, that from that moment on all merchant vessel were built in this fashion.

There were also improvements in the rigging: the typical seventeenth-century spritsail topmast disappeared in the course of the eighteenth century; the mizzen mast grew from a stumpy little mast with only one triangular sail into a much longer one, with square sails as well; the size of the topsails increased, staysails were slowly introduced around 1660 and stunsails at about the same time. The spritsail topmast was replaced by a jibboom before 1740 and the spritsails finally disappeared altogether. The triangular mizzen sail was cut down into a trapezium shape abaft the mast, initially retaining the long mizzen yard until it was finally replaced by a gaff, although it was still without the lower boom of later years.

One Dutch invention should not pass unnoticed: lowering topmasts were the idea of a Dutch skipper, Krijn Wouters, in about 1570. Until then topmasts were lashed to the lower masts, but Wouters designed a large semi-circular block (the mast cap) fixed to the head of the lower mast and crosstrees to cradle the topmast. Masthead tackles and sheaves in the foot of the topmast allowed the crew to hoist and lower the upper mast as required. This invention was adopted very quickly all over Europe, although inshore craft and small seagoing vessels retained their lashed topmasts up to the end of the sail era.

Lasts and lengths

During the first few decades of the period under review, the sizes of ships were not given in terms of hull dimensions but in the number of 'lasts' they could load. A last was not a weight, but a cubic measure for corn; nevertheless the last is supposed to be the equivalent of two tuns, or 2000 kilos. In the first years of the Dutch East India Company ships of, for instance, 50, 100 or 350 lasts are recorded, without giving the actual lengths in feet.

It was not possible to calculate the number of lasts mathematically. What was usually done

13. Anonymous, 'Evenredige Toerusting van Schepen ten Oorlog Bijder See', manuscript dated 1660 in Scheepvaartmuseum Amsterdam. Transcription Herman Ketting.
H Decquer, *Middelen om uit te vinden de ware ladinge der schepen na hare groote* (Amsterdam 1690), VOC publication.

was to fill an unloaded ship with cannonballs. When an acceptable draught was reached the weight of the shot was added up and divided by 4000, which produced the number of lasts. It was, of course, very impractical to do this for every ship built, and vessels more or less similar to the trials ship were listed as being of an equal number of lasts.

A second (theoretical) method to establish the loading capacity was to measure the precise shape of the waterline of an empty ship, then to load the ship before taking the shape of the waterline again; the distance between both levels was measured and the contents of the resulting volume worked out. This produced the number of lasts. The difficulty, again, was the amount of work involved, so a formula was devised: the length (between the outside of the stem and the stern) multiplied by the moulded beam (over the frames, without the planking), by the depth in the hold (from the keel to the underside of the deck planking, measured at the ship's side). This produced far too high a number of cubic feet, so the product had to be divided by a factor. The problem lay with the size of the factor: for inshore vessels the factor differed for each type of ship–for a *wijtschip* for instance it was 180, for certain types of the *kaag* it was 240, and all other types ranged somewhere in between.

For seagoing vessels, however, it was even

more complicated. For both VOC *retourschepen* (East Indiamen) and men-of-war a factor of 250 was used.[13] However, checking the formulae on ships of known length and lasts rarely produces this figure. *Fluits*, for instance, often come to a factor somewhere near 200, whereas early *jachts* or *pinasses* often produce a figure as high as 370. In fact this is not without logic. The carrying capacity of a ship was highly dependant of what else the ship had to take on board: ships with a large crew and guns had much less room left for cargo than ships with only a few men and no artillery. Therefore, it is very unwise to derive the length of a ship from only the number of lasts. This means that for the first decades of the Dutch East India Company only a rough estimate of the size of the ships can be given, unless both the factor and the proportions mentioned above (length : beam : depth = 10 : 4 : 1) are used as a starting point. Then, for a hypothetical ship of 300 lasts, the calculation would be as follows:
(length[L] x beam x depth) / factor = number of lasts.
or: (L x 1/4 L x 1/10 L) / [for instance] 250 = 300.
or: $1/40 \ L^3 = 250 \times 300$.

H C Vroom's painting of the Hollandse Tuyn *and some smaller vessels returning from Brazil in 1598. Though the difference is hard to see, the ship on the left is probably a* 'jacht'. *(Rijksmuseum, Amsterdam)*

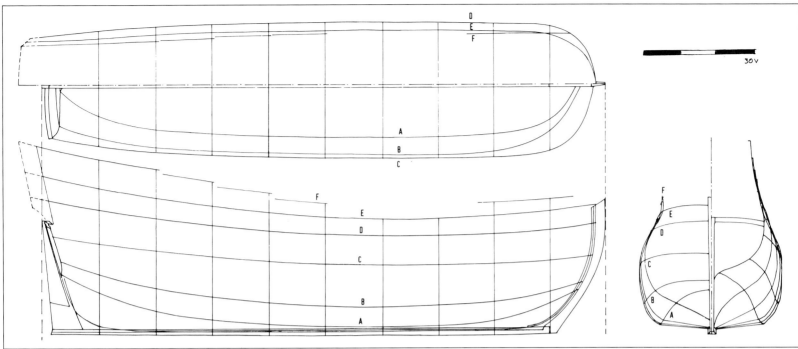

Lines plan after the dimensions the Dutch East India Company settled in the Resolutions of 1697. The lines delineate the floor (A), tops of the bilges (B), height of the 'Scheerstrook' (C), height of the upper deck in the waist (D), and top wale (E). F represents the lines of the rails fore and aft. Each of these datum points (where the lines cross) has been taken from the Resolutions. There were three rates: 160 feet, 145 feet and 130 feet, but the lines were very much alike for all three. Reconstruction by the author.

or: $1/40\ L^3 = 75,000$.

or: $L^3 = 3,000,000$.

or: $L = \sqrt[3]{3,000,000} = 144$ feet

So this ship's dimensions would be 144 x 36 x 14.4 feet.

Standardisation

For the Company itself the issue of ship size must have been just as troublesome, and at a very early stage it tried to standardise the sizes of its ships: mostly about 160ft for the largest charter, 145ft for the medium and 130ft for the smallest type. Standardisation saved money in purchasing, supply and repair. Around 1640 ships were no longer specified by the number of lasts, but by their length in feet, usually over the outside of stem and stern. It remained that way for the rest of the period, except for warships: in the eighteenth century their size was specified in terms of guns, not by length in feet. In the seventeenth century, on the other hand, the shipwright decided on the number of guns that could be carried during construction, although occasional adaptations were made to fit more or fewer guns. Leendert van Zwijndrecht describes how if the eighteenth-century shipwright was commissioned to build, for example, an 80-gun ship, he would begin his calculations as follows:

14 gunports, each $3\frac{5}{11}$ft wide	48ft 4ins
13 inter-port spaces, 8ft each	104ft
distance from first gunport to stem	20ft
distance from last gunport to stern	12ft

Makes a total length of the ship   184ft 4ins

It is obvious that shipbuilding in the eighteenth century increasingly limited the freedom of the master shipwright. More and more rules and regulations determined the nature of his profession. The influence of the management of both the Dutch East India Company and the Admiralties became more obtrusive. No longer did the shipwright make the final decision on the shape and arrangement of his product, but his superiors did. Van Dam's history of the Dutch East India Company, written at the end of the seventeenth century, depicts an ongoing struggle to force the master shipwrights to build according to the chosen criteria: fellow shipbuilders from other cities were even brought in to check whether or not the masters had kept to the specification.[14] Initially only the dimensions were prescribed, but gradually also the shape of the main frame, the rise of the bottom, the length of the transom, etc were specified, sizes being quoted to the quarter of an inch. This process culminated in the *Resolutie* (Resolutions) of the *Heeren Zeeventien* (the seventeen directors) of the Dutch East India Company of 4 April 1697, when so many co-ordinates were given that a complete lines plan can be reconstructed. The rigging was also subject to the regulations: the Resolution of 2 February 1742 gives the data for a complete sail plan, with all the rigging details mentioned down to the smallest rope.

All this may be most gratifying for historians, but the opportunities for the spontaneous introduction of innovations, inventions and experiments became very much reduced within a system that already suffered a lack of flexibil-

ity. Also lost was the speed with which ships were built : construction times escalated from a few months in the seventeenth century to a year or more in the eighteenth. The unbridled energy, the over-enthusiastic belief in the endless possibilities the world had to offer that seemed to characterise the beginning of the seventeenth century, is painfully missing in the eighteenth. Maybe this is one of the reasons why Holland could no longer compete with other European countries, though the products of its shipbuilding industry were by no means of inferior quality.

Having said all this, it must be remembered that the Admiralty and the Dutch East India Company were not the only customers for ships. There was still a lively trade, carried on in a series of smaller vessels in the Baltic and the Mediterranean, that only came to an end when French intervention in the Netherlands made it impossible to carry on.

14. P Van Dam, *Beschryvinge van de Oostindische Compagnie*, edited by F W Stapel (The Hague 1927, 1943; original edition 1701).

Types of ship

The rest of this chapter will attempt to characterise the most important Dutch ship types of the period. It is rarely possible to describe any ancestry because too little is known of the ships before this period to be sure of their evolution. Written sources in archives seldom provide images of the ships they mention and ship portraits with the names of the ship types on them, like those by Reinier Nooms and Lons in the seventeenth century, do not exist for earlier centuries. Models are scarce and hardly trustworthy, and ships in paintings, etchings, drawings and on coins are stylised to the point where interpretation is open to question. Of course, archaeology is valuable, but apart from the cog there are not many ship types in Holland for which a really detailed image is available. Therefore the description of ship types below will be limited to knowledge of the seventeenth and eighteenth centuries gleaned from written sources, models and archaeological finds, without expending too many words on their putative ancestors.

Square-sterned ships

In general Dutch ships can be divided into two groups: with or without a flat-tucked square stern. As stated earlier, the flat tuck is not a typical Dutch feature. In fact it only appeared in Holland for about 150 years. Is it mere accident that it coincides with the Golden Age of The Netherlands? When the first exploratory fleets were sent to India they usually consisted of two types of ship: the large, flat-sterned, armed, three-masted ship and a miniature copy of it: the *jacht* or *pinas*. Both types will be dealt with here.

The East Indiaman

In the early days there was hardly any difference between a warship and a big merchant vessel. In fact, during the period of discoveries the largest ships were men-of-war, hired from the Admiralties. These ships were so large that they could barely operate in Dutch waters, so everybody was pleased that a suitable task was found for them. They are well depicted in Vroom's paintings but, as explained above, their exact dimensions are unknown. Most of what is known about their construction

comes from archaeological finds such as the *Mauritius*,[15] a ship that made the journey to India twice before being wrecked in 1609 near Gabon off the west coast of Africa. Though only a section of the ship's bottom is left, it is very interesting to note that it shows the double layer of hull planks that was mentioned earlier. The ship measured 350 lasts, but it is hard to say how many guns she carried, because part of them were stowed in the hold to serve as ballast.

Another early East Indiaman of which there are remains is the *Batavia*, which stranded in 1629 on the west coast of Australia with 341 people on board.[16] Only a piece of the aftermost part of the ship has been recovered, but as always with ship finds, details are both impressive and puzzling. The double planking of the tuck has been mentioned above, and on board was the complete stone gateway for the fortress which the Dutch East India Company was building in Batavia. The ship probably measured 160ft x 36ft x 17.5ft and carried 36 guns. Since 1985 a replica has been under construction in Lelystad, Holland. Though questions can be asked about the method of building and some aspects of her appearance, the reconstruction indisputably gives a marvellous impression of a ship of that period.

The oldest ship model of an identifiable East Indiaman is the *Prins Willem* in the Rijks-

museum in Amsterdam.[17] The ship was built in 1649 and sank on a return voyage to Holland in 1661. Though the model is exquisite, the hull shape is probably not completely trustworthy, because it seems to have served as a toy boat. The ship was an example of the largest rate East Indiamen of the Zealand chamber of the Company and probably measured 160ft or a little more. The differences between men-of-war and merchant vessels were so small in those days that during the first Anglo-Dutch War (1652-1654) the ship was chartered by the Admiralty to reinforce the fleet. The number of guns was raised from 32 to 40, for which extra gunports were cut. The *Prins Willem* took part in the Battle of the Downs in 1652, during which she briefly flew the flag of Admiral Witte de With.

However, the event marked the end of the period of exchangeability of the two types. Warships became more heavily built, had less sheer in the decks and heavier guns, so that by the time of the outbreak of the second Anglo-Dutch war (1665-1667), East Indiamen were no longer regularly used as battleships. Yet

---

15. M l'Hour, L Long, E Rieth, *Le Mauritius. La Memoire Engloutie* (Grenoble 1989).

16. Anonymous, *De Ongeluckige Voyagie*, edited by Jan Jans (1649).

17. H Ketting, *Prins Willem* (Bussum 1979).

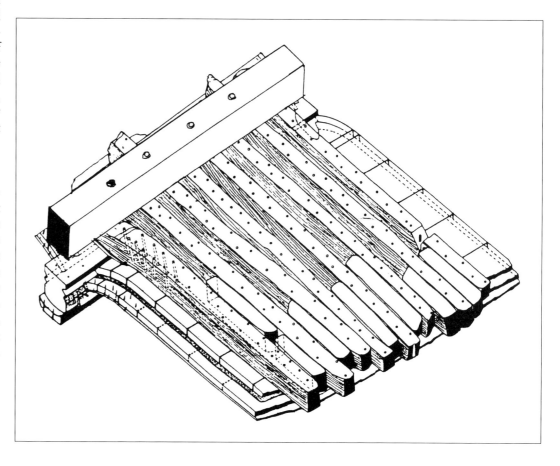

An artist's impression, based on archaeological investigation, of the double planking of the bottom of the Mauritius, *which sank off the west coast of Africa in 1609. (From* Le Mauritius. La Memoire Engloutie*)*

Model of the East Indiaman Prins Willem *of 1649.*
The ship shows many typical mid seventeenth-century
features, including a step down on the gundeck aft, and a
long raking beakhead. These very powerful ships were
often used as auxiliary warships in the Netherlands'
many wars, and required a very skilled eye to tell them
apart from regular ships of the battlefleet.
(Rijksmuseum Amsterdam)

the concept is not necessarily strange: the
Company had the right to make war in Asia if it
was considered necessary, so it is not surprising
that this possibility was a factor in the design of
its ships. However, more and more specialisa-

18. J Gawronski, B Kist and O Stokvis-van Boetzelaer,
Hollandia Compendium (Amsterdam 1992).

tion in ship types was the way forward, and as
outlined below the Company developed its
own men-of-war, which could double as merchant vessels as well.

If nautical archaeology gives the impression
that most of the Company's ships were
wrecked, it must be corrected. During the
almost two centuries of its existence the Dutch
East India Company made 4789 outward
voyages and 3401 return voyages on which
respectively 105 and 141 ships were lost, a
total of a little over 3 per cent. Over that
period 1770 ships saw service, most of them
built in the Company's own shipyards.[18] The
Amsterdam VOC shipyard was the largest
industrial enterprise of its day, with 1500

employees and an average production of three
ships a year. Even in Asia a ship-repair yard was
set up, on the island of Onrust in Batavia Bay.
On arrival every ship was examined to establish
whether it required small or major repairs, or
possibly that it was in such bad shape that it
could only be broken up.

By the end of the seventeenth century standardisation led to detailed directions in shipbuilding and thereafter the shape of such
vessels can be established without doubt for the
first time. Models of *retourschepen* of the first
quarter of the eighteenth century, such as
the *Valkenisse* (1717–Museum of Fine Arts,
Boston, USA), the *D'Bataviase Eeuw* (1719–
Royal Museum of Scotland, Edinburgh),

A contemporary model of the East Indiaman Padmos *of 1721. Compared with the* Prins Willem *the ship has less sheer, a shorter and higher head, and flush main decks. However, the rigging has not altered dramatically, in particular retaining the very vulnerable sprit topmast at the end of the bowsprit, an aspect of the ship rig falling from favour elsewhere in Europe.* (Maritiem Museum 'Prins Hendrik', Rotterdam.)

little information about the construction of the ships. The wrecks of the *Zeewyk* (1727 – Western Australia),[19] the *'t Vliegent Hart* (1735 –Holland),[20] and the *Hollandia* (1743 – Scilly Islands), for example, produced a lot of inventory, but the ships themselves were mostly scattered all over the bottom of the sea, while the wreck of the *Geldermalsen* (1752 – Indonesia)[21] was simply plundered instead of excavated. Therefore the wreck of the *Amsterdam* (1749 – England) should not go unmentioned: the ship rests practically complete in the sands on Hastings beach, ready to be lifted and investigated provided the funds can be raised.[22]

However, it was not just the sizes of ships that concerned the Company. The Resolutions of the Directors show an unusual eye for detail, not only in the obvious areas of prices and storage of goods, the organisation of its shipyards and the cartographic aspects of the trade, but also everything relating to the crew and shipboard conditions: discipline, nutrition,

the *Padmos* (1721 – Maritiem Museum 'Prins Hendrik', Rotterdam) and the *Den Ary* (1725 – Nationaal Scheepvaartmuseum, Amsterdam) do not show revolutionary differences from the earlier image, even though the Company went on making modifications in the size and form of its rates. In the 200 years of its existence the Dutch East Indiaman lost most of its sheer and its high stern, but acquired stronger framing. The Company changed its usual rates from 160ft (sometimes even 170ft), 145ft and 130ft in the seventeenth century to smaller ships in the eighteenth: 150ft x 41ft x 19ft for the largest, 136ft x 39ft x 17ft and 120ft x 33ft x 13ft for the smaller types.

In the second quarter of the eighteenth century the type lost its square tuck and the sprit topsail. Some fine models of East Indiamen survive from that period: the *Bleiswijk* (*c*1740 – Museum Simon de Gijn, Dordrecht), the *D'Gerechtigheid* (1742 – Nationaal Scheepvaartmuseum, Amsterdam) and the *Mercurius*

(1747 – Rijksmuseum, Amsterdam); the *Barbersteyn* (Nationaal Scheepvaartmuseum Het Steen, Antwerp) dates from 1767. Some of these models have their original rigging and every detail is represented.

Most recent shipwreck finds have offered

19. H Edwards, *Het wrak op het Halve-maan's rif* (Baarn 1971).

20. J Gawronski, B Kist, *'T Vliegend Hart Report 1982-1983* (Rijksmuseum Amsterdam 1984).

21. M Hatcher, *The Nanking Cargo* (London 1987).

22. P Marsden, *The Wreck of the Amsterdam* (London 1974).

A ship with draught reduced by camels being towed by a line of waterschepen. *Print by Pierre Le Comte.*

A model of a slighly later East Indiaman, the Bleiswijk *of 1740. Although a cruder model than that of the* Padmos, *it is interesting in its portrayal of some unusual features, including the sails (the model's rigging is believed to be original). These show that staysails were in use, and although the old-fashioned sprit topmast has been retained, the mizzen – originally a full lateen – is now shortened and its luff (leading edge) lashed to the mast. Although the vessel is still well armed, neither tier of guns is complete, which with the coach on the quarterdeck would serve to distinguish the ship from a man of war. (Museum Mr Simon van Gijn, Dordrecht)*

payment, physical care and religion. It is, therefore, not surprising that details about the ships were recorded as well. The Directors kept an open mind about new ideas. The introduction of three British shipwrights from the Portsmouth Royal Dockyard to Amsterdam in 1727 has been mentioned. They were employed not only by the navy, but also developed concepts for East Indiamen, of which a number of fine models survive. In 1741 Gustaaf Willem Baron Van Imhoff (1705-1750) wrote a report on rigging innovations, mostly based on what he had seen abroad, and his suggestions were quickly accepted and introduced at the shipyards. This makes it possible to reconstruct the complete rigging of an East Indiaman of that period.

This is probably the place to mention another Dutch invention: the marine 'camel'. For big ships access to Amsterdam was very difficult, because of the shallowness of the Zuiderzee. The Pampus sandbank at the

A painting by Willem van de Velde the younger showing a West India Company jacht *of the late seventeenth century returning to its home port.* (Rijksmuseum, Amsterdam.)

entrance to the Y, an inlet into which the river Amstel flows out, was especially notorious. As early as the seventeenth century heavy ships were unloaded near Den Helder or at West Terschelling into smaller vessels, *wijd-ships* and *kaags*, but even when empty the draught of East Indiamen was too great. In 1688 Meeuwis Meindertzoon Bakker from Amsterdam invented a method of carrying big ships over the shallow stretch of water. Two large pontoons full of water were strapped one each side of the ship, the inner sides of the pontoons being contoured to fit the hulls of the different rates of East Indiamen and warships as closely as possible. The pontoons were then pumped dry and the ship rose about 9ft, enough to pass the difficult areas. *Waterships*, strongly built fishing vessels from the island of Marken, increased their earnings by acting as tugs. It was clearly an effective solution and in a short space of time the idea was adapted by several countries with similar problems.

Between 1750 and 1800 there are no major developments worth mentioning. The commercial success of the Company slowly declined and though it paid a yearly dividend of 20 per cent even in its last years, it was bankrupted in 1795, which meant the end of the Dutch East Indian trade for several decades, as well as the end of the Dutch East Indiaman as a ship type.

The jacht or pinas

Although etymologically connected to the English 'yacht', the name of this type must not be mixed up with the luxurious vessels that were introduced into England during the reign of Charles II, as a gift from the Dutch authorities to the newly restored British king. The Dutch word *jacht* comes from the verb *jagen* (to chase), which implies 'fast-sailing'. The first *jachts* were miniature copies of the East Indiaman, and like them were three-masted vessels used during the age of discoveries. The ships were 60-80ft long and measured 25-40 lasts. They were fast, of shallow draught, were highly manoeuvrable, relatively heavily armed, and were still able to carry some merchandise if required. According to some sources the type seems to have been developed from a Basque

sailing vessel that could also be rowed. Ships of 300 to 500 lasts with a large carrying capacity served as the military backbone of the fleet, but the *jachts* were used to reconnoitre coasts, bays, rivers and other shallow regions where the heavy ships could not go. They were the eyes and ears of the exploration fleets.

The Company not only earned its money by transporting goods from India to Europe, but also provided a shipping network all over the Indian Ocean area. In the East *jachts* served as warships with additional cargo capacity, as convoy escorts and were much used for voyages of discovery, like Abel Tasman's *jacht* the *Heemskerck*, which in 1642 became the first European ship to reach Tasmania and New Zealand.[23] The *jacht*, or *pinas* as is was also called, was a small man-of-war in private service. The West Indian Company had many of these ships, as they were used for privateering and the slave trade. The galleons of the Spanish silver-fleet were captured by vessels of this type. The size of the *pinas* grew slowly

23. A J Hoving, 'The *Heemskerck*, Abel Tasman's ship', *Bearings* 4/2 (1992).

from 70ft in the earliest days to 134ft in 1653, and when Nicolaes Witsen wrote his book on shipbuilding in 1671 the *pinas* had evolved into a medium-sized armed merchantman, built for speed and with a relatively high cargo capacity. Witsen chose the *pinas* as an example to explain shipbuilding, because it united both the characteristics of a man-of-war and a trader.

By the end of the seventeenth century the archives of the East India Company even refer to *retourschepen* as *pinassen*, but this lasted for little more than a decade. In the eighteenth century the description *pinas* disappeared: the big ships were then called *Oostindiëvaarders* (East Indiamen) and the smaller auxiliary warships were termed 'frigates', as in naval usage. It is not easy to separate the two types, because most of the characteristic differences were found in the underwater shape and in the rigidity of the construction, which are not immediately apparent. The *pinas* usually had a sharply raking stem, and a bottom that rose more than that of an East Indiaman. Apart from the smaller dimensions, the ratio of length, beam and depth also differed. Finally the *pinas* was less heavily constructed than an East Indiaman

and the number and calibres of its guns were smaller. Most of these aspects can only be judged by experts, so it is no wonder that the names were often confused in common usage.

Round-sterned ships

None of the following ship types had a flat tuck. They were all built with rounded hulls, aft as well as forward. Looking at the traditional inshore types like *tjalk*s, this form of construction seems more 'typically Dutch' than the characteristic flat-tucked vessels of the seventeenth century. In some ways the various types may be related, but it is seldom clear in precisely what aspects and to what extent.

The fluit

The *fluit* is a ship type about which a lot of contradictory accounts have been written. That is not surprising: in spite of the fact that it was the most common ship type of the seventeenth century, hardly anything tangible has survived. No complete shipwrecks have been excavated, there are hardly any trustworthy models of the type, and although they do turn up in contemporary paintings, they are seldom portrayed with the loving attention to detail expended on men-of-war or East Indiamen. The type was so common in those days that it became more or less invisible.

Yet it is the only ship type of which we have a report of its 'invention'. In 1595 a prominent merchant, Pieter Janszoon Liorne turned his vision of an ideal merchant vessel into reality.[24] Liorne traded with Livorno in Italy, which probably gave him his name. He was also a politician, became Lord Mayor of the city of Hoorn, and was advisor to the admiral of the Channel fleet, Jan Gerbrandszoon. His talents were obviously not limited to trade, politics and warfare, for he must have been able to brief a shipbuilder in enough detail to allow him to construct a non-traditional type of ship for him, a ship that united all the merchant's wishes: cheap to build, easy to sail and with a large cargo capacity. D Velius, Hoorn's chronicler, reports that the length:beam ratio was 4 to 1, which was obviously exceptional, and that

24. J Van Beijlen, *Schepen van de Nederlanden. Van de late Middeleeuwen tot het einde van de 17de eeuw* (Amsterdam 1970).

A model of the pinas, as described by Witsen. It was reconstructed by the author from a long contract specification given in Witsen's book as an example for how ships were built. (Noordelijk Scheepvaartmuseum, Groningen)

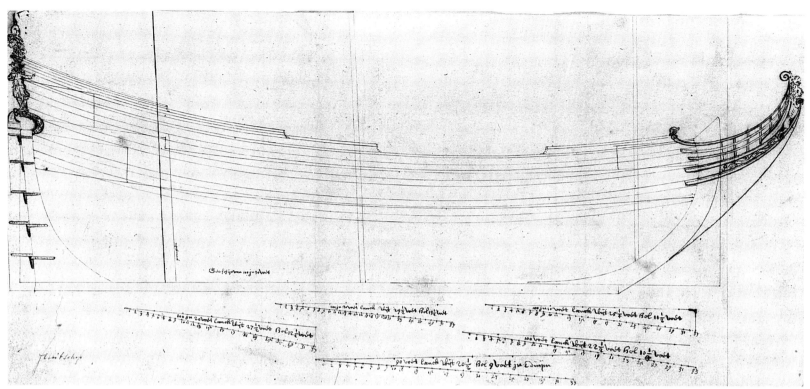

Drawing of a seventeenth-century fluit *by F C Keyzer. The same design served for* fluits *of different sizes. The internal arrangement of decks is also indicated.* (Nederlands Scheepvaart Museum, Amsterdam)

the master shipbuilders and skippers from neighbouring cities came to look at that 'crazy and unusual design'.

What was so crazy and unusual about the ship? It can hardly have been the relative narrowness of the hull. A small model-building experiment carried out by the author threw some light on this question. With a model of a *fluit*, built in exactly the same way as the prototype (*ie* shell-first), up to the lower deck everything is normal and the vessel looks a lot like, for instance, a *hoeker*, but with much less rake to stem and stern and a fuller main frame. However, when the upperworks are added, it almost looks as if the top of a much narrower ship is placed on the bulky lower half of the hull –indeed a crazy and unusual sight. But from a merchant's perspective it was a lucky combination, giving plenty of carrying capacity while minimising tolls, which were calculated on the breadth of the upper deck.[25] Furthermore, the rig was simple enough for the ship to be sailed by only a few men, which was economically attractive as well. Within eight years more than eighty of these vessels were built in Hoorn– and 'much to the citizens' profit', as Velius

An engraving by Reinier Nooms showing (at left) two fluits *in a Dutch harbour. Despite their different sizes, the hull form and rig of both vessels is very similar.*

states. The *fluit* proved to be a complete success. They were constructed not only all over Holland, but were also copied in France, Germany and Sweden. However, the secret of the *fluit*'s success was not to be discovered without that other quality of Dutch shipbuilding: the art of adaptation. For every sort of trade a special type of *fluit* was developed, and because all versions could operate as economically as possible, they became very popular.

The characteristic appearance the *fluit* makes

it easily recognisable: a bulbous hull with exaggerated tumblehome, and a very narrow taffrail with wide 'hips' beneath. The internal arrangement of the smaller examples differed from other ship types. The lower deck had a height of no more than 4ft or 5ft, and was meant as a

25. Shipping entering the Baltic through the 'Sound' between Denmark and Sweden were subject to a toll. This was large enough to give the narrow-decked *fluit* a distinct commercial advantage.

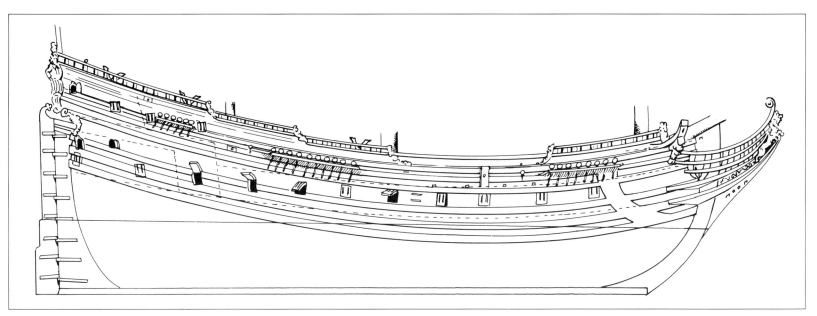

A VOC fluit, *from the second half of the seventeenth century. Traced by the author from an original drawing in the Hoorn Municipal Archives.*

'tween deck' for the dry stowage of cargo rather than accommodation for crew or passengers. Aft of this *koebrugdek* (orlop deck, probably because of its limited height) but not interconnected, was the gunroom, in which there were usually two guns per side. Aft of that was the captain's cabin, with some windows in the stern. The top of the rounded stern ended level with the cabin's deckhead, so that the tiller entered the hull via the so-called *hennegat*, just above. The deck of the upper cabin was laid

over a narrow space which allowed the tiller to swing; the end of the tiller was connected to the whipstaff in the gunroom, the helmsman standing one deck up forward of the upper cabin. The crew were housed in the bow of the vessel, abaft of which the ship usually had a windlass fitted. In general, the *fluit* had no beakhead.

There were many variations in the basic pattern. Ships for transporting timber sometimes had no upper deck, to facilitate loading. They also had a loading port in the stern and sometimes another amidships in the side. The biggest *fluits* were 140ft long; the smallest type, the *boot*, had only one deck and was 86ft at

most. Grain traders were a few feet shallower than timber ships; whalers were doubled forward to protect the hull against ice, carried a beam over the poop to hoist the whaleboats, had heavier masts, and were often converted from old timber or grain traders. The more sophisticated types were the *spaensvaerder* and the *straetsvaerder*, so called because they traded with Portugal or Spain and the Mediterranean (through the 'Straits'). They differed from the

Lines of a hekboot *after the 1697 resolutions, reconstructed by the author. The ship has a round stern at the waterline like a* fluit, *but a wide upper transom, like a* pinas.

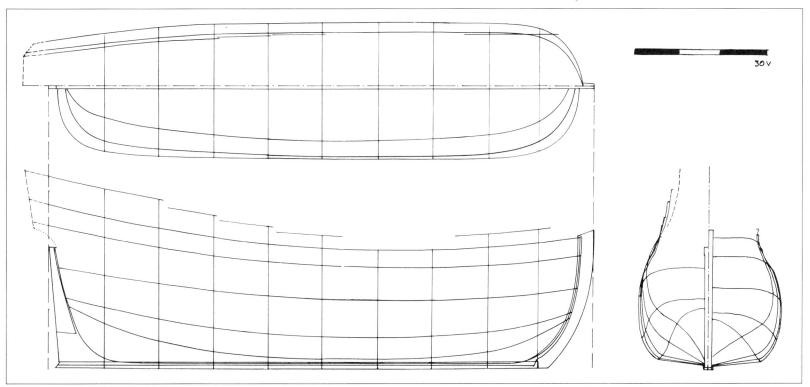

30 v

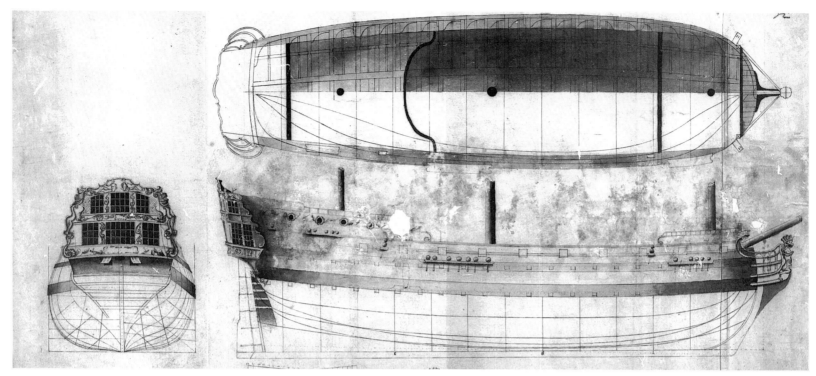

An eighteenth-century Dutch draught of a
hekboot. *The rounded lines of the stern can be seen in*
the plan view, while the wide stern above the transom is
apparent in body plan and sheer elevation. (Nederlands
Scheepvaart Museum, Amsterdam)

standard *fluit* because they had a beakhead and
some modest carving and painting.

There was also the East India Company *fluit*,
which had gratings in its decks to allow air on

the *koebrug*, where Company's soldiers were
billeted during the voyage to Asia. The
Company used *fluit*s in the first half of the seventeenth century for transport tasks in Asian
waters but the type proved less than ideal in
tropical conditions: when the sharply bent
planks in the aftermost part of the hull were
exposed to the sun, they warped and severe
leaking was the result. Therefore they were

gradually replaced by *pinasses* and *hoekers*. The
fluit was also used in times of war–not in the
line of battle but mostly as a supply vessel. Abel

Lines of a kat, *reconstruction by W H Versteeg after*
Witsen. *The hull form is completely flat-bottomed, with*
bluff ends, and a short, fairly narrow taffrail above the
rudderhead, and only modest tumblehome in the topsides.
From Scheepsmodellen 1700–1900, *published in*
Amsterdam in 1947.

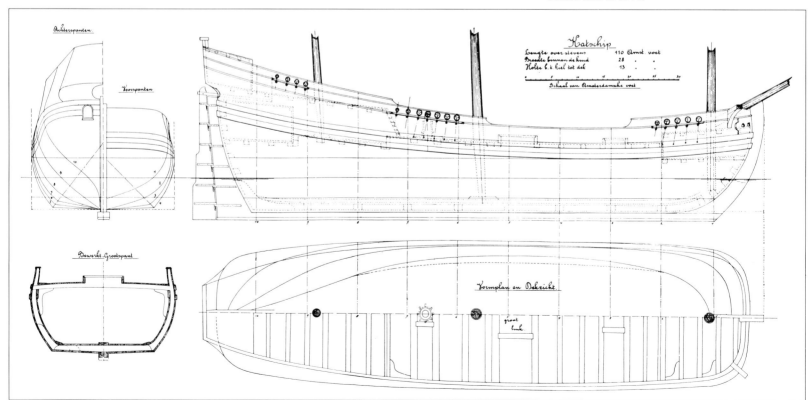

Model of a bootschip, *called* de Goede Hoop *of about 1770; the type was much used in the whaling trade.* (Nederlands Scheepvaart Museum Amsterdam)

Tasman's second ship in his small exploration fleet was a *fluit* of 100 lasts called the *Zeehaen*.

Though *fluits* continued to be built in to the eighteenth century, the heyday of the type was the first three-quarters of the seventeenth century. After 1669 the rules for calculating the Sound tolls were changed, and the principal economic advantage of the typical *fluit* shape disappeared. In 1697 the Rotterdam shipwright Van Yk no longer saw any reason to prefer a *fluit* above a square-sterned ship. The *fluits* of later periods were all wider aft and lost most of the characteristic bulbous shape. In Holland they were sometimes called *hekboot* by the turn of the century, but elsewhere in Europe the type soldiered on for several decades. Chapman includes a 'flyboat'–the English name for a *fluit* –in his great collection of ship drawings known as *Architectura Navalis Mercatoria*.[26]

The *hekboot*

The *hekboot* is an example of a ship type whose ancestry is difficult to trace. The East India Company's Resolution of 4 April 1697, quoted earlier, gives enough data to reconstruct a lines plan of what is called a '*hekboot* or *fluit*', implying that the two terms were synonymous by that time. That is possible, because, as noted above, the reason for the extreme tumblehome of the *fluit* disappeared after 1669, and thereafter the type became wider above the lower deck. Witsen calls the *hekboot* a combination of the lower hull of the *fluit* and the topsides of the *pinas*. However, the word *Hekboot* can be found in Zealand chronicles as early as the thirteenth century.

Its origins may never be known, but the type under discussion here can be recognised by its similarities with the *fluit*, but with a wide topside. Above the stern a transom (*hek*) was fitted (*fluits* never had a transom), which was the basis for the stern superstructure with its taffrail. The type was at most 130ft long and carried a ship rig. In the eighteenth century the East India Company operated *hekboots* in the Indian Ocean. Later the name of the type was changed into *pink*, which should not be confused with the small flat-bottomed fishing vessel of the same name. Pictures of *hekboots* are scarce.

26. F H af Chapman, *Architectura Navalis Mercatoria* (Stockholm 1768).

The *kat*

The *fluit* and *hekboot* may have been austerity ship types, but the *kat* was even cheaper, simpler and more utilitarian, little being spent on decorations. Its maximum length was 120ft, and was constructed of softwood–mostly pine –which was light and resulted in a very shallow draught. The bottom was completely flat and the ship's sides were almost straight with

Two Dutch coastal types depicted in this engraving by Reinier Nooms: a boeier *and a* galjoot.

minimal tumblehome for the top strakes; the bilge was clearly marked by a sharp turn. The rig, known as the polacre, consisted of very long pole masts without tops and separate topmasts. They were typical coastal traders, mostly used in the timber trade from Scandinavia to Holland. They were renowned for their poor sailing qualities, and in heavy weather the *kat* was confined to harbour.

Because of their lack of beauty *kats* are rarely depicted in pictures so that the details of their appearance are unknown, although Chapman's book includes lines plans of eighteenth-century *kats*. By the end of the eighteenth century both the *kat* and the *hekboot* were replaced by the *kof* and the *koftjalk*.

The bootschip

The *bootschip* is probably another variation of the smallest *fluit*-type, the *boot*. Though the name appears in earlier sources, the *bootschip* first occurs frequently in eighteenth-century paintings of whaling scenes. In the seventeenth century the *fluit* was employed in that particular trade, but in those days whales were processed on land, as for instance at Spitsbergen, with *fluits* being only used to transport whale products. In the eighteenth century, however, over-hunting drove the whales away from the coast so that the whole operation, including flensing and boiling the blubber, had to be carried out at sea. This required a wider deck and necessitated changes to the *bootschip*. Like the *hekboot*, it had a relatively low taffrail without quarters. It also had the characteristic whaler's beam over the poop, with which two boats on each side were hoisted, and fenders to

A church model of a hoeker, *from Maassluis. The model is complete with all its canvas and shows off to advantage the robust and seaworthy hull.*

protect the ship's side against damage by the boats. The type had the usual ship rig. There is an excellent model of a *bootschip* in the Amsterdam Scheepvaart Museum: *de Goede Hoop* of about 1770.

The boeier

The *boeier* was a small coastal trader, developed from the *heude*, an inshore vessel. It was a round-hulled ship with leeboards, originally setting a single spritsail, but later it had a form of yawl rig, with a gaff rigged main, often with a topsail in addition, and a small mizzen mast with a lateen sail, a jib and a flying jib and a small spritsail under the bowsprit. Witsen gives a contract for a *boeier* of 86ft by 20ft by 9.5ft dimensions, which reveals that the vessel had an after superstructure.

In the course of the seventeenth century the *boeier* disappeared to be replaced by the *fluit* and its smaller single-decked version, the *boot*. Oddly enough, there is still a traditional ship type in Holland with the name of *boeier*–a Frisian flat-bottomed *jacht* that is still built in the area–but it is very unlikely that this type is related to the old *boeier*.

Reinier Nooms draws both the *boeier* and the *galjoot* in one etching.

The galjoot

Like the *boeier*, the *galjoot* was a round, relatively small coastal trader, with a similar rig to the

27. G Groenewegen, *Verzameling van 84 stuks Hollandse Schepen* (Rotterdam 1789).

boeier, but without the after superstructure. The tiller, therefore, was free to work over the deck. Usually they were about 80ft long. In the fleet they were used as supply and dispatch vessels (*adviesjacht*). The seventeenth-century marine artist Willem van de Velde owned a *galjoot*, which allowed him to witness at first hand some of the great sea battles of the Anglo-Dutch wars. The type slowly developed into the eighteenth-century three-masted *galjoot* and disappeared in the course of the nineteenth century.

The hoeker

Originally the *hoeker* was a fishing vessel, angling for cod with hooked lines. Being out in the North Sea in all weathers it had to have excellent sailing qualities. It was an old type with one large mast with a square sail and jibs, and a small mast aft to steady the ship when fishing with the main mast lowered. Apart from being a fisherman the type evolved into a trader in the seventeenth century. The Dutch East India Company replaced *fluits* by *hoekers*, because the planking of the latter had a better resistance to the warping effects of the Eastern sun. It was a ship type with a large carrying capacity, but nevertheless a well-shaped under-water hull, which allowed it to sail well to wind-ward. The low sides allowed the tiller to work on deck. It was usually 80-90ft long, and when employed in trade it sometimes carried a three-masted ship rig. There are several good models of the merchant type as well as the ship as a fishing craft. Groenewegen depicts the type in both its fashions.[27]

An engraving by Reinier Nooms depicting Herring buizen *(busses) fishing in the North Sea. The usual method of operation when fishing, shown here, was to fold down the fore and main masts, leaving a steadying sail on the mizzen.*

The buis

Like the *hoeker* the *buis* was originally a fishing vessel–in fact it was the most common fishing craft of the North Sea. There are pictures of early *buizen* with a flat tuck, but around 1600 it developed into a round stern, probably under the influence of the success of the *fluit*. By that time there must have been between 1000 and 1500 of them, but after that the numbers decreased. The stern quarters of the *buis* were formed to allow a small opening for the tiller to enter the ship under a narrow taffrail. The *buis* was about 50ft long and was used to fish for herring. For this it had three low masts of which the forward two could be lowered. As an eighteenth-century merchantman the *buis* had one mast with square sails and jibs and a mizzen mast with a lateen sail like the *hoeker*.

Conclusions

Listing ship types in a limited space like this always requires some degree of generalisation, but while it is necessarily incomplete, it does provide an overview of the principal ships that contributed to the Golden Age of the Nether-lands. Although the enormous boom in Dutch economic activity in the first few decades of the seventeenth century was never exceeded, the decline was only relative. Both the seventeenth and the eighteenth centuries can be characterised as most prosperous—one has only to look around Dutch cities like Amsterdam, Hoorn, or Enkhuizen en Middelburg to find proof of Dutch prosperity in the past. Ships may not have generated the wealth directly, but they were certainly instrumental in its creation. Furthermore, they were not merely means to an end, but to the contemporary eye they were objects of great beauty as well; the modern world can count itself lucky to have inherited so many reminders in the form of archaeological finds, models, and the paintings, drawings and prints in which they are so exquisitely depicted.

A J Hoving

Dutch East India Company: Typical Vessels 1600-1800

Name	Description	Built	Launched	Tonnage (Lasts)	Dimensions (Feet)* (Metres)	Remarks
DUIFJE	Pinas	Amsterdam	1594	25		Crew 20
MAURITIUS	Retourschip	Amsterdam	1594	230		Crew 85; made three voyages to the Indies
BATAVIA	Retourschip	Amsterdam	1628	300		300 on board; wrecked 4 June 1629
PARKIET	Galjoot	Amsterdam	1659	40	70.00 x 17.50 x 8.25 19.81 x 4.95 x 2.33	Wrecked off Bimelepatnam 9 November 1665
YSVOGEL	Hoeker	Delft	1667	45	80.00 x 20.00 x ? 22.64 x 5.66 x ?	
UDAM	Fluit	Amsterdam	1668	224	128.00 x 27.50 x 12.75 36.22 x 7.78 x 3.61	Crew of 77 plus 85 soldiers
LAREN	Jacht	Amsterdam	1670	134	105.00 x 25.50 x 10.00 29.72 x 7.22 x 2.83	Laid up at Malacca April 1682
AMERICA	Retourschip	Hoorn	1673	500	160.00 x 39.00 x 18.00 45.28 x 11.04 x 5.09	Conspiracy to mutiny suppressed on board
ENGELENBURG	Kat	Hoorn	1680	182	115.00 x 25.00 x 12.50 32.54 x 7.08 x 3.54	Laid up at Batavia January 1694
STAVENISSE	Pinas	Middleburg	1681	272	130.00 x 31.00 x 13.25 36.79 x 8.77 x 3.75	First voyage carried 88 crew, 69 soldiers, 9 passengers
D'BRIL	Bootje	Rotterdam	1683	70	84.00 x 21.75 x 10.00 23.77 x 6.16 x 2.83	Also called *Den Briel*; crew 31
THEEBOOM	Fluit	Amsterdam	1699	263	130.00 x 30.50 x 13.50 36.79 x 8.63 x 3.82	Crew 104
OEGSTGEEST	Hekboot	Amsterdam	1699	288	130.00 x 33.50 x 14.00 36.79 x 9.48 x 3.96	Crew 87, soldiers 48, passengers 8
AVONTURIER	Fregat	Amsterdam	1707	150	130.00 x 31.00 x 13.00 36.79 x 8.77 x 3.68	Crew 56, soldiers 35, stowaways 5
PATMOS	Retourschip	Rotterdam	1722	405	136.00 x 39.00 x 17.00 38.49 x 11.04 x 4.81	Wrecked 27 October 1752 after 9 voyages
GERECHTIGHEID	Retourschip	Enkhuizen	1742	425	136.00 x 39.00 x 17.00 38.49 x 11.04 x 4.81	Sold in the Indies 5 July 1763 after 6 voyages
GELDERMALSEN	Retourschip	Zeeland	1746	575	150.00 x 41.00 x 19.00 42.45 x 11.60 x 5.38	Wrecked 18 January 1752; 32 saved
AMSTERDAM	Retourschip	Amsterdam	1748	575	150.00 x 41.00 x 19.00 42.45 x 11.60 x 5.38	Beached at Hastings on maiden voyage
BLEISWIJK	Retourschip	Goeree	1756	440	135.00 x 39.00 x 17.50 38.21 x 11.04 x 4.95	Wrecked 1777 after 6 voyages
ZON	Hoeker	Amsterdam	1768	225	120.00 x 33.00 x 13.00 33.96 x 9.34 x 3.68	Laid up 1782
HOOP	Fluit	Purchased 1775		400	135.00 x 32.00 x 14.00 38.21 x 9.06 x 3.96	Wrecked off the Cape 30 June 1784
VEERE	Pink	Zeeland	1786	379	120.00 x 33.00 x 13.00 33.96 x 9.34 x 3.68	Crew 104

* = Amsterdam foot of 28.3cm

3

The Ships of Scandinavia and the Baltic

NORTHERN European trade in 1650 still followed patterns that could be traced back to the medieval period and in some cases to the Iron Age, dictated by the extensive river systems and the geography of the Baltic area. The north and east of Europe were relatively sparsely populated, but rich in raw materials, whereas the west was more intensely cultivated and more industrially developed. This produced ideal conditions for trade, exchanging western manufactured products, salt, cloth and wine for timber, furs, fish, farm produce and metals like copper and iron. Because of transport economics, and the lack of

The busy port of Copenhagen in 1794. The large ship rigged vessel in the foreground is typical of ocean-going merchantmen built throughout Europe and North America at the time, but the smaller craft are more characteristic of northern trades–especially the galeas to the left and the sloop in the right foreground. (Danish Maritime Museum, Kronborg)

good inland communications, much of this trade was waterborne, using the rivers and age-old coastal routes, with occasional open-water crossings to the larger Baltic islands. Expansion in the seventeenth century and later was still based on these underlying conditions and patterns.

Politically, in the middle of the seventeenth century northern Europe comprised a broad geographical area, with several national states. These were political entities of long standing, with territorial interests extending from the northern part of the European continent in the south, to the waters of the Arctic in the north; from Iceland and the Faeroes in the west to western Russia in the east. The area was dominated by two old nation states, Sweden and Denmark. Sweden, at this time also incorporating present-day Finland, was of central importance, since the Thirty Years War left her with extensive territories: besides central Sweden

and Finland, also to the east, the county of Kexholm, inhabited by Finns; the county of Ingermanland, inhabited by Russians; Estonia and Livonia; and to the south of the Baltic four provinces inhabited by Germans.

Denmark dominated the western part of northern Europe, including Norway, the Faeroes and Greenland, all areas with their own indigenous inhabitants. On the eastern borders of northern Europe were two major political powers, Poland and Russia, the former with harbours on the Baltic, and the latter at this time with harbours on the White Sea. In the south the loosely knit empire of German states bordering the Baltic included several important merchant and seafaring towns of long standing.

Topographically the area was very varied, taking in almost every form of water, from inland lake and river systems to the open expanses of the North Atlantic and the White

Sea. This produced a spectrum of seaborne transportation systems, and ship types for overseas, coastal and inland seafaring. This last was of major importance in the overall communications system, although it was often less conscious than the seagoing trade.

Northern Europe also participated in wider international trade, with import/export connections with the most important shipping centres of western Europe such as Amsterdam and London. Arctic whaling and fishing, although based in the Netherlands, was another form of northern external trade which developed significantly during the period covered by this book. Northern trade with more distant countries, like the Americas, the Indies and other colonial areas, also evolved at this time.

The major harbours in northern Europe were also the principal towns of the time. Starting in the south, it seems that the cities of the old Hanse kept their positions in the trading system of the area long after the formal dissolution of the Hanseatic League. In the seventeenth century they were still the dominant trading and seafaring centres of the northern part of the continent. Similarly, to the east in the Baltic states the old ports, like Riga and Narva, retained their position in eastern European trade. These were harbours to which

goods were brought along Russian and Baltic rivers to be trans-shipped into seagoing vessels. In Sweden and Denmark urbanisation in general was less advanced than in the former areas in that the towns were smaller and had fewer inhabitants. Foreign trade was to a high degree concentrated in the capitals.

Beside the coastal towns, there were other types of seafaring centres, namely those devoted to fishing and hunting in the far north. Among these were the seventeenth-century bases at Spitzbergen for whaling in Arctic waters, and also the harbours of the White Sea trade, to a large extent furnishing the European market with fish and furs.

Northern European sea trade 1650-1830

The Thirty Years War (1618-1648) devastated the rural and urban economies of much of northern Europe, and consequently the years following saw a decline in sea trade. Some of the old Hanseatic towns retained their independence, of which Hamburg was the most

Besides the transportation of goods, the other main employment for northern European merchant ships was fishing, and the related activities of whaling, sealing, and hunting. This Danish ketch rigged hukkert *is shown fishing for cod off Iceland with long lines, in an engraving of 1785. The type was also common in Sweden and the Netherlands, from where it probably originated.* (Danish Maritime Museum, Kronborg)

successful during the war, and became the most important regional shipping centre; in 1672 a total of 277 seagoing vessels were registered there. On the other hand, Danzig (present-day Gdansk), Poland's chief seaport, saw its trade decline almost to extinction, owing to lack of export commodities. Russia had no access to the Baltic at this time, and her exports of tar, timber and grain went through ports in other Baltic states or via Archangel on the White Sea.

Swedish (including Finnish) shipping experienced three short periods of prosperity–in the 1660s, the 1670s and 1690s–when its market share was increased thanks to the advantages of neutrality in times of major European wars. In general, this was a period of mercantilism–of protectionist state-sponsored measures designed to promote trade at the expense of the country's enemies or rivals–and Sweden attempted to both regulate shipping and to encourage the building of larger armed merchant vessels that might also form a strategic reserve in times of war. Monopolies on certain trades and goods were widely used to foster the growth of trading companies, and in Sweden this applied to copper and tar.

Seventeenth-century Swedish exports were principally iron, copper, tar and timber, and grew significantly in the second half of the century, accounting for about 10-13 per cent of all northern shipping activity at this time. Trade from Stockholm was mainly with the Netherlands, and from the west coast with England, but English trade became more important as time went on. Finland also exported tar and timber, but until the nineteenth century Finnish ships very rarely left the Baltic, except where the new-built ship herself was the export (a common trade from East Bothnia), when the hold would be filled with tar barrels to maximise the value of the voyage.

Denmark exported agricultural products, such as grain to Norway, and also salted fish. However, the loss to Sweden of the shipowning counties of Skåne, Halland and Blekinge in 1658 crippled Danish shipping until the 1680s, when a gentle recovery began. The state made a number of generally unsuccessful attempts to establish trading companies, and in the 1670s subsidised the construction of large 'defence ships' (see below). After 1680 Danish shipping benefited from neutrality in a number of maritime wars, and the French *guerre de course* was so successful towards the end of the century that many English and Dutch ships converted to Scandinavian flags for the protection of neutrality.

Dutch domination of world trade

A table of Dutch shipping in the 1670s gives an interesting insight into the structure, and the relative size, of Dutch shipping in world trade, including northern Europe.[1]

Trade	No of ships	Total lasts
The Baltic, England, France and Portugal	735	103,000
Norway	200	20,000
Archangel	25	4500
Mediterranean	200	6000
Guinea and the West Indies	100	20,000
East Indies	100	30,000
Greenland whaling	150	20,000
Herring fisheries in the North Sea	1000	30,000
Coastal shipping	1000	20,000

A study of the table give a good impression of how deeply involved the Dutch were in the northern European market in the seventeenth century, including the trade with the Baltic, Norway, Archangel, and Greenland, as well in the herring fisheries and coastal shipping of the North Sea. In fact, the principal part of Dutch enterprise was devoted to these different aspects of northern European shipping.

By 1650 the North Sea was the centre of gravity of the world's shipping. A significant driving force was the western European demand for building materials–especially timber–and the most intensive of all seventeenth-century trades was the export of timber and stockfish from Norway to Holland in return for cloth, wine, salt, tobacco, cheese, spices and manufactured items like bricks and tiles. One-third of all clearings from Amsterdam in 1652 were destined for Norway, and in 1667-68 a total of 5,000,000 pounds of stockfish was imported into Amsterdam. According to one source, there were 350 Dutch ships of over 100 tons in the Norway timber trade in 1635, 387 in 1647, and 300 as late as 1697.

England's notorious Navigation Acts of 1651 and later effectively banned foreign ships from trade in third-party goods, a measure which crippled the world's carriers, the Dutch. England's demand for timber increased enormously in the latter half of the seventeenth century, and by about 1700 43 per cent of all imports came from Norway–but it could not be carried in Dutch ships, thanks to the Navigation Acts, weakening the Netherlands' hold on the timber trade. However, the main beneficiaries were the Norwegians themselves and their Danish masters, since the Anglo-Dutch wars (mainly the product of intense trade and colonial rivalry) made the carriage of timber in neutral ships far safer than those of the belligerents. It was not until after the end of the War of Spanish Succession in 1713 that the British began to take over part of this trade.

The Netherlands also dominated trade within the Baltic before 1651, including the

1. Walter Ried, *Deutsche Segelschiffahrt seit 1470* (Munich 1974).

In 1650 the timber trade was dominated by the Dutch, but after the English introduced the Navigation Acts in 1651 the Hollanders were effectively prohibited from the expanding market of the British Isles. The Norwegians and Danes benefited from this change and this painting by Samuel Scott symbolises that shift. Dated 1736, it shows a Danish timber bark in an English port. The bluff, capacious hull form was typical of these craft. (National Maritime Museum)

The Danish Royal Asian Company was set up in 1722 and like other East India trading companies operated as a state sponsored monopoly. Its East Indiamen were also the largest and best-found ships in the merchant marine. This painting of around 1800 shows the Christianshavn *entering Table Bay, Cape of Good Hope. In contrast to the British East Indiaman to the left, the Danish vessel has a single level of quarter galleries and is probably a somewhat smaller ship.* (Danish Maritime Museum, Kronborg)

export of grain and timber from ports like Danzig and Königsberg, and flax from Riga. Early in the century Dutch ships passing the sound outnumbered English ones thirteen to one, and in 1666 around three-quarters of all investment on the Amsterdam capital market was actively involved with Baltic trade.

One important factor in northern European shipping was the levying by Denmark of the Sound Dues on all ships passing in and out of the Baltic. They constituted a relatively heavy tax and were always subject to intense political negotiation, but they were so valuable a source of income to Denmark that they survived from the fifteenth century until 1857. They even affected ship design, because they were calculated on certain dimensions that could be min-

imised – the narrow deck measurement of flutes is often attributed to a desire to keep down the Sound Dues. One happy consequence for the historian is that the details of ship movements, with basic data on each ship and its skipper, necessary to administer the dues, now form an invaluable record in the Danish state archives in Copenhagen.

After the Great Northern War (1700-1721)

After a boom at the beginning of the century Denmark suffered an economic slump in the years following the Great Northern War, before trade again picked up again about 1740. Thereafter the country was able to steer clear of major wars – and neutrality was good for shipping – until dragged into the Napoleonic conflict in 1807. Copenhagen was the dominant port, concentrating activities on the Baltic and North Sea markets, but was also the centre of the country's long-distance trades. Various government-sponsored measures promoted larger trading companies, the best known being the Royal Asian Company, established in 1722, which was granted a monopoly east of the Cape

of Good Hope. However, as the century wore on the structure of shipowning tended to change, moving away from monopolistic enterprises supported by the state, so characteristic of mercantilist thinking, towards more entrepreneurial private shipowning.

The smaller Danish ports were mainly involved in exporting agricultural products, although southern coastal towns like Flensborg, Söderborg and Åbenrå took part in a broader range of Baltic and North Sea trading. From the middle of the century the Danes developed a virtual monopoly on grain exports to Norway, importing timber, iron and glass in exchange. Trade with Finnmark, in the extreme north of Norway, and with Greenland tended to be confined to Copenhagen, a situation which in the latter case subsisted until this century.

The trading patterns of the old Hanse towns in Germany survived more than two hundred years after the formal dissolution of the League. Exports were principally grain – and rye in particular – from the southeastern Baltic to ports on the North Sea and Europe's Atlantic coast. Hamburg remained most important of the Hanseatic towns, reaching a maximum of 295 merchant vessels averaging 220 tons in 1802, plus major involvement in Greenland whaling. The greatest eighteenth-century change in Germany was the emergence of Prussia, first as a military and then as an economic power, with 190 ships registered in its Pomeranian and north German harbours in 1797. German shipping grew more adventurous during the century, looking at first outside the traditional Baltic routes and eventually across the Atlantic. By 1790 Bremen was taking the lead in developing links with the United States.

For Swedish shipping the Great Northern War was a disaster: by 1723 the merchant navy had been reduced to two hundred ships of which only seven exceeded 100 tons, so Swedish trade had to be thrown open to all comers if the economy was not to collapse completely. This circumstance outraged mercantilist orthodoxy, so the government was forced to act. In 1724 it introduced the *Produktplakatet*, a law inspired by the English Navigation Acts of 1651, granting complete freedom from customs duties to all Swedish ships of 50 lasts or more, and halving the customs duties for smaller ships. More importantly, all Swedish ports were closed to foreign shipping with any cargo not produced in the homelands of the respective ships. This was followed up in 1726 with an act banning foreign ships from the Swedish coasting trade. These protectionist measures were of great benefit to Sweden's merchant marine, and remained in force for over a century, although their restrictions were eased in several stages prior to their final abolition in 1846.

Swedish trade in the eighteenth century

At the end of the 1720s the Swedish merchant marine comprised 480 ships, but this had grown to 900 by the middle of the 1780s, indicating that Swedish shipping was enjoying a golden age. A class of wealthy shipowners grew up in the main seaports, and business contacts with the rest of the world were greatly expanded. In the 1790s Gothenburg emerged as a rival to Stockholm in terms of tonnage shipped, largely as a result of the export of herring,

One of the single most important trades within the Baltic was the Swedish importation of grain from the southern coast. The grain trade was largely carried on in galliots, *a round-sterned type of Dutch origin, as depicted in this engraving by Groenewegen in 1789. This example has the ketch rig of the* galleas, *but three-masted ship rigged versions were known.*

which had been increasing in volume since 1750. Nevertheless, wrought iron remained the chief export, between 1738 and 1808 averaging about 45,000 tons per annum, shipped mainly to Britain, although Russia captured larger proportions of the British market after 1750.

As the timber trade developed from insignificant beginnings, mercantilist regulations required cargoes from Norrland to be transshipped at Stockholm for foreign export. This situation persisted until 1800, although the newly developed East Bothnian tar trade was soon freed to export directly from Finnish ports. Tar and pitch exports trebled between 1730 and the end of the century, mainly to the Netherlands and southern Europe, although Britain became a major market after the loss of her North American colonies in 1783. Finnish seaborne trade, virtually at a standstill during the Great Northern War, expanded after 1721, and was heavily concentrated in East Bothnia. Tar, timber, and locally-built ships were its main exports, and overseas contacts were developed initially with the Mediterranean and eventually in trans-oceanic trades.

Prior to 1750 salted herrings were a major import, but there followed a boom in herring fisheries off the Swedish west coast, so Sweden became a net exporter of salted herring. The greatest volume went to southern Baltic ports,

principally Danzig, but also to Cork in Ireland for re-export to the West Indies plantations as staple food for the slaves.

On the import side, Sweden's most significant commodity was grain, and especially rye, from the southern Baltic coast, its tonnage equalling one-third of all grain exported through the Sound. Salt from Portugal, Sardinia and Ibiza grew dramatically in volume during the century to match the requirements of the new herring curing industry.

The Napoleonic Wars and after

The great European wars around the turn of the nineteenth century affected maritime nations in different ways, according to their allegiances. Sweden lost Finland as a result of war with Russia, but generally benefited from good relations with Britain during Napoleon's imposition of the Continental System and the British counter-attack, the naval blockade. The merchant fleet actually grew by 75 per cent between 1800 and 1810, but much of Sweden's trade outside the Baltic and North Sea was obliterated. Imports were almost exclusively in the hands of foreign-flag ships, and while shipping charges from foreign shipowners went up 150 per cent, Swedish owners' profits declined by 20 per cent.

For Denmark the wars meant the loss of her fleet to Britain, and attacks on Copenhagen in 1801 and 1807. The ensuing British blockade destroyed Danish commerce, and the Baltic trades were largely taken over by British, Norwegian and Prussian enterprise. The end of the war did not reverse the trend, since Norway was separated from Denmark, and between 1800 and 1824 Copenhagen's registered shipping declined by fifty per cent and 150 of the city's larger shipowners went bankrupt. Foreign competition also damaged overseas commerce, so that the Royal Asian Company had to be dissolved in 1844, although the West Indies trade continued to bring in good returns until the 1830s.

Copenhagen's decline was to some extent balanced by Hamburg's expansion, which had already taken over Amsterdam's position as the centre of western European grain exports. After the wars it became an entrepôt for British imports into the continent, the inland waterways in the hinterland providing an ideal distribution network.

The period after 1815 was marked by a growing trend towards the liberalisation of trade, towards disbanding the old bonds of mercantilist legislation. This was neither a smooth nor a consistent transition: protectionists in Britain were able to point to the fact that the British merchant marine was three times larger than that of the German states before Napoleon's Continental System, but eight times larger after it. Nevertheless, individual exceptions to the British Navigation Acts were made by treaty in the postwar years: first Mecklenburg and then the old Hanseatic towns, but notably Prussia in 1825. This eased conditions for German ports, but external factors could have the opposite effect. For example, as its population increased Europe became a net importer of grain, and in the 1820s a number of German merchants and shipowners had their businesses destroyed by the decline in grain exporting. The only answer was to seek new outlets for their enterprise, and to take Hamburg as one example, the 1820s saw the port developing commercial links with the

The Danish merchant marine suffered heavily during the Napoleonic Wars from the effects of the Continental System and the British blockade. Danish commerce was swept from the seas, and the Victoria of Flensburg, shown here in 1807, must have had difficulty making a living for her owner. The ship is a typical medium sized merchantman of the period, with a plain stem, no quarter galleries and a square stern. She carries a defensive armament of six small guns a side on the quarterdeck. (Danish Maritime Museum, Kronborg)

West Indies and South America, as well as Britain, the Netherlands and France. Another feature of postwar shipping was the growth of emigrant traffic, mainly to the United States. Certain ports came to specialise in particular routes: Bremen, for example, inaugurated packet services to New Orleans in 1817 and to New York in 1826.

In Sweden postwar economic conditions proved disappointing, and foreign trade did not revive until the 1840s, although coastal shipping remained active. The British Navigation Acts were rescinded in two stages in 1848 and 1857, and Denmark also abolished the Sound

Dues in the latter year. Britain later reduced duties on timber and other Swedish goods, and these liberalising moves by the world's most powerful economy influenced other European nations in the same direction, stimulating trade and increasing the demand for shipping.

The victory of liberal trade policies in Britain also contributed to Finland's expansion as a maritime nation. Russia had acquired the country from Sweden by treaty in 1809, but Finland retained a degree of independence, so she was able to respond to the increasing demand for raw material and foodstuffs brought about by industrialisation on the one hand and urbanisation on the other. Finland became a major world carrier, and accordingly her merchant fleet increased in leaps and bounds: 270 ships totalling 17,000 lasts in 1826, 380 ships of 38,150 lasts in 1838, and 470 ships of 51,500 lasts by 1850. Furthermore, a parallel development can be seen in the coastal trades: around 1800 about 300 vessels engaged in trade with Stockholm, but this figure had reached about 900 by the middle of the century.

tive foreign influences on traditional shipbuilding, ranging from the innumerable smaller changes in fittings and rig to the introduction of entirely new ship types and novel construction techniques.

Existing knowledge, in terms of available sources and earlier studies, is by no means even for this field of ship history. Little is known about inland shipping in early times, for example, whereas the highly organised deep-sea shipping has been much studied. Therefore this chapter concentrates on a few major trends and ship types in the world of north European shipbuilding, ships and shipping during the two-hundred-year timespan of the book. The most important developments in the area's varied and long-established shipbuilding traditions are summarised below, but the emphasis is on Sweden, since it has been relatively well recorded and may stand as a paradigm for the rest.

Denmark

In the seventeenth century Copenhagen played a dominating role both as the centre of Danish

shipping and of shipbuilding, and even in the following century many large ships were built at the capital's yards: the Royal Asian Company, for example, had its own shipyard there. There were also several active and successful yards on the Danish coasts in the eighteenth century. Important shipbuilding areas were the southern Fyn islands, the island of Fanö, and the coasts of Schleswig and Holstein. The industry was largely developed and managed by several shipbuilders' families.

The old Hanseatic maritime towns

The shipbuilding of the old Hanseatic towns of present-day Germany, Poland and the Baltic states had progressed rapidly during the medieval period. The first successful steps were taken towards the organisation of larger-scale shipbuilding, as a result of advances in techniques of capital investment and management, which made possible bigger shipyards, employing large numbers of shipwrights. These advantages did not vanish when the Hanseatic League came to a formal end in the latter part of the sixteenth century, and the Hanse towns

Northern European merchant shipbuilding 1650-1830

It is impossible to generalise about a 'north European merchant ship' during the 1650-1830 period, since the types are so variegated, but there were several 'indigenous' or 'local' shipbuilding traditions in different areas of northern Europe. These were very much dominated by the traditional, clinker technique and its different, traditional hull forms and types of vessel. For this period it is essentially the story of the vessels built and operated by the smaller, rural seafaring communities, and must include inland shipping, which played an important part in the overall system of trade. Some account must also be taken of new and innova-

Danish state involvement with the merchant marine extended to tax incentives which required navy supervision of ship design for the main trading companies, a process which has been beneficial for modern historians since copies of draughts were deposited in the state archives and have survived. This West Indiaman of 1778 was designed by Henrik Gerner, a Danish Navy constructor of the period, as part of the 1776 'Defence Ships' programme (see page 67). (Danish Maritime Museum, Kronborg)

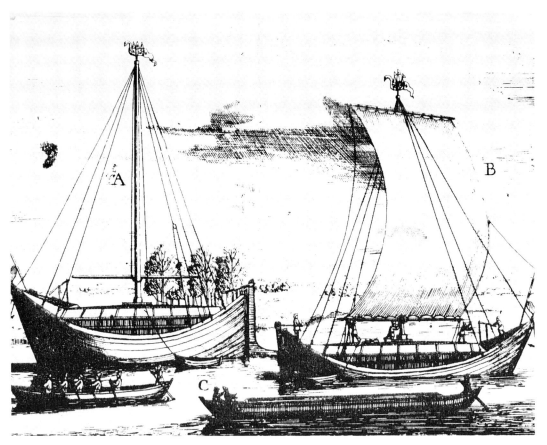

These salt carrying lodjas of the late seventeenth century –as depicted by Nicolaes Witsen in 1671–were widely employed in the White Sea and the river systems of northern Russia. They are typical of the rather crude ship types built in Russia before Peter the Great turned the country's attention seawards at the beginning of the eighteenth century.

carried on as centres of commercial seafaring, including an active shipbuilding industry on a very substantial scale.

German shipbuilding in the seventeenth century was heavily influenced by the Dutch. The ships produced were Dutch types and often built by Dutch shipbuilders employed at shipyards in the individual towns; furthermore, many ships were purchased in the Netherlands. In the eighteenth century the Dutch influence was diminished by a growing reliance on British methods.

Russia

Before the reign of Czar Peter the Great (1689-1725), shipbuilding in northern and western Russia was largely a matter of transport craft, often heavily built using crude, traditional techniques like flat bottoms, for use on rivers or lakes. The vast majority of Russian shipping was confined to the very extensive river systems, and larger seagoing ships and shipping were rare at this time.

However, Peter the Great devoted much of his reign to developing Russian maritime capacity, both in naval and mercantile terms. He enlisted the assistance of Dutch and English specialist shipbuilders, established bigger shipyards, trained shipwrights, and began building seagoing ships. From the early

eighteenth century Russia also had access to the Gulf of Finland, through the Neva river, on which Peter founded Russia's main Baltic harbour and his new capital, St Petersburg.

Sweden

During the seventeenth century Dutch, English and Scottish shipwrights were brought in or emigrated to Sweden. Their work came to influence the construction of bigger ships, and from the latter part of the century the English took an active part in the design and production of larger ships. However, Swedish characteristics persisted in both the dimensions and the rigging. In the late seventeenth century the master shipwright Gunnar Roth, working first in Norrland, later in Kalmar and Gothenburg, employed a style which was said to have been influenced by Spanish or Turkish shipbuilding, acquired through his experience in Algeria.

In 1645 a shipbuilding company was created in the town of Västervik in southern Sweden, in response to mercantilist regulations encouraging the construction of bigger ships. Seagoing vessels, from about 100 lasts to 400 lasts (*c*200 to 800 tons), were its speciality, and similar enterprises were developed elsewhere in the country. This enabled a substantial merchant fleet to be created, which was also augmented by ships bought from abroad.

In 1651 the *kommerskollegium* (the Royal Board of Commerce) was founded. This was a special authority, charged with, among other tasks, the furtherance of shipbuilding in Sweden. Through the peace treaties of this period with Denmark and Germany, Sweden acquired several substantial shipyard establishments in the conquered counties of Bohuslän, Halland, Skåne, Blekinge, on the island of Gotland and in the German Baltic provinces. In the latter part of the seventeenth century a great number of ships were launched from yards in several coastal towns–for example, in Kalmar and Västervik on the east coast, Helsingborg, Malmö, Landskrona and Ystad in the south, and Halmstad, Marstrand and Uddevalla on the west coast. Nevertheless, the centre of shipbuilding remained the capital, with several of the largest shipyard establishments. On the west coast Gothenburg developed its shipbuilding, while the shipyards of Norrland, and especially of Finland (then part of Sweden), also became active during this period. By this time the county of East Bothnia on the northern coast of Finland was already a dominant shipbuilding area, while active shipbuilding also appeared in the Baltic and German provinces.

The structure of shipbuilding enterprise as it was at the end of the seventeenth century seems to have survived essentially unchanged into the early part of the nineteenth century. During the eighteenth century carvel techniques came to dominate ship construction, but a few ships were built in a combination of clinker and carvel–that is with a lap-strake lower hull, and with carvel-built topsides. There were some technological improvements: steaming stoves for the bending of planks were introduced in the 1720s, for example. The building materials were generally oak and pine, with large seagoing ships usually built of oak. Pine was used in areas where oak was rare, for example in Norrland and in Finland.

Shipbuilding in Sweden 1633-1720

The following table of merchant ships built in Sweden gives an impression of the size and distribution of shipbuilding enterprise during the period 1633 to 1720:

	More than 150 lasts[2]	60-150 lasts	20-60 lasts	Total
Towns of:				
Kalmar	42	84	106	232
Västervik	43	102	151	296
Norrköping	8	88	143	239
Stockholm	80	265	342	687
Towns in Norrland	15	66	99	180
Gothenburg-Älvsborg	46	157	154	357
The counties of:				
Blekinge	15	34	81	130
Skåne	12	40	80	132
Halland	2	102	106	210
The island of Gotland	6	10	92	108
Southern Finland	10	27	118	155
County of East Bothnia, Finland	105	361	376	842
The Baltic provinces	63	127	153	343
The German provinces	35	239	715	989
Totals:	482	1702	2716	4900

Beside those mentioned above there were also ships built in unidentified locations. (Source: *Svenskt Skeppsbyggeri*, 1964).

The development and use of ship construction plans

Very few original ship construction drawings have been preserved from before 1700. An idea of the standards of ship draughts in Sweden at this time one can be obtained by studying Åke Classon Rålamb's *Skeppsbyggeri eller Adelig öfnings Tionde Tom*, published in 1691. This was a manual of shipbuilding written for the education of young noblemen, and reproduces a few plans and dimensions of typical ships, providing only a general impression of the size and shape of the ship. The precise ways in which the ship was then shaped and built was to a large extent left to the shipbuilder's own expertise.

In the 1720s there were moves to bring about better standards for ship construction plans. From 1730 the master shipbuilders were ordered to draw up plans and make thorough specifications for all ships to be built, and by the end of the period proper lines and structural plans were commonly produced at the bigger shipyards.

The Sheldons

During the first half of the eighteenth century British shipbuilding principles were widely followed in Sweden, partly due to the dominant position of the English Sheldon shipbuilding dynasty. The first was Francis Sheldon who came to Sweden in 1655, and his decendants were actively employed as shipbuilders into the nineteenth century. When the last Sheldon died in 1817 the family had occupied influential positions in Swedish shipbuilding for 142 years,

2. In Baltic countries the *last* (*läst* in Swedish) was used as a measure of ships' cargo capacity and burden. The last was sometimes used to measure volume, sometimes to measure weight. Its value differed over time and also for different kinds of commodities. In 1726 the definition of the last was regulated: one heavy last (*tung läst* in Swedish) was given the weight of 2448 kilogrammes.

The oldest known draught of a Swedish East Indiaman, the Sophia Albertina *of 1753. This semi-pictorial draughting style, which could be traced back to the Sheldon family, was already regarded as old-fashioned in many parts of Europe, but was still employed even by the Swedish Navy until the advent of Chapman.*

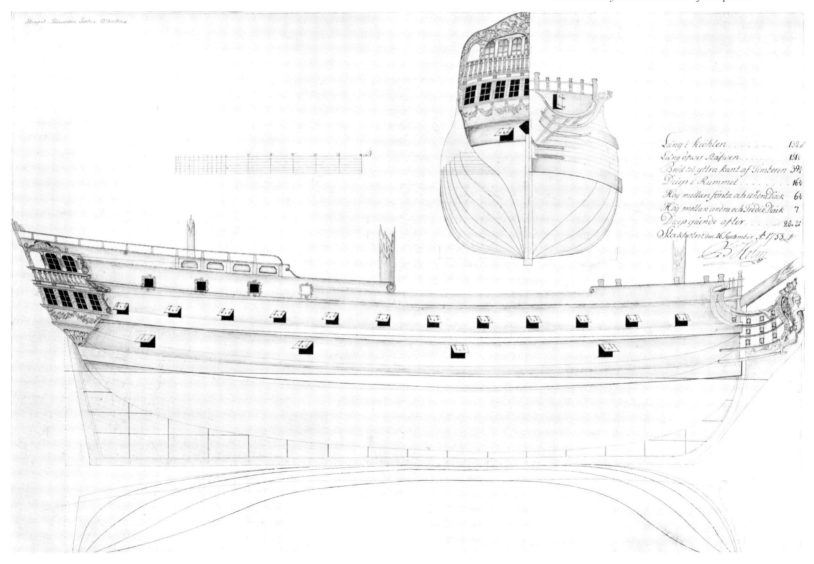

generally promoting a British constructional style.

A French design approach became popular in the middle of the eighteenth century, because it offered sharper ships with better sailing qualities. These principles were introduced by the master shipwright Harald Sohlberg in 1749, when he designed a frigate in the French manner which proved to sail very well. During a government investigation in to shipbuilding principles, Fredrik Henrik Chapman put forward his own system, which combined English and French methods. Chapman's shipbuilding principles became the established norm over a long period, and well into the nineteenth century.

Fredrik Henrik Chapman

The great advances in shipbuilding theory and practice attributed to Fredrik Henrik Chapman during his long lifetime had far reaching consequences.[3] He developed a system for ship design and construction, combining both theory and his own practical experience. He aimed to establish a systematic framework to many of the basic questions of naval architecture: for example, ideal proportions for hull dimensions; the ratio of sail area to hull size and the best sail plan; the appropriate positions for centre of gravity and the metacentre; the shape of the bow underwater to reduce resis-

tance; the characteristics that made ships work and steer well; and the principles of weight distribution for ordnance and cargo. Chapman is widely regarded as the first to put scientific calculation to practical use in ship design, and his concepts were equally applicable to merchant ships.

Finnish shipbuilding enterprise

During the eighteenth century Finland played a very dominant role in Swedish shipbuilding. Total numbers of ships built in the whole of Sweden, including Finland, during the period 1680 to 1814 were:

Area	Number of ships	Total in heavy lasts
Norrland	18	44,610
Stockholm	113	24,520
Southeast coast	137	18,190
West coast	41	5790
Total	*609*	*93,110*
Finland and the Baltic states:		
Finnish Bothnian coast	953	121,330
Finnish south coast	61	12,140
The Baltic states	6	780
German provinces	188	20,000
Grand total	*1817*	*247,360*

(Source: *Svenskt Skeppsbyggeri*, 1964)

In summary, Finnish shipyards produced nearly 54 per cent of the ships built in the whole country. The shipyards north of Stockholm built 18 per cent, and Stockholm produced about 10 per cent of all ship built.

The nineteenth century

Many shipbuilders in the early nineteenth century kept to the proportions advocated by Chapman, but the American trend towards longer ships with a taller rig was also influential. In Sweden clipper proportions were first introduced in shipyards at Sundsvall and Gävle in the north.

In the general European depression of the early nineteenth century virtually all shipbuilding ceased, but from 1824 shipyard businesses in Norrland experienced some growth, although production in the rest of the country was very small. The town of Gävle in the southern part of Norrland achieved an important position both in foreign trade and in shipbuilding. During the period 1815 to 1843 Gävle produced a quarter of all the larger ships built in Sweden.

Local ship types and construction methods

In terms of seagoing ships, northern types were part of the western European mainstream, but even the multifarious local craft at the base of the typological pyramid were influenced by developments elsewhere on the continent. An example might be the clinker tradition of the south and southwest coasts of Scandinavia–Denmark, southern Norway and southwestern Sweden–where the beamy and sturdy hull forms of the Friesian and Dutch coasts made a powerful impression on the local designs. The fore-and-aft rig was another feature originating in western Europe, which spread from the Netherlands along the coasts of the North Sea in the sixteenth and seventeenth centuries. It became the standard rig in smaller vessels, although in a very few situations the square rig survived, most notably in western and northern Norway and in certain inland vessels.

---

3. The standard biography in English is D G Harris, *F H Chapman: The First Naval Architect and his Work* (London 1989).

The ship rigged Danish hukkert Fredericia of the late eighteenth century. The rig is standard for the period, but the hull form is clearly a development of the galliot type, with the round stern and exposed tiller that is ultimately derived from Dutch coastal types. (Danish Maritime Museum, Kronborg)

One measure of the integration of northern shipbuilding into broader European traditions is to be found in the spread of carvel construction in the region. Written and iconographic sources suggest that it was employed in the sixteenth century but largely confined to warships, and to a lesser degree to bigger merchantmen. The rather sparse evidence also indicates that sixteenth-century carvel technique differed in detail from what is known about carvel in the seventeenth century and later, when archaeological finds reveal a technique that was then similar to the standard European tradition. In the seventeenth century, from the Swedish perspective, there is a close connection with Dutch building methods, which were later succeeded by British. By no means all carvel-built vessels in northern Europe were locally built. In the seventeenth century both Dutch shipbuilding and Dutch trade were paramount, so ships were ordered or bought from Holland. Dutch shipbuilders emigrated northwards to exploit their skills in Nordic countries, while local shipbuilders adapted to the new techniques.

It seems probable that carvel construction was already in use in northern Europe in the fifteenth century and grew slowly in the sixteenth century, to become the standard method of ship construction in the seventeenth. From then onwards a spectrum of ship types of moderate size was gradually introduced through the medium of foreign shipping and shipbuilding, most of which were of Dutch origin. These ships were employed alongside local ships, often of the traditional, northern structure. The fact that the shipbuilders of the north took up the new types for construction meant that they were to a certain extent adaptable to Nordic conditions. Conversely, the shipbuilders of the rest of the continent adapted their ship types to Nordic conditions. A good example is provided by the special types of flute –the *Noordsvaarder* for the timber trade with Norway; and the *Ostervaarder* for trade in the Baltic; and the whaling flutes used in the Greenland trade were also specially built and reinforced to withstand the harshness of the Arctic conditions.

The largest vessel depicted on the Björnö map is this three-master with the rather curious mizzen that looks like a modern bermudan sail. However, another depiction of an otherwise similar vessel shows what might be interpreted as a conventional lateen mizzen, so the oddity may be no more than the artist's lack of familiarity with technical details. (Nordic Museum, Stockholm)

Northern European merchant ship types 1650-1830

Vessels of many types have been employed on the high seas, along the coasts, and throughout the inland waterways of northern Europe, and in a great many different trades. The following section outlines some of these in an attempt to show the variety of sizes, hull designs and rigs adopted. To give a balanced picture it is important to stress that northern European merchant ships were by no means all seagoing vessels. Very important trade and transportation was provided by smaller, less conspicuous vessels, operating in sheltered waters. The selection which follows is intended to indicate the diverse nature of northern European shipping.

The boats on the seventeenth-century Björnö map

A map, dated to 1654, of a coastal farm situated not far from the town of Norrtälje, north of Stockholm, gives several representations of smaller coastal transport vessels of the time. These are important evidence for the shape and structure of local vessels on Sweden's central east coast in the seventeenth century. Beside some archaeological remains, very little evidence has so far come to light of the smaller transport vessels of the time.

The biggest vessel on the map is three-masted, with one square sail on the fore and one on the main mast. On the mizzen it sets a triangular sail that looks like a modern bermuda fore-and-aft sail–something that may seem like an anachronism in this period. The vessel has a superstructure at the stern. The position of the helmsman (standing on a deck high up in this structure) suggests that there is a cabin in this superstructure, under the deck.

Judging by the depictions of other vessels on the map, the inhabitants of this part of the coast transported their cargoes in fairly small and beamy vessels with an open hold. They were clinker-built, single-masted with a square sail, and had a crew of three or four men. Cargoes can be seen in two of the vessels. A few of the boats might have a cabin in the stern. One of the boats evidently carries an open cargo of firewood: in the eighteenth and nineteenth

One of the small craft from the Björnö map, most of which are open boats with a single square sail. This one seems to be carrying a stacked cargo of firewood. (Nordic Museum, Stockholm)

centuries this was to become one of the most common cargoes for the coastal vessels of the area, brought from the archipelago to Stockholm.

Hay transport vessels of the Stockholm Archipelago

A report by the Italian diplomat Lorenzo Magalotti after his visit to Sweden in 1674 includes a drawing of a smaller coastal vessel, as was seen in Stockholm harbour during his visit. In all probability this is an illustration of a local transport vessel of the type farmers and fishermen in the archipelago used to transport products from their household to the town or market. This vessel could be compared to the 10-12m long *storbåt*, ('big boat') which was used to bring farmers' produce to town or market for sale during several hundred years, and well into the nineteenth century.[4] At the time of this picture the vessel was double-ended, probably clinker-built, and had a small cabin in the stern. It had two masts with one square sail on each and a jib headsail. It seems to be loaded with a variety of goods for market.

Later depictions, from the years around 1800, of local boats in Stockholm harbour can be found in many of the engravings by the Swedish artist Elias Martin. His aquatints and engravings evidently depict harbour scenes and boats with great care and also with a good

Elias Martin's engraving of Stockholm harbour in 1786. Between the larger vessels are two hayboats, of the storbåt ('big boat') type, which might be seen as a decendant of the craft in Magalotti's drawing. The sail plan, however, was a simple sloop rig, and the stern was square. (Maritime Museum, Stockholm)

The drawing of the small coaster included in Magalotti's report of 1674. These craft were probably used in and around Stockholm for transporting mixed cargoes, but one of the figures on deck appears to be a woman, showing that they also carried members of the owner's family and other villagers on trips to market; there seems to be a gangway over the cargo to the cabin at the stern. (Maritime Museum, Stockholm)

4. See, in this series, *Sail's Last Century*, Chapter 8.

knowledge of the structure of the boat. Vessels arriving from different areas of the coast were moored in different parts of the harbour, so depending on which view the artist depicts, one should be able to recognise boats of a certain origin.

The example from 1786 reproduced here is one of two 'hay boats', also of the *storbåt* type. This was later the prototype of the *roslagsjakt*, the fore-and-aft-rigged light, merchant sloop, typical of the Stockholm archipelago. By the end of the eighteenth century hay boats were clinker-built and single-masted with a square sail. The cabin in the stern was typical of the *storbåt* type, with its rounded, 'shingled' roof. The *storbåt* at this time had a flat stern, which one can only glimpse in this illustration.

The *lodja* on Baltic inland waterways and on the White Sea coast

In his book *Architectura Navalis et Regimen Nauticum* of 1671 Nicolaes Witsen gives a thorough description of the northern European *lodja*. It seems that he based his description on personal observations when he was travelling in the White Sea area, and from observations of earlier visitors there. The term *lodja* in his time was used both for vessels on inland waters in the Baltic states and for vessels on the White Sea coast.

According to Witsen, northern Russian *lodjas* were used both for trading and for fishing and had a crew of eight to ten men. They were

It is a characteristic of nautical usage that ship type terminology often survives quite radical changes in the design of the type itself. One such example is the Russian Lodja, *which developed from the crude single-masted barge depicted by Witsen in 1671 to this quite ship-like three-master reproduced in P Bogoslavsky's* Certezi i risunki sudov *(St Petersburg 1859).*

built in Karelia and thus called 'Karelian *lodjas*'. They carried salt, salted fish, seal train-oil, wood and glass. This type of *lodja* was about as big as the Dutch galliot, with one mast amidships, carrying one square sail. Witsen presents several pictures of *lodjas*. One shows *lodjas* carrying salt, one loaded, and one without cargo. Both have a double-ended hull, straight stem, a distinctive sheer, one square rigged mast and a stern rudder. The hatchway with a high coaming was covered with a roof used as a deck.

Although Witsen mentions the use of a 'sewing technique' in the northern Russian area, he does not connect it explicitly with the *lodja* in many cases. The *lodja* of the Baltic states on the other hand has been said to have been built in many examples by the same technique. These *lodjas* were mainly used for transport on rivers and lakes in Estonia and Latvia, from the inland trading centres, like the town of Tartu, to the harbours on the Baltic coast. This very heavy and sturdy transport vessel was in use into the 1940s and in many instances was recorded in photographs. It had the same main characteristics as the northern Russian *lodja*, except for a wider and squarer shape and less draught, due to its use as a river vessel. The northern Russian *lodja* was also a venerable survivor. Observations of this ship on northern coasts in the nineteenth century makes it evident that by that time the type had been influenced in its structure by Dutch shipbuilding. It had also become larger and had been given a three-masted rig with square sails on the main and fore masts, and a gaff sail on the mizzen.

The 'defence ships' of Denmark and Sweden

Political measures strongly influenced the ships ordered, the shipbuilding methods and ship types of the two major seafaring nations of the Baltic, Denmark and Sweden. One expression of state influence was the building of so called *defensions-skepp* ('defence ships'), merchant ships built and armed in such a way that they could be taken into the service of the navy in wartime. The government supported the building of such vessels by reducing the customs duties for the owners.

After the loss of the counties of Skåne, Halland and Blekinge to Sweden in 1658, Danish trade and shipping was at a low ebb. Few successful merchants were in business and few big merchant ships were in effective employment. The Danish state counteracted this by actively promoting trade. One measure established trading companies, and also encouraged and financially supported the building of so called 'defence ships'. A decree of 1671 declared that all imports of salt into Denmark had to be made in ships that were large enough to be taken up by the navy in wartime.

The decrees furthered the building of bigger trading vessels. In 1676 Copenhagen, which at this time occupied a dominant position in Danish shipping, owned 194 ships totalling 5240 lasts. Four of these were so called 'defence ships'. However, by 1687 there were about forty such vessels registered in the same harbour, nine more in other Danish seaports, and in Norway as many as fifty-eight defence ships. The development of the defence ship as a more common type of bigger merchant vessel was one of the factors stimulating Danish trade and shipping in the 1680s.

The defence ship system was revived a hundred years later to provide the navy with a strategic reserve: in 1776 the Danish state

introduced a law giving support to the building of armed traders, if the same were made available to the navy in war. Regulations were worked out for the construction of one light and one larger type. The ships of this sort put into service were quite heavy and thus less suitable for trade in Danish home waters, but were better fitted for overseas trade routes. Of special importance to the development of the science of ship design in general was the condition that construction plans had to be put forward for consideration before building a defence ship. This drove the master shipwrights to work from draughts to a greater extent than previously.

Similar political support for shipping was developed in Sweden. In 1617 and in 1654 the government introduced regulations for the encouragement of bigger, armed merchant vessels. These edicts reduced the customs duties on Swedish ships if they had been fitted out in Sweden, had been built of oak, had a Swedish crew, and a skipper and mates living in the country, and could be armed with at least 14 guns, later to be augmented to 24 guns. This support by the state was evidently not enough to stimulate the building of sufficient bigger merchantmen; the construction costs were simply too high. The authorities instead established ship companies which were given the

could work. The davits were also used for the lowering of small whaleboats, which had been imported from the Biscay coast, along with the Basque whalers who did much of the harpooning. By the end of the eighteenth century *hekboote* were superseded by new ship types developed by the British and better adapted to the difficult conditions.

Towards the end of the seventeenth century, in each year 14,000 Dutch seamen and about 260 ships headed for Arctic waters, bringing their catch to Amsterdam for further refining, sale and distribution. The Dutch long dominated the whaling trade in number of ships and oil produced, but whaling ships from England, France, some German seaports, and Denmark also worked alongside them. Hamburg was the German seafaring town which came to specialise in this trade: in 1669 there were 37 Hamburg whalers, 2 from Lübeck and 7 from Bremen. At its zenith in 1675 Hamburg had 83 whalers, at a time when the Dutch operated 149 ships.

Another specialised northern European ship type was the cat, which was nearly as common as the flute. Compared to the flute it had a more rounded shape, with a bluff bow and stern. It was flat-bottomed, with a relatively simple rig, and was consequently a slow sailer. It had three pole masts, each carrying two square sails, which were so rigged that the yards could be sent down on deck. This made the setting of sails easier and required a smaller crew. The cat was particularly to be found in Swedish, Norwegian and Danish waters.

Spanienfarare ('Spanish Traders') – vessels of Swedish overseas trade

During the seventeenth and eighteenth centuries Swedish export trade was concentrated on iron, copper, tar and timber. These products were carried in the holds of bigger merchant ships built or bought abroad especially for this trade. The more the volume of Swedish exports increased – to pay the heavy costs of the wars of the time – the more often these big fully laden merchant vessels left Stockholm for London or Amsterdam. Most of these ships were jointly owned in shares by merchants in Stockholm belonging to what was called the

monopoly on different trades and trade goods. This proved to be a more creative solution, stimulating shipbuilding and shipping for a great part of the seventeenth century.

During the following century trade subsidy of a similar character to that in Denmark was applied in Sweden. Up to 1760 a highly mercantilist trade policy was employed. The workings of the *Produktplakatet* of 1724 have been detailed earlier, but to recap in brief, it granted complete freedom from customs duties to all Swedish ships of 50 lasts or more, and halved the customs duties for smaller ships. One reason for including smaller ships in the reduction was that they were fast and handy, so were thus not exposed to the same dangers (especially from privateers), as bigger and slower ships, although the latter were better armed; this made them worth encouraging.

Flutes, *hekboote* and cats

Of the bigger traders in northern waters in the seventeenth century the most common ship type was the Dutch flute. They were principally employed in the timber and the grain trades between ports in the Baltic and western Europe. Special variants included the *Noordsvaarder*, with an elongated hull and ports in the bow and stern for the loading of long beams and timbers; and the *Ostervaarders*, which were designed to be able to use the shallow harbours of the Baltic south coast. In the 1630s about 70 per cent of all the ships passing the Sound were flutes, and this rose to 90 per cent in the following decade. In the eighteenth century the picture became more complex, with English brigs and ships gaining a strong position.

In 1640 the average crew size of a flute in the Norwegian timber trade was between twelve and fourteen men. A minimum of four days was needed for the outward voyage, followed by about six to ten days loading. Discharge of cargo and preparations for another voyage seldom took more than two months, so a ship could usually make five voyages a year. However, the ships were normally laid up from December until mid March, since storms made winter sailings risky in the North. Furthermore, the Baltic was often blocked by ice, and during particularly severe winters the Sound itself would freeze, as would some Norwegian ports.

The flute became less common in general trades in the eighteenth century, but was extensively used as a whaler. The Dutch began whaling in Arctic waters at the end of the sixteenth century. From the 1620s the Dutch, the English and the French carried on a systematic whaling industry in the waters around Spitzbergen. In the first period whaling stations were established on these islands, where the blubber was boiled down and the oil packed in casks. Later, in the eighteenth century, the methods changed and most of the work was performed onboard the whaling ships themselves.

These ships were originally flutes designed for this trade, with a bluff bow protected by an extra layer of planking. In the eighteenth century the *hekboot* replaced the flute in the whaling trade, because the narrow decks of the flutes offered inadequate work space. Although slow, the *hekboot* with its broad decks was much better suited to this work. The masts were reinforced to allow the use of tackles with which to handle the whales alongside the ship. Davits on the sides supported platforms from which men

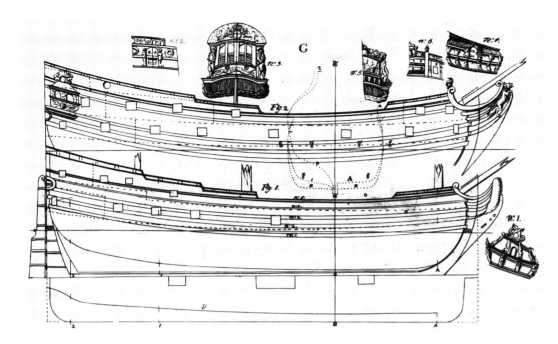

Modifications of the basic flute hull form were employed for the longer-distance trades. These Swedish Spanienfarare of about 600 tons traded down to Portugal, Spain and into the Mediterranean, where they needed protection from Barbary corsairs – hence the larger number of gunports than were usual in northern trades. These examples were reproduced in the first Swedish naval architectural treatise, by Rålamb, published in 1691. (Maritime Museum, Stockholm)

Skeppsbroadeln, literally the 'Ships' Bridge nobility'. This was a word for the most prosperous merchants who lived in palatial houses along the 'Ships' Bridge' (*Skeppsbron* in Swedish) at the eastern side of the Old Town of Stockholm. This long quay was the main harbour for the export trade from Sweden for several hundred years, during the mercantilist era beginning in the Middle Ages.

The ships leaving Swedish harbours with export goods were often built in the Netherlands, or purchased there by Swedish merchants and shipowners. These merchantmen – in the seventeenth century often the larger flutes – followed a regular trade: from Stockholm to Amsterdam or London to unload the export cargo; from there to ports on the Atlantic coast of Spain or Portugal, or to Mediterranean ports to take in salt, wine and other merchandise as return cargo to Stockholm.

A typical vessel of this trade, the big flute *Anna Maria*, built in Amsterdam on the orders of a group of wealthy Stockholm merchants in 1694, survives to the present, well preserved in 18 metres of water on the bottom of the old customs port of Dalarö in the Stockholm archipelago. The ship became trapped by the ice on her way to Amsterdam in the very cold winter of 1708-1709. She was moored in the harbour when she caught fire and sank on the night of 9 February 1709.

The flute *Anna Maria* and other 'Spanish Traders' corresponded in hull form and dimensions to plans published by Åke Classon Rålamb in his 1691 work on shipbuilding, where two versions of the type are described. These vessels were of about 300 lasts (*c*600 tons), with a length of 130ft, and maximum breadth of 28ft. They had the general characteristics of bigger flutes: for example, a 'tween-deck with gunports where several guns could be placed, forecastle and poop. The armament was probably a product of mercantilist regulations giving tax advantages to shipowners with ships which could defend themselves when neccessary, and also could be taken up by the navy in wartime.

Fredrik Henrik Chapman and the *Architectura Navalis Mercatoria*

In August 1766 the Swedish ship designer Fredrik Henrik Chapman asked the commander-in-chief of the Inshore Fleet for an extension of the leave of absence he had been granted a couple of years earlier in order to finish his book *Architectura Navalis Mercatoria*. This now-famous work is a collection of 64 engraved plates of ships and boats of all types and sizes. They are described by categories of data, with information ranged under headings. There are five principal groups of which one is merchant vessels, eleven different types being illustrated.

The plans are very early examples of thorough and scientific presentations of ship designs, forms and qualities, all of which may be gleaned from the plans. Chapman's basic concept was that when a new vessel of a specific cargo capacity was to be built, the ship designer could find all important data in one place in the *Mercatoria*. As Daniel Harris points out in his book on Chapman's life and work, his intention was to present a comprehensive synthesis of the results achieved by shipbuilders

through many generations of traditional design.

Along side the many drawings of bigger traders in the *Mercatoria* there are smaller types from, for example, Greenland, Norway, Finland and Sweden. As an historical source this work is unsurpasssed, and it is worth listing some of the relevant types illustrated by Chapman.

'A scoote used by the Finlanders to carry firewood to Stockholm'

This craft (Plate LX No 9) has a shallow draught, straight sternpost and curved stempost. It is 64ft long and thus significantly bigger than the coastal vessels depicted in the earlier illustrations of vessels in Stockholm archipelago, carrying firewood and hay. On the other hand it has a similarly wide beam and flat stern like the hay vessels in Elias Martin's engraving. It has three masts, probably for a bark rig, but it may have been rigged like the Finnish *kray* in Chapman's plate on rigging (LXII, No 10.).

'The galleas – a vessel used in the Baltick'

From the eighteenth century onwards, one of the most common smaller cargo vessels of the Baltic was a type Chapman calls a 'galeass' (*galeas* in Swedish), which has survived in

Chapman's galeas *rig plan from* Architectura Navalis Mercatoria.

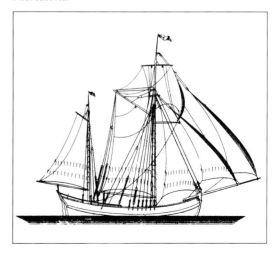

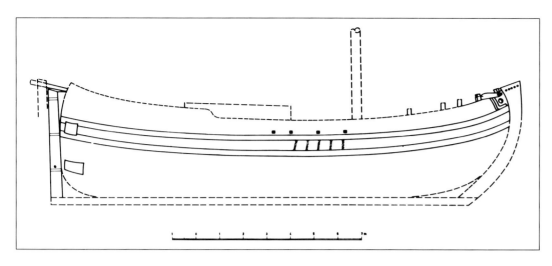

A profile of the Älvsnabben wreck, now known to have been the grain galliot Concordia of Stralsund, *which sank in 1754. The dotted lines represent reconstructed areas; furthermore, the ship may have had a mizzen mast and certainly had a bowsprit. From C O Cederlund,* Vraket vid Älvsnabben. Fartygels byggnad *(Stockholm 1981)*

varying forms into the twentieth century.in some areas around the Baltic. Plate LXII, No 9 depicts a seagoing type of *galeas* in a rigged elevation drawing, showing the standard sail plan of the type: mizzen and considerably taller main, with gaff sails on both masts, and a topsail over the main, and fore stay sails. A sturdier variety of the *galeas* type is a 'vessel used on lakes and rivers to carry merchandise and passengers' in Plate LVI, No 19, with length between perpendiculars of 50ft.

The Jacobstads Vapen – an eighteenth-century galeas of East Bothnia, Finland

In the middle decades of the eighteenth century the development of the *galeas* was influenced in its form and fittings by the galliot. It was used not only in Sweden and Denmark, but also in the merchant fleet of Hamburg and in Holland. The appearance of the *galeas* coincided with the transition in the Baltic from clinker to carvel construction of smaller ships.

The *galeas* became common in the period when the shipbuilding of Jacobstad in the county of East Bothnia in northern Finland expanded to become the most important in Sweden. A ship draught, drawn around 1760, for a two-masted hull, has been located in the archives of the magistrates' court of Jacobstad. It is very similar to one of Chapman's plans in Plate XXII, but also closely matches the type of

two-masted ships which were built in the Jacobstad area in the 1760s and 1770s. It seems to have been a standard model for vessels offered for sale by the local shipbuilders. The two-masted hulls were often rigged as brigs, as snows or as a *galeas*.

The two-masted rig of the *galeas* had a main mast with a height three times the maximum breath of the hull. At this time the mizzen was short and stepped fairly far aft. The hull of the *galeas* had a flat stern, and differed in that respect from the double-ended galliot, which had a rig similar to the *galeas*.

The rig of the *galeas* differed from the galliot in the shorter bowsprit, so that the *galeas* did not carry a flying jib. The outer jib stay ran to the top of the main topmast, and the inner jib to the head of the lower mast. The main mast only carried a square topsail and a gaff main sail on a boom. The latter was somewhat narrower than the galliot main sail.

Eighteenth-century grain galliots

From the reign of Charles XI during the latter decades of the seventeenth century Sweden developed a requirement for imported grain, and for nearly a hundred years this demanded more tonnage than any other trade, amounting to about a quarter or a third of total Swedish imports. The most important variety was rye, followed by corn, rye being imported largely

from the Swedish province of Pomerania, and from Russia. Rye from Pomerania was encouraged by reductions in customs duties.

This extensive and long-standing trade was carried on in smaller vessels, especially galliots, built and owned in the small seafaring villages and towns of Pomerania. The galliot was a double-ended, Dutch ship type which existed in a two-masted *galeas* rigged version, and a three-masted variant with a ship rig. The galliot was usually under 100 lasts cargo capacity, and in the eighteenth century was built in the Swedish provinces on the southern shores of the Baltic, as well as in East Bothnia in the north of Finland. The galliot became less common in the middle of the eighteenth century.

One Pomeranian grain galliot, the *Concordia* of Stralsund, en route to Stockholm was lost in a gale in 1754, and the wreck has been located off Hundudden (Dogs Point) on the island of Älsvnabben. The hold is still full of grain.

Barks for timber and grain

Barks were shallow-draught merchant ships, widely employed in North Sea and Baltic trades in the latter part of the eighteenth century. They were strongly built and cheaply finished, without stern galleries or head; low costs and a capacious hull form made them ideal for bulk cargoes. Barks, therefore, often carried timber from Norwegian ports and grain in the Baltic. Chapman illustrates the type in Plate XXX, No 13, which shows a bark, with a *galeas* rig, of 39 heavy lasts burden and a length of 68ft. With slight modifications this could be used for either of the two trades: for timber it had stern loading ports to be able to take in long baulks; slimming down the stern lines produced a grain carrier with somewhat better sailing qualities. Chapman also describes two smaller barks with sloop rig of 13 and 7.5 heavy lasts burden respectively, for use on lake Mälar inland of Stockholm (Plate XXIX, Nos 9 and 10). These

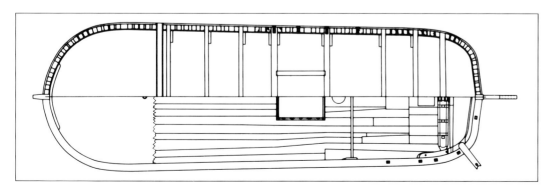

A deck plan of the Älvsnabben wreck. There was a deckhouse of undetermined size abaft the main hatch; as excavated the stern was partly broken down, but had incorporated a cabin whose roof line probably rose higher than the deck. A pump and the main horse (a traveller for the main sheet block) were also discovered. (Author)

vessels were presumably used in the very intensive trade between the smaller towns on the inner parts of the lake and the capital, largely taking iron and metal for export to Stockholm, returning with food, salt and assorted merchandise to the small Mälar towns.

The pink was similar in many respects to the bark, but was characterised by sharper lines and, particularly, a narrow 'pinched' stern.

During the eighteenth century the term bark (sometimes spelt barque) came to imply a three-masted rig, in which the mizzen carried no square canvas, just a gaff sail and sometimes a gaff topsail. This required fewer seamen for sail handling and so reduced costs compared with a ship.

The 'Denmark sloops'

The lack of timber in Denmark and the need for agricultural products in Norway created a persisting pattern of trade between the northern part of Jutland and southern Norway. From the seventeenth century Danes exported grain, meat, pork, textiles, and other merchandise to Arendal and other ports in southern Norway, returning with timber, often in the shape of pine beams of different sizes. Wrought iron was also brought south from Norway.

The shortage of tonnage, caused by the British blockade of Danish waters during the Napoleonic Wars encouraged the Norwegians to build more ships. This was the inspiration for the small sloops that were developed from earlier and more primitive vessels. By the middle of the century they had found their final form, and from then on they were known as 'Denmark sloops'.

They were small, but wide and beamy, designed for big deck cargoes. They were clinker-built with thin planks of oak, intended to give them the necessary elasticity to survive being beached for unloading on the open, shallow sands of the west coast of Jutland. They seldom measured more than 4½ commercial lasts (*c*9 tons), which was an advantage in terms of customs duties. The sloops carried a gaff main sail, a topsail on a separate topmast, fore staysail, jibs in two or three different sizes, and sometimes a flying jib.

The traditional coastal cargo carriers – *jekt* and *storebåt* – of Sogne Fjord, Norway

Sogne Fjord, north of Bergen, has a total length of about 180km. This fjord with its high shores was a central communications route for

local trade in the area into the twentieth century. Many of the farmers in the inland mountain valleys had boat-sheds down by the fjord, where they kept boats used for carrying goods to the town of Bergen.

Of these traditional, clinker-built cargo vessels , the coastal *jekts* were numerous in the Sogne area. No Sogne *jekt* has survived from the nineteenth century, but some of them were photographed in the 1870s. Many large farms had smaller vessels, the *storebåt* ('big boat'), for the purpose of transporting farm produce. They were smaller but otherwise shaped like the *jekts*.

The wind and currents of Sogne Fjord often set up a nasty sea, and the wind is squally. The local boats were built for these conditions, as Arne Emil Christensen points out in his book based on Öystein Faeröyvik's collection of plans of traditional Norwegian boats.[5] The strong sheer fore and aft kept out any spray, and the boats were light and flexible. The sails

---

5. A E Christensen (ed), *Inshore Craft of Norway* (Oslo and London 1979).

The plans of a Denmark sloop as reproduced in Paris's Souvenirs de Marine *in the nineteenth century. The beamy, shallow-draught hull is evident. They were usually clinker-built, although this example is carvel.*

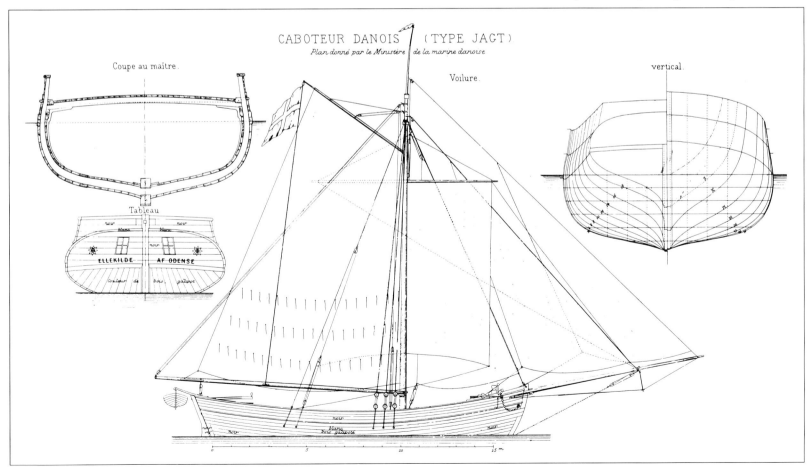

were cut low and wide, and the boats were considered very fast on the wind, although they did not tack well. The *storebåt* was used for the same purpose as the bigger *jekt*, namely to take farm surplus to the market in Bergen. While the *jekts* were regular freighters, taking cargo for many customers, the *storebåt* served only the farm owning it.

Other common types of merchant ship in northern European waters

The *bojer*, of Dutch origin, was a common vessel in Swedish waters in the seventeenth century, usually carrying a fore-and-aft rig with a topsail on the main mast and jib headsails; sometimes it also had a small mizzen mast.

Swedish seventeenth-century sources also mention another Dutch vessel, the *byssa*, a fishing craft better known in English as the buss. The *koff* was yet another typical Dutch ship, common in Scandinavian waters since the seventeenth century, where it usually had a fore-and-aft rig with spritsails on both masts. The *smak*, common among the Dutch, the Danes and Swedes, was very similar to the *koff* but the mizzen mast was positioned at the extreme stern.

The *hoeker*, which was somewhat larger than the *galliot*, became common in the Baltic from the middle of the eighteenth century. It had a flat bottom and a double-ended hull, and like the *galliot* was built in two types. The larger was three-masted, and similar to the three-masted *galliot*, except that it had a head. A smaller type was the so called single-masted *hoeker*, which actually stepped a small mizzen mast far aft. The latter was very similar to the *koff*, but had taller masts. Several varieties of the *hoeker* existed, one for instance used for fishing.

Some traditional vessels in northern waters were known as *skuta*.[6] In the seventeenth century this applied to a type of smaller transport vessel for coastal waters with one or two square rigged masts, and a crew of five to eight men. It was similar to the *craier* or *krayer* which was a very common vessel in the Baltic. It had a sharper hull than the *galliot* and a flat stern, two pole masts, and a mizzen mast. On the fore and main masts it set square main and topsail, and on the mizzen a gaff and a square topsail. Another relatively small type was the *pråm*, a barge-like transport vessel for heavy goods, of which there were both sailing and unrigged towed versions.

Finally, it should be mentioned that although the term 'frigate' in eighteenth-century Britain was almost exclusively reserved for naval cruisers, elsewhere in Europe it was applied to a particular type of merchant vessel as well. Rather like the warship, this had a low profile hull with one flush gundeck, a square stern and quarter galleries and a full head. It carried a full ship rig and was usually employed in the prestige trades where faster passages were at a premium.

6. See in this series *Sail's Last Century*, Chapter 8.

A Sogne Fjord jekt, *a Norwegian open boat design that can trace its ancestry right back to Viking era ships, although its flat transom and cabin reveal greater development than other local types like the Nordland boat or the Åfjord boat. The* jekt *was a coastal trader rather than a farm boat. From A E Christensen's* Inshore Craft of Norway.

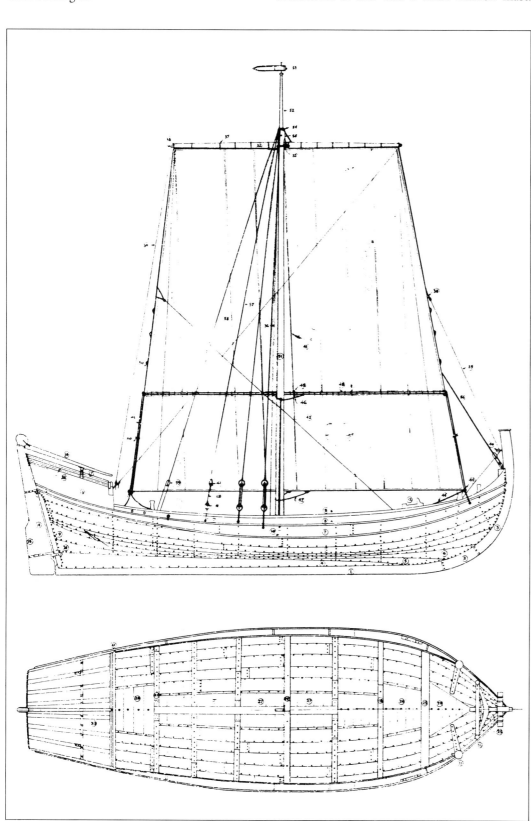

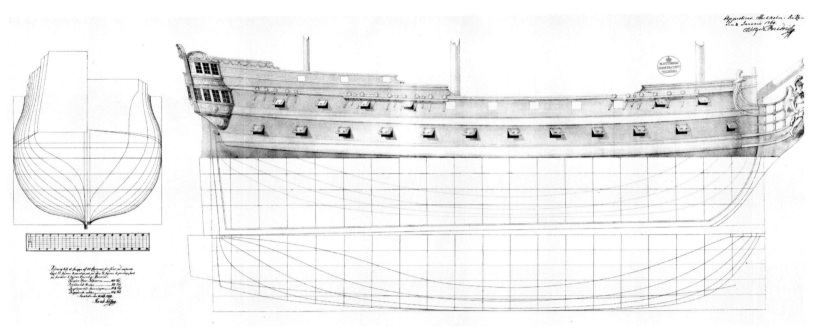

The ships of the Swedish East India Company

As is not unusual in other contexts, because Swedish East Indiamen were the products and vehicles of highly organised shipbuilding and seafaring, they are fairly well recorded. They have also attracted the attention of historians with an interest in Swedish maritime and technical history.

At the end of the Great Northern War in 1721 Swedish shipping was in a parlous state. The government supported efforts to rebuild an active foreign trade, based inside the country. Through several initiatives the merchant navy grew from practically nothing around 1720 to about 480 ships under the Swedish flag in 1727. However, of these most were small, and not fit for ocean-going shipping.

State and private interests in this situation co-operated in plans to revive Swedish shipping for markets outside Europe. This had been in the interests of every Swedish government for a hundred years, but a few investors could now make capital and experience available. In 1731 the Swedish East India Company was founded and survived for 82 years until 1813, making in total 132 voyages. Nearly all the ships used by the company were built in Sweden, but one exception was *Ulrika Eleonora*, which was bought from the English East India Company. She was the second ship the company sent out, but made only one voyage.

A few examples of the Swedish East India Company's ships are described below, and also a few ship projects developed for the company which were never executed. These latter some-

times provide an insight into the ship designer's intentions as they were expressed at certain points in time, but can also be used to sketch the evolution of the ships the company built and used. From a broader perspective this might be seen as an indication of how the big merchantmen of northern Europe were designed during the course of the eighteenth century.

Friedericus Rex Sueciae

The first ship that sailed from Sweden for the Swedish East India Company in 1732 was the *Friedericus Rex Sueciae*, which was building at Grill's shipyard in Stockholm at the time of the company's foundation. The ship was of 200 lasts burden, but little else is known about her. Although very successful in trade, she was quite small for the East Indies. On the basis of the burden the ship designer and engineer Hugo Hammar calculated the dimensions to have been about 115ft over the posts, maximum breadth 31ft, and a depth in hold of 20ft. She was supposedly originally intended for a Spanish trader, for which her size would have fitted her very well.

Thomas Rajalin's ship design of 1730

Hugo Hammar's research into Swedish East Indiamen suggests that the earliest ships were very similar in design to contemporary ships of the same size in England and Holland. Hammar believes that the approximate appearance of early Swedish East Indiamen can be gleaned from a ship project whose plans were published in Commodore Thomas Rajalin's *Nödig underättelse om skiepsbyggeriet* of 1730, one of the first manuals on shipbuilding pub-

Sohlberg's original draught for the Lovisa Ulrika *as a 50-gun ship. During construction the ship was acquired by the Swedish East India Company and converted for their purposes. The lower deck gunports were sealed – except for a few loading ports – and a superstructure built over the waist, but the relatively sharp lines of the warship remained. From Hugo Hammar's* Fartygstyper i Swenska Ost-Indiska Compagniets flotta.

lished in Sweden. It aims to summarise the state of shipbuilding in the early eighteenth century, and is now assumed to represent the most modern views of shipbuilding just after the Great Northern War.

In the same work Rajalin also reproduces the plans of a 60-gun ship of the line, measuring 372 lasts. It is not an East Indiaman of course, and is also much larger than *Friedericus Rex Sueciae*; nevertheless, it has been supposed to represent the new trends towards bigger ships in Sweden at this time, especially in relation to the rigging. Compared to the bigger ships of the seventeenth century, the rig of the 60-gun ship was modern in that the spritsail mast on the bowsprit had been replaced by a jibboom and staysails, with the spritsails transferred below the jibboom. Staysails were introduced on the bowsprit and jibboom and also between the masts. One can assume that the hard lessons of war had taught seamen the value of ships that sailed closer to the wind, and thus replaced the spritsail mast with staysails instead. It is probable that the first Swedish East Indiamen had this pattern of rig. Rajalin was active in Stockholm when the first East Indiamen were built there and it is very likely that they followed his ideas in their design.

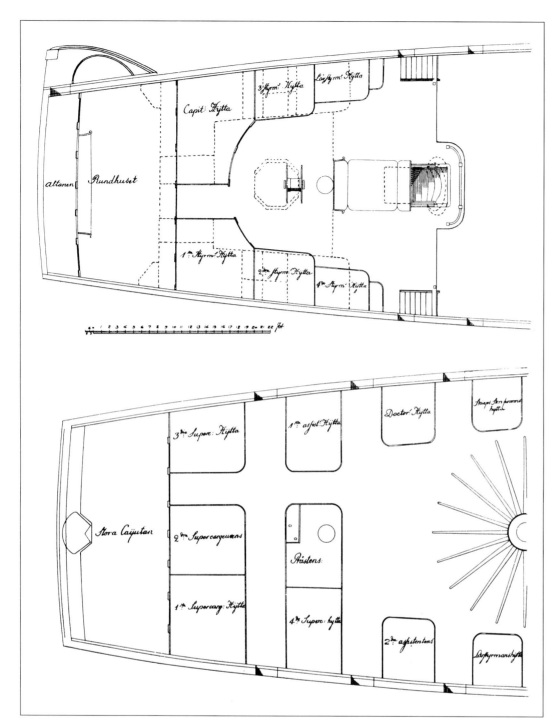

The arrangements of cabins on the upper and quarterdecks of Chapman's first East Indiaman, the Cronprins Gustaf *of 1760. Note that the upper deck cabins are positioned between the ports so that the whole wardroom area may benefit from the light and ventilation they provide. From Hugo Hammar's* Fartygstyper i Swenska Ost-Indiska Compagniets flotta.

Sophia Albertina

The first Swedish East Indiaman of which design plans have been preserved is the *Sophia Albertina*. The plan is signed by the master shipwright B Holm, and dated 1753; the ship made her first voyage in 1755. The hull is still traditional in form, with a fairly steeply raked cutwater, and with a high, heavily adorned after superstructure, and also other kinds of decorations. The gunports on the lower gundeck have been removed, leaving only four loading ports on each side.

Lovisa Ulrika

The design and adaptation of the *Lovisa Ulrika* is interesting as it shows how close was the similarity between an East Indiaman and a ship of the line. The construction plans of the *Lovisa Ulrika* were draughted in 1753 by Harald Sohlberg, one of the best known master shipwrights of the Swedish navy of the time. When started in 1757 it was intended to become a 50-gun ship of the line. The building progressed slowly, and in 1763 the East India Company expressed a wish to take over the ship and convert it into an East Indiaman. It was launched as such in 1766.

The lines of the hull were drawn for the

Chapman's Gustav III, *a large East Indiaman built in 1779. By this date the lower deck ports have disappeared altogether, but the beakhead bulkhead was retained up until the opening years of the nineteenth century. From Hugo Hammar's* Fartygstyper i Swenska Ost-Indiska Compagniets flotta.

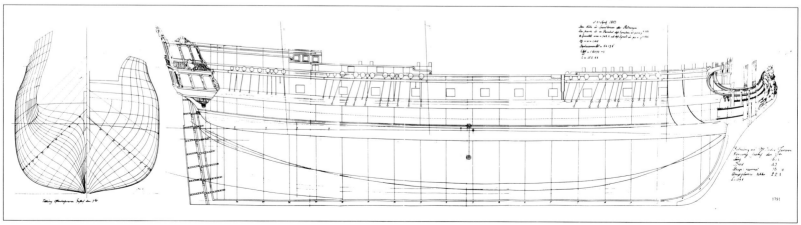

At 540 lasts the Gothenburg *of 1786 was the largest of all Swedish East Indiamen. This body plan and structural section gives a good impression of the capacious hull form of these ships, as well as their warship-like scantlings and appearance. From Hugo Hammar's* Fartygstyper i Svenska Ost-Indiska Compagniets flotta.

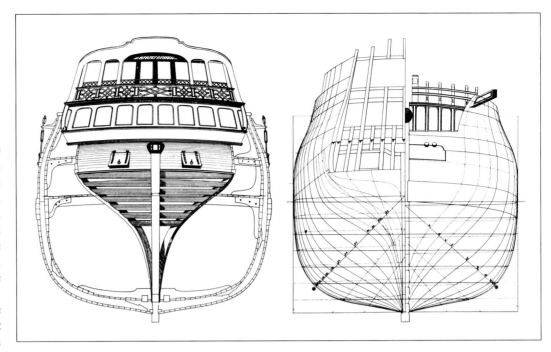

sharper form of a man of war, so when the ship was transformed into an East Indiaman little could be altered in this respect. However, the gunports of the lower gun deck were closed, except those which were to be used for loading, and a structure built between the forecastle and the half-deck, covering the main deck in the waist, which was common on East Indiamen. The half-deck was also raised, to provide more room underneath it.

The *Lovisa Ulrika*, which was designed to be of 385 lasts, and a length overall of 147ft, left Gothenburg on her first voyage to China in 1766. After a total of four round-trips, in 1789 she was bought back by the Swedish navy at the time of the Swedish–Russian war of 1788-1790 to serve in the squadron stationed at Gothenburg. Soon afterwards she sank outside Vinga on the west coast with a cargo of guns, supposedly due to decay in the hull resulting from the extended construction period.

The *Lovisa Ulrika* was built as a man of war with heavy oak frames of substantial scantling. Sharper underwater lines meant less buoyancy than a merchant ship, while the hull weight of a warship was too great and its displacement too small to carry the cargo one could expect of a merchant vessel of the same dimensions. It was also more difficult to arrange enough cargo space in the finer underwater form of a man of war. Furthermore, stability and sailing qualities were also very different from those of a merchant ship. On several occasions in Swedish history the possibilities of joint construction of warships and East Indiamen were discussed, in an attempt at a more effective organisation for the building of bigger ships, but because of the differences between the ship types this was never possible to achieve.

Cronprins Gustaf

In the 1760s the fleet of the East India Company was enlarged with three new ships, *Adolph Friederic*, *Lovisa Ulrika* and *Cronprins Gustaf*. The two first mentioned were designed by Sohlberg, while the *Cronprins Gustaf* was the first East Indiaman to be designed (in 1760) by F H Chapman. According to Chapman's notes on the design plans construction began in 1763. The plans show that Chapman was still strongly influenced by the old shipbuilding concepts

with regard to hull form. This is particularly true for the shape of the stemposts which were very similar to that on the older ships. He does not seem to have been using his parabolic design method in this project.

The construction plans of *Cronprins Gustaf* include an interesting arrangment sketch of the officers' quarters on a Swedish East Indiaman. At this time plans of this sort were not deemed necessary; instead the shipwright's mate marked out the interior fittings with a piece of chalk on the deck.

The Gustaf III and the Gothenburg

The *Gothenburg*, built by J F Roempke in Gothenburg in 1784-87 was the biggest ship ever built for the Swedish East India Company. Like the *Gustaf III*, she was designed by Chapman, and the two ships were similar both in design and size. The *Gothenburg* measured 540 lasts and had a length overall of 166ft. The plans were still in Chapman's hands in 1803, when he calculated certain qualities in her hull shape using the then fully developed parabolic method. The plans were also accompanied by detailed building specifications.

The two ships have been seen as proof of the excellence of Swedish shipbuilding at the time, in terms of both the lines and appearance as well as the structural strength. There is a model of the *Gustaf III*, which reveals a novelty in the rigging of the ships which does not show in the designs plans. The vessel had been given a royal above the usual sails, something which evidently was not used on the East Indiamen at this time, although it had been used by the British navy much earlier. The standing royal

became more common in the merchant marine around the turn of the century. The lateen sail on the mizzen mast had also disappeared to be replaced by a gaff sail with a boom.

Chapman's East India ship project of 1807

Finally, a survey of the development of Swedish East Indiamen would not be complete without mention of a project which was never completed. In 1807 F H Chapman was requested to design a ship suitable for the East India trade. Although the ship was never built, the plans show what was thought to be the most modern and seaworthy ship for this long-distance trade in the early nineteenth century, seventy-five years after the founding of the Swedish East India Company.

Times had changed and the ship was much smaller than those designed in the eighteenth century, at only 350 lasts. The company was no longer the brilliant business it had been and considerations of economy dominated the design. Many features and fittings were simplified and rationalised. The design of this late East Indiaman, with its clean and elegant unornamented profile, seems to prefigure the clippers of some decades later. The bow is shaped in a simple curve towards the figurehead; the tumblehome is greatly reduced compared with earlier designs, a development which continued until the topside became more or less vertical. A peculiarity of this project is the inclusion of an unusual plan showing how to store cargo on the lower deck for the return voyage from Canton to Sweden.

Carl Olof Cederlund

Scandinavian and Baltic Ships: Typical Vessels 1650-1850

Name	Description	Built	Launched	Tonnage (in lasts)	Dimensions (Feet) (Metres)	Remarks
KALMAR NYCKEL	Ship of the New Sweden Company		?1637	130	*115.00 x 25.00 x 13.00* *33.35 x 7.25 x 3.77*	One of the first fleet that sailed in 1637 to the New Sweden colony in Delaware
HAFSFRUEN	Ship of the 'Lilla Saltkompaniet'			250	135.00 x 30.00 39.15 x 8.70	Belonged to the Stockholm 'Small Salt Co'; mostly in Portuguese trade, but taken up by Swedish navy in 1676
DERFFLINGER	Flute	Netherlands	1675	170	110.00 x 23.00 34.10 x 7.13	Owned in Gdansk, Poland from 1681; traded with La Rochelle, W Indies and W Africa
ANNA MARIA	Flute	Amsterdam	1694	274	132.00 x 28.50 38.28 x 8.27	Built for Stockholm merchants, trading with London and Amsterdam; sunk 1709 at Dalarö and wreck identified in 1987
SCT JOHANNES	Sandskuta ('sand vessel')	Norway	1726	5	40.10 12.43	Common type in the trade between southern Norway and Jutland until the last century
FRIEDERICUS REX SUECIAE	East Indiaman	Stockholm	c1730	200	*115.00 x 31.00 x 20.00* *33.35 x 8.99 x 5.80*	First ship of the Swedish El Co to sail to China; purchased on stocks at the Grill yard
SANKT MIKAEL	Three-masted galiot		c1740		*83.00 x 20.60* *24.07 x 5.97*	Lost in Finnish archipelago in 1747, en route to St Petersburg; wreck located 1960s
CONCORDIA	Two-masted galiot	?Stralsund	c1750		*70.00 x 20.00 x 9.25* *20.30 x 5.80 x 2.68*	Owned in Stralsund, lost in 1754; wreck located in 1968 and identified in 1994
SOPHIA ALBERTINA	East Indiaman	Stockholm	1755	412	151.00 x 39.00 x 23.00 43.79 x 11.31 x 6.67	Designed by B Holm; traditional Indiaman of the early part of the century
JACOBSTADS WAPEN	Galeas (ketch rig)	Jakobstad, Finland	1767	65	65.00* x 21.00 18.85 x 6.09	Earliest ship plans in Finland include this vessel; first Finnish vessel to trade abroad after 1765 freeing of commerce
Unidentified	Sump	Sweden, Åland Is and Finland			44.00 x 13.50 x 4.50 12.76 x 3.92 x 1.31	Chapman's Plate LX,4. A common Swedish wet-well fishing craft into the last century
Unidentified	Skuta	Sweden, Åland Is and Finland			64.00 x 25.50 x 7.50 18.56 x 7.40 x 2.18	Chapman's Plate LX,9. A common Swedish coaster, especially in firewood to Stockholm
HERZOG VON BEVERN	Merchant frigate, 40 guns	Stettin	1770		132.00 x 32.00 x 17.00 40.92 x 9.92 x 5.27	Built for Frederick the Great's Prussian Shipping Co; European and overseas trade
ANNA MARIA	Hukarjakt ('hooker sloop')	Åbo, Finland	1777	51.66	57.00 x 23.50 16.53 x 6.82	Bordeaux trader from Åbo, 1777-1788
PROWINSIEN GOTHLAND	Ship	Visby, Gotland	1784	300	113.00 x 33.00 32.77 x 9.57	Largest ship ever built on the island of Gotland; designed as a warship for Spain but served as a cargo ship until loss in 1788
DE FIRE BRÖDRE	Sloop	Marstal, Denmark	1794		44.20 x 13.20 x 5.00 13.70 x 4.09 x 1.55	Survived from 1794 until loss in 1943 with minimal changes; no engine ever fitted
CUXHAVEN	Ship	Cohr Shipyard, Hamburg	1798	109	96.00 x 27.00 x 16.00 29.76 x 8.37 x 4.96	Traded from St Petersburg, to Britain, and across the Atlantic; ex-*Margaretha Cornelia*
ORA ET LABORA	'Denmark sloop'	Klitmöller, Denmark	1799	8.1	46.30 14.35	Measured 13.1 lasts in 1825 and 14.5 in 1851; owned at Thisted from 1839
FREDEN	Barque	Björneborg, Finland	1807	142	96.00 x 27.00 27.84 x 7.83	Owned in Åbo, Finland 1807-1821; sold to Hull in 1825
SEVERN	Brig	Chepstow, Britain	1815	51	66.60 x 20.00 19.31 x 5.80	Found drifting off Sweden in 1825; then owned in Karlskrona until lost in 1832
KRONPRINZ VON PREUSSEN	Brig				86.00 x 24.00 x 15.30 26.66 x 7.44 x 4.74	Aquired by the Prussian Shipping Co in 1827 and sailed overseas for the company
FÄDERNESLANDET	Schooner	Fogelvik, Sweden	1837	44	67.20 x 21.00 x 8.00 19.49 x 6.09 x 2.32	Lost in southern Swedish archipelago 1845; wreck identified in 1992
SKÅSHEIMBÅTEN	Storebåt	Sogn, Norway	1840		34.60 x 11.00 x 3.00 10.03 x 3.19 x 0.87	Farm boat, now in the Amla Museum, Sogn. Built at the farm of Inre Slide
Unidentified	Estonian lodja			c55	*75.00 x 45.00 x 6.00* *21.75 x 13.05 x 1.74*	Reconstruction of a larger *lodja* of the late nineteenth or early twentieth century

Hull dimensions are in the local feet, the Swedish foot equalling 0.29 metres and those of Germany and Denmark 0.31 metres approximately.

Dimensions given *in italics* are reconstructed from archaelogical or other data. * = keel length.

As a measure of tonnage the *last* could be either a unit of weight or volume, and varied from place to place and over time. The value used in the table is that in use when the ship was measured.

4

Mediterranean Ships and Shipping, 1650–1850

ANY SURVEY of Mediterranean ship- ping in the age of sail faces particular difficulties in the great variety of ship types to be covered, the diversity of cultures involved, and the significant technical changes over time. No approach is entirely satisfactory, but this chapter is organised by geographical area, which in many cases is more or less identical with separate maritime traditions, starting in the east with what is loosely called the Levant and working westwards. The nominal limits of the period covered have been breached in some cases, if the development of a specific ship type requires it, or if source materials permit.[1]

Source materials themselves are also a problem, since there are few preserved records or accurate illustrations before about 1700. There is some information on ship movements, and these often quote ship types, but most records are at best partial and confined to single places and short periods of time. This forces the writer to make assumptions about other times and places based on this scarce evidence. This makes it very difficult to generalise about the characteristics of each ship type: these might be identified at a particular place and date—and even then on fairly thin evidence —but clearly the same details cannot be held to apply throughout the Mediterranean and across three centuries. Differing geographical conditions dictated variations, and the passage of time produced improvements.

Of the means of measuring improvements, only tonnage is sufficiently documented to be meaningful, although even here the figures are often in obscure units like the *salma*, which measured 3 *kantara* (or quintals), equal to 300 pounds. Total tonnages of merchant fleets tend to increase over time, reflecting both larger individual hulls and a greater amount of trade. As the hulls grew in size, so did the amount of canvas necessary to drive them, and ease of handling required dividing this greater area into more individual sails, necessitating changes in the sail plan. Greater efficiency may be measured in terms of speed (shorter journey times), or the crew size required, but this brings qualitative aspects into the discussion of developments, and as far as hull forms are concerned there is virtually no evidence on the subject. Nevertheless, hulls seem to be subject to less development than the rig. To quote only one example, the Greek *bratsera* carried lug sails two hundred years ago but in the last century, was rigged as a *brig-schooner*, on an identical hull. The overriding consideration in all that follows is that any description of a ship type is confined to the time and place specified, and may not apply across the whole period or area under consideration.

Shipping in the Levant

The 'Levant' is a relative term in geography, as it does not refer to a well-defined expanse of water, with islands and a shoreline with ports. Like 'west' or 'east' or 'Orient' it refers to a direction, a course to steer, in this case 'into the rising sun'. For the Maltese it began east of Valletta; for the Genoese it was much the same, but only after changing course on leaving Messina. Venetian influence prevailed, however, since they did not steer eastward until they left the Ionian Sea. The Adriatic, Corfu and the Ionian Islands were not originally in the Levant, but Crete or Smyrna (modern Izmir) and the Aegean most definitely were, certainly as much as Coron and Modon, the Venetian strongholds in the Peloponnese, where even before 1700 captains of galleys and

1. Full details of sources and useful further reading are given in the Bibliography.

A late example of the Greek bratsera, *with what was termed locally a* brig-schooner *rig. In earlier centuries this characteristic hull form would have carried a pair of lug sails but would have still been called a* bratsera, *highlighting the problem of ship-type terminology which could have rather different significance in different places or at different times.* (Author)

skippers of merchantmen waited for orders or news. It is clear then, that the term has not the same meaning as the purely hydrographic 'Eastern Basin'. Only the Maltese would see the two as synonymous.

Occasionallly it is possible to make judgements on shipping and seaborne trade before 1700, but for shipbuilding this is exceedingly difficult, unless the ship type is mentioned together with a painting or drawing. This is often done in the case of *ex-votos*, but votive paintings are *anathema* in Muslim lands, and hardly occur in Greece. Moreover, many emphasise the devotional aspect rather than the nautical accuracy historians would hope for.

For the Turks themselves a term like 'levant' has no meaning. With their predilection for speaking in oppositions, they tend to stress the contrast between 'Black' and 'White Sea' (their name for the Mediterranean), implying notions like 'sinister' versus 'bright'. This is carried over into their maritime organisation, where they dub masters of big merchant vessels 'Black Sea captains', reserving 'White Sea captains' for those in command of galleys and other men-of-war. Corsair captains licensed to plunder would also belong to this latter maritime guild. Skippers belonging to the first category would therefore include Orthodox Greeks trading with Alexandria or Salonika, without ever making port in Odessa or any other Black Sea harbour. The captains of the eight *karamürsali* arriving at Venice from the Aegean a few years before 1600 must have been Greeks, as Turks on the whole did not venture that far west, this in contra-distinction to the Latins, who since time immemorial had penetrated into the Levant.

On the whole the term 'Turkish' refers to shipping under the Ottoman flag. For port statistics no other interpretation can be expected, and this always includes Greeks unless otherwise stated, at least before 1820. Apart from the Laz who lived east of Trebisond (modern Trabzon), and who anyway style themselves Turks, there is no other strong maritime tradition besides Muslim or Orthodox Greeks, even today. Greeks dwell on both sides of the Bosporus and all along the Sea of Marmara but then, in the past most of the Greek world in the widest sense was part of the Ottoman empire. Even the War of Independence in the 1820s

One of the most common sights of the Ottoman empire was the saïka, *or* saique, *as depicted in this late seventeenth-century example from the* Album du Levant *of 1679 by Jean Jouve. The rig is a Levantine form of ketch; note the relatively austere hull. (Musée de la Marine, Paris)*

did not liberate more than half the country, leaving most of the Greek islands under Turkish domination. Moreover many of these islands have been resettled by Arnauti (Albanian tribesmen), after their virtual depopulation at the hands of the Ottoman government in the course of the sixteenth century. To apply ethnological criteria in the context of shipbuilding traditions seems an impossible task.

Turkish sea transport

The mainstay of Turkish seaborne trade found its *raison d'être* in the feeding of Istanbul, the biggest town in the whole of the Mediterranean, with more than half a million people in the seventeenth century. This kept many crews busy, both on the long-haul run from Alexandria and Odessa, and on the coastal routes from Smyrna, Saloniki or the Archipelago. The grain carrying-ships in the so-called Cairo caravans, huge convoys of *karamürsali*, *mahonas* and *jermas*, sailing twice each summer season, were matched in the coastal trades by *caïques*, *peramas*, *bergantins* and *saïkas*, transporting timber and firewood, olives and fruit from the islands, horses from Anatolia and all kinds of merchandise, including cargoes imported from western Europe arriving in foreign ships.[2]

After 1650 the larger of the indigenous craft tended to give way to more modern types, large sailing ships from the West like *kalyons*–recog-

nisably the familiar 'galleon' in Turkish guise. The largest of the galleons were known to the Turks as *mogarbinas*, 'ships of the Western (seas)'. These were not only larger and stronger, they also carried more guns and developed a better turn of speed. The first galleons at Istanbul are recorded as early as 1580, half a century later than at Venice. Originally they were employed to protect the convoys, but later they themselves were used as transports or as corsairs, cruising against enemy ships. The small entrepreneurs in this form of predatory trade preferred the *bergantin*, in fact a small type of *kalite* or *galleot*, usually with two lateens, ten or twelve oarsmen a side, in this case not slaves but armed freemen, and two pieces of artillery in the bows. The *galleot* itself–sometimes referred to as a 'half-galley'– had at least fifteen banks, each oar this time manned by two rowers, but normally these men would be convicts, at least when the *galleot* was fitted out for war.

On the whole our knowledge of typical 'Turkish' craft leaves much to be desired. There is little information about their large trader, the seventeenth-century *karamürsal*. Its average capacity seems to have been between 1000 and 1500 *salme*, a unit of weight, the equivalent being one-eleventh of a ton. The rig was simple enough, with two square sails on both fore and main masts and a lateen on the

---

2. F Braudel, *The Mediterranean and the Mediterranean World in the Age of Phillip II*, 2 vols (London 1972).

A late seventeenth-century engraving by Abraham Casembroot of a fishing boat at Messina. The steep sheer and extended 'wings' in which the bulwarks terminate are typical of early Mediterranean ships and Turkish types in particular.

mizzen. The bowsprit had one square sprit-sail rigged below. A raised forecastle and a high poop gave the *karamürsal* an old-fashioned look. Up to 20 guns for beating off enemy corsairs are mentioned, for which a crew of 50 or 60 would be considered sufficient. To make matters complicated, the term *karamürsal* in Turkish records after 1800 refers to the *bombarda*, by then a 'modern' ship of French origin.

The *mahona*, another big ship in the long-distance trade between Egypt and Istanbul, was a grain carrier rather than a man-of-war. The overhanging poop deck extended well aft, and the sheer was very pronounced. A vessel like this, with a length overall of 120 *palmi* or 30m, depended not only on her two or three lateens, but also on her rowers, the 20 to 26 banks of oars being handled by convicts or prisoners of war, captured or bought in the slave market. *Mahonas* could only compete in trade as long as slave labour was cheap or otherwise easily available. Moreover, they were weak adversaries in naval engagements against corsairs, let alone against the squadrons of the Knights of St John from Valletta. In modern Turkish simple harbour lighters are spoken of as *mahonas*.

Every now and then the sources also mention the *londra*, a ship the size of a *galleot*. Three of them were captured by Maltese galleys in 1674 whilst cruising in the Levant; one *londra* with 44 Turks on board was taken near Sicily in 1794. This is scant information, and certainly not enough to define the characteristics of the type. According to Spanish records they combined oars and sail, although in merchant ships this went out of fashion before 1700, at least in the long-distance trades. At first they were open vessels, but later they were partially decked. They seem to have had up to 50 oarsmen to twelve banks of oars.

There is little information from Turkish sources on another freighter in the so-called Cairo convoys, but then the *jerma* or *germa* was essentially an Egyptian vessel. It is known that it was low in the water, carried one tall pole mast and a bowsprit of great length and considerable steeve, with a square counter and a length-to-beam ratio of 3 to 1. In 1592 a Maltese ship belonging to the Order of St John captured a *jerma* with a cargo of linen and rice and 150 Muslims on board who were all enslaved. As late as 1768 the Maltese captured two *jermas* together with two *karamürsals*, but

whether these later vessels were of the same type is not known. In 1812 about 200 *jermas* were still employed in the coastal trade around Alexandria, but would no longer normally sail beyond the ports of Syria.

There is frequent mention of a fifth type, the *saika*, a vessel of medium size, half-way between *caïque* and *karava*. But then *caïque* or *kayik* is a very general (originally Turkic) term for any small ship, like *karava* for a big one. The *saika* had a curved stem, and something approaching the 'Baltic' bows of the present century, including the long curving forefoot. A long bowsprit with a fairly steep angle of steeve carried a baggy square sail underneath.

The hull had a fair amount of sheer, but the rise of the half-deck was not very marked and lacked the pronounced wings in which the bulwarks aft often ended in early Mediterranean ships. The transom in these craft was shallow. The tall mainmast, always a pole mast, usually carried both a course and a topsail; the short mizzen was rigged with a small lateen. More often than not these craft were Greek-owned or held in joint ownership, which always implies a Greek crew. Many were fitted out as corsair vessels, some with Turkish crews on board. To that extent thay were neither Greek nor typically Turkish. The vessel is often mentioned in the published accounts of European travellers before 1800, as this was their preferred means of getting about in the Levant.

Although information on the near-namesake *saëte* or *sagete* is limited, and no descriptions seem to exist, it can be assumed that both types

must have been more or less similar. The term crops up quite frequently in ports like Barcelona or Marseille. A late eighteenth-century version with three pole masts, a large ship this time, is both mentioned and depicted. Main and fore masts are crossed by three yards; the mizzen carries a large lateen and a square topsail. Bowsprit, steeve and overall sheer are much more noticeable than in western European ships, or even in Genoese *polaccas* and *pincos*.

Less generally present was the *perama*, which before the days of reduction in rig still dominated the eastern Aegean. The term crops up even before the fall of Constantinople in 1453, but to judge from the context it refers to small ferries crossing the Golden Horn or the Bosporus. The word itself is even cognate with western words for ferry and travelled widely through Russia, Scandinavia, and finally the Low Countries in the guise of 'praam', and similar words for small ships.

Peramas are typically ships of the islands off the Anatolian coast, notably Chios, where the walls in both mansions and rural cottages are often adorned with the framed pictures of these colouful craft. Their average capacity would have been between 50 and 100 tons. The men of Chios had a greater dominion over the sea than the short-sea traders of the Marmara farther north, who manned the *tsernikis* to be mentioned later. However, *tsernikis* operated as carriers of goods for the Istanbul markets, whereas *peramas* were busy in the medium-haul traffic around the Aegean, or in the cross trades

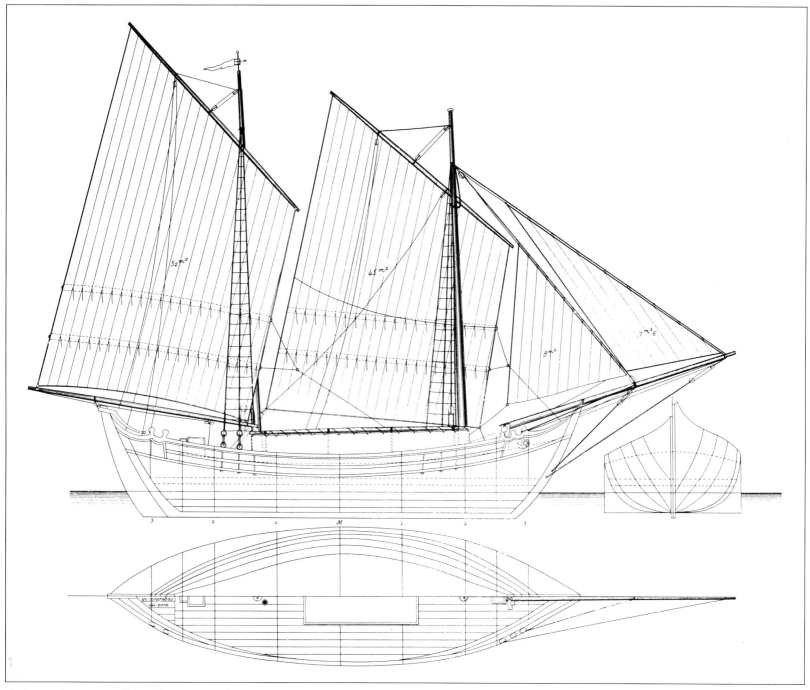

A nineteenth-century rendition of a perama, *as drawn for* Souvenirs de Marine *by Admiral Pâris. Dated to 1878, the vessel carries two lug sails; hull dimensions are given as 14.9m by 3.8m, drawing 1.3m when laden.*

between Smyrna, Saloniki and Crete. A *perama* cannot be mistaken for any other ship type, chiefly because of her hull. Even as late as the middle years of this century, with pole masts and rig cut down to the minimum of two gaff sails, identification was easy. Other medium-sized vessels were also mainly double-enders, but she alone had an almost straight stem with a considerable rake; the sternpost also featured this to a marked degree. The bowsprit was seated on top of the stem-head on the centre-line of the ship. Another characteristic trait was the gap between the ends of the wooden bulwarks and the upturned extremities of both stempost and stern.

The rig has been described as a *goleta-briki* (as the brig-schooner, or brigantine, was known amongst the Greeks), yet there were a few differences. For one thing, brig-schooners of the last century would not normally carry one pole mast, and neither would they be ketch rigged, with the fidded mast aft (technically the main mast) shorter than the fore mast – indeed, exactly the opposite in most cases. Apart from these differences the ship portraits painted around 1800 show familiar features: two stay-

sails amidships and three headsails forward, the main mast crossed by three or four yards and a gaffsail or spanker set aft. This sail is lashed to a boom, whereas a triangular loose-footed topsail is lashed fore and aft. Originally the *perama* had had a simpler rig, consisting of two spritsails and one or two headsails.

Regarding the *tserniki* (or *chektirmè*, as the Turks would say), there were at least two variants of hull type, and three contrasting types of rig, although all carried only one single mast. The largest were broad-beamed double-enders with a high poop, convex bows, a deep waist, and sturdy bulwarks. As motor coasters they still ply as far as Cyprus and Mersin or far along

This photograph of a late example of a caïque shows a rig of two gaff sails, but the hull form has remained very similar to the perama depicted by Pâris in 1878. (Author)

the spritsail (if a spritsail at all) underslung. The heel of the sprit reached to the deck a little forward of the mast itself. Bowsprit and jibboom supported a staysail and two elongated headsails, both reaching to a point above the single square topsail. The bowsprit was fixed to starboard of the high stem which curved slightly inward above the bluff bows. Sometimes a bumkin aft and the heel of the bowsprit came some distance inboard, both being supported by crutches. Technically speaking the single tall pole mast was in fact a topmast with its heel reaching the deck and fastened to an upright stout post. This post, which functioned as main mast, had a length of three or four metres, and

3. Edmond Pâris, *Souvenirs de Marine conservées*, (Paris 1878, reprinted in 3 vols 1972). It contains a great number of plans, some of them from the Mediterranean. They were drawn after 1850, and in some cases the author doubts their accuracy.

4. Sir Alan Moore, *Last Days of Mast and Sail: An Essay in Nautical Comparative Anatomy* (Oxford 1925). The author's own field notes go back to 1961 and 1963, and there must now be few knowledgeable informants left.

the Black Sea coast. In design they are Greek ships, strongly built, and well adapted for sailing the Sea of Marmara and the stormy Black Sea north of the Bosporus. Some compete with schooners in size, measuring up to 100 tons. Admiral Pâris, in his *Souvenirs de Marine*, mentioned a peculiar trait in the construction of some ships of the Pontic (southern Black Sea) coast, where the hull planks were not fastened to the timbers directly, but connected to each other first, edge to edge, by means of staples, a shell-first type of construction also found in some vessels from the upper reaches of both the Danube and Ganges.[3] There were some that still carried sail in the 1960s, but always on a reduced plan, which makes reconstruction of the original rig difficult. Moore made an attempt, but as he did not know Turkish, it is not always convincing.[4]

Turks, Greeks, and even Arnauti from the local shore villages, seem to have been keen on experimenting with rig. One of their solutions resulted in a combination of main course and topsail and a very efficient high-peaked sprit,

A Turkish Black Sea coaster based on an original in Souvenirs de Marine *by Admiral Pâris. Examples of similar single-masted vessels, with a main spritsail and square topsails, are recorded well into this century. (Karl Heinz Marquardt)*

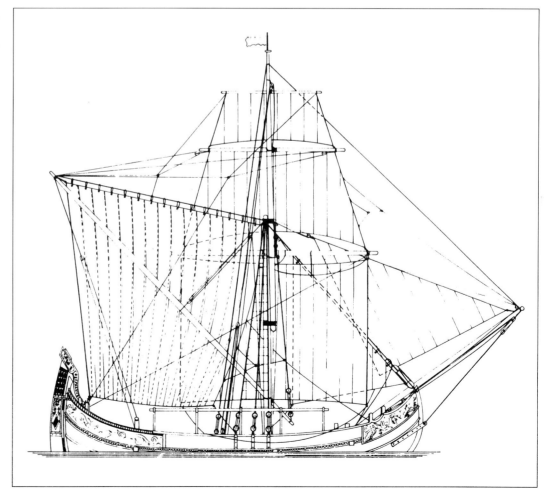

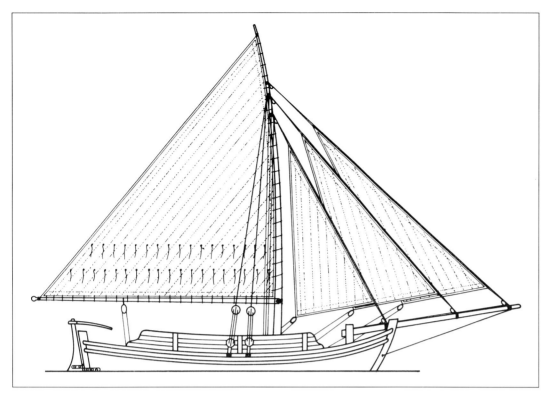

A sail plan of the Turkish chektirmè *with the sliding gunter version of the* pena *rig, known to the Turks as* sheytan ayagi *or 'evil ghost'.* (Wolfram zu Mondfeld)

stepped through the deck–crossed for the occasional two square sails, in addition to a spritsail, a low-footed fore staysail and an equally low-profile jib. The low profile was enhanced by the low angle of the sprit, not more than 30-40 degrees from the deck. This left a considerable gap between the sprit and the mast. Moreover, the sprit had now to support a four-cornered loose-footed spritsail, not the triangular sail of the big *chektirmè*.

These then are the main variations, each type of hull carrying one type of rig, the first with the high peaked triangular sail or *pena* rig, the other with low-peaked four-cornered sail, known as *hasir yelken*. There were two sub-variants of the rig in daily use, however. Of these two the first was also known as the *pena* rig, but had in fact become a sliding gunter. It may well have evolved from the high-peaked triangular Turkish 'lateen' already mentioned, but with the gap between mast and yard reduced to zero. On the other hand the *bacagi yelken* derives from the local low angle sprit sail deprived of its upper quadrant.

penetrated the deck. Four shrouds on each side, crossed with ratlines, supported the perpendicular pole mast. In addition to the shrouds there were two topmast backstays attached to a deck beam aft. This sail arrangement is known as *pena* rig, a word derived from the French *penne*, the upper end of lateen yards, not of sprits; and with reason this type of 'sprit rig' has always

been considered as a lateen by the Turks themselves, even before square sails were abandoned a century ago.

A second variant of the *chektirmè*, with less sheer and with a straight raking stem, had matting or canvas weathercloths instead of wooden bulwarks, a simple bowsprit and no bumkin aft. This type had a real main mast–

Thirty years ago it was still possible to discuss these details with knowledgable elderly locals. Certain rig types tended to be dominant in merchant vessels registered in home ports situated at different ends of the Bosporus–assuming for present purposes that the capital itself had no home-based fleet to speak of. Thus Silivri and Gallipoli craft from the Marmara beat to windward and against the current, which permanently sets to the southward, when fully loaded and heading for Istanbul. Similarly Pontic craft from Sile and Inebolu sailed with the wind on the starboard beam or aft, and generally with the current when the capital was their destination. In adverse conditions of weather and waves, weathercloths would be erected on the top of the stout bulwarks, *chektirmè* not being renowned as dry ships. On the homeward run, with their empty hulls high out of the water, the situation was of course altered. Gemlik, the third important home port for coasters, again on the Marmara, was in a halfway position meterologically speaking, its vessels having the wind abeam both ways. A small *chektirmè* from Silivri on the southern Thracian coast would

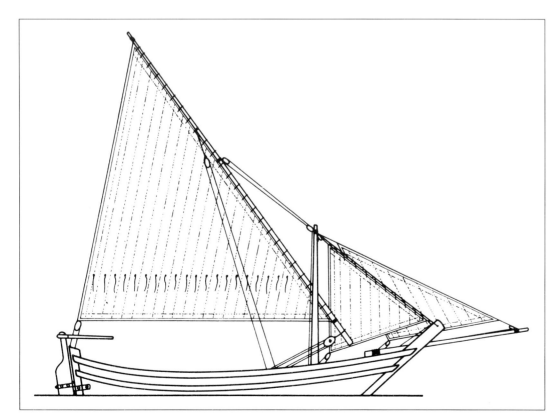

A small version of the Turkish chektirmè *called the* mahone, *with the* bacagi yelken *version of the rig.* (Wolfram zu Mondfeld)

have used the *hasir* rig both ways, but only as a fair-weather combination. When conditions deteriorated she would have reduced sail by adapting to a *bacagi* arrangement, the so-called 'bear paw rig' of the Turks. Big *chektirmès* from Gemlik or Gallipoli, on the other hand, would make use of the high-peaked *pena* rig, or even reduce sail by clamping yard and 'topmast' together, the sliding gunter rig approaching the 'leg of mutton' sail. This rig arrangement is known as *sheytan ayagi*, the 'rig of an evil ghost'! It may seem surprising that definition always relates to the fore-and-aft rig, not to the square sails, but the latter seem secondary in importance. Many *chektirmès* never used them much or even dispensed with them altogether.

This section concludes with the *taka*, designed for the indented Pontic coast, with

A general arrangement drawing from Souvenirs de Marine *of a Turkish coaster of about 1855, called a* gagali *by Paris. The hull is traditional in shape, but the rig is more international – a polacca (ie pole-masted) brig*

many sandy beaches, yet without tidal movement to speak of. The winged transom, although somewhat outmoded, was (or still is to some extent) useful for handling cargo whenever the vessel was beached stern-first. Four of the deck beams were protruding, so as to enable the crew (or a couple of muleteers) to make fast and drag the *taka* above the water's edge. The high bulwarks would make it difficult to handle cargo otherwise. The rig – either one or two *perama*-like sprit sails (nowadays including a low-footed jib or staysail) – was not remarkable for vessels with the wind practically always abeam. However both the hull aft and the keel were unusual. The midship section underwater showed her to have a gull-wing hull. The keel plank, in resting on two skids, curving away amidships, showed similarity with an elongated fish, an eel maybe. Friction between the sand of the beach and the skids underneath was greatly reduced in this way. A similar solution was not only found in small

ships of the Baltic, but also in the French Midi. Whether this would indicate contact in the Classical period, Marseilles being an early Greek colony, remains a debatable point. The Pontic Greeks, before they were expelled in the 1920s by the Turks, knew these ships under the name *taphes*.

Greek mercantile enterprise

As far as sources regarding Greece proper are concerned, there is a synopsis of information not easily found elsewhere in a survey of maritime enterprise sponsored by the Bank of Hellas, the Greek National Bank in Athens, at its centenary jubilee.[5]

There are a large number of more or less

5. *Ellenikè Emporikè Nautilia, 1453–1850* (Athens 1972). The reader is referred to the excellent chapter on the Greek merchant marine by G G Leon. An English translation was contemplated at one time.

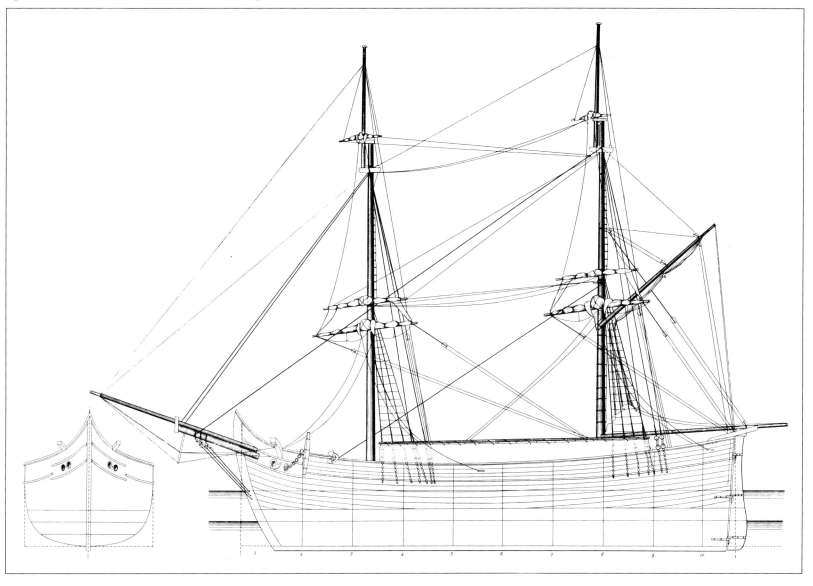

A view of the polacca *under sail, as depicted in the Album du Levant of 1679 by Jean Jouve. Notable is the combination of typical Mediterranean craft forward– with raking lateen fore mast and the* sperone *prow derived from the galley–and a conventional northern hull aft, with the square rigged main and mizzen topsail, plus lateen mizzen course. (Musée de la Marine, Paris)*

typically Greek ships to deal with under this heading. The most common seem to have been the *polacca* and *tartana*, *pinko* and *sakoleva*, but also *bratsera* and *perama*, and, among small craft, the ever-present *trekandiri*. Less frequently ship type names like *moulos*, *péniche* or *lefke* are mentioned. After the Napoleonic wars a large fleet of brigs, brigantines, *barko-bestias*, (*ie* barquentines) and schooners was added to the tonnage. These ubiquitous vessels were close kin to similar ships all over the oceans. Even *polaccas* and *pinkos*, especially those between 100 and 200 tons, resembled some of their sisters elsewhere–they had been built at Livorno or Genoa as early as 1730 in the initial years of Greek maritime enterprise, and were later copied at home. Skippers from Hydra traded not only with Venice, but also with Livorno, for a long time the chief centre of British Mediterranean commerce. In the Dodecanese ten out of twelve ships belonging to Patmos operated under the flag of Menorca, in the middle of the eighteenth century a British possession, like Malta in later years.

Around 1800 more than half of the external trade of the Levant was captured by Greek merchants, replacing the French of earlier years. Of nearly 500 small ships entering Alexandria almost 300 flew the Greek *rajahs*'s flag, as allowed them by the Sultan. The flag consisted of three horizontal bands–red, light blue and red–to distinguish the Greek Orthodox Christians from the Muslim Turks. Half the trade of Istanbul itself was carried in Greek ships. In the west of the Mediterranean the picture was different, but there too one-fifth of all tonnage entering, for example, Ancona was owned by Greeks. Even at Marseilles about sixty ships carrying grain were expected annually in the years between 1820 and the Greek War of Independence. The Black Sea trade, in grain mainly, with Malta after the British occupation of 1801, was also largely in Greek hands,[6] sometimes in fairly small ships like the *trekandiri*.

The first *trekandiri* had been launched as early as 1660, after a group of ransomed seamen from Hydra had decided to have a vessel built on the lines of their Tunisian captors' ships. The first two big lateen rigged

vessels, *pinkos* of over 100 tons, had been built on the island of Hydra itself in 1745, fifteen years after their introduction from abroad. Hydra was clearly a centre for the dispersion of novel ship types within the local maritime culture. Both craft sailed as far as Istanbul and Trieste, and occasionally Venice. In those days it was still a novelty for ships to be ordered or purchased from abroad–the occasional *polacca* or *pinko* at Naples, Messina or Marseilles, or a *karavo-saïka* (in fact a brigantine) at Fiume, as happened for example in 1787. In the same year Missolonghi had fifty ships, decribed as *tartanas*, *polaccas* and *barques*, that is to say eighteenth-century *barques de négoce*.

Of Hydra, Spetsai and Psara, the three main island ports around 1800, the first, with only 35,000 inhabitants, had as many as 120 ships with a total capacity of 45,000 tons, half the tonnage of Marseille! The two other ports owned sixty ships each. Other small islands had less than twenty ships, and even these ranged from 40 to 200 tons. At Corfu, the most important of the Seven Islands of the Ionian Republic, there were probably as many as 250 ships around 1815, ranging up to as much as 300 tons. Included amongst them were *bratseras*, very similar to large *trekandiris*, with two masts and lugsails, *tartanas*, *polaccas* and *martingos*, built on the pattern of ketch rigged *bombardas*, and even a few *chébecs*. By the end of the

Napoleonic wars the Ionian merchant marine relied for its seaborne trade upon no less than a thousand ships, the majority being small *caiques* for the inter-island trade. After the Greek Revolution the centre of mercantile trade shifted eastward, to Syros mainly and to the Piraeus. At Syros alone more than 250 ships were built in the period between 1827 and 1834.

It is convenient to begin descriptions of the individual types with the *polacca*, originally a vessel in the *nave* or galleon class, although rigged as a lateener. When first mentioned by Furttenbach around 1620, it seems to have had two masts–at least at Genoa–but soon the three-masted variety became common. The name (or so it is said) derives from the *polaccone*, the huge lateen fore sail, but as the name *polacre* occurs as well, this may be an etymological stopgap. Later Greek *polaccas* crossed yards on both fore and main masts, and had either a lateen rigged mizzen or a spanker, with a square topsail added in light winds. They had a good carrying capacity, the frames amidships indicating a flat bottom, or very nearly so, like medieval cogs. Heavy cargo was carried in the

---

6. *Mutatis mutandis*, scholars had to use Greek sources, at least for the period after 1800. An example is F C H L Poucqueville, *Histoire de la régéneration de la Grèce depuis 1740 jusqu'en 1824*, 6 vols (Brussels 1843).

A later development of the polacca, *as illustrated by Lescallier in his* Traité Pratique du Gréement *of 1791. The hull form preserves many of the features of earlier* polaccas, *including the* sperone, *but the rig has become a standard three-masted ship, except for the pole main and fore masts. This combination of single-piece lower and topmast became the most characteristic feature of the* polacca *in later years, and the term was extended to describe other rigs in which pole masts were used–a* polacca brigantine, *for example, would denote the usual brigantine rig, but with pole masts.*

hold, whereas general merchandise and fruit would be stowed on the upper and quarter decks. If rigged lateen fashion, it would still have a square rigged short main mast, but if carrying two masts with square sails–as was normal in the late eighteenth and most of the nineteenth centuries–without a *polaccone*, the type would still be called a *polacca*. In the latter case two or three headsails were carried on jibboom and *sperone*, a triangular structure forward of the curvature of the bows. It is clear, therefore, that rig alone was not the definition of a ship like the *polacca*, although the pole masts themselves may have been so.

Also common was the *tartana*, the smaller sister of the *polacca*, with a crew of six to ten. Rig was simple, with either one or two lateens, and a third lateen on the mizzen; alternatively (in Greece at least), the main mast was rigged with a square course, topsail and topgallant. The huge single headsail was also known as *polaccone*. Sometimes a topmast was fidded to the main mast. The Turks rarely mention *tartanas* before 1700, and if they do at all, it is always suffixed by 'ships of the unbelievers'.

Another medium-sized vessel, the *sakoleva*, is a good example of an early type identified by the spritsail rig. The term occurs even before 1600. In contrast with other small or medium-sized ships of the period, some *sakolevas* had a small transom, sometimes combined with an overhanging poop deck of gratings. If fully rigged, it would carry seven sails: a huge spritsail, a main sail with topsail and topgallant, a staysail and a large triangular jib on the bowsprit. The topmast could be removed easily, as could the upright mizzen mast aft, on which a smallish lateen was slung. A *sakoleva* could easily be distinguished by her straight stem with great rake, the flaring lines of the

The Greek sakoleva *was a distinctive sight in the eastern Mediterranean as far west as Malta, combining a sprit main with lateen mizzen and jigger, square topsails, and triangular headsails–almost every configuration of sail known to man. This large example was engraved by Baugean around 1800.*

bows and the forward rake of her main mast. Psara was well known for building fine *sakolevas*. Later the transom received more attention, the poop deck was shortened and a quaterdeck added. The small lateen aft was retained, and a second one added about one foot off the centreline.

The *trekandiri* is always defined as a double-ender with high poop, high rudderhead, curved stem–the so-called 'Baltic bow'–and a fairly low waist, protected by a weathercloth. Originally it carried square sails, lug sails and one jib, but from 1850 occasionally gaff sails, or a combination of both. In nineteenth century

A late example of the Greek trekandiri, *rigged with a lug fore and gaff main. Earlier versions carried square canvas on the fore mast, with a lug main, but as sail gave way to power they were often reduced to a single mast.* (Author)

ship portraits *trekandiris* can easily be mistaken for Ionian *bratseras*, the main distinction being in the mast arrangement: in the first the fore mast raked forward and the main mast aft, whereas the *bratsera* had parallel masts. *Trekandiris* were on the whole smaller than *sakolevas*, and towards the end of their existence only the main mast was retained, first rigged with a lateen but later replaced by a gaff sail.

The *pinkos* is possibly a more modern version of the lateen rigged *polacca*, as it is not mentioned by Furttenbach. An earlier, smaller single-masted version was known as *latinadiko*, because it had introduced the lateen sail in Greece less than 300 years ago, Greece being originally outside the cultural sphere of the lateen. Two-masted *lefkes* from the Sporades were also similar. In contrast to the white and blue of the *trekandiri*, the *pinkos* had a bright yellow hull, blue sides to the afterdeck, and

black linings forward, a remarkably beautiful ship. The cargo space was up to 200 tons, more than would have been expected in a vessel with such graceful lines, but this was largely the result of the wide transom and the raised quarterdeck, despite the tumblehome of the hull. Whereas *polaccas* changed their rig, Greek *pinks* seem to have stuck to their three lateens. The first mention of them, in 1764, notes Missolonghi as their home port.

When the *felucca* (*phelouka* in Greek) was introduced into the Greek archipelago it was already a fully developed ship, with a very deep waist and propelled by three lateens. In the seventeenth century it had stepped only a single mast, carrying a spritsail and a low-footed jib, in addition to eight oars; but, as so often, at a later stage the capacity (still mainly for booty) was increased. The type was very fast–still a true corsair ship until the 1830s–her speed in light winds increased by topsails above the two lateens, with one or two headsails to add to manoeuvrability. On the whole a *felucca* was longer proportionally than a *tartana*, but they were similar in the bows, including the curved stempost and *sperone*. However, they had different pedigrees, the first being in the line of descent of oared vessels like the galley, the *tartana* of the *nave* or round ship.

This chapter does not need to cover the relatively modern ships in the Greek merchant fleet introduced after 1800, which are dealt with in the *Sail's Last Century* volume in this series. These types were often referred to as *corvettes* in a very general way. This also applies to the Hellenic navy for that matter, as many men-of-war in the 1820s were originally built as merchantmen. The modern merchant fleet included a medley of craft like *briki* (spelt *mpriki*) and *brigantini*, *goleta* (the French term was borrowed rather than the term *skouna*), and *briko-goleta*, sometimes referred to as *karava*. Barques of the mid-century type were very rare, but in later years the barquentine was rather common (they were always referred to as *barko-bestia*). To be more precise, in naval employment, barquentines were spoken of as

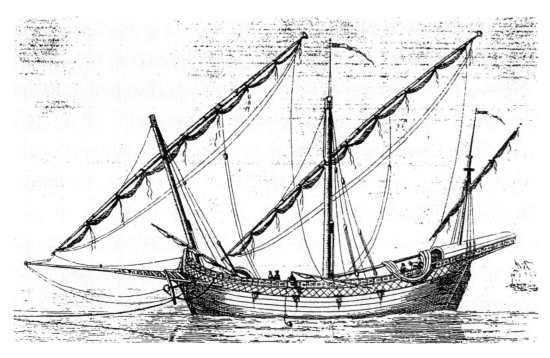

A mainstay of the Greek merchant marine in the eighteenth century was the pinko *or* pink. *This engraving is from Lescallier's French work of the 1790s, but the main features of hull and rig were similar in Greek versions.*

A Greek brigantine from the last days of commercial sail in the Aegean. By this date both hull form and rig were essentially similar to brigantines elsewhere in the western world. (Author)

fregatas, and *polaccas* and brigantines as *corvettes*; but then, this was a question of guns mostly, or of number of crew. The appearance of the *moulos* or *mulos* was very similar to the *brig schooner* with more pronounced steeve of the bowsprit, but with the same numbers of head-sails (usually four). The *mulos* rig seems to have been a little different, however, with a triangular topsail above the spanker aft, instead of the trapezoid one in the *briko-goleta*. Furthermore, the number of yards on the *mulos*'s fore mast was two or three, in contrast to the five crossing the much taller mast in the other type. The main difference is obvious at first sight, in the low gaff trysail aft of the fore mast replacing the lower staysails forward of the main found in the *brig schooner* or brigantine.

The final task for this section is to contrast *goleta* and *péniche*, the rig arrangement following two different conceptions. On similar hulls there may well have been little difference in performance between the two rigs, the one a normal topsail schooner's, the other a two-masted topsail *settee*, always assuming an overall similarity in the flush-decked hulls. After all, a heavily rigged *goleta* could carry almost as much canvas as a settee rigged *péniche*.

The Syrian schooner

When Admiral Durand-Viel began his study of Egyptian naval supremacy in the first half of the ninteenth century, he added some information on the merchant marine. The sudden rise to naval power and maritime mercantile influence during the vice-royalty of the Albanian princes at Cairo is a complete historical surprise. Alexandria, a small port without much significance before 1800, underwent a sudden commercial revival without precedence.[7] In 1817 Alexandria already had fifteen large ships, long-distance traders purchased abroad, with two more building in Austrian yards. Commercial agents for what in fact was a state monopoly ordered more ships in ports like Genoa (1 corvette, 2 brigs), Venice (1 brig, 2 brig schooners), Leghorn (1 frigate), and Marseilles (2 frigates, 1 brig). A few *polaccas*, *misticos* and *sakolevas* were also registered at Alexandria. This does not include the many indigenous *jermas* still registered at Rosetta or Damietta; indifferent performers, they were used for trading up and down the coast. These vessels, probably with a single mast carrying a

lateen (later a gaff) in combination with a topsail, a smaller mizzen, and not more than two headsails, may well be the forerunners of the later *shaktouri* and schooners. They are mentioned (*jerem*, plural *jrâm* in Arabic) as troop transports in 1824, during the war against the Greeks. The squadron even includes a number of prizes recently taken, two *golctas* and one *briki*, but this means little if one compares their numbers with the forty Turkish *sakolevas* destroyed by the Greek forces that year in the roadstead off Samos. The Egyptian transports included brigs, schooner brigs, schooners and even *sakolevas*.

A number of chance remarks from the year 1827 are of crucial importance. Referring to privateers, armed for war as well as the transport of merchandise, there is clear equation of *sakolevas* and *shaktouras*, but a distinction is made between *goélettes* of traditional (clearly French) build as opposed to *schooners*. There is a necessity apparently to discriminate between *schooners* and *goélettes*, but the circumstances that may well have led to a re-appraisal of rig are now unknown.

To equate the Syrian (rather than Egyptian) *shakhtoura* (*sakhtûr* in Arabic; also *kyk*, from Turkish *kayik*) with the *sakoleva* seems far-fetched, as both types could be seen together in Cypriot ports like Limassol or Larnaca. Typically they shared the double-ended hull, often with a square tuck, but later they had a round poop with the rudder underslung. A straight or slightly curved stem and an almost horizontal jibboom were other traits they had in common. Of the two headsails, the one attached to the forestay was rather small, but

the other was a large piece of canvas, suggesting kinship with the *polaccone*. The square sail set on the perpendicular main mast was also very large. In comparison, the spanker and the flying gaff topsail aft were relatively minor affairs. Although a third high-peaked headsail was normally set to balance the sail plan, yet in contrast with the *sakoleva*, the impression of an over-canvassed ship cannot be escaped.

The *felucca* (*flûka* in Arabic; also *mbatné*) is, at least in this part of the world, the smallest of the locally-built craft. A double-ender with a curved stem and either one or two masts, its length cannot have been more than 7m or 8m. The single-masted variety carried a lateen on a short upright pole, together with one jibsail, or else a somewhat taller mast inclining well forward. In the last instance a spritsail was common, the sprit itself being the longer of the two spars. A third spar in this arrangement consisted of a very long and slender bowsprit, carrying a low-profile single jib. A third type of *felucca* was slightly bigger, and could do without a bowsprit as she was rigged with two sprit-rigged masts, the long fore mast inclining forward, the short main mast stepped in an upright position. Both sprits were somewhat taller than the respective masts. Apart from carrying sail–the fore sail known as *tenda*, the after one as *bûmé*–this *felucca* shipped two oars. Both terms for sail may well be of Greek origin, the

7. G Durand-Viel, *Les campagnes navales de Mohammed Aly et d'Ibrahim*, 2 vols (Paris 1935). It is abundantly clear that the author had access to French records of the period, French (not Arabic, at that time) being the language of both the Egyptian port administration and foreign correspondence.

One of the last strongholds of commercial sail in the Mediterranean was the schooner fleet based on coast of Syria and the Lebanon, and especially the island of Ruad off the port of Tartus. In its final guise, as photographed here, the Syrian schooner tended to have bermudan courses, although gaff headed sails were common earlier. (Author)

last one certainly so, as the Greeks had a Cypriot type of smallish vessel known as *boumè*.

This brings us to the subject of the Syrian schooner,[8] or as some prefer, Levant schooner. The more inclusive term points to the fact that there was an Egyptian sub-variety as well, with a flatter head, a curiously crooked counter and less sheer, after the fashion of other ships built in the lower reaches of the Nile. This sub-variety apart, the local Arabs used to refer to one type of schooner as *skûna* in a proper sense

(plural *skâyen*), whereas the other type[9] was known as *gyz* (plural *gyâz* or *agyâz*). Both hulls were identical, but the tophamper differed to such an extent that it was even reflected in the terminology. However, *skûna* did not refer to a schooner proper but to a brig-schooner; similarly, *gyâz* referred to genuine schooners, always bermuda rigged nowadays but gaff rigged with single topsails above until the beginning of the century. One should thus beware of local usage, but this does not come as a surprise, considering how the Syrians loosely refer to their *sakolevas* (they owned a few of 100 tons) as *shakhtouras*.

Bermuda schooners were still employed in great numbers around the middle of this century, and even then one or two sailed with the original tophamper of enormous dimensions, with small square topsails above in light winds. Most sailed under reduced rig, however, with spars shortened and with engines installed. The brig-schooners have gone, but some of them may well have been rerigged as schooners (not as *skâyen*, but as *gyâz!*) as all hulls were essentially similar. The main operational difference consisted in the size of the crew. A schooner (in the usual sense of the word) would not need more than six hands, apart from the skipper, as no man needed to go aloft; but the brig-schooner for that reason required eight. On the whole the first type of schooner would not measure much more than 150 tons, whereas the second might reach 200 tons. The average tonnage, one or two brigs included, would not exceed 100. The really big ships would have a length of keel of up to 18m, with a length overall of nearly 40m, and a beam of over 7m. The masts could measure 30m and 25m respectively in some cases.

The main port for schooners has always been the island of Ruad, a small maritime community off the Syrian coast, where out of 5000 inhabitants a thousand were seamen. The second important port was Tyre (more so than Sidon), followed by Beirut, but at Tyre the vessels were smaller. Both Beirut and Tyre have an extensive hinterland and much of the seaborne traffic was directed to these two ports. Ruad, on the other hand, is one of those typical home ports, like Hydra or Psara in Greece, where most of the lives of the men were spent at sea in a network extending over the whole of the Levant and beyond, to Odessa and Malta, or latterly to Suez or Aden.

The Venetian Gulf

Venice, *la città dominante*, aspired to the lordship not only of the Venetian Gulf–their label for the Adriatic–but of the whole of the Levant

8. Reference is to A H J Prins, 'The modified Syrian Schooner: Problem formulation in maritime change', *Human Organisation* 24, Special Issue (New York 1965).

9. For the nautical terminology see H Charles and A M Solayman, *Le parler Arabe de la voile et la vie maritime sur la côte Libano-Syrienne* (Beirut 1972). The book was organised around a questionnaire distributed by the Cini organisation of Venice, and shows all the negative aspects of a less than well-arranged piece of serious research. The terms are valuable, but not all the other information can be trusted.

The Venetian archives preserve a number of pictorial draughts of local ship types, including this late eighteenth-century hull plan of a polacca. *Judging by the positions of the masts and the arrangements of the deadeyes, the vessel probably carried a square rig on the main and mizzen with the large* polaccone *fore lateen.* (Museo Storico Navale, Venice)

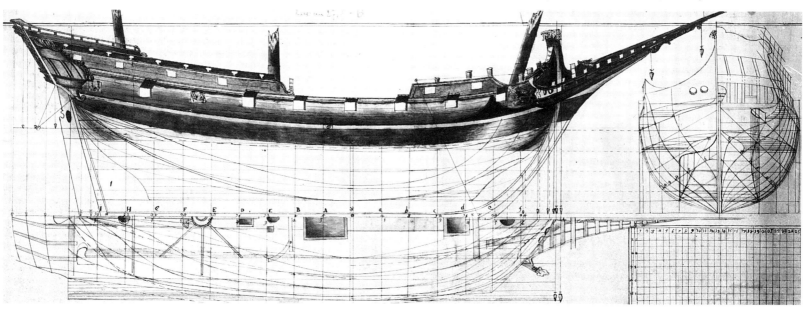

For many the typical sailing coaster of the Adriatic was the trabaccolo, *a two-masted, usually lug-sailed, vessel that survived well into the twentieth century. This example is not radically different from those illustrated by eighteenth-century artists like Baugean.* (Author)

(or at least of the Levantine trade). The city had never been successfully challenged by the other Latin powers, and the supremacy of her maritime power was only actively contested by the Turks, but silently asserted elsewhere. To disregard her influence after 1800 (when the city became part of Habsburg Austria) would be misleading, even if it is true that Greek mercantile ascendancy had made increasing inroads into her Levant trade since 1700. Before the turn of the century Ragusa–as Dubrovnik was known at the time–was, with 30,000 inhabitants for the whole coastal strip, the main competitor, but the Croatian archives of this maritime city-state, are not always easily accessible. Ragusa, first occupied by the French and later annexed by Austria, did not form part of the Venetian empire after 1350, as it was nominally tributary to Turkey until the Napoleonic wars.

For Venice the flag had originally followed trade. But even if trade continued after 1650, and occasionally even grew, the concept of dominion dwindled, a good deal of her seaborne trade with destinations in the Levant being carried in Dutch or English *bertones*, of up to 500 tons. Trade also continued beyond the straights of Otranto, to Naples and Sicily, and as far as Alicante, although Leghorn, Genoa and the parts of Ligurian Sea were no longer visited by ships flying the flag of San Marco. Marseille, too, was outside the network.[10] Maritime trade in big vessels now being the exception rather than the rule, the merchants of Venice chartered or bought smaller types, *marciliani* for instance. State subsidies or loans induced shipowners to build them in great numbers. The *saetia* also belonged to this class, some obtaining permission outward bound to sail as far as Crete. Both types were also built at Ragusa in great numbers. If indeed identical with the *saikas* farther east, *saetias* were possibly of the three-masted variety, at least after 1700. Ports farther east than Crete were to be destinations reserved for *bertones*. *Marciliani*, on the other hand, despite their capacity of 100 to 200 tons, were forbidden to sail beyond Taranto, only half-way to their former destination of Marseille, the town from which they took their name. Bluff in the bows, but narrow aft, they had a curved stem like a *trabaccolo*. In rig they resembled *polaccas* though, as they carried three

pole masts, two crossed by three yards each, the one aft carrying either a loose-footed lateen sail or else a lugsail lashed to a boom. However, this is really a reconstruction, as no good engravings exist. By the time of the Napoleonic wars they had vanished from the Venetian merchant fleet.

The two-masted *trabaccolo*, mentioned in 1711 and still extant after the last war, had a proportionally long bowsprit and a large headsail, whereas both lug sails were lashed to a boom. Characteristically these ships sailed with the lugs hoisted *al terzo* or even *al quarto*, with little sail surface aft of the mast exposed to the wind. The hull was typical for the Adriatic, a double-ender sitting low in the water, bluff in the bows, the stem curving inward, but with an angular forefoot instead of a long one gradually curving away, as was normal among the Greeks. The Venetians employed these small traders extensively. Sometimes the main mast aft carried a spanker instead of a lug sail, with a fore-and-aft topsail above. In that case both masts had fidded topmasts, replacing the original pole masts. This variant went under the name of *peligo*, at least at the head of the Gulf. Ports on the Dalmatian side harboured this craft as well, making occasional appearances in Ragusan accounts.

Another type, equally reminiscent of the *trabaccolo*, was known as the *pielago*. Around 1860 about 600 were registered in ports like Bari, Ancona and Rimini, and in Venice itself. They

hardly ever exceeded a capacity of 100 tons, 60 tons being the average, with a length usually no more than 17m. However, they carried three lateens and a jib on a short boom, in contrast to *trabaccolos*, their two-masted sisters, which normally carried lug sails. One term in one and the same culture area for two very different rigs.

Smaller craft frequenting the Adriatic (or in the case of the *rascona* also the Venetian lagoon), include the *paranza*, with one lateen rigged to an upright mast, later replaced by the Adriatic lug sail. When employed in the fisheries, characteristics would also include a rudder of great depth and a bowsprit of extreme length. The older *paranza* suggests a degree of similarity with the *tartana*, but always without the *sperone*. They could be found as far afield as Tunisian waters, their home ports being in the vicinity of Bari, but also in Messina. Although they had less deadrise than a *tartana*, they were good sea boats, as they were provided with bilge keels, or rather with vertical skids half-way between the keel and the bilges.

The *bragozzo*, finally, is a version of the *trabaccolo*, sometimes employed as a fishing vessel. The main differences between the two vessels

10. For Ragusan maritime trade during the sixteenth century: J Tadic, 'Le port de Raguse et sa flotte au XVIe siècle', in *Travèaux du deuxième colloque international d'histoire maritime* (Paris 1957). Most studies of Dubrovnik as a maritime city, even if written in one of the modern languages, generally cover the Middle Ages, however.

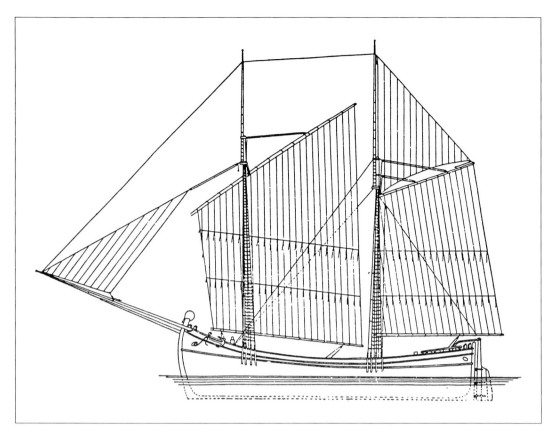

This trabaccolo, *drawn by Scribanti for his 1916 book* Tipi di scafi di legno, *shows a modified version of the basic rig, with a gaff main and fidded topmast carrying a gaff topsail. This was not uncommon in the later generations of this type.*

vided with a keel. The 'real' *bratsera*, of course, was a much larger ship, and, in contradistinction to the small one, did belong to the Ionian Sea, traversing Greek waters farther east, in competition with *peramas* from Chios.

Apart from craft mentioned above, Venice, Trieste and Fiume harboured large modern vessels as well, shortly before or at least after 1800: brigs, brigantines and schooners or *navi* on the one hand, *polaccas* and *tartanas* on the other. None were typical representatives of the Adriatic, though. The few *chébecs* and *tartanas* mentioned for the final years of the Venetian republic, however, were men-of-war. *Navi*, or full rigged ships, were occasionally encountered in the merchant fleet, but not at an early date. Nevertheless, Venice employed them in the years before the Napoleonic conquest. Genoa likewise possessed two in 1815, vessels of between 300 and 500 tons. More typical were *polaccas*, whereas Venetian *feluccas* are never mentioned.[11]

relate, once again, to the enormous rudder, and the fact that the area of canvas carried on the fore mast is less than on the main, exactly the reverse of what would be expected. A third difference regards the lack of keel or keelplank, as all were flat-bottomed craft. They were quite long, measuring anything from 10m to 20m. By the middle of the last century a thousand were registered on the Italian side of the Adriatic, 600 in Venice alone. A smaller variety (probably included in the statistics) went under the local name *brazzera*. This was also the name given on the Dalmatian side to the single-masted variety of *trabaccolo*, but in this case pro-

The Two Sicilies and the Ligurian coast

About 1820, the Kingdom of Naples and Sicily had 5000 ships, with an aggregate of 110,000 tons according to the statistical office. Fifteen years later the tonnage had almost doubled, and it then comprised nearly 9000 vessels. Of these, 6300 measured 10 tons or less, whereas 2400 had a capacity of between 11 and 100 tons. A mere 400 were bigger than this, and consisted exclusively of brigs, *brigantini*, *brigantini-goletas* and also a few *goletas*, although some of these were a bit smaller than 100 tons. Of course, there were Adriatic luggers represented, as Bari for instance belonged to the Kingdom of Naples as well, but they would anyway be of limited tonnage. If bigger than

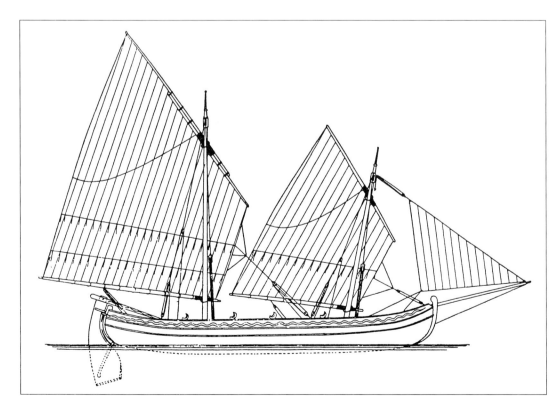

11. In the discussion of Italian craft of the nineteenth century, C De Negri, *Vele Italiane del XIX secolo* (Milan 1974), is a useful guide. For Venice, the well-illustrated work by the director of the Venetian Maritime Museum, G B Rubin de Cervin, *Bateaux et Batellerie de Venise* (Lausanne 1978), has a tendency to stress small boats and galleys, rather than the merchant marine. Scarce, but very much recommended is A Scribanti, *Tipi di scafi di legno* (Genoa 1916).

Scribanti's drawing of a bragozzo, *a small fishing craft with a rig somewhat similar to the* trabaccolo. *Note the over-size rudder.*

A Dalmatian brazzera, *a form of single-masted* trabaccalo *that set a large main lug sail and a jib headsail carried on a very long bowsprit. The hull form is typical of the Adriatic.* (Author)

100 tons they might have been grouped with either of the then modern ship types mentioned, as bureaucrats are not seamen. Most craft of between 30 and 100 tons were apparently *feluccas*. Neapolitan maritime statistics were a transient piece of history, unlikely to survive the beginning of Italian unity around 1860.

The same would be true for the Kingdom of Sardinia, which at that time included Savoy, the Ligurian coast and Genoa – or, rather the other way round, as Sardinia was an annexe of Savoy. The picture is rather different there, and Genoa in particular appeared on the brink of maritime growth. In 1815 there were only two *naves*, but ten years later sixty-seven large ones were building in yards in the vicinity, thirty-three being ships of over 100 tons. At that time the whole of the Ligurian Riviera had almost one thousand ships registered, although admittedly 800 were of small tonnage (less than 50 tons). Nevertheless there were big vessels as

well, as seventy measured between 100 and 200 tons, eleven being even larger than this, with a tonnage of between 200 and 300. Ten years later this category had increased, as there were now almost 400 vessels of over 100 tons. The returns after 1815 are broken up into classes of vessels, showing that there were 158 *pincos* in the merchant marine, as against 155 *sciabecchi*. A number of factors must have contributed to the popularity of these craft, certainly in the case of the *chébec*, a ship that hardly can claim to be of indigenous design. The *pink* may well be Genoese by origin and differs from the *chébec* in

Two typical merchantmen of the Italian west coast, the Neapolitan barque (at anchor), and the Genoese pinco *under sail. Both combined lateen and square canvas, since the latter could set square sails in certain favourable conditions, and some later variants crossed square yards permanently. The* barque, *on the other hand, usually had at least one mast set up for square canvas, although this might be either fore or main. Engraving by Baugean.*

many respects, its design representing a different boatbuilding conception. Amongst the 53 *brigantini* were included a number of brigs as well as *brig-schooners*; to complete the picture, there is even a three-masted *brigantino a palo* mentioned in this category. It is noteworthy that this is not referred to as a *barkentine*, but as a 'brigantine with a third *palo*', which means here one extra mast.

Apart from statistical surveys there are regional overviews. The Ponente–in Arabic known as Maghreb–is in many respects a different world, cut off from the Levant and the Adriatic by the Italian peninsula, yet connected through the Sicilian Straights and the Channel of Malta. It is not surprising, therefore, that Italian ships of a western type are different from those farther east, especially small craft. In the nineteenth century only two vessels belong to this almost parochial category in

Liguria. One is known as the *navicello*, the other as the *liuto*, a term recurring in Tunis as *lûd*, in Malta as *luzzu*, but for different types of craft.

Navicelli with their rig taken down would not be remarkable craft to the casual observer. Their hulls would resemble those of an Italian *tartana*, clipper bows included. Their top-hamper is rather remarkable, however. The main mast in the middle is a composite spar, the lower mast supporting a large spanker or *randa*, with a triangular fore-and-aft sail rigged to the topmast above; originally a lateen was rigged instead of the gaff rigged spanker. The foremast, a short spar forward in the bows of the ship, inclines forward, in length hardly surpassing the bowsprit, so the single jibsail is rather small. Both sails between the two masts are much larger: one, a triangular flying kite slung from a stay connecting both mast heads, blankets the other one, a trapezoid sail under-

neath. Neither spanker nor trapezoid sail are in any way connected with a boom. It seems that the latter went under the name of *polaccone*. Their southern limit is Tuscany, where the term seems to go back to 1600, but around 1815 *navicelli* could still be found along the Ligurian coast about a hundred miles west of Genoa. The rig may well be an adaptation to circumstances of wind and weather in the Leghorn region, as with Turkish craft on either side of the Bosporus. Not very many were left by about 1860, Leghorn still having around thirty-six, the island of Elba a mere three. Some reached a length of 20m with a beam of between 5m and 6m. They were true cargo boats, employed in the transport of marble.

The *liuto* does not figure in the local port statistics as a separate entity. Often it is included under more general headings like *tartana* or *bilancella*. This was a somewhat smaller vessel that the *navicello*, and was employed as a wine carrier. The names seem to refer to different craft, or at least to craft under different rigs, probably changing as time went by. On the other hand, two other terms, *liuto* and *lembo*, seem to have been used to indicate similar ships at a given time. Essentially all were two-masted, lateen rigged small cargo craft, in which the main mast was less inclined forward than the one in the bows. With the introduction of a very large jibsail, the fore mast was given up entirely, whereas the main mast was given more inclination. It stands to reason that the addition of a jibboom was implied in this change, as was the shortening of the overhanging poop aft. The *liuto* resembled a dimunitive two-masted variant of the older type of *polacca*, but without square sails. This would strengthen the geographical argument as to the origin of the bigger ship. The average capacity of these small vessels may have been 20 tons, more than enough to transport twenty casks of wine.

Other small ships operating within a local *ambiente* can be found in the Kingdom of Naples, largely in Sicily. All were used both in the fisheries and in the small-scale carrying trade, like the *lautello*. Both masts featured a rake which contrasts with the *liuto* rig, since the main inclined forward and the mizzen aft. They carried a lateen on both masts, the mizzen being rigged almost as a gunter. Also in contrast to the *liuto*, both sails were rigged to a boom, not lashed like Adriatic vessels. A long boom supported two loose-footed jibsails, but

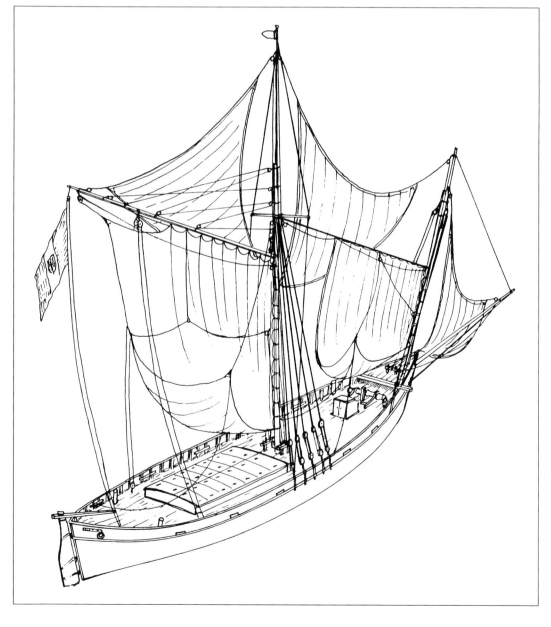

A navicello *from Viareggio from about 1910. The short fore mast, with its two staysails is the most unusual feature of the rig.* (After Marco Bonino, in *Le Petit Perroquet* 20)

A detail from the background of a Baugean engraving, showing a Tuscan liuto. *The type was a coastal bulk carrier, moving cargoes of wine, wood or coal.*

built as a double-ender the *martingana* had a narrow poop with a small transom extending beyond the rudder head. The upright main mast showed her to be a square rigger, with main course and two topsails, all set below the mast cap. The fidded topmast did not normally carry sail. One single jibsail of large dimensions resembled the *polaccone* of craft already mentioned. The mizzen mast with a lateen sail had not yet (at least in the early nineteenth century) evolved into a spanker. Of a mizzen topsail there seems to be no trace. Even if it is true that the *martingana* is characteristic of southern Italy, the type nevertheless spread to Malta and some islands in Greece, where it was known as a *martigos*. In Malta it was very popular with local shipowners until its final demise around 1880.

More confined locally was the *schifazzo*, of which there were still 120 in existence in 1860, almost all based at Trapani in Sicily. Many were built but they apparently were not a design much copied abroad, with the exception of Tunis. They were not designed for fast sailing, as *feluccas* were, which were more or less similarly rigged at that period. Descriptions of the vessel stem from a study of craft employed in the Tunisian trade, but nevertheless Sicilian in build.[13] In many respects *schifazzo* and *lautello* resembled each other, and ideas on how to design ships must have been coloured by identical notions.

The same cannot be said of the *velaccière*, the last limited-tonnage regional sailer of Naples (but also found in southern Spain). On the whole their capacity was less than 80 tons with a length hardly ever exceeding 20m, although they were three-masters. Their sail arrangement was conventional and resembled a rig type known in Italy as *nave-goletta* or even *brick barca*, in Greece as *barco-bestia*, but in all essen-

lacked a bowsprit proper. The hull was rather peculiar, as the straight stem had a negative rake, not so much curving inward as inclining aft near the cap.

At first sight the *lautello* is not unlike the much bigger *martingana* of the Gulf of Naples. These ships of up to 60 or even 100 tons, reached the size of a *sacoleva*. A small one of 21 tons had a length of 14m and a beam of 4m. Such tiny craft could also be rowed with four oars if need be. Around 1860 at least 200 belonged to Naples, 100 to smaller ports in the vicinity, whereas about 90 were registered in Sicilian ports like Messina or Trapani. Those were the smaller craft, none exceeding 60 tons.[12] In hull form these ships resembled the *felucca*, retaining the ram-like bowsprit of the galley, enveloping a high-rising stem showing a convex curvature–as opposed to the concave clipper bow of the Italian *tartana*. Although

12. For the preceeding century see R Romano, *Le commerce du Royaume de Naples avec la France et les pays de l'Adriatique au XVIIIe siècle* (Paris 1951).

13. P A Hennique, *Caboteurs et pêcheurs de la côte de Tunisie* (Paris 1888, reprinted Nice 1989). Both the illustrations and the text are of great value.

Baugean's engraving labelled a Neapolitan 'tartane' is in fact a martingana. *Notice the* felucca-*like hull form, the square rigged main mast and lateen mizzen. The vessel is loaded high with a cargo of hay, much like the Thames spritsail barges often carried well into this century.*

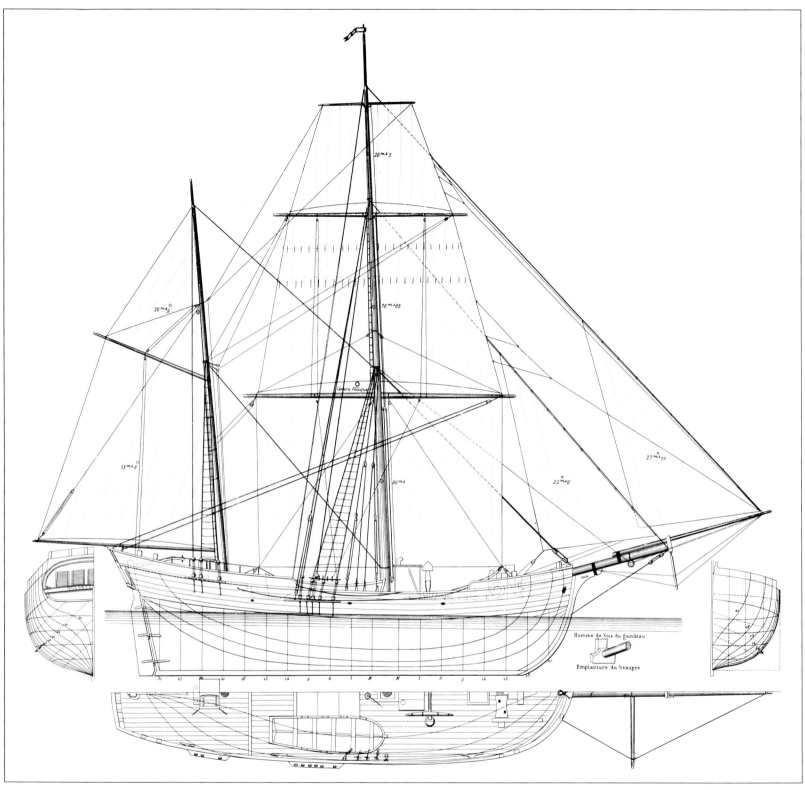

Derived from the first French bomb vessels of the 1680s, the mercantile bombarda *or* bombarde *was a widely used cargo vessel in the Mediterranean. They always carried a version of the ketch rig, although the mizzen developed from a lateen to a gaff, as shown in this drawing of the* Volonté de Dieu, *built at La Ciotat in 1816.*

tials identical with the barquentine rig. The main differences were in the fore mast being crossed by three yards instead of the usual four,

and in the two lateens hoisted on the other two masts, where a barquentine would have gaff sails. A *velaccière* looked distinctly old-fashioned, and this was accentuated by the short jibboom (there was no bowsprit) serving one huge loose-footed jib, attached to the forestay and reaching down from the cap of the pole mast forward. In 1855 they numbered a mere eighteen, but by 1864 had increased to forty.

As they could not compete with modern barques and barquentines they disappeared gradually after 1870, probably because they were too expensive, requiring a crew out of proportion to the limited tonnage.

Five other craft of traditional Mediterranean build are mentioned in nineteenth-century Italy, but none were exclusively Italian. *Bombardas*, *pincos*, *tartanas* and *feluccas* could be seen almost everywhere. *Chébecs* were typical ships of the western basin, rapidly spreading northward since their inception in the Maghreb. But even the Bay of Cattaro in Dalmatia had its *chebécs*, as had Malta and one or two islands in the Aegean.

The *bombarda* was conceived as a bomb ketch or mortar ship by a French engineer in 1682, when Louis XIV attacked Genoa. At the time she was also referred to as a *pallandra*. Because of her cargo space she was adopted in the various merchant marines over the next fifty years. As late as 1830 the French navy chartered a number of them as transports during the final reduction of Algiers. In that sense the ship is certainly more typically French than Italian, although Ligurian vessels were included in the transport convoy. The hull betrays Atlantic influence, the low but quite lengthy quarterdeck ending in a transom, and with a beakhead forward. The very tall main mast was rigged with main course, square topsail, and sometimes a topgallant. The mizzen had a lateen with a square topsail set as well, whereas two large triangular headsails provided balance. Later the steeve of the bowsprit was reduced and a jibboom added; the lateen on the mizzen was replaced by a gaff sail, as occured widely on late eighteenth-century square-riggers. A mizzen staysail amidships and a flying kite between both topmasts, gave the modern *bombarda*, when all sails were set, a well-proportioned appearance. On the whole these ships measured less than 100 tons, although their tonnage increased in the course of the centuries. Ships measured around 1810 hardly exceeded 14m in length, whereas they approached 18m by 1890. Curiously enough shipowners at Camogli in the south of Liguria, referred to some of their brigs (always *bergantini* in Italian, Maltese or Spanish) as *bombard brigs*. In fact in two of these ships the main mast was taller than the one forward, making it difficult to detect any semblance of a *bombarda*.[14]

In referring to the *tartana* one must keep in mind that our attention is drawn to a single-masted ship, bigger than the *bombarda* (at least by the end of the last century). It too was a double-ender, and in the nineteenth century no longer employed as a corsair. As often amongst relatively small ships, it could be used in the fisheries as well as in local trade, usually in the Tyrrhenian sea. Rig was very simple: one single upright mast supported a large lateen, whereas a jib which was at the same time a staysail, functioned as the single headsail. By the end of the century a jibboom was added, the headsails then numbering three. Moreover, a triangular fore-and-aft topsail above the peak of the

lateen yard, known as *freccia*, served to keep steerage in light winds. In a following wind a fair-weather sail could be added when needed, an auxiliary jib being rigged out on a transverse boom. This form of studding sail was referred to as a *pallone*. Around 1700 an average *tartana* would not exceed 70 or 80 tons, but as almost always, ships tended to increase in size over time, and this applied here as well. In about 1850 these vessels would have had a length of 20m and a beam of 6m, whereas at the beginning of the century a *tartana* had a length of less than 17m. They carried three lateen rigged masts, like the nineteenth-century *felucca*. Before 1800 they had been the favourite vessels of Maltese owners who handled the cargoes on behalf of the Order of St John, provisions being bought not only in Sicily, but also in Lisbon or Venice. They were also frequently used as corsairs against Muslim ships. In the middle of the eighteenth century larger examples were rerigged as *polaccas*. One such large vessel had a crew of 30 and transported 40 soldiers. Similarly crewed was a Maltese squadron of four, transporting timber for shipbuilding from France to Valletta.

In some instances, and certainly so before 1800, it must have been difficult to denote the differences between *tartana* and *felucca*, as at an early date single-masted specimens of the second type had already occurred. However, from the beginning of the last century a fully decked *felucca* was always characterised by two or three masts and these lateen rigged. In a case where a *felucca* had only two masts, she was often referred to as a two-masted *tartana*! This

The Italian tartana *of the nineteenth century often featured a clipper bow, as in this drawing from Scribanti's* Tipi di scafi di legno, *of 1916. Later developments included a jibboom (allowing up to three headsails to be set), and a triangular topsail.*

is not surprising, as many *feluccas* were less than 30 tons, and even single-masted *tartanas* were bigger than that. The rather short pole masts were either upright, or else raked slightly forward, in three-masted ships the foremast more noticeably so than the main. They were always double-enders with a *sperone* rather than a bowsprit, and with the characteristic overhang of the poop deck ending in a tiny transom. By the middle of the nineteenth century this poop deck was gradually given up, following a general shipbuilding fashion. The *sperone* was retained, though, and a jibboom even added, so as to bring the luff of the headsail further forward. In some cases it must have been possible to mistake a large *felucca* for a *pinco*, although Greek *feluccas* had more sheer. The main difference between the two was in the raised quarterdeck of the second type and, on the other hand, the bulwarks in the first, which clearly show the line of descent of the *felucca* from its oared ancestors. In fact, in the seventeenth century it was as much a rowing craft as the *galleotta*. Many *feluccas* were registered in Sicily or especially in the Gulf of Naples; most of the northern ones had Lerici on the Gulf of Spezia as home port. Shortly after 1860 about 140 *feluccas* still frequented Italian waters.

Another version with a more pronounced afterdeck and rather high poop–and hence with a more pronounced sheer–was known as *feluccone*. As the vessel resembled a lateen rigged *chébec*, confusion may well have been caused in that case as well. She was not only employed by the Genoese, but also to some extent by the Venetians, where they were simply registered as *feluccas*, all being of the three-masted variety and measuring approximately 100 tons. Even the Kingdom of Naples had seventy registered in 1825, but by 1860 all had virtually disappeared.

Passing mention has been made of the *pinco*, but the ship is of sufficient interest to merit closer scrutiny. Although typically a Genoese vessel, it could be seen off Marseille, Barcelona and other Catalan ports as well. Even Greece, Tunis and Malta had their *pinchi*. The Order of St John owned three by the middle of the eighteenth century, one being referred to as '*fluyt* or *pinco*' in the Valletta Archives! It is believed that the type is decended from Spanish *caravelles*, and can be traced as far back as the seventeenth century. The term *pinco* may well be related to the Dutch term *pink*, but these latter were very

14. A catalogue of ship portraits in the local museum of this maritime town was published a few years ago: P Schiaffino, *The Sailing Ships of Camogli* (Genoa 1987). In 1853 as many as 126 out of a total of 145 registered vessels were brigs.

This illustration by the English marine artist John Serres is labelled a 'Settee off Genoa' but actually depicts a felucca. *This fairly small example nevertheless sets three lateen sails.* (National Maritime Museum)

different small vessels, more tubby in shape and trading (or rather fishing) under a different rig. It is a far cry, therefore, from the three lateens which were a recurrent feature in the Mediterranean *pinco*. Neither the flush-decked hull with its large transom, nor the elongated quarterdeck, resemble Dutch craft either, and the marked tumblehome is a feature more reminiscent of Dutch *fluits* than of Dutch *pinks*.

The first Greek *pinchi*, like the very first *polaccas*, may well have been ordered from Ligurian yards, but not much before 1700. That the North African corsairs also made use of the *pinco*, captured no doubt, is shown by an *ex-voto* in one of the chapels in Malta. In the year 1826 *pincos* were still being built in Italy, as five were on the stocks in the vicinity of

Varazze, an important boatbuilding town in Liguria. In 1797, when Napoleon set out on his expedition to Egypt, seventeen *pinchi* from Genoa accompanied his fleet as transports, all having a capacity of between 100 and 200 tons. But of the 155 Genoese ones registered locally in 1815, as many as 142 were smaller than this. The dimensions survive for an exceptionally large one of 250 tons, including the size of the canvas: 270m^2 when carrying square sail on both masts forward and a lateen on the mizzen – not a typical *pinco* arrangement. When all three masts were lateen rigged in the customary fashion, this amounted to 410m^2. The hull of this ship had a length of 23m, the breadth was 7m, the depth from the after deck to the

keel measured near the poop was also nearly 7m, whereas the same distance forward hardly exceeded 4m, part of the difference being the necessity for deeper draught aft for good sailing qualities, and part the height of the afterdeck.

In 1866 the last *pinco* was broken up, implying the end of the lateen rig in Italian ships of any size: a period of over two centuries had come to an end. One small *pinco* was still employed in the Mediterranean trade between Marseille and Palermo as late as 1860. She was merely a flush-decked vessel with a very tall fore mast, carrying four (!) square sails and two headsails, whereas both the rather short main mast and the mizzen were rigged with lateens.

An interpretation by Karl Heinz Marquardt of a pinco *carrying square canvas on the fore and main masts, having sent down the heavy lateen yards, which are then stowed on deck. This was sometimes done by* chébecs *when the wind was astern, since the big lateens could be dangerous in this situation. From the occasional setting of square canvas, to the permanent conversion of at least one mast to cross square yards is an obvious progression, and was the way the Genoese* pinco *developed.*

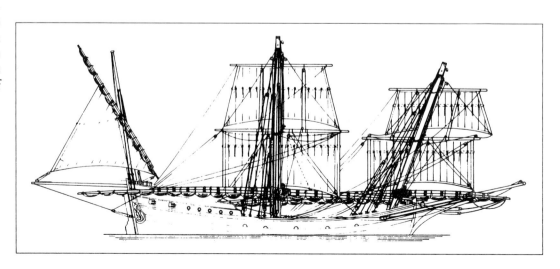

17.

Even if both masts forward might on occasion be crossed for square rig, the *pinco* was essentially a lateener. Both composite yards for the triangular sails could be stowed on deck almost continuously, but ready for an immediate change of rig whenever conditions permitted.

The last traditional sailing ship to be mentioned in an Italian context is the *sciabecco* or *chébec* (Spanish: *xebeque*), a term derived from the Arabic *sambuk*, a single-masted dhow from the Red Sea or even far-off Zanzibar.[15] In a number of languages the pronunciation with an *mb*, as in *xambekk* in Maltese, is still preserved; but, once again, word derivation does not imply similarity in design. The *sambuk* represents a simple, and possibly early stage, whereas the *chébec* is the end product in a long and complex evolution.

The Italian *chébec* almost ousted the *pinco* during the Napoleonic wars, in which a ship originally devised as a corsair, proved eminently suited for hit-and-run operations conducted by smugglers running contraband wares through both British and French blockades. But the origin of the type is without doubt to be found in the milieu of Algerine privateers. If the displacement of a *chébec* was enough to ship the necessary armament of, say, 14 or 16 guns (6-pounders being the minimum for a fast corsair), they proved very successful in their trade, even during the winter. The hull had fine underwater lines, was easy in the bilges and had a sharp entry. If anything, some of these ships were over-canvassed, but fast both in a moderate swell and in a choppy sea, at least as long as the wind permitted. A classical *latina-chébec* carried three lateens without headsails, but there were three other variants, one rigged as a *polacca*, another one as a so-called *mistico*, and finally, there were even square-rigged *chébecs*. All three of these last carried headsails, topsails and topgallants wherever required, but with some variation in the arrangement and some confusion in the terms. The *polacca-chébec* had square sails on both main and mizzen, but a *polacone* lateen on the foremast, the *quadre* version being rigged the other way round. The known case of one particular vessel, with dimensions of 38m by 10m, with three different suits of sail, shows the area of canvas in square metres ideally required. In the *latina*

version it amounts to 780m², in the *polacca* version this has risen to almost 1100m², and in the *mistico* finally to 1345m². The square rigged version is not mentioned separately, but this must have been identical with the *mistico*, instead of the *quadro*. Normally no *chébec* would ever reach such limits, neither in length of hull, nor in sail area, as the vessel mentioned must have measured over 200 tons. The average small vessel would hardly reach a length of 16m and a medium one 25m. Ships would not require such enormous sail areas, and hence the comparison with a *pinco* driven by 400m² cannot be made, unless more information about the hull was available. However, the *chébec* was clearly the faster of the two, and the addition of oars must have been and asset in light winds during any encounter with a more powerful enemy.[15]

Malta and the Barbary Regencies

Taking a recent study of votive paintings as a starting point, it seems possible to get an overview of maritime developments in the central Mediterranean during the past century and a half, with Malta as a cultural focus. As none of the *ex-votos* is much older than 1700, and as steamships, fishing boats such as *firilla* and *luzzu*, and war galleys will be excluded, the original analysis of 400 paintings will be reduced by a little over half.[16] Even so, warships belonging to the navy of the Order of St John are depicted quite often: galleys between 1630 and 1793, twenty times, and half-galleys,

from 1700 to 1796 five times, but always in or after a storm. After these deletions the collection contains mostly Maltese ships, but there is a sprinkling of ships under foreign flags. This distinction will be disregarded. One or two *trabaccolos*, *barques* or *sacolevas* do not alter the picture appreciably. What is striking, however, is the near-total absence of *feluccas*. But then, *feluccas* in Malta at least were small open boats (certainly before 1750), often carried on board and never operating independently of the *galleys*. They were certainly not traders. The simple fact that galleys are under-represented can be attributed to the religious consideration that fighting the Turk was an everyday hazard and not sufficient reason to commission such paintings, whereas a fierce thunderstorm was. Small freighters certainly feared corsair attacks, but men-of-war were invulnerable in that respect – and moreover, no corsairs infested the seas after the reduction of Algiers in 1830.

In the following enumeration the year of first appearance of a type is given, together with the number still present in the churches and chapels of Malta and Gozo today. Most types of vessel have already been dealt with, and will not cause further comment. It should be stressed that only those paintings that permit

15. W Mondfeld, *Die Schebecke und andere Schiffstypen des Mittelmeerraumes* (Bielefeld and Berlin 1974), provides a well-illustrated introduction addressed at the model builder. The drawings are not always as detailed as one would wish.

16. A H J Prins, *In Peril on the Sea: Marine Votive Paintings in the Maltese Islands* (Valletta 1989).

an exact dating are included. The *chébec* (including *mistico* and *polacca-chébec*) is depicted nineteen times, the first instance being 1752, although mention had been made in the archives as early as 1726, then with a crew of 140. The *bombarda* (including the *martingana*), first appearing in 1736, follows with thirteen entries; the *polacca*, 1735, with twelve; the *tartana*, 1731, with eleven; the *pinco*, 1745, with seven. It is worthy of note that the last picture of a lateen rigged *chébec* was donated in 1809, the last *mistico* in 1812, and the *polacca* form in 1830; the last *bombarda* appears in 1837, the *polacca* in 1811; the *tartana* was depicted for the last time in 1847 and the *pinco* in 1809. To conclude from this that, for instance, the *tartana* was not used before 1731 is palpably wrong: its first appearance in the archives dates from 1620. The implication here is only that the first time the type was shipwrecked and recorded in a surviving painting was 1731. The record is of a pictorial series.

Bergantino and *speronara*, from 1789 and 1740 respectively, occur forty and thirty times, much more frequently than any other type. To this must be added that in Latin countries of the western basin brigs are usually included in the first category, in contrast to the usage in Greece. *Barques*, 1812 – a very early date indeed – are depicted seven times, as frequently as the *pinco*; brig-schooners, again very early, 1769, six times; schooners, 1825, the same; full-riggers and *navi* or *vascellottos* five times. *Corvettes* and *frigates* are mentioned twice each, but in this context it is not clear if they are actually merchant ships. No 'last years' are given, as this chapter does not pretend to deal with the second half of the nineteenth century, but some types continue to be present in the recorded series after 1850. Thus the *brigantino* is still present after 1866, as is the *brig-schooner*. The schooner appears after 1862, the *barque* after 1851, and the full-rigger after 1865, all also occuring a few times in subsequent years. The lateen rigged *Gozo boat*, a very typical Maltese coaster, is not represented in the series, as it was developed out of the *speronara* after 1870. The same is true of the *trabaccolo* and *sakoleva* (and of some late large *feluccas*), because they could not be exactly dated. The *speronara* still appears in the paintings in 1857. This means that of all the early small merchant vessels mentioned here by the end of the century only the *speronara* survived. The last one was photographed in 1910, rigged with one spritsail, one topsail and still sound enough to carry passengers.

The *speronara* (*xprunara* in Maltese) has always been mentioned as a specifically Maltese

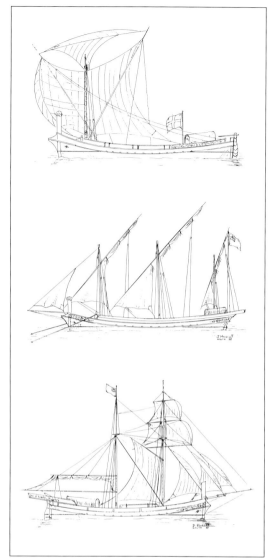

Three of the many variants in the rig of the Maltese speronara: *a single mast with a pair of spritsails and a triangular topsail; a three-masted lateen rig with jib; and a topsail schooner rig.* (Drawings by J Muscat of the Valletta Maritime Museum)

type,[17] even if some were built in Sicilian yards and on occasion were employed in the Neapolitan navy. In the Sicilian merchant marine about thirty still survived around 1860, but the majority belonged to Malta. On the whole they were not built in excess of 25 tons, with a length of about 15m, and a beam a little over 4m, but some had a capacity approaching 40 tons. They were often employed as packets, but were also used for the transport of passengers and general merchandise, just like the lateen rigged *Gozo boat* of later years. They were certainly seaworthy, for in one stormy week in the winter of 1829 Valletta registered three arrivals and six departures. The hull was in no way remarkable; they were double-enders, largely undecked, without overhang, almost flat-bottomed, with easy bilges, and

with very little sheer, except for some flare forward. As in all Maltese craft the stempost was extremely tall. They derived their name from a rudimentary *sperone* or ram, supported by knees, the stemhead knee underneath serving as support timber, the one above having an aesthetic function only.

In the course of almost two centuries tophamper changed quite considerably and more than one variant must have existed at any time. According to the votive paintings, the *speronara* of 1740 carried one single mast with two spritsails and a flying kite. A detail in the Maltese sprit arrangement not visible in the paintings is the position of the heel, assuming at least that the arrangement as found in present-day *luzzus* applied two centuries ago. The heel of the sprit could be adjusted as circumstances required independently of the mast, as it was not lashed to its heel, as is the convention in Britain or Holland. Its lower end was placed instead in one of five hemispherical depressions in a curved beam abaft the heel of the mast, superimposed on top of the mast beam; this was certainly an improvement over the northern rig, where the sprit is permanently lashed or locked on the starboard side. Judging by the next painting, by 1830 the rig consisted of one spritsail and a jib, but another one had two masts, both rigged with lateens, and once again one jibsail. Two two-masted vessels depicted in 1850 show slightly different kinds of rig, which does not of course imply that the earlier sail plan suddenly went out of existence. Both paintings show a small lateen on the mizzen and two nearly rectangular spritsails on the main mast, one extended on the sprit itself, the other one on an outrigger boom forward. Both vessels show the flying kite. Sail plan and hull silhouette in a print dated 1860 are both different. Three lateens and a jib are a new phenomenon, as is the extended afterdeck, reaching well beyond the tiller. Finally, around 1904 the Maltese experimented with the topsail schooner rig in at least one *speronara*, but this was a vessel with a cargo capacity of 100 tons.

Ships like brigs, *brig-schooners* or brigantines, extensively used by the Maltese under the British flag (after 1800), have been described in sufficient detail in other volumes in this series. Originally the Maltese had also used *tartanas*, frigates, and brigantines with oars as well as sprit rig or lateen, in their seaborne trade – according to the archives as many as ninety-nine by the end of the seventeenth century.

17. Details are to be found in J Muscat, 'Le xprunara, un bâtiment traditionnel maltais', *Neptunia* (1992), pp22–32.

This of course, had been before the trend toward bigger vessels, such as *polaccas*, *pincos* or *chébecs*, had set in. To these ninety-nine merchant ships present in the records for 1697, between twenty and thirty privateers should be added, in many respects similar ships, but fitted out for a slightly different trade. On the whole they were slightly bigger, and armed with a few additional guns. Around 1670 some thirteen were involved in one naval engagement, with 1774 men on board, and this in a period that the average number of crew on board a mere merchantman was only thirteen. This means that more seamen were engaged in the *corso* than were earning their keep in a more peaceful way. However, 'slightly bigger' relates, to an average, as many corsair vessels were of medium size – *tartanas*, *polaccas* and *petachios* of 100 to 200 tons. Some 'western' ships, like the *bertone* were bigger than this. This was also true of early full-riggers like the *nave* or *vascello*, and yet licences for the *corso* to be conducted in the Levant were limited to this class of large sailing vessel. The smaller type of craft, lateen rigged and with up to twenty-three pairs of oars, brigantines and frigates or even *feluccas* with five benches, obtained their permits for the more immediate surroundings, bordering on Sicily and the Barbary coast. Even so, from 1700 the

A Spanish chébec, *under both oars and sail, attacking a galley of one of the Barbary powers; another galley is coming up fast, firing from her bow battery. (Museo Naval, Madrid)*

oared ships mentioned became rare in those waters as well, and certainly when operating on their own.[18]

Of the Barbary States Algiers was in many ways similar to other maritime cities like Valletta or Ragusa, but in two major respects it differed. In the first place it was almost entirely dependant on corsairs, as it had hardly any trade of its own; and secondly its seafaring population consisted of foreigners to such an extent that native ship design hardly existed, a constant stream of captured ships being converted into corsairs. Converted merchant ships must have shown cultural influences from almost every corner of the earth, as many sea captains were renegades from England, the Low Countries or the Christian shores of the Mediterranean. A list has been preserved, and though it antedates 1600 by a few years, its contents are telling. Of thirty-five corsairs owning *galleots* at the time, ten were Turks, six Genoese, three Greeks, three south Italians, two each came from Venice, Spain and Durazzo. One was a Jew, and one each came from Hungary, France and Corsica. Three were of unknown extraction and may have come from Atlantic ports, but the heyday of Dutch and English renegades was still to come. To talk of an indigenous maritime culture is impossible, the only contribution made by the Regencies being the introduction of the *chébec*. This also applies to Tripoli, and, to a much lesser degree, to Tunis. Only Tunis had a

seaborne trade of its own and a fertile hinterland as well. But trade goods either captured by or destined for Algiers were largely carried in French ships.

The strength of the North African fleets have been estimated for Algiers at six galleys and 100 sailing ships, varying from *feluccas* with crews of twenty men, to 60-gun galleons with 400; Tunis had ten *brigantines* of 20 benches and fourteen sailing ships; and a mere three sailing ships are recorded for Tripoli. These were the nunbers in 1625, but by 1650 these were already greatly reduced, and in 1720 Algiers had no more than six *galleots* and eight sailing ships with 6-18 guns like *petaccios* or *polaccas*, employed not only as corsairs, but occasionally as merchantmen.[19] Tunis had less than that, but had at least a few local coasters called *sandal*, very similar to a single-masted *tartana*. The term itself is of Turkish origin, and was used on the Bosporus for a mere rowing boat, but in southern Spain it meant a small freighter with two or three masts.

18. P Earle, *Corsairs of Malta and Barbary* (London 1970), made extensive use of Maltese archive records.

19. The main sources for the Maghreb are: J Mathieux, 'Sur la marine marchande barbaresque au XVIIIe siècle', *Annales* XIII (1958); and the much older A Devoulx, 'La marine de la Régence d'Alger', *Revue Africaine* XIII (1869). For studies of Islamic maritime life, also in the Indian Ocean regions, A H J Prins, 'The Maritime Middle East, a Century of Studies', *The Middle East Journal* (Washington 1973), may be of some use.

Spain and the Balearic Islands

Along Spain's Mediterranean coastline, there is one Catalan region, facing the rising sun, referred to as the 'Levant'. From this region the shipbuilding registers of the province of Mataró in Catalonia–an important area as far as shipbuilding is concerned[20]–survive from 1816 to 1875. Apart from a number of entrepreneurs specialising in the building of fishing boats like the *llaut*, between thirty and forty yards are represented, all builders of merchant vessels, their output totalling over 560 ships over a period of sixty years. During those years 150 *polaccas* were built, the tonnage increasing from 60 or 70 in 1816 to 200 or 250 around 1850. *Bergantines* follow with over 140, but as elsewhere brigs and brigantines are both included under the term. They range from 100 to 150 tons before 1830, but also increase in tonnage in the final years, reaching over 200 tons after 1850. The *polacca-goleta*, of which fifty-five were built, shows the same tendency to growth, from 60 or 70 tons around 1835, to 150 or more around 1850. As the type does not appear in the registers before 1834, it must have started rather late, the schooner rig on a *polacca* hull probably needing adaptation. Of the *goleta* itself, comprising both topsail and gaff schooners, only thirty-eight left the stocks, ranging from 60 tons in 1820 to over 100 thirty years later. An equal number *berganti-goletas* were launched in the course of the years. The *mistico* on the other hand, a three-masted lateener not unlike a *chébec*, was comparatively small, never exceeding 70 or 80 tons. A total of about forty were launched, but none after 1840, so presumably phased out before the middle of the century. At the other end of the scale is the *brickbarca*, also with three masts, rigged as a barquentine or barque in the modern sense of the words, and at least for the period under review, a vessel of enormous dimensions. The disappearance of the *mistico* around 1840 is almost simultaneous with the appearance of the first *brickbarcas* (sometimes called *bergantin-corbetas*), their size increasing from 250 to 400 tons ten years later. Full-riggers known as *fragata* were exceptions, nine being launched from 1849–all large vessels between 300 and 800 tons. Only eight *faluchos* left the building yards between 1828 and 1846, all between 70

With its three lateens the Spanish mistico *resembled the* chébec, *but was generally smaller. They were essentially coasters, and the type disappeared around the middle of the nineteenth century, apparently replaced by the* brickbarca *or* barque. *This example from the 1790s was engraved by Baugean.*

and 160 tons. Of the so-called *pailebot* fifteen were built, and of the '*barca de tràfic*' (similar to the *barque longue* of Marseille with three lateens) a mere twelve. To this should be added four *balandras*, six *quetxes* (underneath the curious spelling one recognises the *ketch*!) should be added two *bombardas*, both built shortly after 1820.

It is worthy of note that neither *tartana* nor *chébec* appears in the building records of the time, but most of the other types, or terms at least, have cropped up before. Only the *pailebot* (or *paquebot*), and the *balandra* are exceptions; but the first resembled a small brig, whereas the other looked very much like an English cutter. Furthermore it is not likely that Mataró built every type engaged in the seaborne trade of Spain. Elsewhere, for instance, there are references to craft like *sagetia*, *canari* or *llondro*, the last (but possibly under a different guise) also mentioned in Turkey.

Another important source refers not to the building of ships but to ship movements in the eighteenth century.[21] The period under review only covers the last eighteen years of the century, centred on Salou, a port about the same distance from Barcelona as Mataró, but not in this case in the Levant, but in the 'Ponente' of Catalonia. According to the port administration exactly half of the arrivals could be attributed to fishing vessels of the *llaut* (or *llagut*) type, usually of a little more than 10 tons. Small cargo carriers like *llondro* and *canari* accounted for almost a quarter of the movements, with a mere 3 per cent for the medium-sized *pinco*. Large ships like *berganti*, *xabec* and

pollacra (or *polacca*), and a sprinkling of other ships accounted for nearly 20 per cent. The total of the arrivals over the whole period being almost 3900, this means that more than 1900 *llauts* were entering; some were not selling their catch, but other commodities, vegetables, and fruit, for instance, imported from Valencia. Also in the case of this vessel tonnage was on the increase, resulting in ships as large as 80 tons. A good number of *llondros* also arrived, in total as many as 500; very similar to the single-masted lateener already mentioned, but of less restricted tonnage, some *llondros* measured 75 tons. Records note about 400 *canari*, a double-ender of similar size, but with three lateens; this is a good overall number, and in one top year (1785) there were as many as fifty-two entries. Of the 100 *tartanas*, nearly 60 were foreigners, showing how relatively unimportant the craft really was in Spain. The class of '*falugues*' is even more negligible than this, as 33 were registered, an average of only two every year! Just over 3 per cent of all entries were medium-sized vessels, ie 130 *pincos*, but again, 91 were vessels under foreign flags, all being vessels of between 120 and 140 tons. Salou was not a regular port of call for them: in 1788 as many as 27 *pincos* arrived (22 foreign), but in other years no more than two or three. Neither *balandra*, nor *mistico* are worth mentioning, as only eight and one respectively arrived in the course of

20. J Llovet, *Constructors navals de l'ex-provincia maritima de Mataró* (Mataró 1971).

21. J Morell i Torrademè, *El Port de Salou en el Segle XVIII* (Tarragona 1986), and sources quoted.

A Spanish tartana *off Gibraltar, as depicted by Serres about 1807. Unlike the later Italian version, the Spanish* tartana *usually set only one headsail and no topsail.* (National Maritime Museum)

eighteen years. *Bergantins* give a much better account of themselves, as 260 arrived in that period, 91 being foreign vessels. Brigantines in those years were of smaller size than *xabecs* (some of which reached 300 tons), more than 260 arriving over the years. Less than half that number refers to *pollacres*, ships averaging between 200 and 250 tons. In contrast to their namesakes elsewhere, they were rigged with no more than two masts, and hence known as *pollacra rodondo*. Their rig resembled a brigantine's, with the fore mast square rigged and the tall main mast rigged fore-and-aft, in combination with a trysail and a topsail. Another name sometimes used for this vessel, is *bergantin-pollacra*, although there is a small difference in rig. The 40 *sageties* do not represent more than 1 per cent of the arrivals, and would hardly merit attention, if the first regular voyages to America had not been made in ships of this type, usually measuring between 200 and 300 tons. Finally schooners should be mentioned, not because of their numbers (only 14 arrivals are recorded) but because of the terminology of the entry, the type being referred to as '*escunar* or *goleta*'!

This brings us to the island of Mallorca, and some quantitative aspects of its mercantile trade in the eighteenth and nineteenth centuries,[22] with an appended section on the *corso* from 1702 to 1808. This section amounts to a virtual diary of encounters between corsairs and merchantmen and local *laudes* covering the whole of the western Mediterranean and forming an intriguing chronicle of events. Moreover, an interesting comparison as to ship types can be made with the port of Salou in 1795 and 1796, these being the only years for which records survive. The numbers between brackets refer to both years. Arrivals from Malaga comprised *pinques, londros, navios* and *tartanas*, but never more than one or two. From Catalonia entered *canarios, pinques, polacras, tartanas, navios, bergantins, londros* and *jabeques*, but again, never more than three or four. This is also true of similar ships arriving from Valencia, but the figures were higher for *laudes* (22,9). A good number of vessels arrived from Menorca, amongst them *bergantines* (17 in one year) and *jabeques* (8, possibly 9), *tartanas* (5,0), *canarios* (4,1) and *polacras* (4,0), apart from *laudes* carrying merchandise (7). The greatest number of arrivals refers to Mallorca itself, *jabeques* and its small sister *javega* topping the list (160,72 and 110,93), followed by about 100 *laudes*. Other entries such as *bergantines, tar-*

tanas and *polacras* are less well represented. The arrival of one brig and one schooner from the Barbary Regencies, possibly Tunis, is unusual. Venice, with *bergantines* (2,2), Genoa with one *tartana*, and Ragusa with *navios* (1), *bergantines* (1) and *polacras* (2,3) make-up the foreign-flag vessels present. In earlier years Holland and England, the Hanseatic cities and Denmark, Malta, Tuscany, France and Naples had provided foreign visitors, but 1795 and 1796 were meagre years because of revolutionary turmoil in France.

Half a century later Mallorcan entrepreneurs discovered the lucrative trades across the Atlantic, to Cuba and Puerto Rico in the main, transporting their merchandise–industrial goods and textiles outward-bound, tobacco, coffee and sugar back–in Mediterranean ship types. Some can be found back in the trade registers of 1837 and 1838. *Polacras* of between 60

22. J L Sureda Carrión, *Apuntes para la Historia de la Marina de Vela Mallorquina de los Siglos XVIII y XIX* (Palma de Mallorca 1940).

and 190 tons and *bergantins* from 100 to 190 tons, head the list. The first type appears 29 times in the registers, the second 22, followed by 12 *goletas*, ranging from 45 to 150 tons, and 14 *polacra-goletas* or *berganti-goletas*, ranging from 60 to 100 tons. Six ketches and three *balandras* are the smallest craft in the Atlantic trade, their capacity being 60 to 150 tons, or (for the last type) 50 tons. The two *corvettes*, on the other hand, are large ships, one with a tonnage of 190, the other one of 320 tons. Twenty years later, in 1856, most sailing vessels registered in Mallorca have generally reached that capacity. The tonnage of eight *fregatas* ranges from 400 to 800 tons. For the 15 *corbetas* the limits are between 350 and 540, although there are one or two of 140 tons. The 16 *bergantines*, 12 *polacres* and 9 *goletas* have a capacity of between 160 and 370 tons. As an indication of development, this large schooner of 370 tons can be compared with the earlier one of 150 tons engaged in the Atlantic trade in 1837.

The French Midi

Admiralty records survive for a limited number of years in the seventeenth century, which provide a glimpse of shipping movements at Marseille, divided per type of vessel (arrivals in 1613, 1615 and 1636; departures in 1614, 1647 and 1651).[23] *Barques* arrived in great numbers (352, almost one per day) in the year 1615, but only 77 during 1636. Their departures reached a peak (228) in 1647. *Tartane* arrivals numbered 140 during 1636, but only 49 in 1613, whereas the departures were highest in 1651 with 357 vessels leaving, against 147 during 1614. The *polacca* (*polacre* in French) is of less importance, as the annual shipping movement never exceeded 17 vessels. Other craft mentioned (but not counted separately) under the heading 'diverse', include *feluccas*, *frégates*, *galeots*, *brigantins*, *leudes*, *pétaccios* and '*bateaux*' and also *galleons*. A separate category comes under the heading '*vaisseaux*' (undoubtedly identical with *vascello*, *vascelotto* and *nave*), 117 arriving in 1613, 118 leaving next year, their numbers declining to 53 departures in 1636 and 63 during 1651. The fact that the *pinco* is nowhere mentioned should not come as a surprise, as

there is great similarity between this type and the Provençal *barque de négoce*, so the entries concerning that category may have sometimes included *pincos*.

The Spanish connection was very important, as was the link with the Languedoc; but Genoa also ranked high, as did both Arles up-river and the Levant. Provence was less important in the earlier years, with an annual average of 10 ships, but rising to unprecedented heights during 1647 and 1651, with nearly 300 ships departing. Venice ranks lowest of all, with only the occasional ship, but even then not every year. Malta, the Barbary Regencies, Sardinia, Naples and Sicily and the Papal State are well below average; Nice and Tuscany fare somewhat better, with an average annual movement of almost 40 ships. French policy almost consistently favoured political and commercial links with the Turkish Levant—and even with the Barbary Regencies—over connections with Habsburg Spain, the Italian principalities or Malta, at least before 1700. French consuls were present everywhere in the commercial ports of the Levant, their main task being the promotion of the trade of Marseille and the protection of the Christian minorities. During the six or seven years under review, slack years still meant 30 vessels returning from these ports, 40 departing (respectively 3 and 13 for the Barbary States). When trade was brisk the

numbers increased to 64 and 67 for destinations beyond the Ionian Sea, and to 24 and 43 for North Africa. Levant ships numbered one-third compared with those trading with Spain, but they were often at least ten times as big in carrying capacity: *vaisseaux* of over 400 tons as compared with small *tartanes*. Only when the French position *vis à vis* Turkey was weakened did an increase in shipping with Spain and Italy, or also with Malta, suggest a possible alternative. A permanent interest in the markets of Malta did not arise before 1700, but thereafter Valletta became jokingly known as an outstation of Marseille. Many French vessels in the Levantine trade were *vaisseaux* of up to 700 tons, some chartered in Holland, a custom prevalent in Venice as well.

In sheer numbers the *tartane* was top of the list in Marseille as well as in the small ports of Languedoc or Provence, where the majority were built. This vessel, when used in the fisheries, had only one lateen and a jibsail; in the coastal trade there was often an additional

23. G. Rambert (ed), *Histoire du Commerce de Marseilles*, Tome IV: *De 1599 à 1660* (by L Bergasse), and: *De 1660 à 1789* (by G Rambert), (Paris 1954); Tome V: *De 1660 à 1789*, *Le Levant* (by R Paris). *La Barbarie*, by J Reynaud (Paris 1957), Vol IV contains an interesting paragraph on French practice in measuring ships' tonnage, often used in other Mediterranean ports as well. It seems to be a short *resumé* of P Pezénas, *Theorie et pratique du jaugeage*, (Avignon 1778).

One of the most common French Mediterranean merchant ships of the 1600s and 1700s was the barque de négoce. *They offered more cargo capacity than the* chébec, *with a similar lateen rig. This rather large and well decorated late seventeenth-century example is from the* Album du Levant *of 1679 by Jean Jouve. (Musée de la Marine, Paris)*

more distant trades; their size reached 300 tons on occasion. *Pinques* fitted out in Marseille were mostly built at Genoa, however.

In 1670, when the Marseillais began their transatlantic trade with the West Indies, both lateen rigged types had not yet reached the required strength and dimensions, and so a number of *vaisseaux* were fitted out. Apparently the adaptation of vessels of the 'Atlantic' type was a success, at least in some trades where low freights had to be matched by transport in bulk, as for example in the soda trade with southern Spain. Three *vaisseaux* from Marseille were initially employed in 1680 on the Valencia run, soon to be augmented by another four. Nevertheless, nine or ten big vessels sailing for Alicante do not really compare with the 150 *tartanes* or *barques* departing for Spain every year. By 1717 ships of great size no longer sailed from Marseille: the reverse now obtained, *vascellos* from Spain being engaged between the two ports. By 1780 the term even disappears from the port registry, being replaced by *navire*, and this has a wider meaning, encompassing all kinds of large ship. For France there was now a tendency to return to medium-sized vessels, to *polacres* in this case rather than to *pinques* or *barques*, especially after 1750, and this trend is also markedly apparent in the long-distance trades with the factories of Smyrna, Salonica or Syria, and also with Istanbul. The lines of the hull, the capacity of 200 tons, and the *polacca* rig made the type an ideal combination. The traditional sail plan of a *polaccone* forward, two square sails on the main, and a lateen on the mizzen, with a square topsail added, was preferred apparently by the local skippers–driving their ships hard, outrunning the corsairs and earning money.

This is not to say that no other vessels could be seen in the Golfe du Lion, the Ligurian Sea or off Corsica. Some were flat-bottomed river craft like the *allège*, others chiefly fishing

mizzen mast, or a short mast forward–more of an outrigger in reality–to give lateral support to the *polacron*, the large loose-footed jibsail. Their capacity of a mere 20 tons in 1680 increased to 50 during the next century, and even to 100 tons when trading between Marseille and destinations like Malta or Tunis.

Soon after 1700 the first lateen rigged *chébecs* built at Toulon, were in competition with the largest *tartanes*. Shipbuilders from Mallorca are thought to have designed the first French-built *chébecs*. French shipowners, however, preferred to invest in *barques* (also rigged with three lateens) when more cargo space was needed than could be accommodated on board a *tartane*. After all, *barques*, which began their careers with a capacity similar to the average for a single-masted ship of 1680 (not more than 40 tons) had increased their size to 200 tons by 1750. Merchants might be even more attracted to the broad-beamed *pinques* of that period, which were very similar vessels but destined for

vessels, like *bateau boeuf* or *bovo catalane*.[24] To some extent these single-masted vessels could also be employed as small traders. Large

Sardinian *bovos*, carrying a lateen mizzen aft, have on occasion been fitted out as men-of-war. To conclude on a terminological point: the apparently tautologous 'mizzen aft', is used with a purpose, since the French, in contrast to Spaniards or Italians, refuse to follow interna-

tional practice, preferring to call a mizzen *artimon*, preserving *misaine* for the fore mast! However, the original meaning of *misaine* was 'middle', so the French usage is illogical.

A H J Prins

24. For coastal craft one should consult F Beaudouin, *Bateaux des côtes de France* (Grenoble 1975).

Mediterranean Shipping: Typical Vessels 1650-1950

Type	Description	Nationality	Area	Date	Typical Tonnage	Typical Dimensions (Feet) (Metres)	Remarks
NAVICELLO	Single-masted river craft (lug sail)	Italian	Tiber and estuary	1680		35.43 x 8.20 x 3.12 10.80 x 2.50 x 0.95	Example given by Bonino in *Le Petit Perroquet* 20 (1976)
MISTIQUE	Lateen fore, square main and mizzen	French	Western Mediterranean	1750-86	279	98.49 x 25.26 x 9.19 30.02 x 7.70 x 2.80	Draught reproduced in Pâris' *Souvenirs de Marine* as a 'chébec'
BARQUE	Three lateens, square mizzen topsail	French	Western Mediterranean	1778	220	79.72 x 21.49 x 11.81 24.30 x 6.55 x 3.60	Privateer *Fileuse* built at Marseille; draught in Pâris' *Souvenirs de Marine*
TARTANE	Single lateen and jib	French	Coast of Provence	1789	c180	66.93 x 21.98 x 8.76 20.40 x 6.70 x 2.67	Draught reproduced in Pâris' *Souvenirs de Marine*
PINCO	Three masts, lateen or square	Italian	Genoa	1800	c250	75.95 x 23.23 x 7.38 23.15 x 7.08 x 2.25	Draught reproduced in Pâris' *Souvenirs de Marine*
BOMBARDE	Ketch rig	French	Coast of Provence	1816	177	66.70 x 21.65 x 11.61 20.33 x 6.60 x 3.54	*Volonté de Dieu* built at La Ciotat; draught in Pâris' *Souvenirs de Marine*
FALUCHO	Main and mizzen lateen, plus jib	Spanish	Spanish coast and Balearic islands	c1820	50.7	58.56 x 16.90 x c6.56 17.85 x 5.15 x c2.00	Coaster related to the *llaut*; example from Pastor's article in *Model Shipwright* 60
CHÉBEC	Three lateen masts	Algerian	Throughout Mediterranean	1830	68	58.14 x 19.19 x 7.35 17.72 x 5.85 x 2.24	*Boberich* captured 1830; draught in Pâris' *Souvenirs de Marine*
SAKOLEVA	For rig see text	Greek	Greek Islands	1835		41.34 x 11.48 x 4.33 12.60 x 3.50 x 1.32	Draught reproduced in Pâris' *Souvenirs de Marine*
ALLÈGE	Single lateen river craft	French	Arles, Rhone estuary	1840		76.11 x 24.05 x 7.97 23.20 x 7.33 x 2.43	Draught reproduced in Pâris' *Souvenirs de Marine*; flat bottomed river craft
PERAMA	Two lug sails, plus jib	Turkish	Levant	1855		48.88 x 12.47 x 4.99 14.90 x 3.80 x 1.52	Draught reproduced in Pâris' *Souvenirs de Marine*
TRABACCOLO	Two lugs, two square topsails, two jibs	Italian	Adriatic	1870s		56.43 x 21.33 x 7.22 17.20 x 6.50 x 2.20	Draught reproduced in Pâris' *Souvenirs de Marine*
'COASTER'	Single sprit mast, square topsails, jibs	Turkish	Black Sea	1878		59.05 x 14.11 x 4.86 18.00 x 4.30 x 1.48	Draught reproduced in Pâris' *Souvenirs de Marine*
SPERONARA	Three lateen masts	Maltese	Malta	1882	17	50.85 x 14.44 x 3.94 15.50 x 4.40 x 1.20	*La Concetta Immacolata* recorded by Lt Hennique in 1882
BRAGOZZO	Two lugs plus jib	Italian	Adriatic	1880		58.40 x 16.08 x 5.74 17.80 x 4.90 x 1.75	Draught reproduced in Pâris' *Souvenirs de Marine*
VELACCIÈRE	Square fore mast, lateen main and mizzen	Italian	Sicily	1882	30-35	52.49 x 14.76 x 6.56 16.00 x 4.50 x 2.00	Called a *chitika* in North Africa; recorded by Lt Hennique, 1882
PAILEBOT	Two-masted schooner	Spanish	Mallorca	1885	132	92.81 x 24.64 x 7.55 28.29 x 7.51 x 2.30	*Nuevo Corazón*, example from Pastor's article in *Model Shipwright* 70
PARREGIA	Two-masted lateen plus jib	Italian	Ligurian coast	c1900	c35	55.38 x 17.95 x 7.38 16.88 x 5.47 x 2.25	A form of *bovo*; example from Morino's article in *Model Shipwright* 30
NAVICELLO	Two-masted coaster (see text)	Italian	Viareggio (Tuscany)	c1910		63.32 x 18.04 x 7.55 19.30 x 5.50 x 2.30	Example given by Bonino in *Le Petit Perroquet* 20 (1976)
LIUTO	Navicello rig	Italian	Tuscan coast	1925	20.9	49.54 x 14.70 x 4.86 15.10 x 4.48 x 1.48	Example given by Bonino in *Le Petit Perroquet* 20 (1976)

European Inland Sailing Craft

IN THE DAYS of the medieval Hansa trading community the appearance of seagoing sailing ships in inland ports, tens of miles away from the coast, was a common occurrence. The principal medieval merchant vessels like the cog were small enough to make most western European rivers navigable for deep-sea vessels. However, after 1500 the growing size of the three-masted ship made it more and more difficult to penetrate into the hinterland, and in the sixteenth and seventeenth centuries the division between seagoing ships and inland craft became more marked. Despite the fact that river navigation in Europe was already of great antiquity, stretching back to prehistoric and Roman times, and notwithstanding the continued existence of 'low air-draught'[1] coasters into this century, a clear division between the working areas of the deep-sea and the inland ship became established.

coming of the railways, most regions of Europe were relatively isolated, and this isolation promoted the continuation of indigenous habits of clothing, decoration, folklore, house construction, and of course shipbuilding. In spite of a phenomenon recognisable as a 'European inland ship', the variation in types of ships in the period between the seventeenth and the twentieth century is tremendous. This applies not only to Europe as a whole, but also within some individual countries–such as France–where historians have only recently discovered their own rich culture of river craft of the past centuries. It is possible to argue that the variety

of hull forms in European inland craft is much larger than in seagoing craft, because of this regional isolation and the far more diverse geographical factors which apply on the continent. The result is that more than a thousand distinct types of inland craft can be identified in Europe during the period under review.

This chapter can give only a general survey of the development of the European inland sailing ship, hardly doing justice to the cultural richness of this aspect of European life during

1. The modern term for vessels with low profiles and folding masts for riverine navigation.

The European inland vessel

The riverine vessel evolved certain uniform characteristics in the shape of the hull and rigging which can be distinguished as 'European', in contrast to other traditions of inland shipbuilding, for example in Asia. However, within Europe itself, the detail design differences were considerable; perhaps even more than in the case of seagoing ships, where the international exchange of experience and knowledge had a standardising effect. Until well into the nineteenth century and the

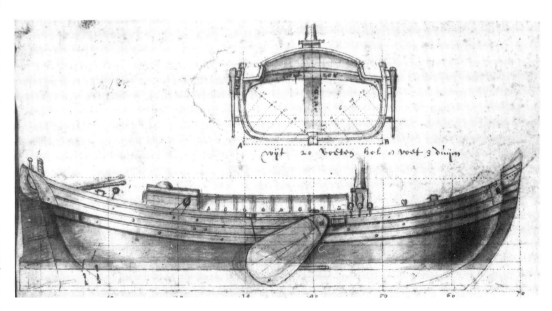

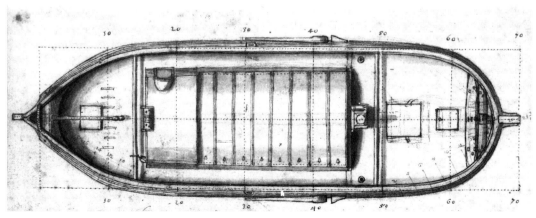

Plan of a wijdtschip. *The oldest known plans of Dutch inland ships were published by Nicolaes Witsen (burgomaster of Amsterdam) in his study of Dutch shipbuilding, published in 1671. The dimensions of this* wijdtschip *were 70ft × 20ft 3in (in Amsterdam feet of 0.283m). (Nederlands Scheepvaart Museum, Amsterdam)*

three centuries. Moreover, it is necessarily confined to one application of river vessels, the transportation of cargo: fishing and pleasure craft are left out of consideration.

Many parts of Europe had navigable rivers and lakes, but only a few of these waters were appropriate to sail under all circumstances. Seen from a technological (and not a cultural) viewpoint, most European inland vessels were simply-built hulls of primitive design. There was one region that especially favoured the development of the inland sailing vessel, thanks to economic, geographical and meteorological conditions that endured far into the twentieth century: these were the so-called Low Countries, including the lower Meuse, Scheldt and Rhine, where a mass of small streams, rivers, lakes and canals offered a network for water transport with sailing vessels which was unequalled in Europe. The focus of this network was the Netherlands. There is hardly any place in this country that could (and can) not be reached by water; and there was hardly any trade that did not use water transport in some way. For this reason–not the neglect of the cultural richness of other countries–this region of Europe receives most attention in this chapter, as the accent will be on the *sailing* inland ship and not towed and poled craft.

In fact, the Dutch inland sailing ship developed so much *after* 1830 that the 'heyday of sail' endured here until the end of the Second World War. Between 1880 and 1925 the Dutch were still building efficient sailing ships with large carrying capacities (up to 250 tons) which could be sailed by two people. Many of

Plan of a veerkaag *(ferry kaag), seventeenth century. Dimensions: 60ft×14ft×7ft. From the seventeenth century the* kaag *transported goods and passengers across the inland lakes and canals of Holland.* (Nederlands Scheepvaart Museum, Amsterdam)

these vessels still survive and prove to be real 'speed-machines' in today's sailing regattas. That is the reason why in this case the volume's end-date of 1830 has to be extended–in the Netherlands, the last decade of sail only began after 1945.

Although this continuity was unusually protracted in the Netherlands, in one respect the phenomenon can be discerned more widely: handling inland craft by means of sails, poling and towing persisted into the Industrial Age, even in those countries which were at the forefront of industrialisation. Nearly everywhere inland navigation was a one-man or family business, which could be made to work with relatively low costs and incomes. Large-scale capital investment for modernisation was not common and only occurred in specific branches of river navigation, for example on the river Rhine. In general the bargemen of Europe compensated for their relatively inefficient methods and their modest incomes by means of longer working days and very simple living conditions, often on board their own vessels.

For inland navigation, the pre-industrial modes of propulsion–sailing, towing and poling–lasted longer than was the case with the seagoing sailing ship. Tradition, relative cultural isolation, and the family basis of trade–and in the Netherlands the presence of an extremely favourable network of waterways–were the main reasons for the long continuation of sailing and other non-mechanised river craft in Europe after 1850.

Basic hull characteristics

Although the range of hull forms of traditional European river craft is kaleidoscopic, certain uniform patterns can be discerned in the construction and division of the hulls and the various methods of propulsion. It is obvious

that common features were encouraged by similar geographical circumstances, even if there was no actual contact between individual shipbuilding traditions. For example, wherever the depth of rivers was limited but where a large carrying capacity was required, shipwrights built long, flat-sheered vessels of limited draught.

Most river vessels had a flat bottom, which resulted in a shallow draught, large block-coefficient hull which was easy and cheap to construct, because most of the frames could be straight. For bargemen who worked in tidal waters and harbours, a flat bottom allowed them to dry out without any potential danger of oversetting. However, there were some exceptions: for example, in certain French coastal areas, where the *barques* used on the lakes of the Rhone delta and ships of the Gironde had sharp hull forms and were actually more coasters than river vessels; the same applies to the sailing ships on the Swedish lakes.

From a viewpoint of hull construction, the European inland vessels can be divided into two categories:

1. Vessels built with a stempost, which formed an essential part of the hull construction.

2. Ships without such a stempost; at the ends, the bottom planks were raised and the sides fixed to the edges of the bottom planks.

In general, group 2 was common on rivers, whereas the ships of group 1 were more appropriate for the navigation of larger areas of inland waters, where good sailing capabilities were remunerative, including being able to beat into the wind well and to cope with quite steep waves.

In the Low Countries the word for the curving-up of the bottom planks at the ends was *heve* (Dutch) or *hebe* (German), related to

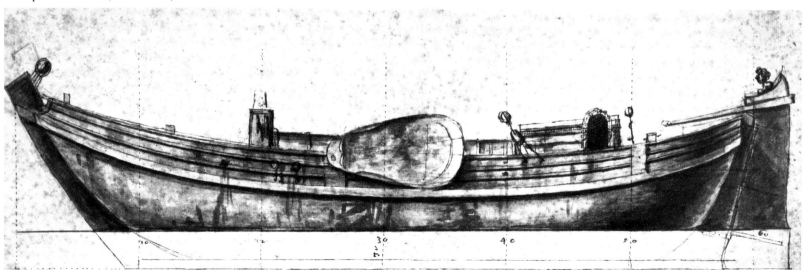

the English word 'heave'. Ships which were constructed in this manner were called *aak* (Dutch) or *aake* (German). By outsiders in the Netherlands and Germany, these two words are frequently used in the same way the word 'barge' has become a general term for 'cargo vessel for inland navigation'. However, barge-men and shipwrights from the seventeenth to the twentieth centuries used the word *aak* to indicate specific types.

The bottom planks of an *aak* were bent up in the fore and after part of the ship, and against these bottom planks the side boards were fixed; this form of construction was called 'swim-headed' in English. Small *aak*-type boats had this form at both ends, especially when no rudder was necessary, but large river vessels needed a rudder and the shipwright sometimes contrived a flat transom (for example, the French *chaland* of the river Loire), or a stern-post, as on the *Dorstense-aak* of the river Rhine.

This construction method of uplifted bottom planks in both of the ends, or only the fore part of the ship, was widespread throughout the continent of Europe. It resulted in a light, relatively cheap vessel, with maximised carrying capacity. The dimensions of an *aak* could vary from about 2m (6ft) for a simple boat to 40m (130ft) in length. It is easy to understand that the result was a structurally weak ship which was not suited to rough waters or high waves.

The other method corresponded with the way in which seagoing ships were normally built: with a stempost to which the planks of the hull sides were fastened, although in most cases the hull bottom was flat. This stempost could have a more or less vertical orientation and be curved or straight, but the result was a more expensive and heavier ship, with less carrying capacity than an *aak* of similar overall dimensions. However, it was also a more sea-worthy ship, and examples of this type could be found particularly in river deltas, tidal waters, estuaries and areas with large lakes, where their hull and rigging would be exposed to more powerful natural forces. Prime areas were the British estuaries, the Low Countries, northern Germany and the deltas of several French rivers, such as the Rhône.

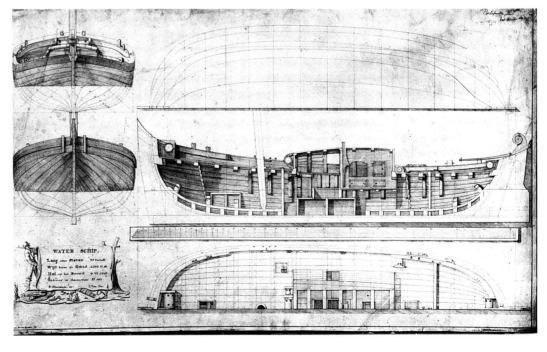

Model of a nineteenth-century Dorstense-aak. *This ship was build at Dorsten on the Rhine near Wesel in Germany and was the successor of the* samoreus. (Maritiem Museum Prins Hendrik, Rotterdam).

Rigging

With the wind in any one direction, a very good sailing ship can make progress over only about 300° of a circle, and for the average cargo-carrier at most 260-280°. An angle of about 40-50° off the wind is the best that can reasonably be expected, and even for this a large investment had to be made in a complete rig. For inland navigation between the seventeenth and twentieth centuries it was a general rule that this investment was only made where the geographical conditions were favourable enough for sail to be actually usable most of the time. On fast-flowing rivers with prevailing feeble winds it was pointless to invest in and to maintain an expensive rig. Moving against the stream under sail alone was often impossible and then the vessel had to be hauled by men or animals; sailing downstream the current provided enough speed. When the river was full of shoals, and a strong wind was absent, tacking with the usual fore-and-aft rig was out of the question. That was the reason why most of the barges on rivers like the Loire, Danube, Elbe or Oder had very simple rigs: a single mast for one square sail or to fasten the towing line. Fully developed sailing rigs were only seen in

Model of a Hollandse Zoomaak, La Belle Alliance *of about 1850. A two- masted ship of the Rhine, and although akin to the* Dorstense-aak, *the* Hollandse-aak *was shorter.* (Nederlands Scheepvaart Museum, Amsterdam)

areas where large, linked lakes and waterways existed. In the seventeenth century the spritsail was common in the Low Countries, and was later replaced by the gaff rig. In England the spritsail survived on the Thames sailing barges (although these were more coasters than genuine inland ships).

In most cases, riverine navigation and shallowness went together. The draught of an inland vessel was always limited. A keel was impractical and the bottom had to be flat, making the hull very leewardly under sail. This potential disadvantage was partly overcome by the use of leeboards, especially in the Low Countries, northern Germany and some parts of England. These were large, flat keel-substitutes which were pivoted from each side of the vessel so they could be lowered or lifted as appropriate. The board lowered was always the one on the lee-side of the ship when sailing– hence the name. Although leeboards may give the impression of primitiveness, in reality they were a very efficient invention. They normally allowed a ship to sail as close as 40° to the wind, even when unladen and drawing only one or two feet. A short, broad pattern was used in shallow waters, while in estuaries long and narrow leeboards were preferred.

Ships of the Rhine, 1650-1925

The long-distance transportation of goods by means of river vessels on the Rhine goes back to at least the Roman period. The discovery of the so-called 'Zwammerdam Ships' in the Netherlands in 1971 proved that around 300 AD the shipbuilders of the Upper Rhine were able to construct barges of 20-35m (65-115ft) in length using caulked planks. Very little is known about the ships of the Rhine between Roman times and the Middle Ages, but in 1930 the 'Utrecht ship' was excavated. This was an oak-built sailing ship of 17.8m length, and 4m width (58.4ft by 13.1ft). The construction was a massive, dug-out hull bottom with sides extended upwards by individual planks.

It seems probable that from the beginning of our era long-distance transportation on the Rhine was carried out by large specialist river vessels. In the Middle Ages seagoing vessels like cogs and hulks were still common in river ports, but when seagoing sailing ships grew dramatically in size after 1500 it became necessary to trans-ship into riverine craft, a characteristic of Rhine navigation down to the present day. Some information survives for the big Rhine vessels of the sixteenth century.

These ships of 20-30m length transported coal, wine, cereals and timber. Upstream they transported more and more manufactures from the industries in Holland into Germany. Navigation on the river Rhine was always on a large scale: today's 12,000-ton pusher-convoys of six barges on the Rhine are the giants of modern Dutch and German inland navigation, and their seventeenth-century equivalents, the *bovenlander*, Dordrecht collier and *samoreus* must have been conceived in the same way.

The samoreus

With her length of 20-30m (65-100ft), two masts and large cabin, the *samoreus* must have been an impressive sight, even for people in the seventeenth century for whom it was commonplace. There is no evidence of the exact origins of the *samoreus*, but without doubt it evolved from older Rhine-built craft. The *samoreus* is a typical member of the *aak* family and follows the tradition that ships of the Rhine have always been bigger than other inland ships. Two factors are responsible for the large dimensions of the *samoreus* and her successors, the *Dorstense-aak* and the iron or steel *Rhineclipper* of the nineteenth and twentieth centuries. First, the river Rhine had very few navigational limitations–no narrow bridges, dams or locks, the only restriction being on the draught of ships, because of occasional shallows, especially in summertime. In the second place the *samoreus* was employed in the international transit of goods, for centuries almost by definition the nature of Rhine navigation. This long-distance traffic made the exploitation of large ships profitable. As early as the seventeenth century, Amsterdam bargemen sailed all the way to German cities like Cologne, so the *samoreus* was also known as the *Keulenaar*.

Plan of a 130ft samoreus *or* Keulsche aak, *eighteenth century. From the seventeenth into the nineteenth century this was the most important type for long-distance navigation between Amsterdam and German Rhineland towns.* (Nederlands Scheepvaart Museum, Amsterdam)

The *samoreus* was a genuine and effective sailing ship, unlike the big ships of German origin on the Upper Rhine, which were called *bovenlander*s and mostly had to be hauled from a towpath. The famous contemporary writer on seventeenth-century shipbuilding in the Netherlands, Nicolaes Witsen, called these *bovenlander*s 'high, rude and large-limbed' (*ie* primitive). From Amsterdam to Cologne, the *samoreus* first had to cross the Zuyderzee to the mouth of the river Vecht and the prevailing favourable wind (westerly) meant that the bargemen could usually sail on the Vecht and the Rhine, but if the wind failed the ship could be hauled by horses. On the return trip, the current could be used, even when the wind was contrary. Contemporaries wrote that a journey from Amsterdam to Dusseldorf took at most fourteen days, but only eight days in the other direction. The *samoreus* carried colonial goods, butter, cheese and other manufactures upstream to Germany, returning with wine and bulk cargoes such as timber, coal, cereals and bricks.

Constructional details relating to the *samoreus* are very scarce. Only one building plan survives, in the collection of the Netherlands Maritime Museum in Amsterdam; and in the Maritime Museum in Rotterdam is a model of a *samoreus*, probably dating from the beginning of the nineteenth century. In 1831 the Dutch artist and engraver Le Comte gave a description of a *samoreus* which had a loading capacity of 100 to 300 lasts (tons of 2000kg) in a hold which occupied most of the ship. Typical were the round-topped hatches, which gave more cargo volume than the more usual slightly cambered hatch covers, and the relatively large cabin on deck. Unlike most Dutch inland sailors of the seventeenth and eighteenth centuries, the bargemen of the *samoreus* lived on board with his family. The family occupied the cabin, which according to Le Comte, had various rooms and offered a well-appointed home. The bargeman's crew lived in the forecastle, and in the stern was stowage for

victuals. In the hold, two sail lockers were contrived before and abaft the mast. The rig comprised two masts, the main mast with topmast, and a mizzen mast, setting the following sails: jib, large jib, fore staysail, square mainsail, spritsail (which was called the 'ferrysail') with topsail, a mizzen and a mizzen staysail. With a fair wind on the long reaches of the Rhine, this large sail area could propel the ship against the strong current. The square mainsail and the big jib were only used with the wind aft: close-hauled the jib, fore staysail, 'ferrysail' and mizzen were set.

The *samoreus* was a good example of traditional Dutch naval architecture, which succeeded in producing sailing ships of small draught but large carrying capacity, coupled with good sailing qualities. The *samoreus* had a fine reputation under sail, because the leeboards made the ship weatherly. The section of traditional Dutch leeboards was rather like the wing of a modern aeroplane: the external surface was flat while the internal form was convex. The resulting aerofoil produced a lifting force.

The usual inventory of a *samoreus* included between eight and fourteen anchors of different weights and several anchor cables, and 300 fathoms of towing line, which had to withstand the strain of twenty towing horses. If necessary the barge's deckhands could run out small anchors, to kedge the ship over a short distance.

Around 1850 the *samoreus* disappeared and was replaced by more modern types like the *Dorstense-aak* and the *keen*.

Table 5/1: Dimensions of a Samoreus, 1831

	200 tons	300 tons	600 tons
Length (m):	31.144	33.975	42.469
Breadth (m):	4.246	5.662	6.794
Depth (m):	2.972	3.114	3.397
Loaded draught (m):	1.768	2.405	2.548

Note: Data from Le Comte.

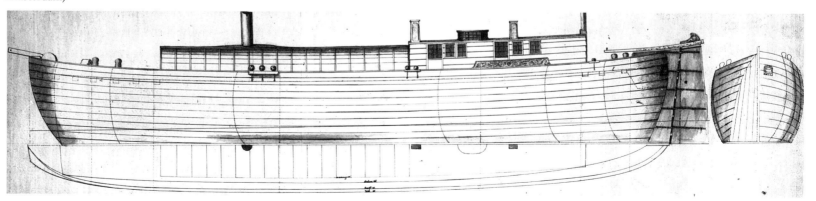

A samoreus *under sail, in an engraving by G Groenewegen, 1789.*

The keen

Although the *keen* (pronounced 'kane') was a sizable inland vessel, it was smaller than the *samoreus*. This permitted the type to sail not only on the Rhine, but also on the smaller inland waters. The *keen* was a pure *aak* hull form, in the fore part of the ship as well as in the stern. The rudder had a very characteristic shape and was called *klaphekken* ('swing-gate'). The hull bottom was flat but the leeboards gave the vessel excellent performance to windward. There was a main and mizzen mast with a jib, fore staysail, mainsail with gaff, and a mizzen sail. The biggest *keen*s had a cabin which was positioned just aft of midships, while smaller examples had a living-space in the stern of the ships called the 'pavillion'. A variant was the *Moselle-keen*, a two-masted vessel with a cabin, but of shorter length.

The Dorstense-aak

In the nineteenth century this type replaced the old-fashioned *samoreus*, though there were similarities between the two: both were *aak*-shaped in the fore part of the ship and had a sternpost; and both had the one-and-a-half mast rig, which was so characteristic of Rhine ships, but the hull of the *Dorstense-aak* was more streamlined and carvel-built. These ships were built in the village of Dorsten in Germany. The rise of heavy industry in the area around the river Ruhr greatly stimulated the transportation of bulk cargoes and the *Dorstense-aak* benefited from this trade. However, cargoes like coals and ores placed great stresses on relatively long wooden hulls, especially in the open waters of the Lower Rhine and in the province of Zeeland, where these vessels also sailed. When iron shipbuilding developed around 1840-1850, the large wooden sailing ships of the Rhine were quickly replaced by new types of ships which were specially designed to be built in iron and steel. Eventually, the *Rhineclipper* or 'river-clipper' became the most important sailing ship of the Rhine.

The 'river-clipper'

The construction of inland sailing ships in the Netherlands reached its zenith with this type of

Model of a nineteenth-century keen, *a two-masted ship of the rivers Rhine and Meuse. The model was built to the lines of a ship that was broken up in 1918.* (Nederlands Scheepvaart Museum, Amsterdam)

vessel, which combined a large carrying capacity, excellent sailing qualities and high speed under sail, with a crew of only two or three, made possible by a rationalisation of the rig. All these qualities were achieved with the large two-masted river-clippers of 30-40m (100-130ft) length which originated in the 1860s and 1870s. The ancestry of the big *Rhineclipper* is still not entirely clear, but it can be assumed that it was produced by combining aspects of the contemporary seagoing clippers with the iron towed barges, or lighters, of the Rhine, which were built from 1841 onwards. These barges (which were called *kast*) had sharp hull forms so they could be towed by the early tugs with relatively small steam engines. From these

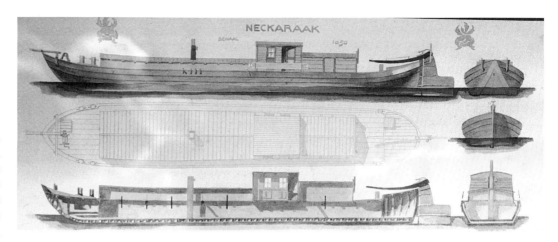

Plan of a Neckar-aak *by E van Konijnenburg, nineteenth century. The Neckar was a tributary of the Rhine, and this* aak *was akin to other ships of the Rhine, like the* keen *and the* Dorstense-aak. *(Maritiem Museum Prins Hendrik, Rotterdam)*

barges the river-clipper borrowed its modern stern, while the S-shaped stempost was inspired by the seagoing clipper ship. Because the bottom was flat, these inland clippers were fitted with leeboards. The first river-clippers were built by shipbuilders along the rivers Noord and Lek near Rotterdam and Dordrecht. Later, smaller inland clippers were built as well, and the clipper became one of the most common sailing barges in the Netherlands.

Two-masted clippers had a minimum length of 30m, the breadth being about 6m, but this was actually determined by the size of certain locks and bridges on canals. With these dimensions the carrying capacity was about 150 tons, but the biggest clippers for inland navigation had a length of about 40m, with a capacity up to 300 tons. The rigging of the two-masted clipper consisted of a jib, fore staysail, mainsail and mizzen sail. The main mast and the topmast of the mizzen could be lowered, allowing the clipper to 'shoot' the Rhine bridges with a partially-lowered main mast and mainsail, and the mizzen sail. The use of efficient winches meant that these clippers could be sailed with only two or three men. The first *Rhineclipper*s of the nineteenth century still had the wooden cabin amidships, as was usual on Rhine vessels, but on later examples a steel cabin was placed on deck abaft the hatches.

Although originally confined to the river Rhine, the two-masted clipper later became common in all parts of the Netherlands, and some parts of Belgium and Germany. They were used, for example, to transport basalt from Germany to the coastal provinces of the Netherlands for the construction of dykes. At the beginning of the twentieth century, some big river-clippers were built or adapted for the coastal trade to northern Germany, the French

Atlantic ports and Scandinavia. But not without some serious accidents and losses–a flat bottom, a hold with many wooden hatches, and vulnerable leeboards made them only moderately successful seagoing ships.

Smaller ships of the *aak* type

Although the *aak* family were originally river vessels, the smaller variants in particular were common throughout the Netherlands. The reason was that these ships were lightly constructed and relatively easy to build, so they gave a high carrying capacity for a modest capital outlay. They also had good sailing qualities on a small draught–an *aak* of about 20m length drew around 50cm (20in) empty and 1.50m (59in) laden. Every region had its own variants. The nineteenth century saw the development of the *hagenaar* ('Hague vessel'), which owed its name to the fact that it could pass the very narrow bridges of The Hague. These vessels were built along Dutch rivers where brickworks were abundant. The *hagenaar* was developed because millions of bricks had to be transported to The Hague – and also Rotterdam–during the industrialisation of the Netherlands in the second half of the nineteenth century. A bargeman of a *hagenaar* could also pass the extremely low and narrow 'Wagen-bridge' in the centre of The Hague. The width of this bridge was 4.20m, the height little more than 2m, so a sailing ship with

dimensions of 22.0m x 4.17m x 1.60m came about: the type had a loading capacity of 85-90 tons, and a surprisingly fine underwater shape. When passing the bridge, the mast had to be lowered, as well as all the gear; the leeboards were also removed and after the cargo was unloaded, to keep down the 'air draught' of the hull, water ballast had to be admitted to the hold, which was pumped out by hand later. The last wooden *hagenaar*s were built up to 1880, but iron and steel examples were constructed down until 1918.

Ships of the Meuse and Scheldt

Until well into the nineteenth century there were no channels between the basins of the Scheldt and the Meuse. Because of this isolation, the ship types of the Meuse formed a distinct and easily recognisable sub-group of the *aak* family. While the inland ships in the Scheldt basin were akin to Dutch prototypes, the ships of the Meuse were more French, with vertical side planking and ends that were quite flat. In the valley of the Meuse, sailing was a matter of secondary importance. There was a square sail, but the mast served mainly to fasten the towing line. For centuries, types like the *mignole*, the *spitsbek* and the *herna* sailed on the French, Belgian and Dutch Meuse. These were

Model of the spitsbek, Josephine, *probably from 1843.* (Nederlands Scheepvaart Museum, Amsterdam)

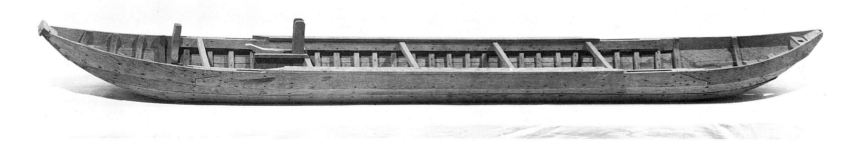

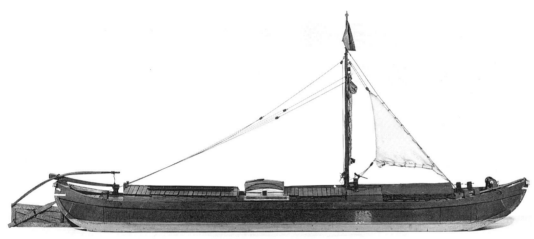

Top: An old postcard showing a mignole *under sail on the Meuse near Namur, about 1900.* (Henk Dessens Collection)

Lower: Model of a herna, *of about 1850. Used on the Meuse, this ship was mainly built in Belgium, but sometimes near Maastricht in the Netherlands. The ship was mostly hauled by horses, although with a favourable wind it could be sailed with a small square sail or lugsail, and a fore sail.* (Maritiem Museum Prins Hendrik, Rotterdam)

long, narrow and structurally weak vessels that could only be used on the upper Meuse and the canals that opened the rest of Belgium for inland navigation. The maximum dimensions of the *herna* were about 45m x 6m x 1.80m (148ft x 20ft x 6ft). The *herna* was a pure *aak*, in the forward hull as well as aft; the *spitsbek* or *mignole* were smaller variants, the smallest being 15m x 2.50m (49ft x 8ft). The last wooden examples were built in the second half of the nineteenth century.

The inland vessels of the Scheldt were unmistakably akin to the Dutch *tjalk* family and these will be discussed later.

Inland sailing ships of the Netherlands

The *wijdschip* and *smalschip* of the seventeenth century belonged to a group of Dutch inland sailing ships which were commonly called 'kromstevens', which meant 'ships with curved stemposts'. In the nineteenth century all these types would eventually coalesce under the general heading of *tjalk* (the word *tjalk* is akin to the english 'keel'). The terms *wijdschip* (broad ship) and *smalschip* (narrow ship) were related to the ability to pass certain locks in seventeenth-century Holland–especially the locks near Harlem and Gouda, which were of impor-

tance in the north-south water transportation routes. A *smalschip* could pass these narrow locks and were true canal craft; the *wijdschip* was bigger and was adapted to sail on the Zuyderzee, which could be a dangerous expanse of water. Like many seventeenth- and eighteenth-century Dutch inland sailing craft these ships had a high stern, which was called *staatsie*. The top of the rudder ran through an opening in the steeply-sheered stern, above which was an ornamental taffrail called the *hakkebord*. A biblical scene would be carved in wood on the forward side of the *hakkebord* ; on the other side there were usually representations of the coats of arms of the cities the ship sailed between.

Like most inland sailing ships of the Netherlands in the seventeenth and eighteenth centuries, these ships had a spritsail, a fore staysail and a jib. Originally a tall sprit rig was common, but in the eighteenth century a second, squarer, variant arose, which was called the 'ferry-rig'. The leeboards were broad, which reflected the shallow waters in which the vessels operated. The *smalschip* was employed moving cargo on canals and small lakes, and as lighters. Larger were the *smakschips*, which were also used to cross the Zuyderzee and the Waddenzee to ports in northern Germany.

In the seventeenth century the Netherlands underwent a true transport revolution. More and more cities organised ferry services with fixed times for departures and strong regulations controlling prices and quality. In Holland an important ferry type was the *kaag*, which for

The baquet *of Charleroi was designed by the Belgian canal engineer Vifquain in 1832, for the opening of the Brussels-Charleroi Canal. The* baquet *fitted in the small locks of this canal and transported mainly coal from Charleroi to Brussels and Antwerp. On the canals the* baquet *was horse-drawn, but in Brussels sails could be hired and with the help of the tide the* baquets *sailed on the rivers Rupel and Escaut to Antwerp. The* baquets *were so narrow that they had to be lashed together when empty to prevent capsizing.* (Henk Dessens Collection)

Model of a smakschip, *marked '1676'. The oldest known model of an inland ship in the Netherlands. Rigged with spritsail main and gaff mizzen. These ships sailed on the Zuyderzee and Waddenzee, which could be rough in heavy weather. (Nederlands Scheepvaart Museum, Amsterdam)*

example sailed from Amsterdam or Harlem to the city of Leyden, across what was then a substantial lake called the Haarlemmermeer. The seventeenth-century *kaag* had a straight stempost, but in the eighteenth century this name was used for a sailing ship with a curved stem.

After 1500 the inhabitants of the Netherlands were increasingly forced to contend with soil erosion and a rising sea-level. An intricate system of weirs or dams in the mouths of rivers, and dykes along the rivers were used to keep the water out of agricultural land. The result was that Holland had several water-boards each

Plan of a kaag, *of about 1800. Dimensions: 68ft×16ft 6in×8ft (Amsterdam feet). At the end of the eighteenth century the kaag had a curved stempost and was a sturdy vessel, able to sail on the Zuyderzee. The bulwarks near the after-deck, the 'staatsie', were made higher. (Nederlands Scheepvaart Museum, Amsterdam)*

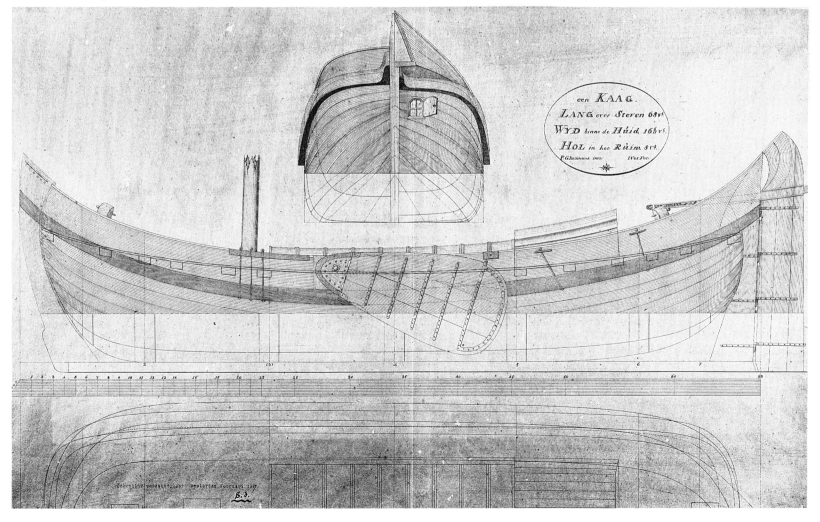

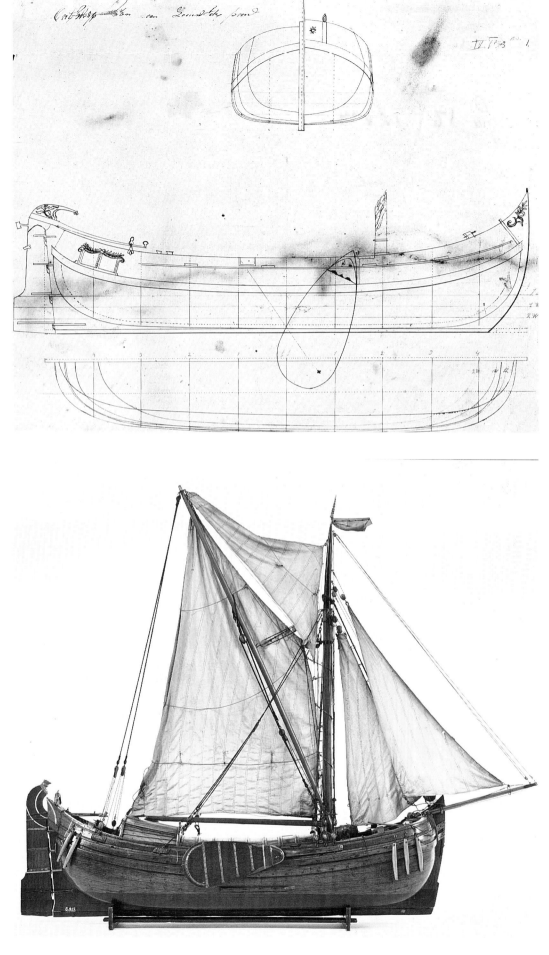

A nineteenth-century plan of a Zeeland poon. A relatively wide and high hull made the poon *a good ship for the rough Zeeland estuary. Unlike most of the tjalks, the* poon *had considerable tumblehome, which made it akin to Flemish sailing craft. This plan represents a* poon *with a pavillion (cabin) beneath the after deck.* (Nederlands Scheepvaart Museum, Amsterdam)

with independent jurisdiction, so that individual regions had their own water-levels. Before locks became common, the Dutch were used to pulling small boats and larger craft over the dams in the rivers. Such a place was called an *overtoom* ('pull-over'). The *damloper* ('dam-walker') was a ship of about 15m (50ft) length which could be hauled over these dams. A smaller variant was the *damschuit* ('dam-barge'). *Damlopers* were also designed to pass the very narrow lock of Leidschendam (between The Hague and Leiden).

The *poon* was also an example of the *kromsteven* type. This craft was built in the provinces of Holland and Brabant, and was mainly seen on the rivers and in the estuaries of the southwest of the Netherlands. Many of them served as ferries from Rotterdam to the surrounding villages and cities. The *poon* was noted for its capabilities in rough waters, especially in the Zeeland estuary. Its principal characteristics were a hull of relatively large breadth and depth, and a stempost which was strongly curved. The length could be 12-20m (39-66ft).

During the nineteenth century most of the old variations of the *kromsteven* type amalgamated into the *tjalk*, which became the most common sailing barge of the Netherlands after 1850, even if regional differences were still

Model of a tjalk, *dated '1818'. This model represents the Amsterdam to Enkhuizen ferry,* Des Koopmans Welvaren *(Merchant's Welfare). The main sail is still a spritsail, but in the nineteenth century the spritsail was gradually replaced by a gaff. The second photo shows the 'staatsie' and 'hakkebord', the decoration above the helm.* (Nederlands Scheepvaart Museum, Amsterdam)

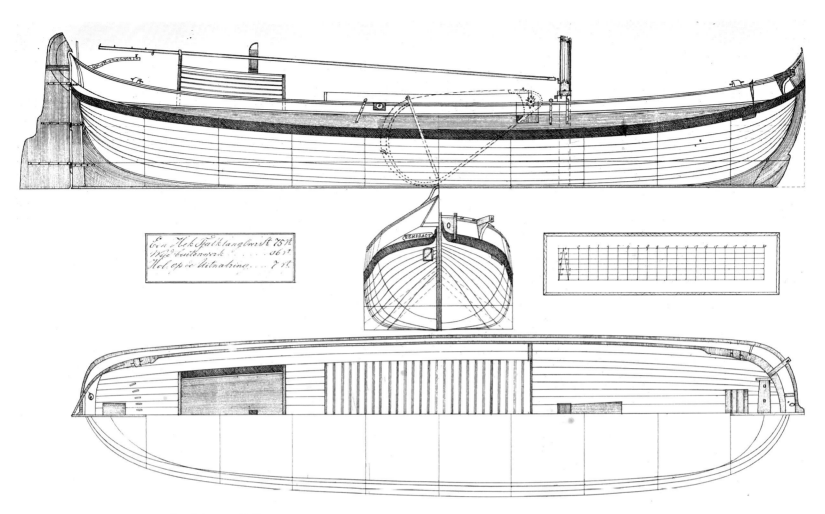

Plan and a model of a staatsie-tjalk, *of about 1850. In the beginning of the nineteenth century the various types of Dutch sailing ships with a curved stempost merged into the general term* tjalk. *This plan represents a design that would hardly change until the last (steel)* tjalks *were built around 1920, but the* staatsie *on the after deck was seldom fitted on the iron and steel* tjalks. *Later in the nineteenth century the bulwarks of* tjalks *would become more and more vertical (without tumblehome).* (Nederlands Scheepvaart Museum, Amsterdam)

obvious. Most of the smallest *tjalk*s were built in the northern provinces, especially Friesland (Frisia), and usually measured between 12m and 20m. In the provinces of Holland and Zeeland the *pavillion-tjalk* was common. Most of the biggest *tjalk*s came from the northern province of Groningen; they measured about 22m x 4.80m (72ft x 16ft) with a loading capacity of 120-150 tons. Very similar to the inland *tjalk* of Groningen was the *koftjalk*, a sailing coaster which in England was called a 'galliot'.

The ships of the inland waters of Flanders were clearly related to the ships of the south-west of the Netherlands. Examples were the 'Flemish *pleit*' (pronounced 'plite') and the *otter*. From the thirteenth century onwards the

Above: Model of a Flemish pleit *of about 1825. The* pleit *was the biggest Flemish inland sailing craft, serving on the Escaut and the smaller rivers in Flanders, such as the Dender and the Rupel. The* pleit *became extinct around 1900.* (Nederlands Scheepvaart Museum, Amsterdam)

Right: A Damloper, *engraving by G Groenewegen, 1789.*

word *pleit* was used for various ship types, both seagoing and coasters, but from the eighteenth century, its meaning was confined to a Flemish inland sailing ship, with one or two masts, depending on the dimensions.

The Flemish *pleit* was built in Flanders and sailed on the Scheldt and its tributaries, the small rivers and canals of Flanders as well as the Zeeland estuary of the Netherlands. Most of them had one mast, only the biggest having

two. Many *pleits* were employed transporting the products of the brickworks along the Rupel, a tributary of the Scheldt. The tidal range in the Scheldt basin was 3-5m (10-16ft) and all these ships had flat bottoms and leeboards to dry out easily. The biggest inland *pleits* were about 180 tons loading capacity, and the last of the type saw service at the end of the nineteenth century.

Originally most inland vessels of the Netherlands were relatively small. In the seventeenth century a *damloper* with a length of twelve metres represented quite a big ship. Dams and locks exercised a particular restraint on the size of ships, but after 1850 there was a distinct tendency for inland ships to became larger, because of an expanding economy and improving infrastructure. Increasing carrying capacity was mainly achieved by making the ships longer, as shallowness and existing bridges and locks still limited hull depth and breadth.

Notwithstanding this tendency towards greater size, small sailing ships of about 10-20 tons cargo capacity still played a role right down into the twentieth century. One of the oldest types was the *bok*, which had its origins in the provinces of Holland and Utrecht, where from the seventeenth century onwards extended peat-digging areas existed. The *bok* was used to transport the peat to the surrounding villages and cities, like Amsterdam and Utrecht, but their bargemen also earned a living by the carriage of agricultural goods and produce. They often had to creep through very narrow canals and channels with very confined bridges and locks. The mast could be lowered very simply with a counterweight by one man. In the eighteenth century the *bok* had a small living space in the forecastle, which was displaced in the nineteenth century by a *pavillion*, or small cabin, aft. Most *boks* had a gaff mainsail and a fore staysail; some of the larger examples also had a jib. The hatches were slightly cambered and stretched from gunwale to gunwale–the *bok* had no gangways–lying on tall vertical coamings, which could be removed together with the hatches during loading and unloading. These ships were very efficient in small polder areas with narrow waters, combining excellent sailing qualities with easy handling during punting, towing and loading.

Inland craft of central Europe

For centuries the only German waterways were the natural rivers, which in the main flowed from the south or southeast to the north or northwest. Until the nineteenth century there were hardly any connecting canals between these rivers and their tributaries, producing relatively isolated shipbuilding traditions which persisted even after the interlinking waterways were completed. Greater uniformity only came about when iron shipbuilding began to turn out big towed river barges.

Left: Engraving of a bok, *by P Le Comte, 1831, and (right) a photograph of a* westlander, *in about 1950. The* bok *probably dates from the seventeenth century, but at the end of the nineteenth century it was replaced by the* westlander. *The photograph shows one of the last active sailing* westlanders, De Vrouw Cornelia, *near Rotterdam.* (Maritiem Museum Prins Hendrik, Rotterdam).

Model of an East Frisian mot, *nineteenth century. This model of a sailing ship from northwest Germany, belonged to the former collection of the Museum für Meereskunde in Berlin. The hull form and rigging is akin to the sailing ships of the northern Netherlands.*

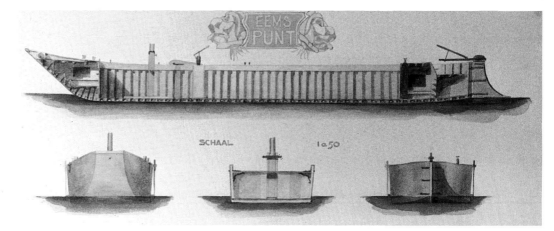

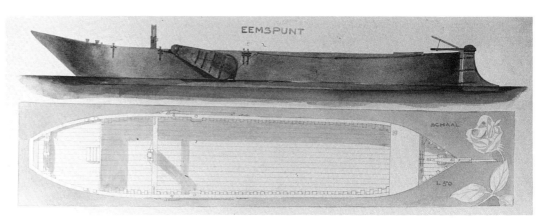

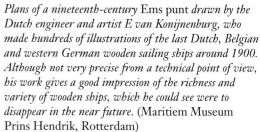

In central Europe the following were the main areas of navigation:

The Weser and the inland waters of East Frisia
The Elbe
The Oder
The Danube
The Vistula and the 'haffen' along the Baltic coast.

In the seventeenth century the river Weser in northwest Germany accommodated an extensive inland navigation. Because of shallowness and the rise and fall of tides on this river, flat-bottomed barges were predominant. In the eighteenth century the biggest barges were the *Böcke*, with dimensions up to 36m x 2.80m (118ft x 9ft). So called *Hinterhänge* with 40-50 tons carrying capacity measured about 33m x 2.20m (108ft x 7ft), and *Bullen* of 20 tons were 20m x 1.50m (65ft x 5ft). The *Harener punt* survived until the twentieth century; this was a scow-like barge with spritsail, which was used

for the transport of peat in Ostfriesland (East Frisia). Another peat-barge from the nineteenth century was the *mot* (length about 15m, or 49ft), which showed similarities with the *tjalk*s from Groningen.

The original *Oder-kahn*[2] (*kahn* is a common German word comparable to 'barge') of the seventeenth century was small: 20 to 25 tons, but later a cargo capacity of 100-150 tons was not unusual. Two main types could be discerned, the *Kaffekahn* and the *Stevenkahn*. The *Kaffekahn*, which was built as an *aak*, was not only used on the Oder, but also on the tributaries and canals in the surrounding region.

Plans of a nineteenth-century Ems punt *drawn by the Dutch engineer and artist E van Konijnenburg, who made hundreds of illustrations of the last Dutch, Belgian and western German wooden sailing ships around 1900. Although not very precise from a technical point of view, his work gives a good impression of the richness and variety of wooden ships, which he could see were to disappear in the near future. (Maritiem Museum Prins Hendrik, Rotterdam)*

Dimensions were 40m x 4.60m x 1.90m (131ft x 15ft x 6ft). Curved 'grown' knees were used for the frames, together with oak for the bottom and hull-side planking; the decks were made of deal. As canal building in Germany advanced, the sizes of *Kähne* were increasingly dictated by the dimensions of locks. Important among these were the 'Finow dimensions' (40.20m x 4.60m, 132ft x 15ft) and the 'Berlin

---

2. Teubert, *Die Binnenschiffahrt. Ein Handbuch fur alle Beteiligten* (Leipzig 1912), Abschnitt II, p272.

Plan of an inland mot *by E van Konijnenburg, nineteenth century. This East Frisian type (Germany) had the living space beneath the after deck, like many inland ships in the neighbouring Dutch province of Groningen. The* mot *sailed on the tidal river Ems and East Frisian inland waters, but also visited Dutch waters occasionally. They mainly transported peat. (Maritiem Museum Prins Hendrik, Rotterdam)*

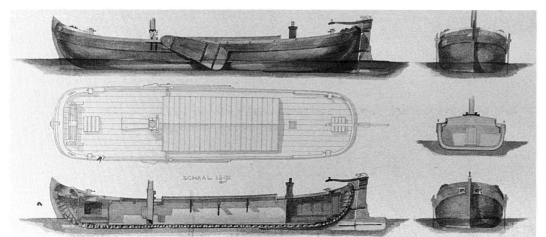

Plan of a Kaffenkahn *of the river Oder, from*
O Teubert, Die Binnenschiffahrt, *Leipzig 1912.*

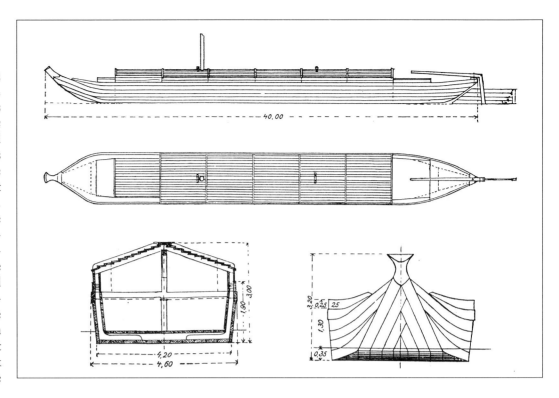

Plan of a Kaffenkahn *of the river Oder, from*
O Teubert, Die Binnenschiffahrt, *Leipzig 1912.*

dimensions' (46.60m x 6.60m, 152ft x 21ft); unladen draught was about 35cm, or 13in. Most of the *Kaffekähne* had a deck and hatches which could be sealed. Originally the *Kaffekahn* was a sailing ship, with a fairly tall mast and spritsail, but with the appearance of steam tugs in the nineteenth century and fixed bridges, the rig became more and more exiguous. By about 1920 the wooden *Kaffekahn* was almost extinct.

The second type of *Oder-kahn* was the *Stevenkahn*, of which there were several variations characterised by the shape of the stempost, which could be curved or straight, the latter being further subdivided into vertical stems or those with varying degrees of overhang. The illustration shows a *kahn* of the Berlin dimensions with an open hold and a cabin. The last generation of *Kähne* was built with steel frames because naturally-curved oak became very scarce. The rigging was the same as the *Kaffekahn*.

The *Kurische Reisekahn* was a ship native to the region between the lower Vistula and Danzig (modern Gdansk) and the Haffen along the Baltic coast. According to Teubert the carrying capacity varied between 100 and 250 tons and his drawing of a *kahn* shows a genuine sailing ship with a hull which was fine-lined for a river vessel. The greatest breadth was at the main mast–itself a long way forward–and abaft the mast the hull became gradually narrower. The considerable sheer and the presence of decks and hatch coamings prove that the ship was designed to operate in waters where the waves could be high. The loading volume of the after part of the hold could be increased by a raised wooden deckhouse over the hold,

Plan of a Stevenkahn *of the river Oder, from*
O Teubert, Die Binnenschiffahrt, *Leipzig 1912.*

which the hatches could be placed upon. The biggest *Reisekähne* measured 35m x 6.40m x 1.90m (115ft x 21ft x 6ft), and were rigged with a main mast and mizzen, setting a jib, fore staysail, gaff mainsail and mizzen. Leeboards guaranteed good sailing capabilities, even with a flat bottom.

Of feebler construction was the *Boidack*, a Prussian undecked vessel which was only fit for navigation in sheltered waters. The hull was relatively long, with no sheer and a completely straight bottom. Nevertheless it was a true sailing ship, with leeboards and a two-masted rig, setting a jib and fore staysail, and two spritsails. In Teubert's drawing the ship has no hatches, an indication that the ship was intended for a calm sailing area. The cargo capacity varied between 150 and 300 tons, with the cor-

responding dimensions of 35m x 5.50m x 1.30m (115ft x 18ft x 4ft) and 50m x 7.50 x 2.00m (164ft x 24.5ft x 6.5ft). For the crew there was a cabin aft, and accommodation under the forecastle.

Most of the ships on the Continent were not full sailing ships but were generally hauled by animals or men, or drifted downstream with the current. A very curious example was the *Zille* of Bohemia. This open vessel operated on the Vistula, the Elbe and Oder, but originated on the river Moldau in Bohemia. The first-stage construction of the *Zille* was only taken up to the point where it was fit to drift downstream with a makeshift rudder to Prague and from there further downstream to Bodenbach. On arrival the bare hull was hauled up onto a slipway on the river bank and completed as a

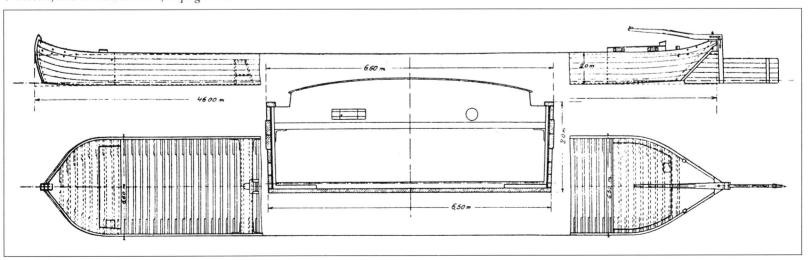

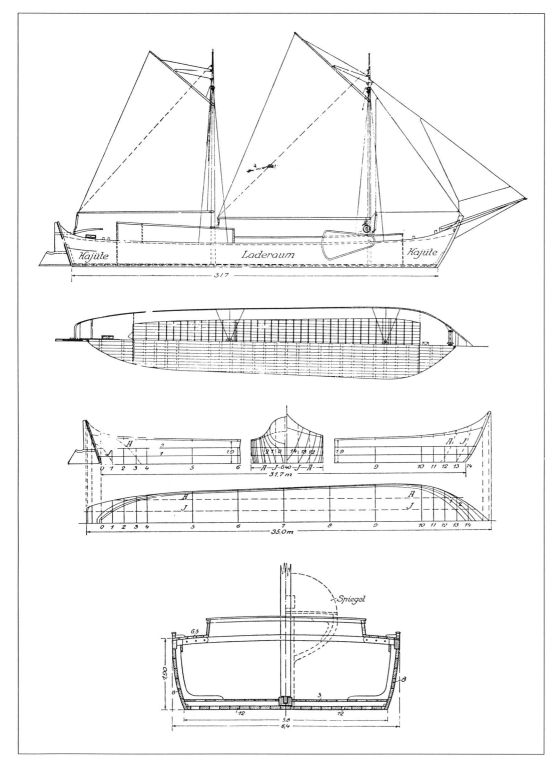

Kajüte   Laderaum   Kajüte

317

31.7 m

35.0 m

Spiegel

Plan of a Kurischer Reisekahn, *from O Teubert,* Die Binnenschiffahrt, *Leipzig 1912.*

the so-called Canal Age there were many inland working craft–usually referred to as 'narrow boats'–but most of them were permanently horse-drawn, until later mechanised by steam engines or internal combustion machinery. The sailing 'barges' which could be seen on many rivers were in fact sailing coasters, with good seakeeping capabilities, and not really inland ships. Examples from the nineteenth and twentieth century are the Thames barge from the east coast, and the Tamar barge, which worked on the river Tamar and along the westcountry coast around Plymouth.

However, genuine inland navigation with river vessels was widespread throughout the waterways known as the 'Broads', in Norfolk and Suffolk. From medieval times ships carried manufactures from Norwich to the North Sea harbour of Lowestoft,[3] a distance of some 30km, and returned with a cargo of coal. Keels also transported peat from the Broads to clients all over East Anglia. The keel was mentioned in written sources as early as the seventeenth and eighteenth centuries, and although little is known for certain about the type, it may be assumed that the continuous use of the word 'keel' throughout those two hundred years did not necessarily denote exactly the same type of vessel–at least, this is what is suggested by depictions on old maps and prints.

In illustrations from the eighteenth century keels are shown as open vessels without leeboards, rigged with a single square sail on a mast placed amidships. With such a rig the sailing capabilities of the keel could have been, at best, only moderate. However, from around 1789 a more effective sailing vessel evolved: this type, the wherry, could beat into the wind, thanks to a better formed hull and a single-masted gaff rig. So-called keels endured into the nineteenth century, although little is known about them, but from the few contemporary illustrations it seems that this variety of keel and the wherry were related: the keel is shown with flared hull sides like those of the wherry. The keel had a small flat stern.

The mast was stepped right forward, and could be lowered with a counterweight because of the many bridges on the Broads. The rig of the Norfolk wherry was unique in Europe: a cat, with one large gaff sail. The smallest wherry could carry about 15 tons, and the biggest 40 tons. The hull was clinker-built,

Markt Zille. The bows were made more ship-like and all the original fastenings were replaced. The hull sides were raised to 1.60m, a more effective rudder was fitted and a cabin was constructed; the hull was then sealed with a coat of tar. They were loaded with brown coal or basalt, and drifted down the Elbe to Magdenburg or made the 500km trip to Hamburg, or even to Berlin. When they arrived at their destination, the *Zillen* were broken up or sold to small German bargemen,

who sailed with them for about another four years. They could be generally divided into the *Kaffen Zille,* built like an *aak,* and the *Steven Zille* with a stempost. The *Zille* had a mast to which a towing line could be secured.

Great Britain

The small-scale geography of Great Britain restricted the employment of genuine sailing vessels on rivers and inland waterways. During

3. Robert Malster, *Wherries and Waterways* (Lavenham 1971).

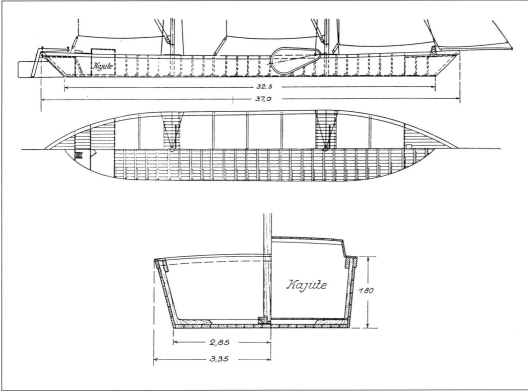

Plan of a Boidack, *from O Teubert*, Die Binnenschiffahrt, *Leipzig 1912.*

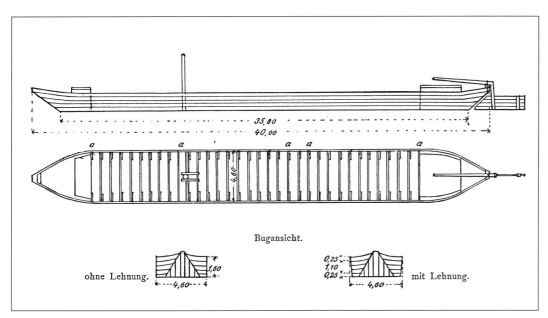

Plan of a Kaffen Zille *from Bohemia, from O Teubert*, Die Binnenschiffahrt, *Leipzig 1912.*

Two views from H Warrington Smyth's Mast and Sail in Europe and Asia *(1906) of a Norfolk wherry; in one the wherry is shown with the sail reefed; the other shows its whole sail, plus the 'bonnet', an additional strip of sail added to the foot in light conditions. This ancient method of adding sail in fair weather was largely replaced by shortening sail through reefing in seagoing ships but survived on this inland type.*

most of the wherries having a stempost and a sternpost; some had a transom stern. The wherry could sail close to the wind, but better laden than empty because there were no lee-boards. The V-shaped bottom gave sufficient lateral resistance when sailing close-hauled. The Norfolk wherry is a good example of the long isolation of regional shipbuilding tradi-tions, because nowhere else in Britain could a similar vessel be found.

From the nineteenth century, other 'keels' were used on the river Humber and its tribu-taries, like the Ouse which gives access to the city of York. Rigged with a single mast and two square sails (mainsail and topsail) and equipped with leeboards, this type was able to tack, but they always benefited from the effects of tide and current. In fact, their sailing patterns were dictated by the tides, in order to profit from the strong currents and because many of their des-tinations dried out at low water. The working area of this type of keel was confined to the

Humber estuary, and they did not venture out to sea. The bows were round, the hull sides nearly vertical, and the bottom was flat. Under the weather deck aft was a very small cabin, and the hold was protected by hatch covers. The biggest keels had a loading capacity of about 80 tons. A later variant of this keel, the sloop, had a fore and aft rig, but the hulls of keels and sloops were otherwise similar.

France

Interest in the history of inland navigation on rivers and canals has been aroused only very recently in France, as part of a new-found general enthusiasm for maritime culture in that country. Research has shown that France used to have a rich tradition in this respect. Between the seventeenth and twentieth centuries shipping activities were common on most rivers. Many different types of ships have been defined, and every region had its own characteristic methods of shipbuilding. In many cases, a basic regional form could be discerned, but with many major and minor variations. Most of the present knowledge is related to the nineteenth and twentieth century, however, and literature about older inland navigation is still scarce.

For a long time natural rivers and their estuaries formed the only French waterways, but from the seventeenth century connecting canals began to be constructed. The first two rivers to be joined – by the Canal de Briare in 1642 – were the Seine and the Loire basins, and many canals were to follow. This stimulated a rich culture of inland navigation in France, although the canal craft themselves were mainly hauled by animals and men, pure sailing being limited to only a few areas. More or less developed sailing ships could be found on the river Loire, the lakes in the Rhone delta, and the Garonne. In general, it can be said that the pure riverine vessels were characterised by a swim-headed bow of 'heaved bottom planks', and that the ships of river deltas were constructed with a stempost. Examples of the last category could be found in the Rhone delta and the estuaries of the Garonne and the Loire.

The most important sailing ship of the Loire itself was the *chaland*.[4] This French word occurs as a general term for inland ships, like 'barge' does in English, but in the Loire region it defined a specific kind of ship, of which the oldest illustrations (carvings on walls of buildings) and descriptions date from the seventeenth century. *Chalands* could measure 22-30m in length, 3-4m in breadth and 1.50-2.20m in depth (72-98ft x 10-13ft x 5-7ft), with a cargo capacity varying between 25 and 50 tons, although the last *chalands* of the nineteenth century could measure 100 tons. During the centuries the basic form of the *chaland* was the same: a long, narrow open ship without hatches, with a single mast setting one square sail, which in the nineteenth century could measure about 170-200m² (1800-2150sq ft). The hull bottom was flat and the swim bow, which was called *levée* in France, was typical of the European river vessel. When laden the *chaland* could sail with the wind on the beam. In many cases however the *chaland* was towed.

Conclusions

From the seventeenth to the twentieth centuries Europe enjoyed a rich diversity of shipbuilding culture with respect to inland navigation. Such a huge variety cannot be covered in any detail in a single chapter, but it is a reasonable generalisation to state that two basic styles of bow construction prevailed: vessels with 'heaved bottom planks', and those with a stempost. The first were usual in sheltered waters like the upper reaches of rivers; the second category – which was more expensive to build – was capable of sailing on open rivers and estuaries where winds could be strong and waves might be higher. The development of genuine sailing ships for inland waterways was

A painting by Reuben Chappell (1870-1940) of the Humber keel Willie. *The Humber sloop was similar, but had a gaff-headed main sail and a single jib.* (National Maritime Museum)

4. F Beaudoin, *Bateaux des fleuves de France* (Douarnenez 1985), pp119-133.

not universal throughout Europe, but was confined to those regions where geographical conditions made it worthwhile to invest in such relatively expensive ships. Nevertheless, for European inland navigation the 'heyday of sail' endured longer than on the high seas. In several regions of Europe transportation by sailing ship was important well into the twentieth century–no more so than in the Netherlands where an extremely dense network of waterways existed–but in other areas inland navigation was extinguished by the rise of the railways. Furthermore, the transition to iron and steel construction in the second half of the nineteenth century reduced the variety of inland craft, and with the transition to steam-towed craft and motorbarges the modern European inland vessel is becoming a more and more standardised type.

Henk Dessens

Inland Craft: Typical Vessels 1650-1950

Type	Description	Nationality	Area	Period	Typical Tonnage	Typical Dimensions (Feet) (Metres)	Remarks
WIJDSCHIP	Sloop rig	Dutch	Zuyderzee, Waddenzee and other inland waters	c1650	80	64.30 x 18.37 x 7.61 19.60 x 5.60 x 2.32	One of the most important and numerous sailing barges of the seventeenth century
KAAG	Sloop rig	Dutch	Dutch lakes, rivers and canals	c1650	15-20	36.75 x ? 11.20 x ?	Typical ferry between Dutch cities; cargo and passengers
CHALAND	One square sail	French	River Loire	1650-1880	100	98.43 x 13.12 x 7.22 30.00 x 4.00 x 2.20	Typical swim-headed river vessel
HEKTJALK	Sloop rig	Dutch	Dutch lakes, rivers and canals	c1795	60-80	63.98 x 16.08 x 7.71 19.50 x 4.90 x 2.35	Most common type of *tjalk* 1700-1850. Built by C E Duyts, Amsterdam
SAMOREUS	Ketch rig	Dutch	Rhine (Netherlands and Germany)	1800-1850	300	139.34 x 22.28 x 11.15 42.47 x 6.79 x 3.40	Typical swim-headed sailing ship on the Rhine, for regular ferry services
TJALK 'JOHANNA PETERNELLA'	Sloop rig	Dutch	Dutch lakes, rivers and canals	1800-1850	60-80	66.60 x 15.62 x 6.89 20.30 x 4.76 x 2.10	Most common Dutch sailing barge of the century; after 1880 iron and steel built
DORSTENSE-AAK	Ketch rig	Dutch	Rhine, Zeeland estuary	1800-1900	250	127.95 x 19.03 x 5.91 39.00 x 5.80 x 1.80	Swim-headed bulk carrier. Largest known was *Justitia* of 650 tons
NECKAR-SHIP	Sloop rig	German	Neckar, upper Rhine	1825-1900	120	82.02 x 12.47 x 4.59 25.00 x 3.80 x 1.40	Swim-headed wooden vessel
KURISCHE REISEKAHN	Ketch rig	German	Lower Vistula, Baltic coast	1800-1900	250	114.83 x 21.00 x 6.23 35.00 x 6.40 x 1.90	Flat-bottomed sailing vessel with leeboards
KEEN	Ketch rig	Dutch	Rhine and Meuse	1825-1900	265	137.80 x 19.69 x 5.74 42.00 x 6.00 x 1.75	Swim-headed sailing barge, smaller than a *Dorstense-aak*
HERNA	One square sail	Belgian	Meuse and canals	1850-1900	200	114.83 x 16.40 x 5.58 35.00 x 5.00 x 1.70	Swim-headed barge, mostly hauled by horses
OTTER	Sloop rig	Belgian	Flanders: Scheldt estuary and canals	1850-1900	100	60.70 x 16.93 x 7.45 18.50 x 5.16 x 2.27	Smaller than the Flemish *pleit*
PLEIT	Sloop rig	Belgian	Flanders: Scheldt estuary and canals	1850-1900	100	77.10 x 16.40 x 4.79 23.50 x 5.00 x 1.46	There were also two-masted *pleits*
HAGENAAR 'HEILTJE'	Sloop rig	Dutch	Dutch rivers and canals	1895-1953	89	72.31 x 13.68 x 5.25 22.04 x 4.17 x 1.60	Iron-built, swim head; specially adapted for river navigation, esp around The Hague
NORFOLK WHERRY	Cat (single mast)	British	Norfolk Broads	1790-1900	23	58.00 x 15.00 x 4.60 17.68 x 4.57 x 1.40	Cargo carrier between Lowestoft and Norwich
MERSEY FLAT	Sloop rig	British	Mersey and local canal system	1740-1900	67	66.10 x 17.10 x 7.70 20.15 x 5.21 x 2.35	Stem-headed sailing barge
HUMBER KEEL	Two square sails on a single mast	British	River Humber	1800-1900	100	62.50 x 15.50 x 8.00 19.05 x 4.72 x 2.44	The Humber sloop was similar but had a fore-and-aft rig

6

Pleasure Craft

UNTIL some two centuries ago, with the advent of railways and improved methods of road construction, water carriage was not only the cheapest but also the most comfortable method of transportation. It is not surprising, therefore, that those mortals who nowadays are honoured with the description 'VIP' were whenever possible conveyed by water. A reminder of the fact is provided by a medieval poem which, in the words of G M Trevelyan, reveals 'so pleasant a picture' of Canute, the eleventh century king of a great Anglo-Danish empire.

> Merry sungen the monkës in Ely
> When Cnut King rowed there by.
> Row, cnights, near the land
> And hear we these monkës sing.

It is no wonder that on the other side of the North Sea, where there are so many waterways and where the shortest route between two loca-tions is so often by water, there was developed a special vessel for the transportation of gov-ernment officials and similar important people. It became known as a *jacht*, a word which is derived from *jagen*, 'to hunt', and has the con-notation of 'fast movement' (a reminder that before the nineteenth century water transport was also relatively fast).

The type first makes its appearance in docu-ments and other written sources at the end of the sixteenth century (in England apparently in 1643-44[1]). We know, for instance, that in 1595 the Rotterdam admiralty had a large yacht built, the *Neptunis*.[2] This was used by Prince Maurice, the Stadholder of Holland and as such also Commander-in-Chief of the Nether-lands' armed forces, during the expedition to Flanders in 1600. It is interesting to note that the last European monarch who commanded his battlefleet in person, Gustav III of Sweden (1746-1792), possessed a similar 'headquarters ship', designed by F H af Chapman. The stern

1. Documents in the archives of Hurstmonceux Castle dating from the years mentioned refer to a vessel which may have been a yacht in the sense we use the term. There are also Prince Henry's 'pleasure vessel' mentioned below and the 'Rat of Wight' built for Queen Elizabeth in 1588. Ernle Bradford in *Three Centuries of Sailing* (London 1964) mentions both of them, but he also stresses the all-impor-tant Dutch contribution to the subject. The author is inclined to agree with him.

2. In the Netherlands Republic naval administration was in the hands of the five admiralties with their headquarters in five different locations divided over three provinces. Although they were considered organs of the central gov-ernment, the influence of the province where they were located was very strong, so naval administration was much less centralised than in, for instance, Britain or France. For the negative aspects of the Netherlands situation, see Herbert Richmond, *Statesmen and Sea Power* (Oxford 1947), pp38-39.

The original Dutch jacht *was a small fast vessel that may have been used as an official transport but was not necessarily a pleasure craft. This Verbeecq painting from the early seventeenth century shows one such vessel: despite the fore-and-aft rig, it has a rather ship-like hull form, with three gunports a side.* (National Maritime Museum)

A painting by Hendrik Corneliszoon Vroom of the arrival of the Elector Palatine Frederick V and his consort Princess Elizabeth at Flushing in 1613. In the centre foreground is the yacht Neptunis *that belonged to the Rotterdam Admiralty. This sprit-rigged vessel is an early example of the Dutch official yacht.* (Frans Hals Museum, Haarlem)

decoration and the saloon of this *Amphion* can still be admired in the Maritime Museum at Stockholm. Also on view there is a painting by J T Schoultz, showing the battle of Svensksund (1790), with the *Amphion* in the foreground.

This category of ship can be best called an official yacht although the description States'

yacht, Prince's yacht or Government yacht is used more often. They were not only owned by government bodies, but can also be found in the ownership of, for example, the Directors of the great chartered Companies or of polder boards (the corporations which were in charge of a particular drained area). They were usually flat-bottomed, to be able to navigate shallow waterways. In their construction comfort was

of course a primary consideration, so they usually had a large day cabin, under the raised poop. Very often they were rigged with one mast, with a spritsail, but there are also early examples which seem to have been ketch rigged (there is a picture of the *Neptunis* with that type of rig) or have sported what has been called a 'bezan cat-schooner rig'.[3]

3. See the caption to the reproduction of Sav(e)ry's print in Hans Vandersmissen, *Holland and the Origins of Yachting* (Nijmegen 1986), p12. This is a most informative little book.

An engraving from Pâris' Souvenirs de Marine *of the last Venetian* Bucintoro *based on a surviving model. Most of the topsides were carved and gilded, and for the annual 'Marriage with the Sea' ceremony the vessel was further decorated with sumptuous flags and arming cloths.*

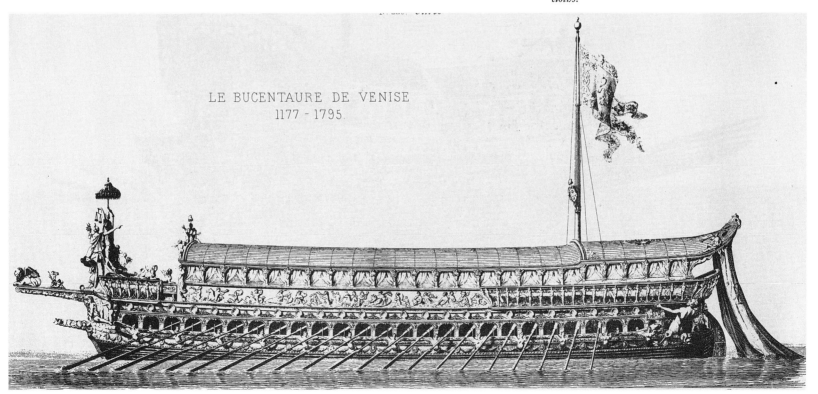

LE BUCENTAURE DE VENISE
1177 - 1795

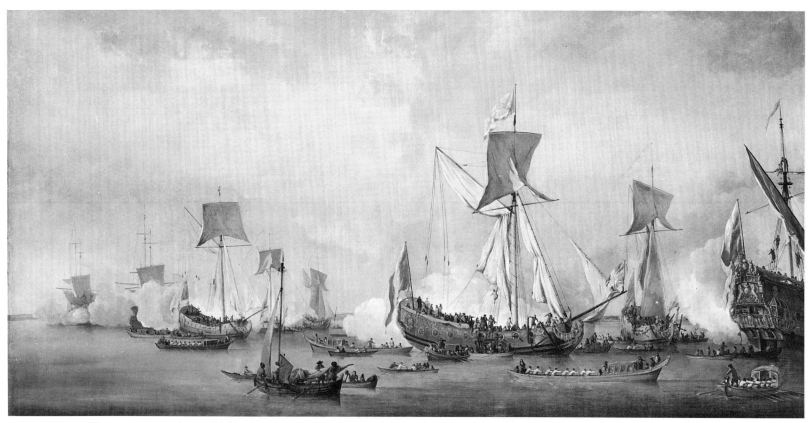

Prince William of Orange returning home with his bride, Princess Mary, in 1677. He is aboard the British royal yacht Mary *in the centre, while the* Charlotte *astern carries the Princess. The* Mary *is not the original yacht presented to Charles II but a brand-new, and rather larger, vessel showing the rapid development of the type inspired by royal patronage. In the foreground are a number of the wherry-like official barges that were used to convey dignatories on rivers and sheltered waters –the limosines of their day.* (National Maritime Museum)

Pictorial sources like contemporary paintings and drawings are a primary source for the appearance of these official yachts. A spectacular example is the large painting by Hendrick Corneliszoon Vroom depicting the arrival of Elector Palatine Frederick V with his English bride, Princess Elizabeth, at Flushing in 1613. In the middle foreground is a vessel identified as the *Neptunis*, in this case depicted with a spritsail rig. Ceremonial occasions like the one Vroom painted were nothing new or uncommon in 1613. Even in the Middle Ages rivers and roadsteads were often used for pageants and the like: since at least 1453 on Lord Mayor's Day a procession was held on the Thames (it was continued until 1856). When in 1487 Henry VII's Queen, Elizabeth, was crowned, she arrived from Greenwich by water; when Anne Boleyn was crowned in 1533 and again later that year when her daughter Elizabeth was born there were water processions. And London was certainly not the only

European city where for centuries its river was also its main highway.

The most famous aquatic ceremonial occasion in Europe has undoubtedly been the annual 'Wedding of Venice to the Sea'. This was instituted during the reign of Doge Pietro Orseolo (991-1008). In its final form the Doge was rowed out into the Adriatic on a splendid state barge, the *Bucintoro*, ablaze with gilded carved works. After the Patriarch had blessed the sea the Doge threw a gold ring into the water, saying, 'We espouse thee, O sea, in token of perpetual sovereignty'. The last wedding ceremony was held in 1796. Two years later the last *Bucintoro*, which had been built in 1728, was stripped of her decorations and left to rot on an island in the lagoon. However, other of these ceremonial barges are still in existence (and in Europe at least one is still used on occasion: *Vasaorden*, the Swedish royal barge). The Museu de Marinha in Lisbon possesses a particularly striking collection: five state barges from the eighteenth and three from the nineteenth century. Pride of place is held by the 'Bergantim Real' (royal barge) from 1778, designed to be rowed by 80 men. In the National Maritime Museum at Greenwich can be seen the Queen's shallop, built in 1689, Prince Frederick's barge, designed in 1732, and the seventeenth-century barge of the Admiralty Commissioners. Another English royal barge is preserved in the Victory Museum at

An emblematic engraving by D E Lons, perhaps after Salomon Sav(e)ry, of an early Dutch pleasure yacht of about 1640. The caption reads 'Earnings made by sailing in trade are often lost by sailing for pleasure', a somewhat cynical reflection of the passion for sailing as a sport in the Netherlands. This two-masted rig, with two sails set from short gaffs, has been seen as a prototype for the schooner rig which came to prominence a century later. (Nederlands Scheepvaart Museum, Amsterdam)

Een Speel-jacht

T'geen dickwils i'varen heeft vermeert Wert dus al'varende verteert

A model of the boeier *yacht presented to Czar Alexander I by King William I of the Netherlands at the end of the Napoleonic War, reviving a connection between the low countries and Russian sailing that went back to Peter the Great. Apart from the well-documented example of the present to the British royal family, the Netherlands introduced the yacht to many other northern European ruling dynasties.* (Nederlands Scheepvaart Museum, Amsterdam)

Portsmouth. It was built for King Charles II and later used to convey Nelson's mortal remains from Greenwich Hospital to St Paul's.

Prince Frederick's barge is a particularly splendid example. Like many other it is of wherry-type design, extremely long and narrow (some 52ft by 7½ft), originally designed for 12 oars (this was later changed to 21). The design was the work of the shipwright John Hall, whereas the decorations were designed by no less an artist than William Kent. Two late examples of state barges are on show in the maritime museums of Paris and Amsterdam respectively. The 'Canot Impérial' in the Musée de la Marine was built in a hurry for Napoleon I at Antwerp in 1810. The 'Koningssloep'[4] (royal shallop) in the Scheepvaartmuseum was built in 1818. Interestingly there is evidence that the sculpted decoration of both these barges was, at least partly, executed by the same craftsman or team of craftsmen.[5]

Perhaps an ancestor of these barges was the pleasure ship *Disdain*, built at Chatham for Henry, Prince of Wales, in 1604, to the design of the famous Phineas Pett. She was '28 feet by the keel, and in breadth 12 feet, garnished with painting and carving, both within board and without, very curiously'. It is quite possible this little vessel was in the first place intended to enable the Prince to take part in water pageants; it is also possible that it was primarily intended for pleasure cruising. It is probable that the same two purposes were uppermost in the design requirements for the vessel depicted in an engraving by Salomon Sav(e)ry (about 1594-after 1664).[6] It is clear that the artist did not intend to depict an official yacht: in that case there would have been a day cabin, not an open poop. We may imagine this ship as

4. Initially this was officially referred to as the 'Koninklijke chaloup', but the translation given here is warranted. The word *chaloup* is, of course, of French origin.

5. See G R Kruissink, *Scheepssier* (Baarn 1977), p77.

6. For the exhibition 'Mensch und Meer', held in 1972 at Kiel on the occasion of the Olympic Games, the Amsterdam Scheepvaartmuseum had a model built which was intended to represent the ship depicted in the Sav(e)ry engraving. This is the only 'non-contemporary' model on public display in the museum.

leisurely cruising on one of the inland waterways of the Netherlands, taking part in the welcoming of an important personage or participating in a mock battle. The last-named form of aquatic entertainment has been popular in the Netherlands for a long time – and is still occasionally practised even today.

Perhaps one of the first of these mock battles was performed in 1580 when William the Silent visited Amsterdam. Another was organised on the occasion of the visit of Queen Marie de Medici to that city in 1638, but most famous are those arranged for the two visits of Peter the Great, in 1697 and 1717. There is a painting in the Amsterdam Scheepvaart Museum, by Abraham Storck, depicting the 1697 show. In the foreground one sees a number of representatives of a type which one still nowadays can

A painting in the style of Abraham Storck of shipping off Amsterdam in the second half of the seventeenth century. Official yachts are much in evidence, but in the foreground is a 'glass shallop', one of the cabbined rowing barges used as transport for important persons. (National Maritime Museum)

The progress of King Charles II through the Netherlands in 1660 on his way to take up the throne of Britain. In the centre is the former yacht of the Princes of Orange which conveyed the king. Details of the sprit rig and the highly decorated hull are evident. Charles was to build very similar vessels for his own use after his Restoration. Painting by Willem van de Velde the Younger. (Mauritshuis, The Hague)

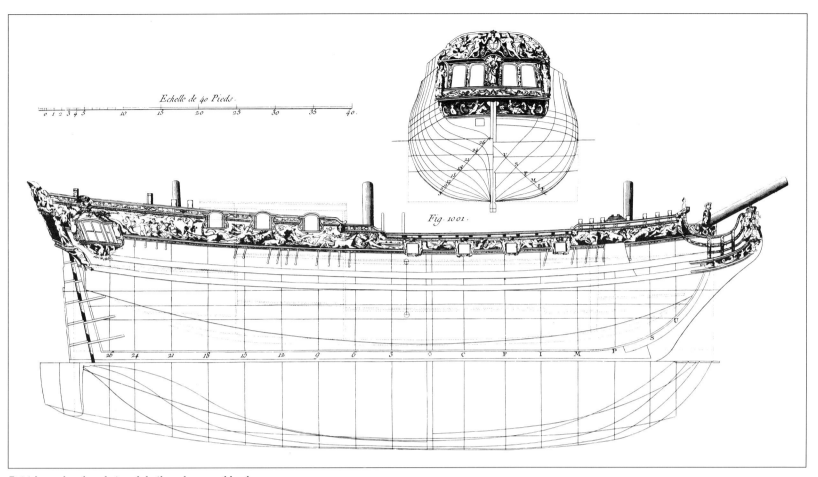

Echelle de 40 Pieds.

Fig. 1001.

British royal yachts, designed, built and operated by the navy, inevitably took on some of the characteristics of small warships. The Royal Caroline *of 1749 resembled a sloop of war in many respects but was far more comfortably fitted and elaborately decorated. Although later monarchs did not race their yachts with the passion of Charles II and James II, speed was still a desirable quality in these vessels, and the lines of this yacht formed the basis of a number of small warship designs in the 1750s. This engraving is from a French encyclopaedia but copied from Chapman's* Architectura Navalis Mercatoria *of 1768.*

encounter in the Netherlands.[7] It is called a *boeier* ('boyer' in English): a carvel-built, shallow-draught, round-bottomed vessel with a low day cabin amidships and an open cockpit aft. The boyer has become more or less *the* classical yacht of the Netherlands. One of the finest ever built in the Amsterdam naval dockyard found its way to Russia when it was presented to Czar Alexander I by King William of the Netherlands in 1815.

Not all 'classical' Netherlands yachts were sailing craft: one also occasionally encounters oared pleasure craft. The horse-drawn yacht (sometimes called a 'glass shallop'[8]) can be regarded as the aristocratic version of the horse-drawn passenger barges which from the seventeenth century until well into the 1800s

were an efficient and reliable element in the Netherlands transportation system.[9] The horse-drawn yachts seem to have been at the peak of their popularity during the eighteenth century when many members of the upper strata of society owned country houses on rivers like the Amstel and the Vecht. The Amsterdam Scheepvaartmuseum owns a horse-drawn yacht from the second half of the eighteenth century and an oared yacht of somewhat later date (early nineteenth century?).

The yachts of King Charles II

In 1660 Charles II, who had just been proclaimed King of England, made a kind of progress from Breda to Delft. The royal party travelled in a fleet of yachts and on this occasion the king expressed the wish to have one built for himself. When this was discovered by his Netherlands hosts they decided to give him two yachts.[10] One of them was the *Mary*, a typical official yacht; the other was the *Bezan*, a boyer-like vessel.[11] Shortly after his restoration to the throne the king had a similar vessel to the *Mary* (although without leeboards[12]), built at Deptford, called the *Katherine*. Apparently the races between the *Katherine* and the *Ann*, built to a similar design at Woolwich for his

7. The Provincial Government of Friesland owns the *Friso*, a *boeier* built in 1894 as the private yacht of the then Queen's Commissionner (governor), as its official yacht. See Rienk Wegener Sleeswyk and Arend Jan Wijnsma, *De boeier Friso, Fries Statenjacht 1894-1954-1994* (Leeuwarden 1994).

8. On account of the conspicuous range of windows in the deckhouse or day cabin. The Amsterdam Scheepvaartmuseum holds a good model (No 154 in its 1943 catalogue).

9. An authoritative study is Jan de Vries, 'Barges and Capitalism', *Passenger Transportation in the Dutch Economy, 1632-1839* (Utrecht 1981).

10. The larger one, the *Mary*, was a present from the municipality of Amsterdam (not, as John Evelyn writes, from the Netherlands East India Company). There appears to be no conclusive evidence regarding the donor of the smaller vessel in printed sources.

11. 'Bezan' is derived from the Dutch word *bezaan* which means 'miz(z)en' or 'spanker'. That the King was given two yachts may have something to do with the custom (which was not unusual in the Netherlands) of one owner maintaining two yachts, one for really narrow waterways and one for rivers and coastal waters. In an account of the funeral of a general of cavalry in 1749, his mortal remains were carried from Leyden, in the neighbourhood of which city he had died, to Rotterdam in the 'inland yacht' and thence to his ancestral domains in the 'large yacht' (presumably both ships belonged to the Council of State which played an important role in the conduct of army affairs).

12. Leeboards are at their most useful in sailing very shallow waters as are to be found in many places in the Netherlands. For an enlightening discussion of the use of leeboards one should consult Vandermissen, *Holland and the Origins of Yachting*, pp20-21.

A lively painting by Andries van Eertvelt (1590-1652) showing a variety of Dutch pleasure craft enjoying a regatta. Yacht clubs may have been a development of the eighteenth century, but yacht races were clearly of greater antiquity, although it is not certain that these were truly competitive affairs. (National Maritime Museum)

brother the Duke of York, inaugurated the sport of yacht racing not only in England but in the entire world.

The *Mary* was the first in a long line of English royal yachts; between 1661 and 1663 no less than five were built and Charles II appears to have owned a total of twenty yachts altogether. It is interesting to note that the first English royal yachts tended to look very much like Netherlands official yachts–witness Willem van de Velde the Elder's drawing of Prince William, later King William III, and his bride crossing the North Sea in 1677. Later on, during the eighteenth and nineteenth centuries, until the advent of steam yachts, they tended to look more like miniature warships, usually ship rigged and no longer fitted with just one mast and a 'half-spreet'.[13]

An exception among English royal yachts was the *Royal Transport*, built during the Nine Years' War at Chatham. A very fast ship with what has been called an early form of schooner rig, she was specifically built to carry the king swiftly and in safety to the Netherlands and back. This vessel was given to Czar Peter in 1698 and no replacement was built, which gives rise to some questions about its utility.[14]

Perhaps it was in conscious imitation of the King of England that Frederick I, 'King in Prussia',[15] had himself a yacht built in the Netherlands in the early eighteenth century. It was most luxuriously fitted and armed with 22 bronze guns. Frederick's successor, an austere 'soldier-king', did not at all approve of the luxurious tastes of his father, and gave this vessel to Peter the Great, who must have appreciated the gift. Another German prince who had a yacht built in the Netherlands was the Elector Palatine John William. The beautiful model of this vessel in the Amsterdam Scheepvaartmuseum shows that it looked like a Netherlands official yacht with one mast. In this respect it was similar to the Prussian royal yacht.

The first yacht clubs

In England at least, yachting began as a veritable 'sport of kings', but in time it also became popular among the aristocracy. A sign of this is the foundation of yacht clubs, the oldest of which is held to be the Cork Water Club of 1720, nowadays the Royal Cork Yacht Club. Apparently this was intended only to bring together those who wanted to pass part of their leisure time afloat and to organise an annual aquatic procession–it is tempting to see this as yachting in the old Netherlands fashion, without any idea of competition. A historian of yachting, Ernle Bradford writes 'the club seems to have been social rather than designed for promoting competition among its members',[16] and there is certainly no record of its having organised sailing races during the firsts decades of its existence.

The 'first recorded race for a silver cup' seems to have been held from Greenwich to the

13. This expression is used by G P B Naish in his *Royal Yachts* (London 1964), caption to plate 1. It is more often referred to as 'standing gaff rig'.

14. Was it perhaps, although very fast, for another reason or reasons not so much of a success? Was it perhaps not replaced because William's great passion was definitely not yachting, but the chase? This vessel is extensively discussed in the *Line of Battle* volume of this series.

15. The Holy Roman Emperor did not dare to allow him to call himself King 'of' Prussia for fear of offending Poland which still exercised sovereignty over western Prussia.

16. Ernle Bradford, *Three Centuries of Sailing*, p36.

Nore and back in 1749. It was also on the Thames that in 1775 the 'Cumberland Fleet', the present Royal Thames Yacht Club, was founded. It was followed in 1815 by a club of owners of sailing yachts of no less than 10 tons with its headquarters at Cowes, Isle of Wight. This organisation, which earned for itself the sobriquet of 'the most exclusive club in the world', was granted the right to fly the White Ensign in 1829 and in 1833 it was renamed the Royal Yacht Squadron. Not long afterwards the devotees of what was still a rather exclusive pastime started to form the first yacht clubs outside Britain: in 1830 the Kungliga Svensk Segel Sällskapet was founded, in 1844 the New York Yacht Club, one year later the Koninklijke Nederlandsche Yacht Club,[17] in 1847 the Royal Yacht Club d'Ostende, and in 1853 the Société des Régates Parisiennes.

The period in the history of yachting covered in this book can be said to have ended in 1851, with the arrival of the famous schooner *America* in England. During its last

In Britain yachting began as the sport of kings, but then developed an aristocratic following. The first yachts were large and ship-like craft that only the very wealthy could afford, but in the late eighteenth century more democratic yacht clubs sprang up. This painting by William Havell shows a race between gaff cutters of the Cumberland Society, established in 1775 and the direct ancestor of the Royal Thames Yacht Club. While not cheap, such craft were well within the resources of Britain's rising middle class. (National Maritime Museum)

half-century there occurred nothing less than a revolution in yacht design, spurred on by 'love of competition'.[18] About 1778 a painting of the 'Cumberland Fleet' by Kitchingman shows most of the yachts as broad-beamed, round-bottomed, shallow-draught, comfortable-looking ships, one or two even sporting leeboards.[19] Most pictures and models of early nineteenth-century yachts show narrow, deep-draught vessels carrying an almost excessive acreage of sail.

Besides those schooners, cutters and the like, there were also yachts which looked like, and in fact were built like, men-of-war. In fact after the Napoleonic Wars there prevailed for a time a curious relationship between the upper stratum of the yachting world and the British navy. A number of aristocratic yachtsmen showed keen interest in naval affairs and even developed the ambition to build ships that surpassed the achievements of the established naval constructors employed by the Admiralty. For a time they exercised great influence on shipbuilding practice in the Royal Navy. It was after all mainly through the influence of such noble yachtsmen as the Honourable George Vernon and the Duke of Portland that Captain Sir William Symonds was 'launched' as Surveyor of the Navy, an appointment he filled in such a way as to earn the reputation of having been perhaps the most controversial member of any nineteenth-century naval administration.[20]

Another of these aristocratic sailors was the

Earl of Belfast, Vice-Commodore of the Royal Yacht Squadron, to whose order in 1831 the 10-gun brig *Waterwitch* was built by Samuel White of Cowes. Lord Belfast had laid a 1000-guinea bet that he could design (or have designed) a vessel of this type that could out-sail any ship of similar size in the naval service – and did his best to prove that point. To quote Ernle Bradford again, 'He would sail idly to-and-fro outside Portsmouth Harbour, waiting until some ships of the Fleet came out. He would then proceed to outsail them in a very ostentatious manner, shortening sail, for instance, yet still maintaining or even increasing his lead over the naval vessels. Their Lordships finally took the lesson to heart and bought the *Waterwitch* so as to copy her lines'.[21]

Dr Philip Bosscher

17. The spelling of the word 'yacht' shows that in the Netherlands it had apparently been all but forgotten that modern yachting had more or less been born there.

18. Ernle Bradford, *Three Centuries of Sailing*, p25.

19. However, at least one of the yachts sporting leeboards – judging from the flags she is flying – looks like a visitor from the opposite shore of the North Sea.

20. This extraordinary, and most controversial, personality is mentioned in many books on nineteenth-century British naval administration. See for a typical reference N A M Rodger, *The Admiralty* (Lavenham 1979), pp101-102. Symonds and his achievements are extensively treated in Andrew Lambert, *The Last Sailing Battlefleet* (London 1991).

21. Ernle Bradford, *Three Centuries of Sailing*, p42.

Pleasure Craft: Typical Vessels 1650-1900

Name	Description	Built	Launched	Tonnage	Dimensions (Feet) (Metres)	Remarks
ROYAL ESCAPE	English smack rigged collier	Purchased by the King 1660	c1650	34	30.41[1] x 14.41 x 7.75 9.27 x 4.39 x 2.36	Ex-*Surprise* in which Prince Charles escaped after the battle of Worcester, 1651
MARY	Dutch yacht, single mast gaff rig	Amsterdam	1660	92	50.00[1] x 18.50 x 7.00 15.24 x 5.64 x 2.13	First English royal yacht; newly built for VOC but presented to Charles II in 1660
'STATENJACHT'	Dutch official yacht, single mast gaff rig	?Amsterdam	1678		62.00 x 18.00 x 6.68 17.55 x 5.09 x 1.89	Draught in the Scheepvaart Museum, signed 'Jacobus Storck 1678'
ELEPHANTEN	Danish snow rigged royal yacht	Copenhagen	1687		92.52 x 22.97 x 9.19 28.20 x 7.00 x 2.80	'Lystfregat' for King Christian V, designed by Englishman Francis Sheldon
DUBLIN	British ketch rigged official yacht	Deptford	1709	148	73.16 x 21.63 x 9.50 22.30 x 6.59 x 2.90	For the Viceroy of Ireland; rerigged as a ship in 1732
MAX EMANUEL	Flemish state yacht, Dutch style gaff rig	Antwerp	1711		89.50 x 20.00 25.67 x 5.74	Built for Maximilian Emanuel of Bavaria when governor of the Spanish Netherlands
SERAFIMS-ORDEN	Swedish royal galley	Stockholm	1719	235	137.00[2] x 20.50 x 7.40[3] 40.69 x 6.09 x 2.20	22-bank galley for King Adolf Fredrik; rebuilt 1769-72
BUCINTORO	Venetian state barge; 42 oars	Venice	1727		115.49 x 24.61 35.20 x 7.50	Last example of the Doge's ceremonial vessel; laid up and abandoned in 1796
'KOPJACHT'	Dutch *boeier* type private yacht	Amsterdam	1752		55.00[2] x 17.50 x 7.00 15.70 x 4.90 x 2.00	Early draught of a yacht preserved at the Scheepvaart Museum, Amsterdam
WASAORDEN	Swedish royal barge	Stockholm	1775	106cu ft	58.66 x 10.17 x 3.90[3] 17.88 x 3.10 x 1.19	Chapman design; original destroyed by fire in 1921 and a replica built in 1923
ESPLENDIAN	Swedish yacht, single-masted rig	Karlskrona	1782	85	56.00[2] x 19.30 x 6.00 16.63 x 5.73 x 1.78	Chapman design for Prince Carl; sister ship of King Gustav III's *Amadis*
DENMARK	Ship rigged yacht for Danish Prince	Deptford	1785	218	89.41 x 23.50 x 10.00 27.25 x 7.16 x 3.05	Gift to the Prince Royal of Denmark
ROYAL SOVEREIGN	British royal yacht, ship rigged	Deptford	1804	278	96.00 x 25.66 x 10.50 29.26 x 7.82 x 3.20	The principal yacht of the British royal family until 1850
LE CANOT IMPÉRIAL	French imperial barge	Antwerp	1811		56.46 x 10.99 x 3.18 17.21 x 3.35 x 0.97	26-oared barge designed by Guillemare for Napoleon I
CLEOPATRA'S BARGE	American brigantine yacht	Salem, Mass	1816	191		First large American yacht; belonged to George Crowinshield, Jr
ROYAL SHALLOP	Dutch royal barge	Rotterdam	1818		55.94 x 8.73 17.05 x 2.66	Surviving example kept at Scheepvaart Museum, Amsterdam; belongs to RNethN
FALCON	British ship rigged private yacht	Fishbourne, Isle of Wight	1824	351	110.00 x 26.33 33.53 x 8.03	Built for Earl of Yarborough, Commodore of the Royal Yacht Squadron
PANTALOON	British brig rigged private yacht	Troon, Scotland	1831	323	90.00 x 29.38 x 12.66 27.43 x 8.96 x 3.86	William Symonds design for Duke of Portland; purchased by Navy in Dec 1831
GIMCRACK	American schooner yacht	Williamsburg, New York	1844		51.00 x 13.50 x 7.50[3] 15.54 x 4.11 x 2.29	George Steers design; NY Yacht Club founded on board in July 1844
FRISO	Dutch *boeier* yacht	Joure	1894		34.61 x 12.20 x 2.79[3] 10.55 x 3.72 x 0.85	'Statenjacht' of the Friesland Provincial Government

Notes:
1. Keel length
2. Unit is local foot which can be converted from the metric equivalent
3. Draught

7

Shipping Economics and Trade

IN HIS DIARY for February 1664 Samuel Pepys records a conversation with a coffee-house acquaintance called Captain Cocke, a hemp contractor, who surprised him with the assertion that 'the trade of the world is too little for us two'–meaning England and the

A bird's-eye view of Amsterdam in 1538 at the beginning of its rise to eminence as a centre of trade. The intimate connection between the city and the water is very clear. The painting is by or after Cornelis Anthoniszoon. (Amsterdam Historical Museum)

Netherlands–'therefore one must down'.[1] From a twentieth-century vantage point the remark has a certain prophetic accuracy, since during the 1650-1830 period covered by this volume the Netherlands declined as a trading nation, whereas England (and after the Act of Union in 1707, Great Britain) acquired a place of almost unrivalled pre-eminence in world commerce. On the other hand, Captain Cocke, with his mercantilist viewpoint, could not fore-see that in the ensuing centuries the volume of

international trade would increase to such an extent as to invalidate his proposition that there could not be enough to support two great economies.

This volume is about ships, but specifically merchant vessels, which would have no *raison d'être* were it not for the economic activities that called them into existence. Therefore, a

1. H B Wheatly (ed), *The Diary of Samuel Pepys*, Vol IV (London 1928), p31.

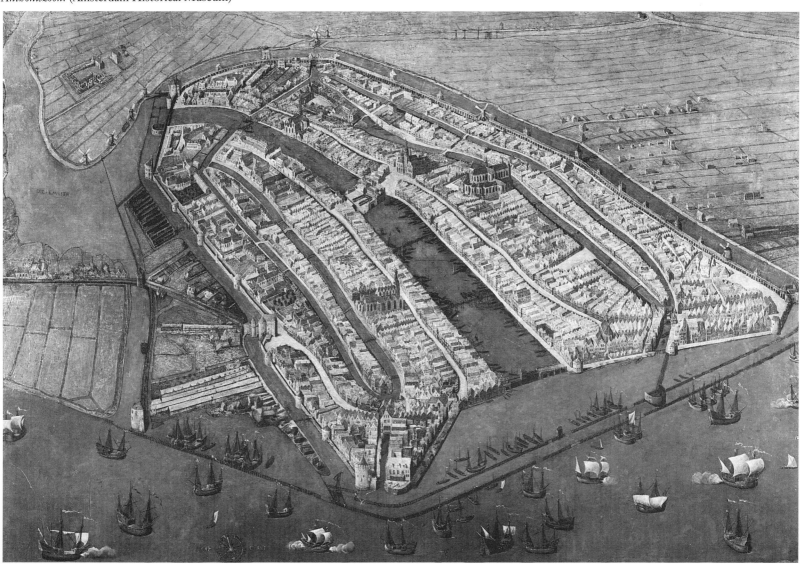

A painting by Andries van Eertvelt (1590-1652) showing Dutch ships loading timber in a northern, probably Norwegian, port. The timber trade was an early staple of Dutch trade: the ships pre-date the flute, having flat transoms and large stern loading ports. (National Maritime Museum)

chapter outlining the economic background is entirely appropriate: this one looks at the shipping industry of the Netherlands and charts the gradual shift of power to Great Britain. It is not that other countries are unimportant, but the emphasis may be justified by an observation of Professor Cipolla: 'If in the age of Leonardo . . . a European could have foreseen the Industrial Revolution, almost certainly he would have placed it in Italy. At the end of the seventeenth century it was obvious that every further economic development of any scale was only possible in the countries bordering the North Sea.'[2]

The Golden Age of the Netherlands

It is generally accepted that towards the middle of the seventeenth century the Netherlands reached the peak of their position as a world power. They had just victoriously concluded their long War of Independence (1568-1648). During the later decades of this Eighty Years' War, from about 1600 onwards, their rulers, the Stadtholders and the States-General,[3] had succeeded in keeping the soil of their 'heartland' (the so-called 'maritime provinces' of

Zeeland, Holland, Friesland and Groningen[4]) virtually free from warlike operations. This was of the utmost relevance to the economic situation, especially in view of the turbulence prevalent at the time in other regions of western Europe.[5] During the same war the country had experienced what can be termed without exaggeration an industrial revolution, which originated on its own soil. This was characterised, *inter alia*, by momentous developments in the field of shipbuilding (exemplified by the introduction of the *flute*[6]) and by innovations in the art of the millwright.[7] Futhermore, there were striking similarities between what occurred in the seventeenth century Netherlands and what is usually called *the* Industrial Revolution, such as the high degree of urbanisation and the 'export' of technical and managerial skill.[8]

In 1604 the Vereenigde Oostindische Compagnie (VOC) was founded, arguably the first joint-stock company in the world[9] and by 1650 it was well on its way to acquiring an extensive trading empire in Asia. During the fist half of the seventeenth century the merchant navy of the Netherlands was the largest in the world. Thanks to the fact that in 1636 a new system of duties to be imposed on shipping was under discussion, a reliable estimate of its strength in that year survives: some 1750 vessels, not counting those in the fleets of the VOC and the West Indies Company. To this should be added about 600 seagoing fishing vessels. The total seafaring

2. C M Cipolla, *The Fontana Economic History of Europe*, Vol II, (London1971), p13.

3. The Stadtholders were originally provincial governors on behalf of the Crown. When the estates of the 'rebellious' provinces concluded the Union of Utrecht in 1579 and repudiated King Philip II as sovereign in 1581 the office of Stadtholder was retained. The Stadtholder became the chief servant of the provincial estates who collectively executed sovereignty. Stadtholder was a 'provincial' office but in practice after the first decades of the Eighty Years' War there were never more than two Stadtholders for the total of seven Provinces which together formed the Netherlands Republic. The Stadtholder of Holland was *ex officio* Commander-in-Chief of the Republic's army and navy. The States-General was an assembly of representatives of all the Provinces who permanently met at The Hague to discuss matters of common interest and, for instance in the conduct of foreign affairs, collectively exercised sovereignty.

4. These are listed here from south to north. Holland was only divided into two provinces, North and South Holland, in 1840.

5. Cf. H Kamen, *The Iron Century, Social Change in Europe 1550-1660* (London 1976), especially Part IV.

6. See, in this series, *Cogs, Caravels and Galleons*, pp115-130.

7. Important developments were the construction of the first sawmill, the adoption of the achimedian screw as a device to transport water to a higher level, and the invention of various types of 'industrial windmills', *eg* for fulling cloth and hulling rice.

8. See Ph M Bosscher, 'The Industrial Revolution in the Northern Netherlands', *Transactions of the Second International Congress on the Conservation of Industrial Monuments* (Bochum 1978), pp216-222.

9. This is the opinion of the leading authority in this particular field of research, the late Professor E J J van der Heijden. See also F S Gaastra, *De geschiedenis van de VOC* (Zutphen 1991), p23. Gaastra's book is the best modern concise history of the Netherlands East India Company.

population at the same time can be estimated at about 50,000.[10]

Amsterdam could be considered the most important commercial centre of the Western World. It was not only the foremost focal point in the shipping industry, but also the centre of many related activities, like map production, to give just one example.[11]

All this makes it understandable that the seventeenth century is often referred to as the Golden Age of the Netherlands.[12] As in so many like instances, the achievement is partly due to circumstances beyond the control of the population, although it should be borne in mind that the phenomena and developments mentioned above occurred in and around a society where the mental outlook was characterisd by keen business acumen and an almost passionate interest in the 'real world'.[13]

Carriers and merchants

One of the features of a country on which its inhabitants can have no control whatsoever is of course its geographical situation. Charles Wilson is prominent among the many authors who have pointed out how important this feature has been in the economic development of the Netherlands. (Henceforth, 'the Netherlands' denotes the area covered by the Republic of the United Netherlands as it came into being during the Eighty Years' War.)[14] In his classic study of the economic background of the Anglo-Dutch wars he stresses that the Netherlands lay astride the estuaries of the Scheldt, Maas (Meuse) and Rhine which connected them with 'the great hinterland' of Germany and that they looked westward towards England and the North Atlantic. 'More immediately significant' than the proximity of the British Isles and the Atlantic, according to Wilson, is their situation 'midway between the great corn areas of the Baltic and the markets of southern Europe.[15]

Indeed, as early as the end of the fifteenth century vessels from the Netherlands, from the Province of Holland in particular, constituted the vast majority of the shipping plying between western Europe and the Baltic: around 1500 some 70 per cent of the ships paying

Sound dues hailed from the Netherlands.[16] From the Baltic region they mainly transported bulk cargoes of relatively low value like grain, timber, pitch, and other 'naval stores'. Originally on the outward voyage they mainly carried salt, herring and wine; they also appear to have frequently sailed northwards in ballast. Towards the end of the sixteenth century there was a significant change: the volume of luxury goods from southern Europe and even further afield carried to the Baltic in Dutch ships increased dramatically. This was a consequence of the fact that Dutch merchants–as distinct from Dutch carriers or shipmasters–had become much more important as participants in this particular form of trade.

This development was to a large extent the result of the fall of Antwerp in 1585. In that year the great entrepôt on the Scheldt, which so far, to quote Jonathan Israel, had been 'a centre of world trade, bolstered by the industrial activities of Flanders and the shipping of Holland and Zeeland',[17] surrendered to the Duke of Parma, King Philip II's Governor of the Low Countries. Thereafter, and until the end of the eighteenth century, the lower reaches of the Scheldt were closed to all seagoing ships. Many people, and not only Protestants,[18] left the city, and their peregrinations often ended in Amsterdam and other trading centres of the 'Rebellious Provinces'. The arrival of these people, comprising a large portion of the Antwerp commercial elite, people prepared to invest large sums in seaborne trade and take the risks involved, greatly stimulated the economic growth of the country. New avenues of trade were opened,

and existing ones broadened, like the Baltic trade in luxury goods previously mentioned. The sudden growth of this trade was perhaps the most crucial factor in the process which made the Netherlands' trade with the Baltic countries the long-standing mainstay of Dutch commercial prosperity. Carriers had become, and remained, merchants–and to such an extent that the Netherlands Baltic trade was often dubbed the *moedernegotie* ('mother trade').[19]

The export of herring referred to above was

10. See J Lucassen, in *Maritieme Geschiedenis der Nederlanden*, Vol II (Bussum 1977), p132.

11. The Amsterdam firm of Blaeu about the middle of the seventeenth century produced perhaps the finest printed maps and atlases that could be procured anywhere.

12. It is not known when this expression was first used. The author's guess is during the nineteenth century.

13 J H Plumb in his introduction to C R Boxer, *The Dutch Seaborne Empire, 1600-1800* (London 1965), pXXIII.

14. The official name of the country today is 'Kingdom of the Netherlands', the matching adjective is 'Netherlands'. Many people who live outside the provinces of North and South Holland object to the use of the word 'Holland' to indicate the entire country.

15. C Wilson, *Profit and Power: a study of England and the Dutch Wars* (The Hague 1978), p2.

16. H P H Jansen, in *Maritieme Geschiedenis der Nederlanden*, Vol I (Bussum 1976), p264.

17. J Israel, *Nederland als centrum van de wereldhandel* (Franeker 1991), p28. Quotes are 'translated back' from the Netherlands version of the authoritative book by Jonathan Israel, *Dutch Primacy in World Trade, 1585-1740* (Oxford 1989).

18. We know that many Catholics went north because they expected better business conditions there.

19. Israel, *Nederland als centrum van de wereldhandel*, p40.

The herring fisheries constituted one of the mainstays of Netherlands maritime prosperity from the Middle Ages to the eighteenth century. This grisaille by Adrien van Salm depicts the herring busses themselves engaged in fishing, plus an escorting warship (centre distance). The vessel in the right foreground is probably a jager, *a buss employed to bring home the early catches.* (National Maritime Museum)

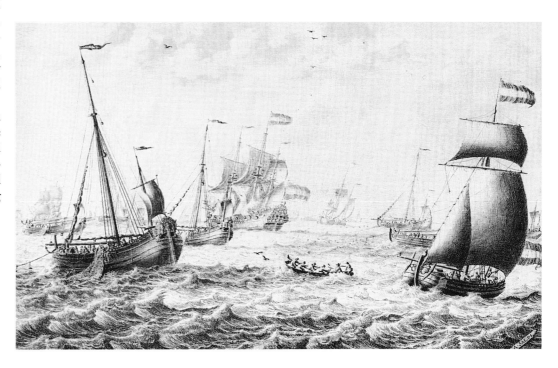

The town of Hoorn painted in 1634, at that time an important harbour on the western side of the Zuyderzee. Since the large ship in the centre is the Eenhoorn (Unicorn), *and the unicorn was the civic crest of the town, this painting by Bonaventura Peeters is probably meant to symbolise the importance of the place. It was the birthplace of Coen and the seat of one Chamber of the VOC.* (National Maritime Museum)

a reversal of the situation pertaining in earlier times. The growth of the Netherlands fisheries in the late Middle Ages and after was mainly due to what Charles Wilson deems 'a mysterious change in the habits of the Gulf Stream'[20] which made the herring shoals migrate from the Baltic to the North Sea and which occured in the early fifteenth century. This, of course, gave great impetus to the growth of the Netherlands fishing fleet, which, as already noted, had reached a strength of some 600 seagoing vessels by 1636. This included a number of whalers: in 1612 two ships from Amsterdam had inaugurated whaling in the Arctic under the Netherlands flag. They were comparatively late-comers in an activity where there was keen international competition. For that reason by 1614 Dutch shipowners engaged in whaling had rapidly formed an association which was called the Noordsche Compagnie ('Northern Company'). This, however, 'silently came to an end' in 1642, although it had not been unsuccessful.[21]

There was already a brisk seaborne traffic

between the Netherlands and the European countries on the eastern Atlantic seaboard by the late Middle Ages, salt and wine being the most important commodities carried northwards. In the 1580s and 1590s Dutch merchantmen began to penetrate into the Mediterranean. The inception of the *Straatvaart* (navigation through the Straits of Gibraltar) on a grand scale is usually put around 1590 when skippers from Hoorn, then a flourishing port on the western shore of the Zuyderzee, started to carry grain to Italy, which had been afflicted by a succession of crop failures. In 1611 the States-General sent an *orateur* (Envoy) to Constantinople, a sure sign that the mercantile community in the Netherlands had become genuinely interested in the possibilities of commercial intercourse with the Ottoman Empire. Smyrna (modern Izmir) soon became the centre of Dutch commercial activity in Turkey. During its long existence the Netherlands colony there experienced periods of great prosperity interspersed with times of real depression. Trade relations between the Netherlands and the Ottoman Empire naturally acquired certain characteristics of their own on account of the extraordinary conditions in the last-named state: a central government which refrained from cultivating diplomatic relations in a manner that had become customary among European States; dependencies like Tripoli, Algiers and

Tunis, over which the Sublime Porte (the central government in Istanbul) had virtually no control. This situation was not without its impact on trade relations because the Barbary States mentioned often indulged in what they professed to regard as warlike operations against the enemies of Islam, but their victims regarded as piracy.[22]

It goes without saying that during the Eighty Years' War commercial relations between the Netherlands and the Iberian Peninsula were also affected by the state of war with Spain which prevailed for the whole period, except the Twelve Years' Truce (1609-1621). Furthermore, in 1580 Portugal accepted Philip II as king and so, in a manner of speaking, became a participant in the war. The Madrid government repeatedly ordered the seizure of Netherlands ships in the harbours under its control, sometimes because it wanted the vessels in question for its own purposes, but mainly because it wanted to damage Dutch economic interests.[23] However, these measures

20. Wilson, *Profit and Power*, p2.

21. See C de Jong, in *Maritieme Geschiedenis der Nederlanden*, Vol II, p312.

22. As is well known these depredations only came to an end in the nineteenth century.

23. Very often these seizures were clearly intended to enforce an embargo, intended to eliminate Netherlands ships from trade with the Spanish Empire.

never achieved the aim of putting an end to commercial intercourse between the Netherlands and the Iberian kingdoms. Perhaps the main reason was that both economies were in a way complementary to each other and that trade with the Iberian Peninsula provided the Netherlands with part of the indispensable 'sinews of war'. Hence the link was never completely broken, subterfuges like fake neutral ship's papers proving of much use.[24]

The Madrid government also failed to keep Netherlands ships and traders out of what could be loosely termed the Iberian overseas sphere of influence. In 1590 a skipper from the Zuyderzee town of Medemblik, on his way to Brazil, was forced by storm damage to call at the island of Principe off the coast of West Africa. There he was taken prisoner by the Portuguese. During a two-year captivity he managed to collect much information about

A painting by Reinier Nooms ('Zeeman') showing Dutch shipping off Tripoli in the mid seventeenth century. Like all of the Barbary Powers, Tripoli was often a thorn in the flesh of Dutch traders in the Mediterranean, requiring merchant ships to be well armed for self-defence, and often convoyed by warships like the two-decker in the left foreground. At various times in the century the Netherlands exerted military, diplomatic or economic pressure on these states, but with no lasting effect. (National Maritime Museum)

that part of the world hitherto known to no Europeans except the Portuguese. He put this knowledge to good use during a voyage to the Gold Coast in 1593 which yielded a handsome profit. Other profitable expeditions soon followed: between 1592 and 1607 more than 200 Dutch ships made one or more voyages to the west coast of Africa. In 1599 a Netherlands ship appeared for the first time on the Venezuelan coast to load salt; thereafter this trade developed rapidly. Within a few years the Spanish authorities came to regard it as a real menace and in 1605 they went to the trouble of mounting a major expedition against this particular breed of intruders, who mainly hailed from ports on the western shore of the Zuyderzee. In later years the East India and West India Companies became the main intruments of penetration into the Iberian colonial sphere (see next section).

The first commercial contacts between the Netherlands and Norway can be traced to the early Middle Ages.[25] In the sixteenth and seventeenth centuries timber and stockfish (dried cod [26]) were the commodities most sought after by Dutch traders. Towards the end of the sixteenth century Netherlands ships ventured further north for two reasons. People had become interested in a north-about route to Asia – hence three expeditions to the arctic in

the years 1594-1597 which got as far as Novaya Zemlya.[27] In 1581 a Swedish force took Narva and so cut off Muscovy from the Baltic; thereafter the Czars attempted to divert the trade between their domains and western Europe through Arkhangelsk on the White Sea. Originally this was mainly to the advantage of the English Muscovy Company, but it appears that Dutch traders who had intermittent commerce with Lapp tribes first became aware of the new opportunities Arkhangelsk offered. At first they very much played second fiddle to the English, but by about 1610 they had aquired a dominant position in the Muscovy trade.

If the pattern of seventeenth-century Netherlands trade is regarded as a wheel, preceeding sections have looked at most of its spokes: the hub was the Netherlands, or Amsterdam, *stapelmarkt*. This expression is not easy to translate. Sometimes the term 'staple market' is used, for instance by Kristof

24. See J R Bruijn, in *Maritieme Geschiedenis der Nederlanden*, Vol II, p232.

25. See Gwyn Jones, *A History of the Vikings* (London 1973), p82.

26. Even today dried cod in Italy is called *stocco-fisso*.

27. The last expedition, led by Jacob van Heemskerck and Willem Barentsz, became famous because of the successful wintering of its participants on 'Nova Zembla'.

The Russian port of Arkhangelsk on the White Sea, painted by Bonaventura Peeters in 1644. Dutch trade with Muscovy via the port began towards the end of the sixteenth century. The rather primitive facilities are readily apparent. (National Maritime Museum)

Glamann,[28] but 'entrepôt market' is probably more accurate because its most important characteristic was that the commodities traded in their great majority were physically channeled through the centre of the market, *ie* through Amsterdam or other Dutch commercial centres. Violet Barbour has pointed out that in its time this entrepôt market offered a unique array of services: 'expert knowledge of market conditions the world over, skill in appraisal and classification of merchandise, informed brokerage, commission and wholesale services, credit, insurance and exchange facilities'.[29] Two institutions more or less constituted the core of its infrastrucure: the *Beurs* (Bourse), which began to function in Amsterdam in the 1580s and for which in 1608 the building of spacious new premises was started, and the Amsterdam *Wisselbank* (exchange bank) which was founded in 1609.[30] Layout and organisation of the (1608) Bourse were to a large extent modelled on those of the London Royal Exchange.[31] The Exchange Bank was inspired by another institution already established elsewhere, the Banco di Giro in Venice. However, both improved on their predecessors and set new standards as regards efficiency and reliability. The Amsterdam Bourse soon became a unique instrument for the regulation of commodity prices. Regarding the Exchange Bank, Violet Barbour believes it was 'the first and long the greatest public bank in northern Europe. Confidence in its stability and integrity was a strong attraction to capital both Dutch and foreign'.[32] In fact, the existence of the Exchange Bank was one of the factors which ensured that Amsterdam maintained its position as a financial centre of the first rank long after the decline of the city as a centre of the shipping industry.

The mercantile community of the *stapelmarkt* gradually came to develop a remarkable degree of specialisation. There were merchants who concentrated on trade with certain specific countries or regions, but the nature of the market produced another category of unique

The courtyard of the Amsterdam Beurs *or* Exchange, *built in 1611 to the design of Hendrick de Keyer. As a centre for the regulation of commodity prices, it became a major contributor to the trading success of the Netherlands. Painting by Job Berckheyde. (Amsterdam Historical Museum)*

importance. These merchants were often collectively called the 'second hand'. They usually did not specialise as regards area or country, but in one commodity or category of commodities. They bought goods from importers, stored, sorted and processed these, and sold them to retailers and exporters. To be able to provide this indispensable service they needed storage space and so became the main initiators of the construction of the many seventeenth and eighteenth century warehouses that still constitute an important part of the architectural glory of the old Dutch trading centres.[33]

The VOC, the Dutch East India Company

In April 1595 four ships, equipped in Amsterdam, left the Texel with Asia as their final destination. More than two years later

three of them returned, with 87 men on board, about a quarter of their original complement. The financial return of this 'First Voyage' is thought to have been mediocre, but several subsequent expeditions fared much better. Up to 1602 a total of 65 ships was sent out, equipped in several harbours of Holland and Zeeland by

28. Author of a deservedly famous book on *Dutch Asiatic Trade 1620-1740* (rev ed, The Hague 1980).

29. Violet Barbour, *Capitalism in Amsterdam in the 17th Century* (Ann Arbor 1963), p21.

30. Barbour, *Capitalism in Amsterdam*, p17.

31. See Israel, *Nederland als centrum*, p91.

32. Barbour, *Capitalism in Amsterdam*, p43.

33. Significantly, they constitute the first category of 'industrial monuments' the architecture of which has become a subject of systematic study. See M Révész-Alexander, *Die alten Lagerhäuser Amsterdams* (2nd ed, The Hague 1954).

The return of the second Netherlands expedition to the East Indies in May 1599. This voyage, commanded by Jacob van Neck, was much more successful than the first, and as such warranted celebration by the artist Andries van Eertvelt in this painting. The ships are the Hollandia, Mauritius, Amsterdam *and* Duyfen. (National Maritime Museum)

associations of merchants who were often in fierce competition with each other. This was damaging to the new Netherlands-Asiatic trade, and the price of Asiatic commodities, especially spices, began to fall in the markets of Europe. It was mainly for this reason that the Grand Pensionary (an office which shows a striking similarity to that of present-day Prime Minister[34]) Oldenbarnevelt brought all the existing associations of Netherlands East India merchants (the so-called *vóórcompagnieën* or 'pre-companies') together into one organisation, the *Vereenigde Oostindische Compagnie*, or VOC. The charter of this new organisation granted a monopoly of navigation east of the Cape of Good Hope and through the Strait of Magellan (Cape Horn being as yet undiscovered[35]). It was granted the right to appoint governors, raise armies, build fortresses and conclude treaties with foreign potentates.

The first charter contained a provision that shareholders were to invest their money for a period of ten years. However, the monopoly was initially granted for twenty-one years and in 1612 the company's *Bewindhebbers* (directors) did not comply with the provision that the initial investors would be reimbursed after ten years, if they so desired. They in fact created a situation in which the shares of the VOC could only be converted into cash by selling them on the stock-market. In this somewhat surreptitious way they generated a permanent capital stock, which was almost a necessity for them in view of the fact that they were engaged in operations that were intended to be of very long duration. Students of the early history of the VOC tend to consider the last-named development as a decisive step on the road towards the modern joint-stock company.

The VOC soon managed to acquire a foothold in Asia. In 1605 the fortress of Victoria on Amboina, one of the 'Spice Islands' (Moluccas) was taken from the Portuguese. In 1619 Governor-General Jan Pieterszoon Coen (perhaps the greatest figure in the early history of the VOC, a man notable for both his far-reaching ideas and his utter ruthlessness) founded Batavia on the site of the conquered Javanese settlement of Jakarta as a headquarters for all the activities of the VOC in Asia. It remained the capital of the Netherlands colonial empire in Asia until that came to an end in 1949, although from the 1730s its original centre was a most unhealthy place, a real 'white man's grave', and also the grave of countless Asiatic servants of the company. It is now understood that this was due to the digging of shallow salt-water fishponds which almost immediately became the breeding ground of a vicious species of malarial mosquito.[36]

The VOC in Asia initially developed on what may be called the Portuguese pattern. Trade being its chief concern, it acquired a number of factories: trading posts which were – if necessary and possible – fortified and garrisoned. In 1609 it possessed 'seven fortresses in the Spice Islands and a small number of factories'.[37] In the same year it obtained permission to establish a factory in the Japanese port of Hirado. By order of the Bakufu, the shogu-

34. In theory the holder of the office was just the legal adviser of the estate of nobility in the Province of Holland and its spokesman in the provincial assembly. In practice he soon became the head of the 'civil service' of the Republic – in so far that there was one – and, together with the Stadtholder(s), its chief political leader. Political institutions in the Republic are discussed in the newest book by Jonathan Israel, *The Dutch Republic: Its Rise, Greatness and Fall, 1477-1806* (Oxford 1995).

35. Cape Horn was discovered in the beginning of 1616 by Jacques Lemaire and Willem Janszoon Schouten. It was named after the birthplace of the latter, at that time an important trading centre on the Zuyderzee.

36. This was recently established by P H van der Brug, in *Malaria and malaise: De VOC in Batavia in de achttiende eeuw* (Amsterdam 1994).

37. J van Goor, *De Nederlandse Koloniën. Geschiedenis van de Nederlandse Expansie, 1600-1975*, (The Hague nd), p60.

nal government, this was transferred to Nagasaki, to the artificial island of De-jima to be exact, in 1641. From that year until after the middle of the nineteenth century 'Decima' remained the only spot where the Japanese government tolerated contact between its subjects and Europeans, and then only under the rigid rules imposed by the Bakufu.[38]

In 1617 it became possible, after many difficulties, to open a factory at Surat, on the west coast of India, terminal point of the two important routes to Gujarat and to Delhi and Agra. In 1621 problems with the supply of nutmeg led to the Banda Islands being conquered, depopulated and resettled (on this occasion Governor-General Coen most glaringly showed *les défauts de ses qualités*). About the same time a fortress was founded on the island of Taiyouan, off the coast of Formosa, the present Taiwan. From 1630 active exploitation of the coastal plains of Formosa began and soon the export of sugar and deerskins became quite profitable. However, in 1662 GuoXingje (or Coxinga, as he was called by his European opponents), a partisan of the deposed Ming dynasty, put an end to the Company's rule in this part of the world. Meanwhile the VOC had been successful in extending its sphere of influence elsewhere. Between 1638 and 1658 the Portuguese were expelled from the coastal areas of Ceylon (modern Sri Lanka), which was important in the production of cinnamon. In 1641 the port of Malacca, one of the focal points of trade within Asia, was taken from them. In 1652 Capetown was founded as 'an inn for travellers to and from the East Indies' where they could obtain 'refreshments of all

The first Netherlands factory on the Indian subcontinent was at Surat, seen here from the seaward side in a grisaille attributed to Ludolf Bakhuizen (1631-1708). (National Maritime Museum)

kinds'.[39] After the Portuguese had been expelled from Ceylon their factories of Tuticorin and Nagapattinam on the Coromandel coast were taken over, and in 1661-1663 Cranganur, Cochin and Cannanur on the Malabar coast followed. In 1666-1667 the southern part of Celebes, modern Sulawesi, was conquered, mainly to put an end to the smuggling of spices through the port of Macassar, the present Uyung Pandan. In 1684 Bantam, the Javanese harbour where the ships of the 'First Voyage' had called to buy pepper, was finally garrisoned, although its sultans remained nominally independent until the middle of the eighteenth century and their rule only came to an end in 1813. By the close of the seventeenth century the sultans of Cheribon, modern Cirebon in western Java, a land of great agricultural reward and promise, became vassals of the VOC.

In this way the VOC had not only acquired a string of factories but also large areas of territory subject to its rule, where it enjoyed—in fact, if not in theory[40]—sovereign rights. The company became interested in these areas because they yielded crops or minerals which were lucrative to trade in or because, in the case of southern Celebes for instance, their possession made it easier to enforce a monpoly it cherished. In the opinion of many, and especially those connected with the VOC organisation in the mother country, this state of affairs where the Company bore the 'white man's burden' (to use an anachronism) of ruling large areas was very much of a mixed blessing. As J H Parry puts it, 'The Company was ill-equipped for such responsibilities' because it was essentially a trading concern, a firm of shipowners. 'The *Heeren XVII* (the Directors in the Netherlands who made the final decisions) on the whole disliked territorial acquisitions, . . . ,

and were unwilling to support the expense of any but a commercial administration in governing them'.[41]

Their real objection was to the mounting costs of the Company's establishment in Asia, where in 1625 the VOC employed some 4500 people. This number had grown to 18,117 in 1700, and to 24,879 in 1753.[42] Especially in the later years a large proportion of the Company's servants consisted of soldiers, who did not contribute directly to the commercial results of the company.

It is safe to assume that many of the Company's servants in Asia, especially in the higher echelons, were of a different opinion. The situation in which 'the merchant had become king' offered them wonderful opportunities for enrichment. A case in point is that of G C Gockinga who in 1793 returned to his native city of Groningen having served for some years as Resident of Cheribon. About 1813 his personal income was estimated at between 40,000 and 50,000 guilders per annum and his stables contained six horses.[43]

Viewed purely as a trading organisation the VOC experienced a long period of conspicuous

38. See C R Boxer, *Jan Compagnie in Japan, 1600-1817* (The Hague 1936).

39. C R Boxer, *The Dutch Seaborne Empire, 1600-1800* (London 1965), p242. The original quote is from the eighteenth-century traveller and writer C P Thunberg.

40. In some cases the VOC exercised sovereign rights, whereas in theory it held the territory in question in fief. See Gaastra, *De geschiedenis van de VOC*, p62.

41. J H Parry, *Trade and Dominion. The European Oversea Empires in the Eighteenth Century* (London 1971), p76.

42. See Gaastra, *De geschiedenis van de VOC*, p81f.

43. We know this from the extensive study of the French (Napoleonic) tax registers for Groningen and district undertaken by the late Professer P J van Winter and published in 1951-1955.

In the Netherlands merchant marine, as in that of their English rivals, the East Indiaman was by far the largest type of vessel. In this Bakhuizen painting dated 1699 two retourschepen *are depicted, one afloat and one careened for graving (scraping and antifouling the underwater hull which before the introduction of copper sheathing was of major importance in reducing friction and protecting the hull). The dockyard is at Amsterdam.* (National Maritime Museum)

success. This was to a large extent due to its profitable operations in the 'country trade'–the commercial traffic within the various regions of Asia. The money earned here was instrumental in solving a problem which had plagued the VOC from its very inception. There was no significant market for goods of European origin in Asia. Therefore the Asiatic goods the VOC wanted to export to Europe largely had to be paid for either in money earned in the 'country trade' or in money supplied from Europe. The calculations of Dr F S Gaastra suggest that the VOC in the period 1640-1688 paid a total dividend of 67 millions to its shareholders. During the same years one fifth of the 'return cargoes' (the goods shipped from Asia to the Netherlands to be sold there on behalf of the VOC) were paid for out of the profits of the country trade. This fifth part had been sold by the Company for a total sum of 84 million. So the entire dividend had been financed out of the profits made in Asia.[44]

This explains why it was so detrimental to the results of the Company when the balance of the country trade took a turn for the worse towards the end of the seventeenth century. There were several reasons why it continuously showed a deficit from about 1690. In Japan the Bakufu took measures which tended to make trade with that country a much less profitable proposition and also reduced its volume: in 1668 it had already prohibited the export of silver, in 1685 it imposed restrictions on imports, and in 1696 it put an end to the export of gold. Stronger competition, notably from the English, was one of the causes of rising purchase prices. For the first decades after 1690 the losses in Asia could be offset by the profits made in Europe. Until the 1720s income (mainly from the sale of Asiatic goods) amply exceeded expenditure (the total cost of the VOC's operations in Asia and Europe). Nevertheless, in some years during that period a greater dividend was paid out than the results warranted, mainly to bolster the Company's credit,[45] and the practice later became quite common, if not actually 'standard'. When the VOC came to an end during the Napoleonic period its total liabilities had reached the staggering level of more than 128½ million guilders, whereas the total value of its assets was put at no more than 9⅓ million.[46]

According to J H Parry the VOC can be regarded as essentially a firm of shipowners,[47] but perhaps it is even better described as a shipping company, the largest of its time. In this connection during the seventeenth century there developed a significant difference between the VOC and its English rival. To quote the Indian scholar Dr Chaudhuri, 'The VOC were joint owners and builders of all its shipping throughout its life' (this is substantially, though not completely, true).[48] The English Company started on the same pattern, but after the middle of the seventeenth century it 'gradually shifted over to the policy of hiring ships for specific voyages'. The former Company yards at Deptford and Blackwall remained in operation, but with (syndicates of) private shipowners as their customers. Only in India did the British Company continue to have ships

44. See Gaastra, *De geschiedenis van de VOC*, p133.

45. Only recently an exact account of the financial vicissitudes of the VOC has become accessible to the general public. It is to be found in J P de Korte, *De Jaarlijkse Financiële Verantwoording in de Vereenigde Oostindische Compagnie* (Leiden 1984).

46. See De Korte, *De Jaarlijkse Financiële Verantwoording*. Regarding the assets it should be borne in the mind that from 1795 onwards most of the overseas possessions were taken by the British (see below).

47. See above and note 41.

48. Towards the end the VOC on several occasions hired ships. See I Dillo, *De nadagen van de Verenigde Oostindische Compagnie 1783-1795. Schepen en zeevarenden* (Amsterdam 1992).

built on its own account, chiefly armed galleys and frigates for police duties.[49]

Nowadays there is considerable understanding of the operations of the VOC as a shipping enterprise, largely as a result of recent work at Leyden University.[50] In the Netherlands the VOC was organised in five 'Chambers', which can be regarded as the successors of the 'pre-companies' mentioned earlier, although they were organised on a municipal basis.[51] Each Chamber possessed its own shipping, constructed in its own dockyard. The largest vessels were called *retourschepen* ('return ships'), which were specifically designed for voyages to Asia and back. They were strongly built, well-armed and of ample carrying capacity. On the outward journey this capacity was mainly used to transport passengers (soldiers and other servants of the Company, sometimes with their families[52]) and to carry money together with the countless articles of equipment of European provenance which the Company needed in order to operate in Asia. On the return journey their main cargo of course consisted of Asiatic goods consigned to various Chambers.[53]

More often than not these ships made their

intercontinental journeys in company, and there soon developed a system of prescribed routes. In the Atlantic a course had to be followed which enabled ships to keep clear of the coasts of both Guinea and Brazil.[54] In the Indian Ocean ships bound for Batavia[55] had to steer approximately along the parallel of 40° south, to take advantage of the trade winds, until they had nearly reached the Australian coast and subsequently to head north. When they returned from Batavia they followed a straight course from the Sunda Strait to the Cape. During the seventeenth century it was common practice for outward-bound ships to depart in groups, some time between September and Easter. During the eighteenth century, as the number of sailings grew, it became the practice to sail individually and all the year round. Homeward journeys usually started some time in December or January, but this period was extended in the eighteenth century to between November and February. Understandably during the return voyages more attention was paid to keeping the ships together as at that juncture they truly constituted a 'treasure fleet'.[56] On the last legs of their homeward journey they were even convoyed by cruisers sent out by the Company or even detachments of the battlefleet.

Thanks to the Leyden research project mentioned above, it is now known that some 4600 voyages to Asia were made by ships sent out by the VOC. Of these voyages some 2 per cent ended in disaster. The percentage of the homeward bound vessls – they were, for obvious

reasons, far fewer in number[57] – who did not reach their destination is about 4 per cent. During the same period the VOC had 1581

49. See K N Chaudhuri, 'The English East India Company's Shipping (c1660-1760)', in Jaap R Bruijn and Femme Gaastra (eds), *Ships, Sailors and Spices. East India Companies and their Shipping in the 16th, 17th and 18th Century* (Amsterdam 1993), pp51, 52.

50. The results have been published by J R Bruijn, F S Gaastra and I Schöffer in three volumes, *Dutch Asiatic Shipping in the 17th and 18th centuries* (The Hague 1979-1987).

51. In principle every city acquired a Chamber where one or more of the 'pre-companies' had had their headquarters.

52. Only the higher servants of the VOC were permitted to take their families with them to Asia. Many of these 'qualified servants' went to Asia unmarried and subsequently married women born in Asia and often of (part) Asian descent. See Leonard Blussé, *Strange Company: Chinese settlers, mestizo women and the Dutch in VOC Batavia* (Dordrecht/Riverton 1986); Jean Gelman Taylor, 'Europese en Euraziatische vrouwen in Nederlands-Indië in de VOC-tijd', in *Vrouwen in de Nederlandse Koloniën*, Zevende Jaarboek voor Vrouwengeschiedenis (Nijmegen 1986), pp10-33.

53. After arrival these goods were sold at auction by the various Chambers to which they were consigned.

54. See Gaastra, *De geschedenis van de VOC*, pp110-111.

55. The VOC 'establishment' at Batavia continuously tried to ensure that all outward bound shipping first called there. However, after 1665 there were 'direct' voyages to Ceylon and later also to China (for a time) and to Hougli in Bengal.

56. To give but one example: the market value of the cargo of the 'return fleet' which took refuge in the Bay of Bergen (Norway) after the battle of Lowestoft (1665) was estimated at 11 million guilders. It comprised, *inter alia*, 3084 uncut diamonds, 2933 rubies, a large quantity of pearls and 16,580 pieces of porcelain.

57. Some ships were lost outward bound.

A splendid evocation of Amsterdam harbour when the city was at the peak of its prosperity. The large ship is the Gouden Leeus, *the younger Tromp's flagship at the Texel, but most of the other vessels crowding the port are mercantile, and represent nearly every type of contemporary merchant ship. Painted by van de Velde the Younger and dated 1686.* (Amsterdam Historical Museum)

A model of the East Indiaman Den Ary, *built in 1725. With 54 guns, the vessel resembled a medium-sized ship of the line in both firepower and overall appearance. The more peaceable nature of the Indiaman was only revealed by the superstructure over the quarterdeck (to shelter the ship's more important passengers) and the break in the regular lines of gunports. (Nederlands Scheepvaart Museum, Amsterdam)*

Facilities also included a rigging and block-making shop, a sawmill, a large smithy and a rope-walk of impressive length, as well as separate warehouses for sugar and saltpetre, and for meat. Some idea of the size of this establishment can be gleaned from the fact that as the VOC was approching its demise the total work force numbered some 1300 men. In the towns where the other Chambers were located, there were establishments organised on the same pattern, but all of smaller size, since the Amsterdam Chamber had to provide half the number of ships the Company needed and also 50 per cent of the Asiatic products which were shipped to the mother country were consigned to the Amsterdam Chamber–and consequently auctioned in that city (the share of the Zeeland Chamber was one-quarter, that of the 'lesser Chambers' one-sixteenth each).

The Dutch West India Company

Except for the treatment of the shareholders when the VOC went into liquidation,[62] the company was never a bad business proposition for investors. From its inception to 1796 it paid a total dividend of 3600 per cent, which is about 18½ per cent a year.[63] In this respect its history was markedly different from that of the other great chartered company, the West-Indische Compagnie (WIC).[64] The root of this differ-

ships built in its metropolitan dockyards. Nearly all of them were 'return vessels' of rather large dimensions for their time. The VOC also owned a well-equipped and efficient dockyard on the island of Onrust in Batavia Bay,[58] but this was chiefly used for repairs and maintenance and also to build smaller vessels for use in Asian waters.

The appearance of these 'return ships' can be judged from models and pictures in museums, but there are also three replicas of large VOC vessels which have been built recently: the *Prins Willem* at Oranda Mura (Japan), the *Amsterdam* in the city of the same name, and the *Batavia* at Lelystad in the area of the former Zuyderzee. It is interesting to note that they not only reproduce originals from quite different periods but also all three reflect a completely different design philosophy, the *Batavia* being closest to 'the real thing'. She is a replica of a ship completed in 1628 which met her end on the Australian coast the following year. The *Prins Willem*, the original of which dated from the middle of the seventeenth century, is based on a model of that ship as it was during the First Anglo-Dutch War when temporarily serving in the Navy of the States-General.[59] The *Amsterdam* was built in 1748 for the Chamber after which she was named and had to be abandoned after she had stranded near Hastings on the English south coast in January 1749. Her

construction was taken in hand after the *Heeren XVII*'s decree of 14 March 1743 that the future building of 'return ships' would be standardised and that no more than three designs would be used, for ships of a length of 150, 136 and 120 feet respectively. The *Amsterdam* belonged to the largest category.[60]

She was built on the 'island' of Oostenburg in the northeastern part of Amsterdam,[61] where in the 1650s the VOC had acquired a large tract of land, and where the Amsterdam Chamber soon concentrated most of its commercial and shipbuilding facilities. One of the sights not only of Oostenburg, but of the city as a whole, was the Great Storehouse, built in 1661 and said to be the largest building in the Netherlands: 122m in length, 20m wide and 22½m tall (with the clock tower 33m). Unfortunately, it collapsed in 1822, being at that time used for the storage of grain, a purpose for which its light construction made it unsuitable. Originally it was chiefly used for the warehousing of Asiatic products like spices, but there was also space reserved for ship and naval stores like barrels, mainly used to pack meat, and rolls of canvas. However, most installations and buildings in the vicinity were used for shipbuilding and related activities. There were three building slips on the site (and on at least three occasions ships were launched on the same day from each one of them).

58. Apparently Captain James Cook was quite pleased with the work done on HMS *Endeavour* by this dockyard when he called at Batavia on his first great voyage of discovery in 1770.

59. During this war the VOC put several large vessels at the disposal of the States-General. The model in question is in the Rijksmuseum at Amsterdam.

60. Peter Marsden, *The Wreck of the Amsterdam* (London 1974).

61. This area, originally part of Amsterdam roadstead, was reclaimed around the middle of the seventeenth century. Its history, and the results of a thorough archaeological survey, have been published in J B Kist (ed), *Van VOC tot Werkspoor: het Amsterdamse industrieterrein Oostenburg* (Utrecht 1986).

62. See below.

63. De Korte, *De Jaarlijkse Financiële Verantwoording*, p67f.

64. After a reorganisation in 1674-75 the Company was officially called the Geoctroyeerde Westindische Compagnie ('Chartered West India Company') or 'GWC'.

ence lay in the working areas of the two companies, which were of very different degrees of importance to the Iberian rivals of the Dutch. In Asia the Iberian interest was represented by a number of factories, where the hinterland was usually under the control of others. The trade of these factories and the profits it generated were not without importance, but in Asia there were hardly any rewarding mining or agricultural activities within the Iberian sphere of influence. In fact Asia was, seen within the context of the Iberian empires, more or less peripheral. The southern Atlantic and the lands bordering it, on the other hand were of paramount importance, constituting the very hub of the Iberian overseas empire. Latin America was immensely valuable because of its mines and agriculture, while Africa offered alluring opportunities for trade, and above all was indispensable as a source of the slave labour needed to work the mines and plantations on the other side of the Ocean.

The West India Company owes its origins to developments during the Eighty Years' War. Willem Usselinckx was a Calvinist of impeccable orthodoxy,[65] who emigrated from Antwerp to Middelburg, the capital of Zeeland in 1591. There he began enlisting support for the idea of a chartered company entrusted with the monopoly of shipping and trade in most of the Atlantic area. One of its foremost aims was to be the creation of colonies for European settlement in the New World. He expected these colonies to develop into most profitable enterprises which also would prove a most effective weapon in the struggle against the enemies of true religion. This anti-Iberian bias also motivated many of Usselinckx's supporters–and it did not escape the attention of those in the Netherlands who were, mainly for commercial reasons, in favour of a more moderate policy towards the Spanish Crown, and also of the Madrid authorities themselves. This is the main reason why the WIC only came into being after the Twelve Years' Truce had come to an end.

The Company's charter, granted on 3 June 1621, reveals many similarities with that of the VOC. There were to be nineteen Directors and five Chambers, three in Holland, and one each in Zeeland and Groningen.[66] It was granted a monopoly in an area defined as Africa south of the Tropic of Cancer, America and the islands in the Atlantic between the meridians of the Cape of Good Hope and of the easternmost tip of New Guinea.

During the first period of its existence the activities of the WIC were not without profit, not even without glory. Privateering expedi-

John Maurice of Nassau-Siegen became Governor-General of the Brazilian possessions of the WIC, and in many ways proved himself an enlightened ruler. One example was the care he took to have the flora and fauna of the country properly documented: these tortoises were painted by Albert Eckhout, one of the painters he took with him to Brazil. (Mauritshuis, The Hague)

tions, embarked upon with zest, culminated in September 1628 in the capture in Cuban waters of a Spanish *flota* on its way home from Mexico. Three years earlier Bahia had been taken from the Portuguese but that important Brazilian port was recaptured by them after a few months. The company's rule lasted much longer in the coastal region to the south of Bahia, where Olinda and Recife were taken in 1630 and subsequently used as bases for the conquest of the adjacent *capitanías* along the coast, valuable prizes because of their cane-fields and *engenhos* (sugar mills). In 1636 John Maurice of Nassau-Siegen, a relative of the Princes of Orange, became Governor-General of the Brazilian possessions of the WIC. During his enlightened, but expensive, rule they reached their greatest extent but he did not succed in winning the allegiance of many of the *moradores* (colonists of Portuguese extraction). In 1637 he organised an expedition which resulted in the conquest of São Jorge da Mina (Elmina), which made the WIC the owner of an important slaving station. In 1641 an expedition to Angola, also an area which was important as a source of slaves, resulted in the conquest of Loanda and the island of São Tomé with its sugar plantations.

In the same year, 1641, the Brazilian possessions of the WIC reached their greatest extent. But there also took place an event which with hindsight proved to have determined the course of the Company's subsequent history. Exasperated by what in their perception was a prolonged period of misrule, the Portuguese revolted against the Spanish Crown. Shortly afterwards the States-General began negotiating an armistice with the new Portuguese government and soon afterwards a form of alliance between the two powers came into being. At first this change did not appear to have put the

position of the Company in jeopardy. Pending the negotiations about an armistice the States-General permitted the WIC to continue its warlike operations against the Portuguese: in fact Angola and the *capitanías* of Sergipe and Maranhão were conquered after the talks had started. However, from 1642 onwards there was a sequence of rebellions by the *moradores* in Brazil. The WIC was unable to cope with these by itself because of cutbacks in its armed forces and only lukewarm State support was forthcoming. The influence of those who were more interested in good commercial relations with Portugal than in the prosperity of the WIC in Brazil was simply too strong. In these circumstances it was not surprising that within a few years the Company not only lost Angola and São Tomé, which were retaken by the Portuguese in 1648, but also all its possessions in Brazil. In January 1654 Recife and all other places still under the Company's rule had to be surrendered.

It goes without saying that this loss caused great financial problems for the Company. In the end it was decided that the only way out of the difficulties lay in drastic reorganisation. In 1674 the 'old' WIC was dissolved and a new company formed. The number of Directors was reduced (from nineteen to ten) as was the staff in the mother country and the capital stock. Subsequently this 'new' company was transformed increasingly from a trading concern into an organisation for the government and exploitation of the teritories it had managed to retain after the Brazil fiasco. In western Africa, on the shores of the Gulf of Guinea, it remained, for the time being, the proprietor of a chain of factories. Those on what was called the Slave Coast were gradually given up during the eighteenth century; those on the Gold Coast, with Elmina as the most important, remained under the Company's sway until the very end. In the Caribbean the WIC continued to exercise sovereign rights over a number of island possessions that still today form part of the Kingdom of the Netherlands. They comprise Curaçao, Aruba, Bonaire, St Eustatius,[67] Saba and part of the

---

65. It is clear that he was largely motivated by the desire to damage the interests of 'Papist' Spain when he tried to enlist support for his WIC project.

66. There were no VOC Chambers outside Holland and Zeeland. That Groningen obtained its WIC Chamber can be explained by pointing out that the city was experiencing a period of economic expansion and also that it, and especially the university, was a bulwark of militant Calvinism.

67. This island was of course the scene of the celebrated first salute to the United States' flag by a foreign nation (16 November 1776).

Itamarca Island with Fort Orangien, in the Brazilian possessions of the WIC. Painting by Frans Post, who accompanied John Maurice to Brazil. (Mauritshuis, The Hague)

island of St Martin (the most valuable portion, on account of the presence of salt marshes; this became the property of the WIC in 1648, the remainder being allocated to France in the same year). The most important of these islands was Curaçao, for many years *the* entrepôt for the importation of slaves into the region. The Company engaged actively in the slave trade until the 1730s, after which her servants in the African factories were permitted to supply slaves to private buyers who had to pay

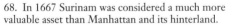

the Company a fixed sum of money for every negro they had been permitted to buy from the 'stock' of the factory in question.

In South America, west of the Amazon delta, the WIC in the course of the seventeenth century acquired a number of plantation colonies: Essequibo, Demerara, Berbice and Surinam. Most of these were Netherlands foundations. Surinam, however, was first settled by English colonists on the initiative of Lord Willoughby of Parham. In 1667 it was ceded to the Netherlands in exchange for Nieuw-Nederland (New York and its hinterlands), which had been taken by an English fleet just before the official start of the Second Dutch War.[68]

By the 1790s the Company[69] was in a moribund condition and indeed of little commercial value. Pensionary Laurens Pieter van de Spiegel, the last gifted statesman of the old Republic, accepted the consequences and

68. In 1667 Surinam was considered a much more valuable asset than Manhattan and its hinterland.

69. As mentioned earlier, this really was the 'second' Company, as reorganised in 1674-75.

70. By the begining of the eighteenth century the Provinces of Holland and Zeeland, which together paid more than half of the expenses of 'central government' (diplomatic service, army, navy) and hence enjoyed a dominant position in the assembly of the States-General, were heavily in debt and their citizens had to carry a correspondingly heavy burden of taxation.

organised its demise, the state taking over the administration of the WIC's former territories. Although the organisation was deeply in debt, the last shareholders fared much better than those of the VOC a few years later: they received 30 per cent of the nominal value of the shares they owned – not a bad bargain considering that at that time the Company's shares sold for only 22 per cent on the Amsterdam Exchange.

Stagnation and decay?

This is not the place to elaborate upon the end of the Netherlands Republic as a political power of the first rank. Let it suffice to state that this more or less coincided with the end of the War of the Spanish Succesion and that it is a point of debate whether that position was 'lost' or 'abandoned' by the States-General of their own free will, and for financial reasons.[70] However, the

An anonymous British painting of Dunkirk in the eighteenth century. Privateers from this port were a constant threat to both British and Dutch commerce in the wars of the seventeenth and eighteenth centuries since the town was almost always in the hands of their enemies – first the Spaniards and then the French. Shoal waters made the place almost impossible to attack from the seaward side, while the town itself was surrounded with formidable fortifications. (National Maritime Museum)

A modern model of a smak, *based on an early eighteenth-century drawing by Adam Silo in the Danish Maritime Museum, Elsinore. Similar vessels were much used by Netherlands shipowners in the all-important Baltic trade. The model is in the Noordelijk Scheepvaartmuseum, Groningen.* (Vos Fotografie)

Republic remained an economic power of the first rank for far longer, although without doubt its subsequent economic achievements in so far contrasted with those of the previous century that they appear much less brilliant and spectacular. Many reputable historians of the past have described economic developments in the eighteenth century Republic as a process of inescapable decline which could only end in catastrophe, which in this case occured during the Napoleonic period. More often than not they stressed that in their opinion what happened was largely the fault of people whose primary task it was to guide the political and economic destinies of the country. It was alleged, or at least suggested, that they had failed to feel the winds of change and had devoted far too much time and effort to feathering their own nests. In a recent survey this point of view is caricatured in summary as: 'a sleepy, bewigged generation whose strength had ebbed away was taking its ease on top of the riches produced by ancestors, who with irresistible willpower and sparkling cultural *élan* had made the seventeenth century a Golden Century'.[71]

Nowadays most historians are of the opinion that the economic decline of the Republic until well into the eighteenth century was more relative than absolute, in the sense that, for example, the size and capacity of its merchant navy did not shrink in any significant way, whereas in other countries there was an absolute increase in that sector. They also tend to emphasise that the decline, if and where there was decline, was primarily due to a formidable combination of circumstances largely beyond the control of the Republic's leaders. Space does not permit a lengthy discussion of these circumstances, but it is worth mentioning some of them, along with a few comments. When its large neighbours started to adopt mercantilist practices (like those embodied in the English Navigation Acts) such moves could only be detrimental to the welfare of the Republic, especially because its internal market was relatively small.[72] The continuation of a period of climatological regression combined with the advent of the teredo made it necessary to invest more money in the upkeep and reconstruction of the sea defences. Successive epidemics of rinderpest had a negative impact on agricultural profits and ruined many farmers.

By the beginning of the eighteenth century the Seven Provinces, especially Holland and Zeeland,[73] were shouldering a heavy burden of debt. This necessitated the imposition of high taxes which in turn had an adverse effect on labour costs. Changes in dietary habits made it more difficult than before to obtain a good price for herring. The export of technical expertise led to the foundation of new industries abroad which often became keen and efficient competitors for similar undertakings within the confines of the Republic.

One would be wrong to assume that those who held the reins of power in the Republic meekly surrendered to these negative develop-

ments and did nothing to meet the novel challenges. Nor were their measures always unsuccessful. A case in point is the reaction of the elite of Amsterdam capitalists to changing patterns of trade which diminished the importance of the *stapelmarkt* as an entrepôt market for certain commodities (although not tropical

71. J A Faber, 'De achttiende eeuw', in J H van Stuijvenberg (ed), *De economische geschiedenis van Nederland* (Groningen 1977), p152.

72. Towards the end of the seventeenth century the total population of the Netherlands was less than 2 million souls (cf. Faber, 'De achttiende eeuw', p120).

73. See above, note 70.

products). Their strong financial position enabled them to move without major problems from being merchants to being merchant bankers, financing the trade operations of others and branching out into other related activities. It was largely due to them[74] that Amsterdam's importance as a financial centre, notably for the floating of bond issues, still increased until far into the eighteenth century.

The capitalists of the Republic also made skilful use of the neutrality that the States-General succeeded in maintaining during many of the European wars of the eighteenth century. They expected to be able to do so again when the North American colonies in the 1760s drifted into conflict with the British Crown. Initially everything went well. Curaçao and even more St Eustatius experienced a boom period as centres of the contraband trade with the rebellious colonies after the War of American Independence had formally broken out in 1776. In the main commercial centres of Holland, notably Amsterdam and Haarlem (much less in Rotterdam, which was perhaps the most 'English' community on the continent) the struggle on the other side of the Atlantic was watched with keen sympathy for the rebels–and awakened great expectations as to the business opportunities an independent America would present. In September 1778 a group of Amsterdam politicians went so far as to engage in talks with American representatives from which a draft commercial treaty resulted. When its text became known to the British Government in September 1780, it

became one of the *casus belli* leading to the outbreak of the 'Fourth English War' in December of that year.

The outcome of that conflict was nothing short of disastrous for the Republic. Many merchant ships were captured by British men-of-war and privateers, and among the captures were twelve VOC vessels, seven of them with valuable 'return cargoes'. Despite the use of subterfuges like 'neutralising' ships or chartering neutral bottoms, the flow of Asiatic goods which arrived in the Netherlands consigned to any of the VOC Chambers diminished to a trickle after the outbreak of war. This not only caused trouble for the Company itself, which by 1782 was faced with a large deficit in its current account, but it also affected the *Wisselbank*, which customarily lent the Company a large annual sum (the so-called 'anticipation money') to bridge its expenses during the period after which a large number of ships had sailed to Asia and the 'return ships' had not yet arrived. The war with Britain ended in May 1784 with the Treaty of Paris. This, again, was disastrous for the VOC. It not only had to surrender Nagapattinam and its hinterland, but was also forced to permit the free passage of British ships through Indonesian waters, including those of the Moluccas. This practically put an end to the monopoly of the export trade from the 'Spice Islands' which the VOC had enjoyed for so long.

This accumulation of setbacks proved fatal for the VOC. Despite massive support from the Provinces of Holland and Zeeland and from

the States-General, who not only furnished large sums of money but also dispatched squadrons of warships to Asia three times in succession when there were altercations with indigenous princes, its situation did not improve. In 1790 Holland and Zeeland agreed another loan, of 31½ million guilders but this time only on condition that henceforth a commission from the States-General would be authorised to scrutinise the accounts of the VOC which so far had been kept a closely guarded secret. The end came in December 1795 when the States-General decided not to renew the Company's charter, but to all intents and purposes to nationalise it. At that time its consolidated debt had risen to the staggering level of nearly 120 million guilders. This was partly the consequence of the long-standing practice of paying substantial dividends even in the years when the results did not warrant this. Like the maintenance of a veil of secrecy around the Company's financial administration this apparently had been at least partly done to bolster the VOC's reputation for solvency. After the demise of the Company the topic of compensation for the shareholders was broached on several occasions but in the end they did not receive anything.

1795-1813: a time of troubles

Towards the end of 1795 it was not clear what exactly the State had acquired when it nationalised the VOC, although the shore establishments, ships and stores in the mother country had passed into public ownership. Many other assets were in fact in the process of being lost, either temporarily or for good, and again war was the cause. During the winter of 1794-95 a French army invaded the Netherlands, forcing the last Stadtholder, William V, to flee to England. When he had found a temporary refuge in Kew Palace, in February 1795, he wrote to those in charge of the various Netherlands overseas possessions ordering

74. This development is well illustrated in the history of an important banking house of Anglo-Netherlands origin, as described in M G Buist, *At spes non fracta: Hope & Co, 1770-1815. Merchant bankers and diplomats at work* (The Hague 1974).

Dutch whalers in the ice, a grisaille by Roelof van Salm (1688-1765). The whalers are of the bootschip *type, a derivative of the flute with wider decks that facilitated the processing of the whales. Whaling was one of a number of trades in which the Netherlands lost out to Britain in the course of the eighteenth century.* (National Maritime Museum)

The VOC Indiaman Zuiderburg *depicted in three positions in Rammekens roadstead off Flushing in 1788. One of the last of the* retourschepen, *the vessel belonged to the Zeeland Chamber of the VOC, the second in importance. Painting by Engel Hoogerheyden.* (Nederlands Scheepvaart Museum, Amsterdam)

them to put themselves under the protection of the British. This was done swiftly in several cases and by 1801 practically everything which had constituted the Netherlands overseas empire, except Java and the factories on the Gold Coast,[75] was in British hands. With the exception of Ceylon, it was all handed back after the peace of Amiens in 1802. Definitively to be written off, however, were the 'return cargoes', worth millions, which had been seized by the British at the beginning of the war, either on the high seas or in harbours under their control. A typical case in point was that of the six East Indiamen which had put into Plymouth in October 1794, at that time a friendly port, and were seized next January.[76] When the war broke out again the British for the second time embarked upon the conquest of the Netherlands overseas territories, on this occasion including Java, which they seized in 1811. These developments were particularly detrimental to the Netherlands economy because the trade in what was loosely termed 'colonial products' during the previous decades

had become the main prop of the *stapelmarkt* system – or what was left of it.

Other branches of maritime trade and related industries also suffered during the Napoleonic period. The Netherlands were allied to France – perhaps it is better to describe it as a kind of satellite status – until 1810 when the country[77] was annexed by Napoleon, a situation which lasted for about two years. The French authorities naturally tried to assure themselves of maximum co-operation from the Netherlands in their policy of isolating British trade from continental Europe, which culminated in the Berlin Decree of November 1806, and thus in inaugurating the Continental System. As might be expected, ship owners and traders reacted in the time-honoured manner: many vessels were transferred to neutral flags, Prussia and northern Germany's 'mini-states', like Kniphausen and Papenburg being preferred choices this time. Indeed until at least 1810 trade with Britain remained reasonably brisk (there was, for instance, a significant export of Netherlands dairy produce to Britain: cheese from the Netherlands remained an important item in the diet of the sailors of the Royal Navy). After the French annexation, however, things took a clear turn for the worse. From 1802 (the year of 'Amiens') the numbers of seagoing ships entering Netherlands ports

coming from abroad diminished every year and the herring fishery became practically extinct.

Perhaps it will never be possible to establish with any degree of accuracy the impact of developments during the Napoleonic period on every branch of the maritime sector of the Netherlands economy. It is certain, however, that the infrastructure was heavily hit. The nationalisation of the VOC and a fundamental change in the system of naval administration[78] provoked the closure of a large number of shore establishments in the widest sense of the word, like dockyards, gun foundries and warehouses. The market for ocean-going ships con-

75. That the British did not bother to conquer them, either before or after the Treaty of Amiens, shows how much their importance had dwindled. Almost without doubt the main cause was the abolitionist movement and the subsequent abolition of the slave trade by the British Parliament (1807).

76. They had taken refuge in the Allied port of Plymouth because French privateers were rumoured to be active in the North Sea.

77. Certain parts of the territory of the Netherlands Republic, like the fortresses of Maastricht, Venlo and Flushing, had been annexed earlier.

78. Briefly, the five 'Admiralties', with their seat in three different provinces, where the influence of the province where they had their headquarters was very great, were replaced by one Ministry of Marine.

tracted and this led to the demise of many privately-owned shipyards: in the Zaan area near Amsterdam[79] where there had been some sixty shipyards in the seventeenth century there was just one left in 1816. There were other communities traditionally oriented towards the sea which were particularly hard hit in terms of vanishing job opportunities. A poignant case is the town of Enkhuizen on the west bank of the Zuyderzee which between 1795 and 1810 not only was hard hit by the decline of the herring fishery but also lost its naval and VOC dockyards. It is not surprising that the total number of inhabitants, which had been 20,967 in 1622, fell from 6803 in 1795 to 5400 in 1811.[80]

Rebuilding an ocean fleet

Towards the end of 1813 the Netherlands regained their independence. The country now became a monarchy with William, son of the last Stadtholder, as 'Sovereign Prince'. This title was soon changed into 'King of the Netherlands' as a consequence of the union with the former 'Southern Netherlands', the country now known as Belgium. This union, however, lasted only until the 1830s.[81] Britain

gave back all the colonies it had taken, with the exception of the Cape of Good Hope, Essequibo, Demerara and Berbice.

When the restored colonies again came under Netherlands rule troops had to be sent to occupy them, but it transpired that large ocean-going Netherlands vessels were in very short supply. This was one of the reasons which inspired the Government to embark upon a deliberate policy of stimulating the growth, if not rebirth, of the shipbuilding industry. Its first move, in 1819, was to prohibit the issue of Dutch certificates of registry to vessels which had not been built and equipped in the country. Much more important was the introduction, in 1823, of a bonus system. This made every Netherlands subject who ordered a new sailing vessel of more than 300 tons eligible for a bonus of 18 guilders per ton as soon as the vessel in question was for the first time and in all respects ready for sea. Soon after this system was extended to the building of smaller vessels, like coastal traders,[82] and of steamships.[83] It remained in operation until 1830 when it was deemed no longer necessary. Indeed from 1826 to 1829 the number of Netherlands-built ships in the country's merchant navy had grown

from 978 to 1166 (from a total of 1176 and 1346 respectively). After that, notwithstanding the abolition of the bonus system, the tonnage of the Netherlands merchant navy continued to increase until, in 1859–two years after the international shipping industry began to be affected by a steep fall in freight rates–it had reached its maximum for the nineteenth century.[84]

A major factor in this continuing growth can be traced to 1824, the year in which the *Nederlandsche Handel Maatschappij* was founded. This 'Netherlands Trading Company' was to a large extent inspired by the great chartered companies of the *ancien regime*. In the inaugur-

---

79. In this region, at Zaandam to be precise, Peter the Great in 1696 started to acquaint himself with the practical aspects of shipbuilding. However, he soon moved to the VOC dockyard at Amsterdam, where he could be better screened from the public eye.

80. We can be sure that in both years a large proportion of the population of Enkhuizen was unemployed. In Amsterdam, which was less hard hit by economic developments, in 1799 more than thirty per cent of the population was dependent on social assistance.

81. The two parts of the united kingdom had grown very much apart. There were deep differences as regards religion, culture, language and economic orientation (Belgium was one of the pioneering countries in the 'second' Industrial Revolution, whereas the northern Netherlands definitely were not).

82. The coastal trade during the eighteenth and nineteenth century became more or less a special preserve of the northern provinces of Friesland and Groningen. Most of the ships domiciled there were, entirely or partly, owned by their skippers. It goes without saying that they were usually of (very) small size.

83. In the Netherlands there were some interesting experiments with the construction of seagoing steamships in the 1820s. In this respect the name of Gerhard Moritz Roentgen is to be remembered: See John Guthrie, *A History of Marine Engineering* (London 1971), pp123-126, where his work on compound engines gets attention, but his name is not mentioned. Steamships capable of transoceanic voyages became an important element in the Netherlands merchant navy after the opening of the Suez Canal.

84. I J Brugmans, *Paardenkracht en Mensenmacht, sociaal-economische geschiedenis van Nederland 1795-1940* (The Hague 1961), p95. Other important statistical data are to found in a book which gives a clear insight in the interrelation of the NHM and the Netherlands merchant navy: E W Petrejus, *Het schip vaart uit. Onze zeilvaart in de negentiende eeuw* (Bussum 1975).

The Charlotte *of Chittagong and other Indian government vessels off Calcutta. The Honourable East India Company, like the VOC, employed vessels of this type as dispatch vessels and VIP transports. Along with the vessels of their defence forces, the Bengal and Bombay Marines, they were the only ships built to the orders of the HEIC as opposed to the cargo carriers which were chartered or hired. Painting by F B Solveyns, 1792.* (National Maritime Museum)

al Royal Decree its aim was proclaimed to be 'the promotion of commerce, navigation, ship-building, the fisheries, agriculture, industry and manufacture in the Netherlands and their over-seas possessions'. This manifesto proved too ambitious and the activities of the NHM were soon almost exclusively directed towards Java. Until the beginning of the twentieth century this island was (to borrow Mackinder's term) the real 'heartland' of the Netherlands colonial empire. Together with Surinam and the Spice Islands it was – at least until tobacco growing in Sumatra became important – the only territory to be intensively exploited; and this exploita-tion was much more successful than in the two other areas mentioned.[85] In fact, for many years Java was, so to speak, the sheet anchor of the Netherlands economy.

85. Surinam during the nineteenth century struggled with an ever-present labour problem due to the abolition of the slave trade and subsequently of slavery itself (which in Surinam took place in 1863). The Spice Islands had become much less important in the world economy since they no longer exclusively produced certain commodities.

This domination came about rapidly after the so-called Culture System was introduced on Java in 1830. Much has been, and is still, written on this system and there is still lively debate on topics like its impact on the welfare and well-being of the indigenous population. However, everybody agrees that it was a very clever device to exact considerable monetary revenue from a society where there was little money in circulation. It was based on the assumption that the Government as owner of the land was entitled to demand from the agricultural population tribute in kind, that is in the products of that land. To become convertible into cash these taxes in kind had to be saleable on the European, or North American, markets.

For that reason the Government exercised the right to determine what particular crops it wanted cultivated by the inhabitants of a particular region, in what quantity these had to be delivered, and within which period of time.

After these products had been harvested, the NHM came in to the picture, since from its inception the company was the sole agent of the Government for their shipment to the mother country and subsequent sale at auction. It was not allowed to own ships itself and could only hire Netherlands vessels, but for a long time it paid freight rates considerably in excess of those obtainable on the world market. For much of its history the company also employed various ways and means to guarantee employment for certain categories of ship. It is clear that all this amounted to a truly protectionist policy.

As pointed out above, the Netherland merchant navy increased in size under this system, which was only abolished gradually after 1849 (a few years before the Navigation Act vanished from the statute book), but in a sense this was a stunted growth. The number of steamships, certainly those of larger size, remained comparatively small: the system did not encourage innovation of that kind. Nor did it encourage fast passages as speed was of no interest in the coffee and sugar trades (the commodities that constituted the bulk of those consigned to the NHM). As a result, many of the sailing vessels under the Netherlands ensign at this time could certainly be called 'well-found' (the experts of the NHM saw to that!) but they were far from fast.

And yet, remarkably enough, there were also Netherlands owners of large sailing ships during this period who operated on other routes besides the 'cart track' between the Netherlands and Java, and who invested in clipper ships. But that is another story which falls outside the scope of this volume.[86]

Dr Philip Bosscher

86. The Netherlands achievement in the building and construction of clipper ships appears to have been rather overlooked by foreign authors. A good survey is to be found in A Blussé van Oud-Alblas, *De geschiedenis van het clipperschip, in Noord-Amerika, Engeland en Nederland* (Amsterdam 1949).

After the French left the Netherlands in 1813-14, much was done to improve the maritime infrastructure. One of the most important works undertaken was a canal linking Amsterdam with the North Sea at the Texel. This painting by Petrus Johannes Schotel shows the lock at the Amsterdam end of the canal, with the city in the background. (Amsterdam Historical Museum)

8

Seamen and the Merchant Service, 1650-1830

THIS FINAL chapter turns its attention from the ships to the crews of the merchant marine, their social background, and–as far as it is possible to describe–their terms and conditions of employment. It is clearly beyond the scope of a single chapter to summarise the situation for every country, for although there were many common aspects of life in the merchant service, there were others which were unique to individual societies. In keeping with the general theme of this volume, the example chosen to represent the human side of merchant seafaring is that of the Dutch Republic, the dominant mercantile force in 1650 and a country for which a reasonable depth of information is available.

Shipping and the Dutch economy

At the end of the seventeenth century Sir William Temple, ambassador of England to the Dutch Republic, expressed his admiration for the still blooming economy of the Netherlands in the following words:

'Tis evident to those who have read the most, and travel'd farthest, that no countrey can be found either in this present age, or upon record of any story, where so vast a trade has been managed, as in the narrow compass of the four maritime provinces of this commonwealth: nay it is generally esteemed, that they have more shipping belongs to them, than there does to all the rest of Europe.[1]

Although Temple also noticed that the Dutch Republic had passed the zenith of its growth, yet trade and shipping were still the backbone of the Dutch economy for many decades to come.

It is not difficult to imagine how much the economy, the social life and culture of the Dutch coastal provinces were permeated by its inhabitants' specialisation in maritime business. The larger ports such as Amsterdam, Rotterdam, Enkhuizen, Hoorn and Medemblik were full of industries and crafts closely connected to shipbuilding, seafaring and overseas trade. Dockers, shipbuilders, sailmakers, carpenters, blacksmiths, ropemakers, brewers, bakers, mapmakers, compass-makers, even public notaries and innkeepers, were all crafts and trades more or less linked to the sea and the riches it generated. The hundreds or maybe thousands of sailors constantly crowding these places must have contributed to the rather cosmopolitan atmosphere of the Dutch ports.

The fundamentals of Dutch shipping success were well rooted in the fifteenth and sixteenth centuries, when Dutch carrying trade began gradually to take over the trading links between southern and northern Europe. Not hampered by any regulations like the shipmasters of the Hanseatic League, their rivals from Zeeland and Holland took whatever cargo at whatever price that might prove profitable to them. Next to wine and brandy, the most important commodity was salt, brought from the southern regions of western France and used for preserving the massive quantities of herring caught by Dutch fishermen. Salted herring and dairy products were exported from the Netherlands to the Baltic region from where timber, tar, hemp, flax and grain were loaded for transport to Holland. In this way the trades to the Baltic and to France were complementary. Seen geographically, the inhabitants of the Dutch coastal provinces were true middle-men. For at least the sixteenth century more than 55 per

1. W Temple (edited by G N Clark), *Observations upon the United Provinces of the Netherlands* (Oxford 1972), p395.

Ships, shipping and seamen were central to the success of the Dutch Republic in the seventeenth century, and as such were common subjects for the great artists of the period. This grisaille by Experiens Sillemans (1611-1653) is dated 1652 and shows the typical appearance of the seamen of the time, including a rough-looking character drinking from a pitcher. (National Maritime Museum)

The seaman was an early example of the 'technocrat', a man whose advancement in his profession depended on his mastery of the latest developments in science and technology. As voyages became more adventurous, this became particularly true of navigation, and officers liked to emphasise this understanding in their portraits. This painting in the style of Hendrik van der Borcht (1583-1660) of an anonymous 'navigator' places prominence on the globe and dividers–the hallmarks of his trade–with his ship in the background. (National Maritime Museum)

cent of all shipping entering or leaving the Baltic was based in the Netherlands.

The end of the sixteenth century saw a new phase in the expansion of the Dutch maritime economy. In 1568 the Dutch had begun a rebellion against their Spanish masters, but by 1580 the newly-formed Republic of the Seven United Netherlands was on the verge of total collapse. However, Philip II of Spain suddenly changed his political priorities, concentrating his efforts on the neighbouring realms of France and England, and allowing the infant Dutch Republic to survive. The grip of the Spanish armies on Dutch territories was loosened and embargoes against Dutch shipping were lifted. The seizure of Antwerp, the ensuing closure of the river Scheldt and the exodus of all sorts of merchants and craftsmen to the northern Netherlands or elsewhere produced an unintended advantage for the economy of the north. While from the 1580s onwards more frequent contacts with the Russian empire were established via the port of

Arkhangelsk in the White Sea, a series of bad harvests in Italy after 1590 sparked off the Dutch penetration of Mediterranean markets. Dozens and dozens of Dutch ships chartered by Italian merchants transported their precious cargoes of grain to the ports and cities of Italy. With the rapid development of this *Straatvaart* –named after the Straits of Gibraltar, the entrance to the Mediterranean–within ten years the Dutch more or less mastered the carrying trade in all European waters.

One of the main characteristics of the Dutch seizure of the carrying trade was their ability to keep shipping costs as low as possible. As pointed out in earlier chapters, the bulk import of wood, tar, flax and hemp made the basic materials for the shipping industry relatively cheap. Furthermore, the use of wind-driven sawmills, the application of multi-bladed saws, and standardisation in the construction of the ship itself had already effected a substantial reduction in building costs. Moreover, the 'invention'–or to put it differently, the final perfection–of the *fluit* or flute type inspired another breakthrough for the shipping strength of the Netherlands. In this type of ship were concentrated all the virtues and advantages of Dutch trade and business. The *fluit* was contructed of relatively cheap timber (fir instead of oak), and was not fitted out with guns; the rig was kept as simple and efficient as possible; and the *fluit* was relatively long compared to the older types of ship. Not only did this design create more space for cargo, but it also improved the sailing qualities of the ship. At the same time, however, the austerely efficient rig and the absence of guns kept crew numbers relatively small. With all these minor or major advantages the Dutch possessed a cargo carrier that would give them the economic lead, and the concommitant political power, for at least a century. Or to put it in the words of Violet Barbour, 'the success of the flute placed the carriage of a large part of European trade, particularly in bulky and heavy commodities, in Dutch hands, and the freights in Dutch pockets'. It may be said without exaggeration that by the beginning of the seventeenth century Dutch shipmasters and sailors dominated the carrying trade in European waters.

Merchant seamen and shipmasters

Who were these men sailing to all corners of Europe and who were the shipmasters? Where did they come from, where were they domiciled? What age were they, what was their social status, how much were they paid for their services? These and so many other questions

relating to seafaring life from the seventeenth well into the nineteenth century are hard to answer due to lack of source material. Very few contemporaries were interested in the life and deeds of seafarers. State or port authorities hardly showed any interest in them. As long as trade was buoyant, all was well; and as long as there were crews to man the ships, there was no specific reason to be interested in them. In fact, apart from the various stories told about life on board the East Indiamen, hardly anything is known about sea life in the merchant marine.

To get a glimpse of these sailors at the very least it is necessary to know how numerous this fleet was. According to the estimate of an agent of the king of Spain the Dutch disposed of a fleet totalling 22,370 ships (including the fisheries) manned by 240,815 sailors and fishermen. In 1609 an Englishman claimed that the Dutch Republic possessed a fleet of 20,000 ships. Even in the twentieth century the merchant marine was thought to have numbered tens of thousands of ships. The actual reality, however, is less exalted (Table 8/1). The fleets that sailed the waters around Europe comprised only a few hundred ships at the most. Although during the period of time covered by this chapter (the seventeenth to nineteenth centuries) various shifts in numbers per destination took place, the global picture changed only gradually and undramatically. The beginning of the Napoleonic Wars, however, brought Dutch shipping to a total standstill by the end of the eighteenth century. It was not until after 1813 that Dutch shipping revived and managed to recover from the years of isolation inflicted by the French occupation.

Table 8/1: Estimated Number of Ships in the Dutch Merchant Marine (1636)[2]

Trade with	Number of ships	Tonnage (average)
Baltic	400	200
Norway	350	200
North Russia	50	240
North Germany	150	40
Dover, London (colliers)	100	80
Rest of England, Scotland	50	60
Calais	10	40
Southwest of France	300	200
Spain, Portugal, Mediterranean	200	300
Total	1750	155,300

2. J R Bruijn, 'De vaart in Europa', *Maritieme Geschiedenis der Nederlanden*, Vol II (1977), pp209-213.

As a subject, the ordinary seaman of the seventeenth and eighteenth centuries rarely attracted the professional artist, who was usually dependent on wealthy patronage. This anonymous British portrait of about 1790 depicting a sailor sitting on a sea chest is unusual. The man is in his shore-going rig, but sailors were usually instantly recognisable among landsmen by their garb and gait. (National Maritime Museum)

Obviously the corresponding earlier estimates of the number of men and boys employed in the various branches of seafaring activities also need to be revised downwards (Table 8/2). While some dramatic changes took place in the numbers employed by the Dutch East India Company, employment in the merchant marine as a whole remained essentially stable during the seventeenth and eighteenth centuries. But these crude numbers only reveal a part of the story of seafaring as a means of subsistence.

As pointed out earlier, knowledge of seafaring life aboard the Dutch merchant marine is very limited, but a welcome exception to this rule relates to the shipmasters and their origins. For an enormous span of time Denmark kept records of all ships entering and leaving the Baltic (the so-called Sound Toll Registers, 1429-1857). Although part of this information has been lost during the centuries, most of it has survived to this day. These registers demonstrate, firstly, the overwhelming dominance of the Dutch in trade to and from the Baltic. Not without reason was this branch of shipping known as the *Moedernegotie* ('mother trade') in those days. The majority of these Dutch masters in their turn was domiciled in the province of Holland, or to be more specific, in its northern part. Secondly, the registers show that during the larger part of the seventeenth century and in the beginning of the eighteenth century most of these shipmasters came from the small villages of the countryside of this part of Holland. At first glance this observation may seem of little relevance, but if it is true that shipmasters used local labour for manning their ships, then the aggregated numbers of the Sound Toll Registers indicate the importance of shipping in at least one region.

Indeed, recent research suggests that Dutch shipmasters recruited their crews from their immediate geographical, and even social, environment. Given the fact that during the sixteenth and seventeenth centuries the main share of Dutch shipmasters originated from the northern part of Holland, it is obvious that shipping was of enormous importance as a source of employment to this region. According to detailed local research in some villages just about half of the male working population earned its daily bread from seafaring.

However, these numbers also prove something else. Too often it is assumed that in the days of sail seamen belonged to the lowest strata of society. With hardly an exception, seafaring folk are depicted as a bunch of fighting drunks, excessively stupid and afflicted with the worst human failings. If this myth were true, it would mean that the villages of Holland were crowded with the lowest kind of humanity. This being not the case, it is evident that these qualifications do not apply to all seafarers. In fact, recent research into the Sound Toll Registers combined with Dutch local evidence reveals that shipping was part of overall normal daily life. Dutch shipmasters recruited their crews from their immediate geographical, and even social, environment. So, to put it differently, the traditional view of sailors needs revision. First of all, seafaring folk cannot be regarded as homogeneous. Secondly, they do not necessarily belong to the lowest echelons of society, at least as far as the merchant marine is concerned. And thirdly, a structural difference can be discerned between the manning 'system' of the merchant marine and that of the Dutch East India Company. While the East India Company recruited its seamen from proletarian city-dwellers, the merchant marine for the larger part manned its ships with men and boys from the countryside, where shipping and sailing was a decent means of subsistence. Indeed, as C R Boxer stated, 'the better class of Dutchmen preferred to seek employment nearer home and only took service with either of the two India Companies as a last resort.'

In many ways Dutch merchant shipping in European waters can be regarded as a regional affair where family ties and local loyalties played a pre-eminent role. These ties are particularly visible in relation to the higher professional ranks such as mate and bosun. This does not imply that only Dutchmen were to be found on board Dutch ships. There are good reasons to assume that even during the seventeenth century when Dutch labour seemed to be abundant, part of the crews of Dutch merchant ships came from abroad. Banns of marriages in Amsterdam record that thousands of foreign sailors came to the Netherlands to offer their labour for a relatively well-paid job in every branch of Dutch shipping. At least part of them found their way into the Dutch seagoing merchant service. By the end of the seventeenth century on average a quarter of the crew originated from abroad. For that specific period the same applied to the composition of the crews of the Dutch East India Company. Looking at the details of the composition of crews on board merchant vessels reveals some interesting features (Table 8/3).

Obviously, the overall numbers make it clear that nearly a quarter of the total crew originat-

Table 8/2: Employment in the Dutch Merchant Fleet in Selected Years[3]

	1610	1630/40	1680	1725	1770	1825
Navy	3000	8000	3500	3500	2000	5000
Merchant marine	21,500	25,500	22,500	22,000	21,000	17,000
East India Company	2000	4000	8500	11,000	11,500	–
Whaling	–	1500	9000	9000	6000	–
Fisheries	6500	7000	6500	4000	4000	2000
Total	33,000	46,000	50,000	49,500	44,500	24,000

3. J R Bruijn and J Lucassen (eds), *Op de schepen der Oost-Indische Compagnie. Vijf artikelen van J de Hullu* (Groningen 1980), p14; J R Bruijn, 'Scheepvaart in de noordelijke Nederlanden', *Algemene Geschiedenis der Nederlanden*, Vol VIII (Bussum 1979), p211.

Although the sailor was often portrayed as rough, if not actually ferocious, there was a sentimental side to his nature, and a romantic appeal to his calling. At a period when few travelled outside their parish, foreign voyaging was considered very exotic, and these sentiments found their expression in popular ballads like this 'Sailor's Farewell' from the 1740s. some of the accoutrements of shipboard life—the tankard, bowl, pipe and the hammock—can be seen in the engraving.

their crews from the ports and villages from the nearby mainland. Although the numbers of Table 8/3 should not be taken too literally, they prove that aboard the ships of the Dutch merchant marine local and regional social relations had the upper hand. The exception to the rule are the masters domiciled in Amsterdam, who could call upon the 'cosmopolitan' labour pool of their city. It is evident that the multitude of foreigners to be found on the quays of Amsterdam was also reflected in the composition of the crews of Amsterdam shipmasters.

To a certain extent the numbers of Table 8/3 also reveal that by the beginning of the eighteenth century, besides North Holland and Amsterdam, other regions within the Dutch Republic played an important role as a reserve of shipmasters and sailors. Until the turn of the century the northern part of the province of Holland had served as more or less the main area of recruitment for the merchant marine. Moreover, this same region also had to satisfy the growing thirst of the East India Company for able bodied seamen: around 1700 the crews of Dutch East Indiamen were still three-quarters Dutchmen, of which about 90 per cent originated from the province of Holland. However, again it must be stressed that these sailors did not come from the countryside, but from the cities of Holland. Finally, in times of war—and the Dutch had to fight many a war during the second half of the seventeenth century—the navy needed all the hands it could get. This kind of demographic burden on the relatively small population of the Netherlands (a maximum of two million around 1670) was to cost more and more effort and strain to carry. 'The years following the Treaty of Utrecht [1713] apparently saw a decrease in the numbers of Dutch seamen available for service in the *navy*, and in *ocean voyages*, and this decrease certainly became obvious after around 1740', Boxer wrote in 1964 in his groundbreaking article on sedentary workers and seafaring folk in the Netherlands.

As mentioned earlier, around 1700 the merchant service also used other regions such as Friesland and the Wadden Islands as recruiting areas for sailors. In fact these regions were

ed from abroad. The so-called 'recruitment pattern' of the shipmasters was characterised in most cases by a strong local and regional cohesion. For instance, masters from North Holland recruited nearly 70 per cent of their sailors from their immediate environment.

With masters from Friesland this cohesion proved even stronger. Although masters from the small Wadden Islands along the northern coast of the Netherlands seem to have had a broader view in engaging sailors than their colleagues from elsewhere, they actually recruited

Table 8/3: Geographical Cohesion on board Dutch Merchant Ships, 1700-1710.[4]

	Origins of crew				
	Group I	Group II	Group III	Group IV	Total
	Nos %	Nos %	Nos %	Nos %	Nos
Masters from:					
Amsterdam	408 18	830 37	986 43	46 2	2270
North Holland	2170 69	521 16	523 16	33 1	3247
Friesland	1279 72	246 14	241 13	20 1	1786
Wadden Islands	1592 50	1010 32	577 18	17 0	3196
South Holland	229 49	121 26	109 24	3 1	462
Zeeland	65 53	24 20	32 26	2 1	123
Groningen	5 –	– –	1 –	1 –	7
Total	5748 52	2752 25	2469 22	122 1	11,091

Groups: I = sailors originating from same place or region as shipmaster, II = sailors originating from other regions within Dutch Republic, III = sailors from abroad, IV = sailors of unknown origin.

slowly taking over the old dominance of the Holland masters and sailors in the Baltic trades. One of the characteristics of the maritime labour of these new regions was their shared dislike of, and aversion to, working with either of the India Companies or the navy. For instance, one source claims: 'In most of the villages . . . farmers were also sailors, mates and masters for the merchant marine, but not for the VOC [Dutch East India Company] or the navy; this was regarded as shameful'. Elsewhere it was stated that 'the sailors from Ameland [one of the small Wadden Islands] sail to all parts of the known world except to the East Indies, only some of them excluded. This is regarded as a source of shame and the consequence of a life of debauchery, which seldom happens to them'. Obviously, the maritime labour market was divided into two systems: an 'agrarian-mercantile' system in which shipping was, in the beginning, more or less a part of an all-year labour cycle, integrated into the social life of a relatively limited group; and an 'urban-proletarian' system, in which shipping was a mere means of subsistence, and family or other social ties played a minor role.

In the course of the eighteenth century some

basic changes took place in the recruitment patterns of the Dutch merchant marine (Table 8/4). The proportion of foreigners within the average crew of the Dutch East India Company rose dramatically from just about 25 per cent at the beginning of the eighteenth century to more than 50 per cent towards the end. The same process took place in the rest of the merchant marine. Between 1700 and 1775 the share of foreigners among the crews rose from 25 per cent to nearly 60 per cent. These radical changes have not been satisfactorily explained by historians to date. It may be that the enormous demand for labour from the Dutch East India Company in combination with a slow

deterioration of the economy put too great a strain on the demographic resources of Holland. Furthermore, because living standards, particularly in the province of Holland, were relatively high, working with the Company was no longer as attractive to the inhabitants of that region as it must have been to the thousands of foreigners who came to the Dutch Republic to offer their labour. Within the indigenous Dutch proportion in the merchant service as a whole, there was a shift from Holland to the islands along the northern coast, but also within the composition of the foreign part of the crews a shift can be observed from the Scandinavian countries towards Germany.

With the turn of the century and the end of the Dutch Republic, shipping as a means of subsistence seemed to have almost vanished. The Napoleonic era made the Dutch turn their attention landward. By the time the sea was open to trade and shipping again the 'new' fleet of the Netherlands and its crews had undergone further structural changes. In particular the domicile of masters and sailors, and the share of foreigners among the crew, were completely different. Firstly, the northern province of Groningen replaced the province of Holland as the main reservoir of seamen. Secondly, the share of foreigners had dwindled down to a pre 1700 level. And with this development, in fact, the social characteristics of the

4. P C van Royen, 'Manning the Merchant Marine: The Dutch Maritime Labour Market about 1700', *International Journal of Maritime History* I/1 (June 1989), pp1-28.

Although the Dutch navy and merchant marine were often short of men, they never resorted to the British Navy's Press Gang, depicted here in all its gory drama by Rowlandson. 'Pressing' certainly caused riots and at times was abused–in this case they appear to be pressing a tailor, whereas strictly speaking only seamen were legitimate targets–but even within its limits it caused much resentment among merchant seamen; the practice of pressing out of ships nearing the homeward leg of long voyages was a particularly sore point.

Table 8/4: Geographical Composition of the Crews aboard Dutch Merchant Vessels (1700-1710, 1774-1775, 1814-1816, 1824-1826 and 1834-1836) [5]

| | 1700-1710 | | 1774-1775 | | 1814-1826 | | 1834-1836 | |
	Nos	*%*	*Nos*	*%*	*Nos*	*%*	*Nos*	*%*
Grand total	8790	100	8926	100	11,372	100	3991	100
Netherlands	6678	76	3762	42	6746	59	2224	56
Shipmasters	–	–	–	–	1957	17	657	16
Foreigners	2112	24	5164	58	2669	24	1110	28
Dutch total	6678	100	3762	100	8703	100	2881	100
Shipmasters	–	–	–	–	1957	22	657	23
Amsterdam	666	10	629	17	1003	12	279	10
N Holland	2200	33	474	13	248	3	51	2
S Holland	420	6	48	1	325	4	190	7
Zeeland	111	2	3	0	26	0	19	0
Friesland	1761	26	987	26	1438	17	355	12
Groningen	–	–	156	4	2217	25	948	33
Wadden	1417	21	1434	38	1380	16	362	12
Various/unknown	103	2	31	1	109	1	20	1
Foreign total	2112	100	5164	100	2669	100	1110	100
Germany	726	34	2675	52	1951	73	1043	94
Scandinavia	984	47	1378	27	379	14	44	4
Baltic coast	353	17	667	13	–	–	–	–
Various/unknown	49	2	444	8	339	13	23	2

An anonymous British portrait of a Mate, dating from around 1805. The navies of the period relied heavily on the merchant service for all manpower, but especially for the technical rates and warrant officers, like masters and carpenters. However, if the late seventeenth-century career of Edward Barlow is anything to go by, men who held very responsible positions in the merchant service could not expect to be so highly rated in the navy. (National Maritime Museum)

Successful merchant captains were men of means, and this was particularly true of East India Company commanders, who could amass huge fortunes through their private trading. This anonymous portrait, dated to around 1690, shows a wealthy and somewhat self-satisfied captain of the English East India Company, with a large Indiaman in the background. (National Maritime Museum)

'agrarian-mercantile' system had returned to shipping. Once again family ties, local and regional relations were the basis of Dutch shipping.

Merchant seamen and society

What social status did shipping give to the masters and sailors involved? As might be expected, within the confines of the seafaring communities masters held a relatively high position, but the social stratification of Dutch society was not typified by sharp and unsurmountable gulfs and barriers. During the seventeenth century in particular the Dutch social system was rather open and dynamic. In the course of the eighteenth century the dynamism slowly wound down into a more static society in which it became more difficult to climb from the bottom to the top. According to the *Observations* by Sir William Temple, Dutch society counted the following 'classes':

... the clowns or boors, who cultivate the land. The mariners or schippers, who supply their ships and inland-boats, the merchants or traders, who fill their towns. The renteneers, or men that live in all their chief cities upon the rents or interest of estates formerly acquired in

their families, and the gentlemen and officers of their armies.

The clowns or boors were 'dull and slow of understanding . . . yielding to plain reason, if you give them time to understand it. The mariners are a plain, but much rougher people, whether from the element they live in, or from their food, which is generally fish and corn . . .'. Be this as it may a shipmaster of the merchant marine at least had some status. Some who had gathered enough wealth were member of the local elite and ruling 'class', but given the nature of his profession, with its frequent absences, a shipmaster was not exactly the ideal type of person to take a part in local government. But at least it seems that the masters belonged to the higher ranks of society.

For the other ranks very little information is available. Older seamen, after they had given

5. P C van Royen, *Zeevarenden op de koopvaardijvloot mstreeks 1700* (Amsterdam 1987), p116 (for 1700-1710, only individuals counted); G K Pielage and M Ramler, 'Wie monsterden aan in 1774 en 1775?' (unpublished MA thesis, Amsterdam 1990) (for 1774-1775); Gemeente Archief Amsterdam, Archief van de Waterschout, PA 38: 91-102 (for 1814-1816), 122-127 (for 1824-1826); A Verburg, 'Zeelieden aan boord van Nederlandse vrachtschepen 1834-1836' (unpublished MA thesis, Amsterdam 1990).

Table 8/5: Monthly Wages of the East India Company, the Navy and Merchant Marine (in Guilders), 1700-1826 [6]

	EIC 17th-18th centuries	Navy	Merchant Marine			
			1700/10	1774/75	1814/16	1824/26
Master	60-80	30	–	–	–	–
First mate	40-50	36	32	31.60	32	32
Boatswain	20	22	–	23.40	29	28
Carpenter	30-36	28	32	31.70	31	25
Cook	20	18	25	19.80	22	21
Able seaman	7-11	11	10-15	14.50	22	20
Ordinary seaman	6 - 7	–	–	–	17	14
Boy	4 - 6	4 - 7	5 - 8	–	9	8

up the sea, are sometimes to be found teaching the younger maritime generation the basics of reading, calculating and navigation. Indeed, it seems that compared to other strata of society the seafaring folk of the merchant marine were more 'literate', particularly in those villages where a large seafaring community could be expected.

As for wages, the picture is also rather vague. The East India Company kept wages as low as possible, and the navy too was bound by the government to pay the sailors a minimal wage. Although it is seldom possible to prove, clearly sailors did not belong to the best paid classes of worker. 'The small pay and great hardships of a sailor's life, together with the uncertainty of promotion, meant that many mariners

could only expect a poverty-stricken old age.' Whether this pessimistic view is entirely true is to be doubted. For instance, as long as shipping was the main occupation in certain villages, living standards seem to have been more or less guaranteed. On the other hand, the story of Sir William Temple, when meeting an old Dutch sailor who refused a financial award for recounting his adventures at sea–'and here I met the only rich man that I ever saw in my life . . .'–is obviously beyond the truth as well.

From the middle of the seventeenth century to the end of the eighteenth wages paid by the East India Company and the Dutch navy remained unchanged. In fact it was the policy of the shipowners and overseas traders to try to keep pay in the navy below the rates prevailing

in the merchant marine, so as to ensure that seamen would sooner enlist in the merchant service. This policy was enshrined in the words of the Grand Pensionary John de Witt (1665): 'It is necessary that once and for all sailor's pay is fixed as an iron law so that no one can nay longer hope for a rise; else the sailor is master and the State at the discretion of the rabble.' Wages in general, and more specifically for the lower ranks, were relatively high in the merchant marine, but more importantly, life on board a general merchant ship must have been far more pleasant than sailing with the ships of the Dutch East India Company or the navy. Signing up with the East India Company implied a journey of at least seven months to the East Indies during which the possiblity of death was far from remote; it also meant service for at least five years. Between 1600 and 1800 one million people were transported from the Netherlands to the East, but only one-third of these servants of the 'Honourable' Company returned to the home country: the rest remained in the East (at best), or perished during the voyage.

For the rest of the merchant marine shipboard life must have been of better quality. A voyage to the Baltic, for instance, may have taken only a couple of weeks. Apart from loading and unloading, the crew had time enough to go ashore for a while. As pointed out earlier, the larger part of the crew already knew one another. But other factors contributed to making life more amenable in the merchant service. For instance, the less dramatic changes in temperature and shorter trips in European waters allowed fresher and better quality victuals in comparison with those provided by the East India Company or the navy. However, this does not mean that seafaring was either easy or uneventful: life under sail has been too often

6. J Lucassen, 'Zeevarenden', *Maritieme Geschiedenis der Nederlanden* II (Bussum 1977), p141; J R Bruijn, *The Dutch Navy of the Seventeenth and Eighteenth Centuries* (Columbia, SC 1993), p199; G K Pielage and M J Ramler, 'Wic monsterden aan in 1774 en 1775. Een onderzoek naar de Nederlandse vrachtvaart en haar bemanning' (unpublished MA thesis, Amsterdam 1990), tables 10-18; Municipal Archives Amsterdam, Rechterlijk Archief PA 5061, 2618; Municipal Archives Amsterdam, Archief Waterschout PA 38, 91-94, 126-127.

Shipboard life was somewhat basic, but perhaps no more so than experienced by similar social groups ashore. These 'domestic' artifacts were recovered from the British line of battle ship Invincible, *wrecked in 1758, but merchant seamen would probably have used similar items. There are wine bottles, a stave-built tankard, turned wooden bowls, a square wooden platter, pewter plate and spoons, and a stoneware jar.*

A group of seamen or watermen gathered around a seventeenth-century navigational mark consisting of a barrel on top of a long pole. Oil painting by J H Koekkoek of Middelburg. (Dordrechts Museum)

regarded in a romantic light, but in practice it was uncomfortable, often wet and always required hard work. It was also dangerous: in times of war the life of a sailor was cheap, while the carrying-trade to the Mediterranean always remained a hazardous business thanks to Muslim corsairs, and hundreds of sailors ended their lives in misery somewhere on the coast of Barbary.

If a sailor wanted to advance in his career and earn better wages, the least he required was experience and nautical knowledge. To become a helmsman or shipmaster literacy was a further prerequisite. Beyond that a sailor also needed good relations with the master or the owner(s) of the ship–but family connections were even better. Indeed, the higher ranks in the merchant marine were virtually a 'closed shop' to foreigners. By the beginning of the eighteenth century the highest rank a sailor from abroad could hope for was that of bosun. However, the enormous influx of foreigners into the service during the course of that century makes it unlikely that these barriers were still in place by its close. By the beginning of the nineteenth century the old system of a closed shop seemed to be back again.

Knowledge of seafaring life in the seventeenth, eighteenth and nineteenth centuries is rather limited. Personal memories or detailed data concerning life on board are very scarce. The information provided by the notarial records of, for example Amsterdam, prove that the Dutch carrying trade in European waters was business done by hard-working men, their family and relatives, or men preferred because of local and regional ties, and in the last resort also foreigners. As the weather was rough in northern European waters, so was the sailing. Knowledge of and experience with the shallow coastal waters, of the tides and the dangers of wind and water, were indispensable. But also the will and the urge to make a profit–whatever profit meant to these men–were necessities. In the seventeenth century an Englishman complained: 'The Flemings [*ie* the Dutch] have eaten us out, by reason that they carry halfe as cheape againe as we can, in regarde that their fashioned shippes saile with so few men'. He could not have been more right.

It is a safe conclusion that Dutch carrying trade in European waters was of pre-eminent importance to the inhabitants of the coastal provinces of the Netherlands. In many respects social, economic and cultural life on local and regional levels was strongly affected by maritime activities. Furthermore, the influence of Dutch shipping and trade can be traced in the historical inheritance of many other European countries. For instance, much Russian mar-

itime terminology is in fact merely Dutch, and geographical names like 'Kattegat' and 'Skagerrak' are also Dutch. Navigational knowledge and shipbuilding technology were exported to all the corners of Europe. Even the votive ship models in churches found along the coast of Europe reflect the influence of Dutch seafaring in former days. These sailors, according–again–to Sir William Temple, were

surly and ill-manner'd, which is mistaken for pride; but is I believe learnt, as all manners are, by the conversation we use. Now theirs lying only among one another, or with winds and waves, which are not mov'd or wrought upon by any language, or observance; or to be dealt with, but by pains and by patience; These are all the qualities their mariners have learnt; their valour is passive rather than active; and their language is little more than what is of necessary use to their business . . . . Their great foreign consumption is French wine and brandy, but that may be allow'd them, as the only reward they enjoy of all their pains . . . .

Dr P C van Royen

Bibliography

Edited by Robert Gardiner from material supplied by the contributors

INTRODUCTION

The well-known general books on ship development like Landström's *The Ship* or the Andersons' similarly titled work tend to have less to say about the merchantman than the warship of the 1650-1830 period. In fact, there is no history of pre nineteenth-century merchant ships based on modern analytical methods, perhaps reflecting the general lack of source materials on the technicalities of the ordinary vessels of the mercantile service. Therefore, no truly general books can be recommended, although those listed below relate to more than one chapter of this volume.

J J BAUGEAN, *Collection de toutes les espèces de Bâtiments de guerre et de Bâtiments marchand* (Paris 1814).
One of the best visual sources for the ships of about 1800 is this collection of highly detailed and convincing engravings of a wide range of warships, merchantmen, and small craft. Reprinted in various editions in recent decades.

HOWARD I CHAPELLE, *The Search for Speed under Sail* (New York 1967, reprinted London 1983).
A general history of ship development between 1700 and 1855 by the *doyen* of American technical historians; examples are mostly Anglo-American, but a good overview of progress in naval architecture.

FREDRIK HENRIK AF CHAPMAN, *Architectura Navalis Mercatoria* (Stockholm 1768).
The classic collection of draughts of typical European, and especially northern European, ships of the period, with designs from Chapman himself. Reprinted in various editions in recent decades.

ALAN MCGOWAN, *The Century Before Steam: The Development of the Sailing Ship 1700-1820* (London 1980).
An excellent short survey (with illustrations) examining the main developments in warships, merchant ships engaged in overseas trade, and coastal and short distance traders. Especially clear on changes in rig and sail patterns. In the National Maritime Museum's series *The Ship*.

SIR ALAN MOORE, *Last Days of Mast and Sail: An Essay in Nautical Comparative Anatomy* (Oxford 1925, reprinted Newton Abbott 1970).
Based on firsthand experience, the author compares rigs, rigging and seamanship in the last generation of working sail in northern Europe, the Mediterranean and the East.

H WARRINGTON SMYTH, *Mast and Sail in Europe and Asia* (London 1906; second edition 1929).

An early example of the firsthand recording of the disappearing art of commercial sail, Warrington Smyth covers a huge swathe of maritime ethnography, from the Baltic through the Mediterranean, to the Indian Ocean and Far East. Written and illustrated with the understanding of a keen amateur sailor.

MERCHANT SHIPPING OF THE BRITISH EMPIRE

In the three decades since the publication of Ralph Davis's pioneering book on the English shipping industry (see below), maritime history as a field of research has expanded significantly. The result has been a notable increase in the number of publications in the area–not only in the many books on shipping, trade, the ports, the merchant community etc, but also in quality articles in journals such as *The Mariner's Mirror*, *The American Neptune*, and *International Journal of Maritime History*. Because of the amount of material available, this chapter has not been able to give equal attention to all aspects of merchant shipping between 1650 and 1830, and certain areas have been ignored. This bibliographic note, therefore, begins by mentioning one or two references to cover the obvious gaps: (1) *The British Whaling Trade* (London 1978) by G Jackson has much material on the vessels which engaged in whaling expeditions, including the numbers of vessels involved, their tonnage and the ports from which they operated; (2) Scottish shipping is dealt with in more detail in the article by G Jackson referred to in the text, and in the same author's *The Trade and Shipping of Dundee* (Dundee 1991); (3) the costs of building ships, various estimates of these costs, and levels of investment in shipping are discussed in R Craig, 'Capital formation in transport in Britain: shipping', in J Higgins and S Pollard (eds), *Aspects of Capital Investment in Great Britain 1750-1850* (London 1971), and S Ville, 'Patterns of shipping investment in the port of Newcastle Upon Tyne, 1750-1850', *Northern History* 25 (1989); (4) the social and cultural conditions within which the seamen lived and worked are most fully discussed in M Rideker, *Between the Devil and the Deep Blue Sea: Merchant Seamen, Pirates, and the Anglo-American Maritime World, 1700-1750* (Cambridge, 1987).

DEREK ALDCROFT and MICHAEL FREEMAN (eds), *Transport in the Industrial Revolution* (Manchester 1983).
The two crucial chapters in this collection are by Armstrong and Bagwell on coastal shipping, and Jackson on the ports. Both can be highly recommended.

WILIAM A BAKER, *Colonial Vessels: Some Seventeenth-Century Sailing Craft* (Barre 1962).
Study of early American ship types by a historically-minded naval architect best known for his design of the *Mayflower* replica in 1957. Some sections of his later *Sloops and Shallops* (1966) is also relevant to the period covered by this book.

HOWARD I CHAPELLE, *The Search for Speed under Sail* (New York 1967, reprinted London 1983).
See remarks in Introduction section above; also useful in a specifically American context are the earlier *History of American Sailing Ships* (1935) and *The Baltimore Clipper* (1930), both of which have been reprinted in recent decades.

PATRICK CROWHURST, *The Defence of British Trade 1689-1815* (Folkestone 1977).
Begins with a discussion of the threat posed by French privateers throughout the period studied, and then concentrates on the organisation and success of convoys, especially in Britain's Atlantic trades.

RALPH DAVIS, *The Rise of the English Shipping Industry in the 17th and 18th Centuries* (Newton Abbot 1972).
Although first published in 1962, this is still the best survey of the English shipping industry over the period studied, and an essential starting point for anyone with an interest in merchant shipping.

CHRISTOPHER FRENCH, 'Productivity in the Atlantic shipping industry: a quantitative study', *Journal of Interdisciplinary History* XVII (1987).
Shipping productivity has received much recent attention – see references mentioned in the text to this chapter–and this particular analysis brings out the ways in which merchants, owners, and hirers of shipping involved in London's colonial trade minimised their costs by concentrating on the timing of voyages and regularising patterns of trade, thereby increasing the productivity of trading ventures.

RONALD HOPE, *A New History of British Shipping* (London 1990).
Solid account of the long history of the British shipping industry based on extensive bibliographic knowledge. For the period covered in this survey, there is useful material on vessel size, size of the merchant fleet, fluctuations in shipping activity etc.

DAVID MACGREGOR, *Merchant Sailing Ships 1815-1850: Supremacy of Sail* (London 1984).

——, *Merchant Sailing Ships: Sovereignty of Sail 1775-1815:* (London 1985).

——, *Fast Sailing Ships 1775-1875: Their Design and Construction* (revised edition, London 1988).
Any bibliographic note on British merchant shipping between 1650 and 1830 would not be complete without reference to the work of David MacGregor. His extensive-

ly illustrated volumes on merchant shipping are an invaluable source for the maritime historian, full of details, analysis, and examples of all aspects of merchant vessels. Unfortunately his work does not cover the first half of the eighteenth century and earlier, although *Merchant Sailing Ships 1775-1815* does make some reference to the decades before its nominal start date.

KENNETH MORGAN, *Bristol and the Atlantic Trade in the Eighteenth Century* (Cambridge 1993).
Comprehensive analysis of the commercial activity of one of Britain's major ports in the eighteenth century. Chapters on shipping and shipping patterns are particularly valuable for illustrating some of the themes raised in this survey.

E P MORRIS, *The Fore and Aft Rig in America* (New Haven 1927, reprinted New York 1970).
Now rather dated, but in its time a highly regarded study of the various small local craft of North America, most of which were merchant ships.

C NORTHCOTE PARKINSON (ed), *The Trade Winds: A Study of British Overseas Trade During the French Wars 1793-1815* (London 1948).
Despite its sub-title, this classic collection of chapters by a previous generation of leading maritime historians examines not only the major trades during the French Wars, but also shipowning, the employment of shipping, seamen, and the seaports. Still an important reference.

SIMON VILLE, *English Shipowning During the Industrial Revolution: Michael Henley and Son, London Shipowners, 1770-1830* (Manchester 1987).
Based on the Henley papers discovered in the 1970s, this case study traces the career of one London shipowning firm which graduated from coal merchanting to specialist shipowning. The material illustrates such themes as capital accumulation, the ships employed and owned by Henleys, the role of the master, the conditions of the crew, and profitability.

SEAGOING SHIPS OF THE NETHERLANDS

Not surprisingly, there is little in English specifically devoted to this subject, so much of what follows is in Dutch. Apart from the published works, there are a number of important manuscript sources, which although inaccessible to the ordinary reader are listed for the benefit of scholars:

Anonymus, 'Evenredige Toerusting van Schepen ten Oorlog Bijder See'. Manuscript in Scheepvaartmuseum Amsterdam. Transcription Herman Ketting. Dated 1660. Manuscript on building of men of war.

P Van Zwijndrecht, 'De Groote Nederlandsche Scheeps Bouw op een Proportionaale Reegel voor Gestelt', manuscript 1757.

ANONYMUS, *De Ongeluckige Voyagie*, edited by Jan Jans (Amsterdam 1649).
Eye witness' report on the dramatic wrecking of the *Batavia*. In Dutch.

J R BRUYN, 'Engelse Scheepsbouwers op de Amsterdamse Admiraliteitswerf in de 18de eeuw— enkele aspecten', *Mededelingen van de Nederlandse Vereniging voor Zeegeschiedenis* (September 1990).
Paper on the introduction of British shipwrights to the Amsterdam Admiralty shipyard.

J R BRUYN, F S GAASTRA and I SCHOFFER, *Dutch-Asiatic Shipping in the Seventeenth and Eighteenth Century*. Rijks Geschiedkundige Publicatien, Grote serie nr 165, 166, 167 (The Hague 1987).
Standard work on the Dutch East India Company, with lists of all outward and return voyages by East Indiamen.

H DECQUER, *Middelen om uit te vinden de ware ladinge der schepen na hare groote* (Amsterdam 1690).
VOC publication, Scheepvaartmuseum. Report on calculating ship's cubic capacity. In Dutch.

H EDWARDS, *Het wrak op het Halve-maan's rif* (Baarn 1971).
Story of the loss of the *Zeewijck*.

J GAWRONSKI, B KIST and O STOKVIS-VAN BOETZELAER, *Hollandia Compendium* (Amsterdam 1992).
Archaeological report on the findings on the *Hollandia* site.

J GAWRONSKI, B KIST, *'T Vliegend Hart Report 1982 –1983* (Rijksmuseum Amsterdam 1984).
Archaeological report on the finds of the *'T Vliegent Hart*.

J GREEN, *The loss of the VOC retourschip BATAVIA, Western Australia 1629. An excavation report and catalogue of artefacts*, BAR Int Series 489 (Oxford 1989).
An archaeological report on the findings of the team investigating the wreck.

ROBERT GRENIER, *Red Bay Project*, Canadian Conservation Institute (in press).
An archaeological report by the leader of the team working on the Red Bay wreck.

M HATCHER, *The Nanking Cargo* (London 1987).
Report on the cargo from the wreck of the *Geldermalsen*.

H DEN HEIJER, *De Geschiedenis van de WIC* (Zutphen 1994).
History of the West Indian Company. In Dutch.

M L'HOUR, L LONG, E RIETH, *Le Mauritius, La Memoire Engloutie* (Grenoble 1989).
Report on the archaeological finds on the *Mauritius* site.

A J HOVING, 'The *Heemskerck*, Abel Tasman's ship', *Bearings* 4/2 (1992).
Article on the reconstruction of the model of the *Heemskerck*.

H KETTING, *Prins Willem* (Bussum 1979).
Book on the model in the Rijksmuseum. In Dutch and also available in German.

TH J MAARLEVELD, 'Archaeology and early modern merchant ships. Building sequence and consequences. An introductory review', in A Carmiggelt (ed), *Rotterdam Papers* VII (Rotterdam 1992).
Latest information on shipbuilding methods based on archaeological finds.

P MARSDEN, *The Wreck of the* Amsterdam (London 1974).
Report on the wreck of the Dutch East Indiamen *Amsterdam*, with details of the background of the company and its ships.

DUHAMEL DU MONCEAU, *Grondbeginselen van de Scheepsbouw of Werkdadige Verhandeling van de Scheepstimmerkunst* (Amsterdam 1757).
Originally a French publication, translated into Dutch under supervision of two Dutch shipbuilders.

R REINDERS, 'Cog finds in the IJsselmeerpolders', *Flevobericht* 248 (1985).
Review of archaeological cog finds in the Zuiderzee area.

W UDEMANS JR, *Verhandeling van den Nederlandschen Scheepsbouw* (Middelburg 1757).

J VAN BEIJLEN, *Schepen van de Nederlanden. Van de late Middeleeuwen tot het einde van de 17de eeuw* (Amsterdam 1970).
Standard work on seventeenth-century ships. In Dutch.

P VAN DAM, *Beschryvinge van de Oostindische Compagnie*, 17de Capittel. Edited by F W Stapel, I, III. Rijks Geschiedkundige Publicatien, grote serie nr 63, 87 (The Hague 1927, 1943; original edition 1701).
Van Dam was commissioned by the VOC to write its history. Voluminous work. In Dutch.

C VAN YK, *De Nederlandsche Scheeps-bouw-konst Open Gestelt* (Amsterdam 1697).
Second Dutch book on shipbuilding. Clearly written by a shipbuilding expert. In Dutch.

L VAN ZWIJNDRECHT, *Verhandeling van de Hollandschen Scheepsbouw, raakende de verschillende Charters de Oorlogschepen* (with an additional part by C de Ruiter, *Verhandeling van 't bouwen van Koopvaardyschepen*, The Hague 1757).
Written as a reaction to Duhamel du Monceau, to prove that Dutch shipbuilders were not inferior to foreign ones. In Dutch.

NICOLAES WITSEN, *Aeloude en Hedendaegsche Scheeps-bouw en Bestier* (Amsterdam 1671).
The first book on shipbuilding in Holland; important but inaccessible. Re-edited with a commentary by A J Hoving as *Nicolaes Witsens Scheeps-bouw-konst Open Gestelt* (Franeker 1994). Due for translation into English and publication in 1995.

THE SHIPS OF SCANDINAVIA AND THE BALTIC

Although many of the publications listed here are in foreign languages, some have summaries in English.

CHRISTIAN AHLSTRÖM, *Spår av hav, yxa och penna. Historiska sjöolyckor i östersjön avspeglade i marinarkeologiskt källmaterial* (Helsingfors 1995).
Dissertation in archaeology analysing the conditions and methodology for the identification of shipwrecks in the Baltic from historical records. Gives a series of examples of such identification procedures carried out on wrecks of old merchantmen.

ARNE BANG-ANDERSEN, BASIL GREENHILL and EGIL HARALD GRUDE (eds), *The North Sea. A Highway of Economic and Cultural Exchange. Character –History* (Oslo 1985).
Comprehensive overview of the story of the North Sea and its culture. For the subject of the present chapter see in particular the contributions of Jarle Björklund, P M Bosscher and Jaap R Bruin (titles listed below), which deal with different aspects of seafaring and maritime trades in the post-medieval period.

KERSTIN G BERG, *Redare i Roslagen. Segelfartygsrederier och deras verksamhet i gamla Vätö socken*, Nordiska museet handlingar 100 (Arlöv 1984).
Ethnological dissertation on the development of shipowning and shipping in and around the northern part of the Stockholm archipelago, particularly the island of Vätö in Roslagen.

JARLE BJÖRKLUND, 'Trade and Cultural Exchange in the 17th and 18th Centuries', in A Bang-Andersen *et*

al (eds), *The North Sea. A Highway of Economic and Cultural Exchange. Character–History* (Norway 1985).
Paper describing the structure and development of North Sea trade in the period.

P M BOSSCHER, '"...except through the Agency and Intermediary of the Aforementioned Sea..." Some Observations on the Development of Dutch Sea Power and the Diffusion of Dutch Influence in North-Western Europe', in A Bang-Andersen *et al* (eds), *The North Sea. A Highway of Economic and Cultural Exchange. Character–History* (Norway 1985).
A description of the social and economic structure of the area around the Rhine estuary in the post-medieval period, as background to study of naval development.

JAAP R BRUIN, 'The Timber Trade. The case of Dutch-Norwegian Relations in the 17th Century', in A Bang-Andersen *et al* (eds), *The North Sea. A Highway of Economic and Cultural Exchange. Character –History* (Norway 1985).
Paper giving an overview of the timber trade between Norway and the Netherlands and Britain during the seventeenth century.

HENRIK BYGHOLM (ed), *Skuder og skippere i Klitmöller. Blade af skudefartens historie* (Fredrikshavn; no date).
Monograph on the coastal society of Thy and the small town of Thisted in Jutland, Denmark, and the local shipping based in this area, trading with the southern coast of Norway (see also Götche below).

HJALMAR BÖRJESSON, *Stockholms segelsjöfart* (Stockholm 1932).
Extensive history of the seafaring of the Swedish capital from the medieval period to the early twentieth century. A stimulating insight into the subject through case studies of the history and fate of particular ships sailing from Stockholm, based on historical records.

CARL OLOF CEDERLUND, *Vraket vid Älvsnabben. Fartygets byggnad*, Statens sjöhistoriska museum, Rapport nr 14 (Stockholm 1981).
Marine archaeological report on the ship structure of the wreck of a merchantman, later identified as the galliot *Concordia* of Stralsund, which foundered in the Stockholm archipelago in 1754. (See above C Ahlström 1995; see also Kaijser 1981 which is a parallel study on the finds of cargo and equipment in the same wreck.)

——, 'The lodja and other bigger transport vessels built in the east-european clinker-building technique', in Sean McGrail and Eric Kentley (eds), *Sewn Plank Boats*, BAR International Series 276 (Oxford 1985).
An overview of smaller and medium sized vessels for transport in western Russia and the Baltic states during the medieval and postmedieval period.

FREDRIK HENRIK AF CHAPMAN, *Architectura Navalis Mercatoria* (Stockholm 1768).
See remarks under 'Introduction' section above.

ARNE EMIL CHRISTENSEN (ed), *Inshore Craft of Norway. From a manuscript by Bernhard and Öystein Faeröyvik* (Oslo and London 1979).
Portfolio of ship design plans of traditional, local and usually clinker-built transport and trading vessels from the Norwegian coast, followed by historical and technical descriptions of them.

MORTEN GÖTHCHE, 'Fra skude til slup', in Henrik Bygholm (ed), *Skuder og skippere i Klitmöller. Blade af skudefartens historie* (Fredrikshavn; no date).

Chapter on the ship types and their development in the trade between northern Jutland and the south coast of Norway since the eighteenth century.

MARKKU HAAPIO (ed), *Seglens Tidevarv* (Pori 1983).
Historical overview of Finnish sea trade.

GUSTAF HALLDIN, (ed), *Svenskt skeppsbyggeri* (Malmö 1964).
Comprehensive history of Swedish shipbuilding from the prehistoric period to the early twentieth century, with many illustrations.

HUGO HAMMAR, *Fartygstyper i Svenska Ost-Indiska Companiets flotta* (Göteborg 1931).
Treatise on the structure and development of the ships of the Swedish East India Company based on a series of ship plans included in the publication.

DANIEL G HARRIS, *F H Chapman: The First Naval Architect and his Work* (London 1989).
Standard English biography of Fredrik Henrik af Chapman, the best known ship designer of the eighteenth century.

——, 'Henrik Gerner and the Danish 1776 "Defence Ship" Programme', *The Mariner's Mirror* 81 (1995).

STAFFAN HÖGBERG, *Utrikeshandel och sjöfart på 1700-talet. Stapelvaror i svensk export och import 1731–1808* (Lund 1969).
Economic history dissertation on the subject of Swedish foreign trade and shipping during the eighteenth century.

INGRID KAIJSER, *Vraket vid Älvsnabben. Dokument-ation. Last och utrustning*, Statens sjöhistoriska museum, Rapport nr 13 (Stockholm 1981).
Marine archaeological report on the finds of cargo and equipment in the galliot *Concordia* from Stralsund, which foundered in Stockholm archipelago in 1754.

SVEN T KJELLBERG, *Svenska ostindiska compagnierna 1731–1813* (Malmö 1975).
The history of the Swedish East India Company.

KNUD KLEM, *De Danskes vej. Rids af dansk söhistorie* (Copenhagen 1941).
History of Danish sea trade and shipbuilding, its structure and development.

GUNNAR LÖWEGREN, *Sveriges sjöfart och skeppsbyg-geri genom tiderna* (Stockholm 1953).
Survey of Swedish sea trade and shipbuilding throughout recent history.

CHRISTIAN NIELSEN, 'Danske båttyper. Opmålt og beskrevet af Christian Nielsen', *Söhistoriske skrifter* VII, Handels- og söfartsmuseet på Kronborg (Helsingör 1973).
Description of Danish coastal boat types with ship design plans and data, including smaller trading vessels.

WALTER RIED, *Deutsche Segelschiffahrt seit 1470* (Munich 1974).
History of German sea trade and shipbuilding, its structure and development.

C RISE HANSEN, *Den danske skibsfart gennem tiderne*, Vi og vor Fortid No 3 (Copenhagen 1941).
History of Danish sea trade and shipbuilding in modern times.

PEKKA TOIVANEN, *Jacobstads Wapen 1767. 'Ett I Smått för Landet värderlig Förmån i Utrikes Seglation'*, Jakobstads Museum Publication No 21 (Jakobstad 1988).
Monograph on the building of a replica of the *Jacobstads Wapen* of 1767 in the Finnish town of Jakobstad.

MEDITERRANEAN SHIPS AND SHIPPING

A major problem for the study of this area is the variety of languages and cultures it encompasses. For terminology, Auguste Jal's classic *Glossaire Nautique* (3 vols, Paris 1848) is still useful, although the ongoing project to update the work is making significant improvements; there is also H R and R Kahane and A Tietze, *The Lingua Franca in the Levant* (Urbana, Illinois 1958), a study of Turkish nautical terms borrowed from Italian and Greek. The Levant is particularly difficult, since proper study requires knowledge of Arabic and Persian, so Western scholars have to depend on works based on old Turkish sources, like R Mantran, *Istanbul dans la seconde moitié du XVIIᵉ siècle* (Paris 1962), or J von Hammer-Purgstall, *Constantinopolis und der Bosporus* (Budapest 1822). H Charles and A M Solayman, *Le parler Arabe de la voile et la vie maritime sur la côte Libano-Syrienne* (Beirut 1972) makes an attempt at a glossary of nautical terms for the Levant coast but its methodology is suspect.

F BEAUDOUIN, *Bâteaux des côtes de France* (Grenoble 1975).
Well illustrated survey of the coastal craft of France. Text in French.

E BLOOMSTER, *Sailing and Sailing Craft down the Ages* (Annapolis, Maryland 1969).
A general survey, but one covering some of the surviving Mediterranean working sailing types.

MARCO BONINO, 'Notes sur les navicelli italiens', *Le Petit Perroquet* 20 (1976).
Well illustrated study of the various local types of the Italian west coast. In French.

JEAN BOUDRIOT AND H BERTI, *Chébec Le Requin 1750* (Paris 1987).
Subtitled 'Chébecs et Bâtiments Méditerranéans', this book is both a modelmakers' monograph on a naval xebec and a study of related lateen rigged craft. In French; an English translation of part of the text is available, but it omits the section on other types.

F BRAUDEL, *The Mediterranean and the Mediter-ranean World in the Age of Philip II*, 2 vols (London 1972).
A masterly overview of the economic and social milieu, but some of the detail has been challenged.

RENÉ BURLET, 'Mistics, Misticou et autres Polacres', *Neptunia* 189 (1993).
Attempts to sort out the various types of craft derived from the *chébec* and *polacre*. In French.

J L SUREDA CARRIÓN, *Apuntes para la Historia de la Marina de Vela Mallorquina de los Siglos XVIII y XIX* (Palma de Mallorca 1940).
History of Majorcan sailing ships in the eighteenth and nineteenth centuries. In Spanish.

G B RUBIN DE CERVIN, *Bâteaux et Batellerie de Venise* (Lausanne 1978).
A lavishly illustrated study of Venetian shipping, although concentrating on local craft and naval galleys rather than merchant sailing ships. French text.

G DURAND-VIEL, *Les campagnes navales de Mohammed Aly et d'Ibrahim*, 2 vols (Paris 1935).
A study by a French admiral of the naval side of Egyptian expansion at the expense of the Ottoman empire in the nineteenth century. In passing has some information on merchant shipping. French text.

P EARLE, *Corsairs of Malta and Barbary* (London 1970).
A study of privateering/piracy that made great use of Maltese archival material.

J VON HAMMER-PURGSTALL (translator), *Evliya Effendi: Narrative of Travels in Europe, Asia and Africa in the 17th Century*, 2 vols (London 1846-50).
Translation of work by Evliya Gelebi, which contains accurate descriptions of the *kadirga*, a large galley, with full dimensions.

P A HENNIQUE, *Caboteurs et pêcheurs de la côte Tunisie* (Paris 1888, reprinted Nice 1989).
A useful illustrated survey of Tunisian coastal and fishing craft from the nineteenth century. French text.

P KAHLE (translator), *Piri Re'is, das Türkische Segelhandbuch für das Mittelländische Meer*, 2 vols (Berlin and Leipzig 1926).
Early Turkish sailing directions translated, with an important introductory chapter to the second volume. German text.

G G LEON, chapter on the Greek merchant marine, *Elenikè Emporikè Nautilia, 1453-1850* (Athens 1972).
An excellent survey, but only available in Greek.

J MATHIEUX, 'Sur la marine marchand barbaresque au XVIIIᵉ siècle', *Annales* XIII (1958).
An important study of the merchant marine of the Barbary states. French text.

W ZU MONDFELD, *Die Schebecke und andere Schiffstypen des Mittelmeerraumes* (Bielefeld and Berlin 1974).
A modelmaker's monograph on Mediterranean ship types; the drawings, however, are not always very detailed. German text.

G MORINO, series in *Model Shipwright*.
Well illustrated articles with plans, aimed at modelmakers, on Italian small craft–the 'Genoese Leudo' in issue 24 (1978), the 'Ligurian Pareggia' in 30 (1979), and the 'Navicello Toscano' in 35 (1981).

C DE NEGRI, *Vele Italiane del XIX Secolo* (Milan 1974).
A useful discussion of nineteenth-century Italian sailing craft. Italian text.

VICE-ADMIRAL EDMOND PÂRIS, *Souvenirs de Marine conservées* (Paris 1878, reprinted in 3 vols Grenoble 1972).
A huge collection of plans and data on historical ship types, but as far as Mediterranean types are concerned doubts have been expressed about their accuracy; at the very least, they represent late examples. Text in French.

XAVIER PASTOR, series in *Model Shipwright*.
Well illustrated articles with plans, aimed at modelmakers, on Spanish small craft, although most are fishing boats rather than coasters–the 'Dorna' in issue 43 (1983), the 'Jabega of Malaga' in 44 (1983), 'A Spanish Jabeque of 1795' in 51 (1985), the 'Mallorcan Llaut' in 57 (1986), the 'Mediterranean Falucho' in 60 (1987), the 'Mallorcan Pailebote *Nuevo Corazón*' in 70 (1989), and the Catalan 'Palangrera' in 83 (1993).

A H J PRINS, 'The modified Syrian schooner: Problem formulation in maritime change', *Human Organisation* 24, Special Issue (New York 1965).
A study of the Levant schooner that survived in to the twentieth century.

————, *In Peril on the Sea: Maritime Votive Paintings in the Maltese Islands* (Valletta 1989).
A survey of ships and ship types in the many ex-voto paintings in Maltese churches.

G RAMBERT (ed), *Histoire du Commerce du Marseilles*.
Relevant volumes of this monumental study of the trade of Marseille are IV: *1599-1660*, by L Bergasse, and *1660-1789* by G Rambert (Paris 1954); and V: *1660-1789 Le Levant* by R Paris, and *1660-1789 La Barbarie* by J Reynaud (Paris 1957).

R ROMANO, *Le commerce du Royaume de Naples avec la France et les pays de l'Adriatique au XVIIIᵉ siècle* (Paris 1951).
An economic history of Neapolitan trade in the eighteenth century. In French.

EUROPEAN INLAND SAILING CRAFT

For most European countries literature in the English language is very scarce on this subject, so the most important works are quoted in whatever language.

BELGIUM

ALEX DE VOS, *Bibliografie van de Belgische binnenscheepvaart*, Parts I and II (Ghent 1972 and 1974).
An extended bibliography of the inland navigation of Belgium.

FRANCE

FRANÇOIS BEAUDOIN, *Bâteaux des fleuves de France* (Douarnenez 1985).
A richly illustrated and well documented book, mainly on French inland craft of the nineteenth century.

Colloques du Patrimoine. Le patrimoine maritime et fluvial (Paris 1993).
Collection of papers, conferences on the French maritime heritage, organised by the Ministry of Culture.

GERMANY

WERNER BÖCKING, *Die Geschichte der Rheinschiffahrt. Schiffe auf dem Rhein in drei Jahrtausenden* (Moers 1980-81).

K SCHWARZ, *Die Typenentwicklung des Rheinschiffs bis zum 19 Jahrhundert* (Karlsruhe 1926).

OSCAR TEUBERT, *Die Binnenschiffahrt. Ein Handbuch für alle Beteiligten*, 2 vols (Leipzig 1912).

KARL-HEINZ WIECHERS, *...Und führen weit übers Meer. Zur Geschichten der Ostfriesischen Segelschiffahrt*, Vol III: *Die Fehne*. (Norden, in press).
Volumes I and II covered the seagoing vessels of East Frisia. Vol III will discuss the ships in the peat areas of this German province.

GREAT BRITAIN

ROBERT MALSTER, *Wherries and Waterways* (Lavenham 1971).
About the Norfolk wherry and keel.

EDWARD PAGET-TOMLINSON, *The Illustrated History of Canal and River Navigations* (Sheffield 1993).
Gives a very complete overview of many British inland and river craft and contains an excellent bibliography.

MICHAEL STAMMERS, *Mersey Flats and Flatmen* (Lavenham 1993).
Covers the local craft of this river and related canals.

ITALY

MARIO MARZARI, 'Vecchie Barche Adriatiche', *Rivista Maritima* CXVII (1984).
Description of the working boats (mainly fishing boats) in the inland waters of the Adriatic. Includes a bibliography.

G B RUBIN DE CERVIN, *Bâteaux et batellerie de Venise* (Lausanne 1978).
Covers Venetian craft in the widest sense, including medieval galleys, but has much material, and some excellent illustrations, on the local craft of the Lagoon.

NETHERLANDS

In the Netherlands a huge range of books about historical inland and fishing craft was written in the 1970s and 1980s. The following selection are the 'classics'.

G C E CRONE, *Nederlandsche jachten, binnenschepen, visschersvaartuigen* (Amsterdam 1926, reprint Schiedam 1978).
Gives a description of many old Dutch sailing craft from 1650 to 1900, with numerous plates of ship models in the Netherlands Maritime Museum, Amsterdam. Includes an extended English summary.

G GROENEWEGEN, *Verzameling van Vier en tachtig stuks Hollandsche schepen* (Rotterdam 1789).

P LE COMTE, *Afbeeldingen van schepen en vaartuigen in verschillende bewegingen* (Amsterdam 1831).
Both contain excellent and detailed contemporary engravings of Dutch seagoing ships and inland craft of the eighteenth century. Many reprints, still available in secondhand and antiquarian bookshops in the Netherlands.

E W PETREJUS, *Oude Zeilschepen en hun modellen. Binnenschepen, jachten, vissersschepen* (Bussum 1971).
Contains many illustrations of ship models.

PORTUGAL

MANUEL LEITÃO, *Boats of the Lisbon River*, National Maritime Museum Monograph 34 (Greenwich 1978).
A study of the *fragata* and related types of Tagus sailing barges.

O L FILGUEIRAS, 'The book of all Tagus Boats', in *Post-Medieval Boat and Ship Archeology*, BAR International Series 256, (Oxford 1985).

————, *The Decline of Portuguese Regional Boats*, National Maritime Museum Monograph 47 (Greenwich 1980).
Covers both seagoing and inland traditional craft.

SPAIN

FRANCISCO CARRERAS CANDI, *La navegación en el Rio Ebro: notas historicas* (Barcelona 1940).

BLANCO BLASCO NOGUÉS, *El Ebro: Navegación y pesca* (Zaragoza 1992).

JOSÉ MARIA MASSO Y GARCIA-FIGUEROA, *Barcos en Galicia: de la prehistoria hasta hoy y del Mino al Finisterre* (Pontevedra 1982).

ANGEL PORTET, 'Raiers d'arreu del món: el transport fluvial de la fusta als diferents països', *Collegats* No 3, pp27-36.

SWEDEN

YNGVE MALMQUIST, *De seglade Pa Vättern. Skutor, skeppare, sjömän och skeppsbyggare* (Uddevalla 1986).

YNGVE ROLLOF, *Sveriges inre Vatttenvägar*, Del 1-4 (Stockholm 1977-1981).

SWITZERLAND

P BLOESCH, 'Die Schiffspläne im Berner Statsarchiv', *Berner Zeitschrift für Geschichte und Heimatkunde* 39 (1977), pp37-65.

G CORNAZ, 'L'evolution de la navigation a voile et a rames', in G Cornaz, N Charmillot and J Naef, *Bâteaux et batellerie du Léman* (Lausanne 1983).

PAUL KOELNER, *Die Basler Rheinschiffahrt vom Mittelalter zur Neuzeit* (Basel 1954).

SCHWEIZERISCHES SCHIFFAHRTSMUSEUM BASEL, *Museumsführer* (Basel 1985).
Guide to Swiss shipping museum at Basel.

ALBERT SPYCHER, *Der Weidlingbauer* (Basel 1988).
Concerns the *weidling*, a scow-like boat of Switzerland.

YACHTS AND PLEASURE CRAFT

The literature of yachting is vast, but since this volume is only concerned with the early years of pleasure boating, the following list is similarly restricted.

ERNLE BRADFORD, *Three Centuries of Sailing* (London 1964).
A general history of the subject, with some information on the early years of the subject.

G C E CRONE, *De Jachten der Oranges* (Amsterdam 1937).
Now somewhat dated, but still a useful survey of the early history of yachting in the Netherlands. In Dutch.

C M GAVIN, *Royal Yachts* (London 1932).
Now rather dated but still the only serious study of British royal yachts.

BROR HALLÁNG, *Slupen Wasaorden* (Stockholm 1985).
A small illustrated book on the Swedish royal barge *Wasaorden*, in both its original form and as rebuilt. In Swedish

G P B NAISH, *Royal Yachts* (London 1964).
A small booklet produced by the National Maritime Museum based largely on their collection of plans of British royal yachts; well illustrated.

D PHILIPS-BIRT, *Fore and Aft Sailing Craft and the Development of the Modern Yacht* (London 1962).
A history of small sailing craft by an historically minded naval architect.

W F RYAN, 'Peter the Great's English Yacht', *The Mariner's Mirror* 69 (1983).
Article about William III's yacht *Royal Transport* that was presented to the Czar.

R W SLEESWYK AND A J WIJNSMA, *De boeier Friso, Fries Statenjacht 1894-1954-1994* (Leeuwarden 1994).
The story of the Friesland Provincial Government's official *boeier* yacht *Friso*. In Dutch.

R STEEN STEENSEN, *De Danske Kongers Skibe* (Copenhagen 1972).
A hisory of Danish royal pleasure craft.

J VAN BEIJLEN, *Schepen van de Nederlanden. Van de late Middeleeuwen tot het einde van de 17de eeuw* (Amsterdam 1970).
Standard work on seventeenth-century Dutch ships, containing a chapter on yachts. In Dutch.

HANS VANDERMISSEN, *Holland and the Origins of Yachting* (Nijmegen 1986).
A small but informative work, with much detail on the early history of pleasure sailing in the Netherlands.

SHIPPING ECONOMICS AND TRADE IN THE AGE OF SAIL

For works concentrating on the British side of Anglo-Dutch commercial rivalry, see under 'Merchant Shipping of the British Empire' section above.

VIOLET BARBOUR, *Capitalism in Amsterdam in the 17th Century* (Ann Arbor, Michigan 1963).
An influential study of the background conditions of Dutch economic expansion.

C R BOXER, *The Dutch Seaborne Empire 1600-1800* (London 1965).
An overview of the various aspects of the social, economic and political history of the Dutch Republic connected with the Dutch maritime expansion over the world. The standard English-language history.

J R BRUIN and FEMME GAASTRA (eds), *Ships, Sailors and Spices. East India companies and their Shipping in the 16th, 17th and 18th Century* (Amsterdam 1993).
A series of essays on European Asiatic shipping. See, for example, K N Chaudhuri, 'The English East India Company's Shipping (c1660-1760)'.

J R BRUIN, F S GAASTRA and I SCHÖFFER (eds), *Dutch Asiatic Shipping in the 17th and 18th Century*, 3 vols (The Hague 1979-1987).
The product of a major reseach project on the operations of the VOC based on a detailed study of its records.

F S GAASTRA, *De geschiedenis van de VOC* (Zutphen 1991).
A good concise modern history of the Dutch East India Company. In Dutch.

KRISTOF GLAMMAN, *Dutch Asiatic Trade 1620-1740* (revised edition The Hague 1980).
An important book on the economic workings of Dutch trade with their Far Eastern empire.

JONATHAN ISRAEL, *Dutch Primacy in World Trade, 1585-1740* (Oxford 1989).
Provides a new approach to the economic and political rise of the Dutch Republic. Inevitably, Israel pays a lot of attention to the merchant marine and other branches of maritime activities in the Dutch Republic.

———, *The Dutch Republic: Its Rise, Greatness and Fall, 1477-1806* (Oxford 1995).
A new and authoritative history of the Dutch Republic, including a discussion of its institutions.

J H PARRY, *Trade and Dominion. The European Oversea Empires in the Eighteenth Century* (London 1971).
A comparative view of the colonial expansion of the major European powers by one of the great names in economic history.

C WILSON, *Profit and Power: A Study of England and the Dutch Wars* (The Hague 1978).
A study of the economic circumstances of the Anglo-Dutch wars of the late seventeenth century.

SEAMEN AND THE MERCHANT SERVICE, 1650-1830

G ASAERT, P M BOSSCHER, J R BRUIJN and W J VAN HOBOKEN, *Maritieme Geschiedenis der Nederlanden* , 4 vols (Bussum 1977-1979).
A four-volume overview of various aspects of Dutch maritime history through the ages. Each volume comprises a particular era, treating as far as possible the same themes and issues. A 'must' for those seriously interested in Dutch maritime history. In Dutch.

VIOLET BARBOUR, 'Dutch and English Merchant Shipping in the Seventeenth Century', *Economic History Review* II/2 (1930), pp261-290.
Seminal article on the importance of the economic advantages of the Dutch flute.

C R BOXER, 'Sedentary Workers and Seafaring Folk in the Dutch Republic' in J S Bromley and E H Kossman (eds), *Britain and the Netherlands*, Vol II (Groningen 1964), pp148-168.
Article on the growing shortage of native Dutch sailors and the decline of seafaring expertise, related to the general economic and political decline of the Dutch Republic during the eighteenth century.

J R BRUIJN and J LUCASSEN (eds), *Op de schepen der Oostindische Compagnie. Vijf artikelen van J de Hullu* (Groningen 1980).
The introduction of this collection of five essays on the various aspects of the social history of the Dutch East India Company treats the problem of seafaring labour and the growing demand of the company in a broader perspective of the overall development of the (maritime) labour market of the Dutch Republic. In Dutch.

J R BRUIJN, *De Admiraliteit van Amsterdam in rustige jaren, 1713-1751. Regenten en financiën, schepen en zeevarenden* (Amsterdam 1970).
A history of the organisation of the Dutch navy at the beginning of the period of the Dutch Republic's decline. In Dutch.

———, *The Dutch Navy of the Seventeenth and Eighteenth Centuries* (Columbia, SC, 1993).
Obligatory reading for those interested in Dutch naval history; primarily focussed on the organisation and administration of the Dutch navy before, during, and after its heyday.

AKSEL E CHRISTENSEN, *Dutch Trade to the Baltic about 1600. Studies in the Sound Toll Register and Dutch Shipping Records* (Copenhagen and The Hague 1941).
The work of Christensen is mainly based upon the working of the well-known Sound Toll Register. This book gives a broad and detailed view of the importance of Dutch merchant shipping by the beginning of the Golden Age.

C A DAVIDS, *Wat lijdt den zeeman al verdriet. Het Nederlandse zeemanslied in de zeiltijd (1600-1900)* (The Hague 1980).

The introduction of this collection of shanties presents a clear overview of the *status questionis* concerning the social side of seafaring labour in the Netherlands. In Dutch.

————, *Zeewezen en Wetenschap. De wetenschap en de ontwikkeling van de navigatietechniek in Nederland tussen 1585 en 1815* (Amsterdam and Dieren 1986).
A survey of the development of the various navigational techniques in the Netherlands. The mutual interdepence of science and seafaring and finding one's way across the sea and the exchange of ideas is the central theme of this work. In Dutch.

JONATHAN I ISRAEL, *Dutch Primacy in World Trade, 1585-1740* (Oxford 1989).
See entry in previous section.

P C VAN ROYEN, *Zeevarenden op de koopvaardijvloot omstreeks 1700* (Amsterdam 1987).

Presents the results of research on a new and unique source of data (notary records) that shed light upon the ships and masters—as well as the previously undocumented common seamen—taking service with the merchant marine operating in European waters. In Dutch.

————, 'Manning the Merchant Marine: the Dutch Maritime Labour Market about 1700', *International Journal of Maritime History* I/1 (1989), pp1-28.
A summarised version of the Dutch written research on seafarers.

————, 'Personnel of the Dutch and English Mercantile Marine (1700-1850). An introductory paper', in J R Bruijn and W F J Mörzer Bruyns (eds), *Anglo-Dutch Mercantile Marine Relations 1700-1850* (Amsterdam and Leiden 1991), pp103-113.

Presents new results of research into seafaring as a source of employment extended with data concerning the nineteenth century.

W TEMPLE (edited by G N Clark), *Observations upon the United Provinces of the Netherlands* (Oxford 1972).
As an influential contemporary diplomat Temple provides some interesting views and statements—and in some respects a sharp analysis—regarding the political and economic state of affairs of the Dutch Republic at the zenith of its power.

R W UNGER, *Dutch Shipbuilding before 1800. Ships and Guilds* (Assen and Amsterdam 1978).
A history of Dutch shipbuilding from the middle ages through the rapid advances in the sixteenth and early seventeenth centuries and finally the stagnation in the eighteenth.

Glossary of Terms and Abbreviations

Compiled by Robert Gardiner. This list assumes some knowledge of ships and does not include the most basic terminology. It also avoids those words which are defined on the only occasions in which they occur in this book.

aak. A family of Dutch ship types originally characterised by a flat, turned up 'swim' bow and stern; usually single-masted, initially with a square sail and later a sprit.

aback. The situation of the sails when the wind bears on the opposite surface from that which will propel the ship forwards. In a square rigged ship the sails can be intentionally backed, to slow the vessel or to hold it relatively stationary; a ship can also be taken aback by a sudden wind shift or due to the inattention of the helmsman.

allège. Flat-bottomed river craft of the Rhône area of southern France, although also venturing along the adjacent coasts; in existence from at least the seventeenth century until replaced by railways in the nineteenth. Lateen rigged with one or two masts.

Baltimore clipper. An imprecise term applied to fine-lined American schooners with an emphasis on extreme speed; not so much a specific type as a concept, their heyday was approximately 1780-1820.

baquet. A barge designed in 1832 by the Belgian engineer Vifquain for use on the Brussels-Charleroi Canal; sometimes sailed but usually horse-drawn.

Barbary powers. North African Muslim states from what would now be called the Maghreb that carried on a sporadic form of maritime guerilla warfare against Christian shipping from the sixteenth until the early nineteenth centuries. Although often referred to in the West as pirates (or less emotively as corsairs), their naval forces carried out state-sanctioned policy, and their privateering and slave-raiding were often the main economic support of their respective states.

barge. Originally a fine-lined ship's boat, but latterly most commonly applied to a capacious riverine or coasting vessel, sometimes with a simple fore and aft rig, such as the familiar Thames spritsail barge.

barko-bestia. Greek form of barquentine (*qv*).

barque or **bark**. Originally a simple, capacious bulk carrier, with a simplified version of the ship rig (*qv*), which sometimes carried no square canvas on the mizzen.Therefore, in the late eighteenth century and later, it came to denote a vessel with three or more masts, square rigged on all but the aftermost, which set only fore and aft canvas. Without further qualification the term usually applied to three-masted vessels, those with more being denominated four- or five-masted barques. Mediterranean barques, or *barques de négoce*, were an entirely different type, usually carrying three lateen rigged masts on a hull form that resembled a xebec; they dated from at least the seventeenth century.

barquentine or, in America, **barkentine**. A nineteenth-century term applied to a vessel with a full square rigged fore mast but fore and aft rigged main and mizzen; some later vessels had four or more masts.

bâteau boeuf. Single-masted lateen rigged fishing craft of the Golfe de Lion, occasionally used as a trading vessel.

bergantino. *See brigantino.*

beak, beakhead. The protrusion beyond the stem proper underneath the bowsprit that characterised galleons and their successors. Probably developed from the overhanging bow of the galley–the *sperone*–the beakhead served as a platform from which to handle the headsails and the site of the crew's latrines. Cut off from the forecastle by the beakhead bulkhead.

Bermuda sloop. An extreme version of the sloop (*qv*) rig with raked aft mast, long bowsprit and relatively large main sail. In eighteenth-century Britain this was known as the Bermudian or Bermudoes rig after its supposed place of origin.

bertone. An Italian description, common from the sixteenth and early seventeenth centuries onwards, of a specific type of vessel hailing from England or, more properly, from the British Isles. The type cannot be identified with any English term, and some scholars feel the etymology of the word may originally denote no more than 'Briton'. In later centuries it seems to have implied the standard three-masted ship rigged merchant ships of northern Europe.

bezan, bezaan. Description of the characteristic Dutch rig of tall sail with very short gaff; by extension, applied to craft that carried it like the *bezanjacht*.

bilander. A two-masted vessel with square rigged fore mast and square main topsail but a main sail set from a lateen; this latter was not triangular but had a vertically cut forward edge or luff. Most common in North Sea and Baltic traders.

billethead. A simple form of abstract decoration to the top of the stem where more sophisticated vessels had a figurehead. It was often carved like the end of a violin, which was then specifically called a fiddlehead; if it turned outwards instead of inwards, it was called a scrollhead.

billy-boy. A bluff-bowed capacious coastal trader associated with the northeast of England. Usually sloop or ketch rigged, it may have been developed from the Humber keel, which, although larger and more seaworthy, it generally resembled in overall appearance.

binnacle. The cabinet housing compasses, log glasses and watch glasses. Usually positioned directly before the wheel and divided into three compartments, with compasses in the outer ones (so that one was visible to the helmsman whichever side of the wheel he stood) and a light box between to illuminate them at night. Originally known as a bittacle, the form became more compact in the nineteenth century, and after the introduction of iron construction, prominent metal spheres were added to either side to compensate for the magnetism of the hull.

bitts. A frame of strong upright timbers and a cross piece to which ropes and cables were made fast. The most important were the riding bitts (double in ships of any size) to which the cables were secured when at anchor but there were others associated with the rigging.

bobstay. Piece of standing rigging between the end of the bowsprit and the ship's stem, designed to counteract the upward pull of the jibs.

Bock. Large barge used on the Weser in northwest Germany in the seventeenth century; up to 120ft long.

boeier, boyer. Sprit rigged Dutch coastal trader; from the mid sixteenth century the usual sail plan was a triangular jib, sprit main with two square sails, and a mizzen lateen (absent from earlier examples). *Boyers* averaged about 100 tons. Smaller examples of the hull form were often commonly used as yachts.

Boidack. Sprit rigged two-masted Prussian sailing lighter.

bok. Small Dutch inland sailing vessel of about 10-20 tons; sloop rigged with a counterbalanced mast for easy lowering.

bolster. Any item designed as a reinforcement against chafing, such as the moulded wooden pieces under the hawse holes or the pads of tarred canvas protecting the collars of the stays from rubbing the woodwork of the masts.

boltrope. Strengthening rope sewn around the extremities of a sail; divided according to position on the sail as head-, leech- and foot-ropes (top, sides and bottom, respectively).

bombarda, bombarde. A merchant ship type of the western Mediterranean whose hull form was based on the original French bomb *galiotes*, which were ketch rigged.

boom. A relatively light spar, such as a studding sail boom; most commonly applied, without qualification, to the spar that extended the foot of a spanker (*qv*).

boomkin, bomkin or **bumkin**. A small outrigger spar used to extend the corner of a sail; if used without qualification the term usually applied to those either side of the bow for the windward corner of the fore sail.

bootschip. A variant of the *fluit* (*qv*), but with wider, lower taffrail and stern windows; there was less tumblehome, so the deck was also broader. Ship rigged; used in many European trades, but in the eighteenth century often associated with whaling.

bovenlander. A large lighter used on the Upper Rhine in the seventeenth century.

bovo. A small craft, most commonly used for fishing, and closely associated with the Catalan coast.

bowline. Rope attached via three or four bridles to the leech (side) of the sail; led forward to hold the leech up into the wind when the ship was close-hauled (*qv*), from whence 'on a bowline' became synonymous with this point of sailing.

bowsprit. Heavy spar (in effect, a lower mast) angled forward over the bow; provided the support for the fore mast stays and allowed sail to be set far enough forward to have a significant effect on the balance of the rig.

bp. Between perpendiculars, sometimes given as pp: modern designer's measurement of length, omitting the overhang of stem and stern structures, as opposed to length overall; roughly equivalent to length on the lower deck as understood in the eighteenth century.

braces. Rigging that pivots the yards; to brace up was to swing them to as sharp (*ie* smallest) an angle with the keel as feasible; bracing in was the reverse.

brails. Rigging lines used to reduce and control the area of sail catching the wind.

bragozzo. A smaller, flat-bottomed version of the Adriatic *trabaccolo* (*qv*); mostly registered in the Italian side of the sea, and usually employed as a fishing boat. Two-masted lugger with larger main than fore.

bratsera. A two-masted Greek coaster of double-ended hull form common in the Ionian Sea, originally lug rigged in the eighteenth century but later carrying a modern brig-schooner sail plan.

brazzera. A smaller version of the *braggozzo* (*qv*); also used to describe a Dalmatian single-masted variant of the *trabaccolo* (*qv*).

brig. A two-masted square rigged vessel but with a fore and aft gaff-and-boom main sail; very similar to a snow (*qv*).

brigantine. Originally more a hull form than a rig, by the nineteenth century it came to denote a two-masted rig, square on the fore mast and fore and aft on the main; it was sometimes called a brig-schooner in some European countries.

brigantino, brigantin or *bergantino*. In the Middle Ages a type of small, fast oared craft, decked and rigged with a single mast and sail, much employed in the Mediterranean; although the origin of the later English term 'brigantine', at this time the word did not refer to a particular rig. Later Mediterranean usage tended to refer to craft descended from the oared type.

brig-schooner. *See* brigantine.

Bucintoro. The Venetian state barge that was used in the annual 'Marriage with the Sea' ceremony; the name supposedly derives from *buzin d'oro*, or 'golden barge'.

Buis. *See* buss.

Bullen. Small barges of about 20 tons used on the Weser in northwest Germany in the seventeenth century; up to 65ft long.

bumkin. *See* boomkin.

buntline. Rope from the foot of a square sail passing over the forward surface to the yard; used to spill the wind from a sail when necessary.

burthen. A measurement of capacity in tons calculated by formula from the dimensions of the ship. The precise formula varied over time and was different from country to country, but usually involved dividing by 94; it greatly underestimated the real displacement but may be regarded as a crude forerunner of gross tonnage (*ie* a measure of internal volume). When more sophisticated rules for tonnage calculation were introduced, tons burthen was designated Old Measurement or Builder's Old Measurement. *See also* measured tonnage.

buss. From the fifteenth century a seagoing fishing vessel with bluff bows, a square stern and a relatively long hull; they were usually rigged with three masts, each with a single square sail, all except one of which were struck when fishing, the one remaining sail gave the vessel enough way to keep the nets taut. *Buis* in Dutch, *byssa* in Swedish.

camel. Developed in response to the special shoal conditions on the coast of the Netherlands, the 'camel' was a primitive floating dock designed to lift deep-sea ships over the shallows and mudflats at the entrance to Dutch harbours and waterways, especially Amsterdam. The camel consisted of two parts, the insides of which were approximately shaped to the outsides of the ship's hull. Both parts were flooded down, lashed to the ship, and when the water was pumped out of the camel, the complete ensemble floated up to a draught that allowed it to be towed over the shallows. The process was reversed to allow the ship to sail on.

carvel. A method of construction in which the strakes of planking butt at the edges, creating a flush hull surface–as opposed to clinker (*qv*) in which the strakes overlap and are clenched through this overlap. Carvel as a method of construction implies the initial setting up of a frame to which the strakes are fastened, which in turn means that some form of preconceived design is necessary in order for a properly faired shape to result. The term is closely associated with caravel and the technique was probably imported into northern Europe from the Mediterranean, where in late Antiquity frame-first carvel had replaced the earlier shell-first structure where mortise and tenon joints formed the connections between strakes.

cat. In modern terminology a fore-and-aft rig that does not include any headsails. In the seventeenth and eighteenth century it was applied to a hull form, a capacious merchant ship type with round stern beneath a relatively narrow counter, and bluff bows; often used as a collier or in other bulk trades. Term probably derives from the Dutch *katschip* (*qv*).

caulk. To ram fibrous material (caulking) hard into a seam to make it watertight and to prevent the planks of the hull from sliding upon each other when the hull is subjected to longitudinal bending stresses.

chaland. A generic French term for barge, but specifically applied to the large (50- to 100-ton) open lighters of the Loire region; swim-headed, they were often towed but could set one large square sail.

channel.
(i) The navigable part of a river or stretch of water.
(ii) The platforms projecting from the hull abreast each mast to spread the shrouds (*qv*) and prevent them chafing against the hull (term derived from 'chain-wales').

chébec. Also called xebec or zebec. A low, fine-lined Mediterranean craft that began life as a Barbary corsair but soon came to be employed as a naval vessel and fast merchant-man in Christian states. Lateen rigged originally, but the hull form was later to carry a combination of square and lateen canvas and eventually even a full ship rig.

clench. To bend the protruding part of a spike or nail over to prevent it pulling out of timber; also, specifically, to rivet the end of a nail over a washer, or rove. *See also* clinker.

clew. Lower corner of square sail or after corner of a fore and aft sail; on square sails a tackle called a clewline (or clew garnets on courses) hauled them up to the yards.

clinker. Method of construction in which overlapping strakes are fastened along the edges (usually with nails 'clenched' over roves, from which the term derives). It is a shell-first technique, without the benefit of a pre-erected frame, although strengthening timbers are sometimes added later.

clipper. Much abused term of no real technical precision, but generally denoting a fine-lined, fast-sailing vessel. First applied to American small craft like the Baltimore clipper (*qv*), the description was widely employed in the mid nineteenth century.

close-hauled. The point of sailing as near to the direction of the wind as possible (about 70 degrees for a square-rigger, although fore and aft vessels can get somewhat nearer).

cog. The classic sailing ship of northern Europe in the high Middle Ages, the cog was developed on the Frisian coast from whence its usage spread to down the North Sea coasts and into the Baltic before reaching the Mediterranean. Its capacious flat-bottomed form, with straight raked stem- and stern-posts, is believed to derive from the technology of expanded logboats, but by the thirteenth century the type had evolved into a seagoing vessel of several hundred tons in its largest form. It acquired a stern rudder on the centreline to replace the steering oars and was powered by a single square sail.

convoy. A fleet of merchant ships gathered together under naval escort; originally, however, the term applied to the escort rather than the escorted.

counter. The area of overhang at the stern, beneath the cabin windows; usually divided into upper and lower counters.

courses. The lowest, and hence largest, sail on each mast; a lateen mizzen or spanker was also considered a course.

crank. Of ships, lacking in stability.

crayer. *See* kray.

crossjack. Pronounced 'crojack'; the lowermost mizzen square yard that extended the clews (*qv*) of the mizzen topsail. Unlike the fore and main yard it did not reguarly set its own sail, the lateen mizzen, and later the spanker (*qv*), being considered the mizzen course.

cryer. *See* kray.

cutter. Sharp lined fast-sailing coastal craft, originally clinker-built in the English Channel ports; carried a single-masted rig of large area, with a bowsprit of little steeve (*qv*). In this century there has been a tendency to differentiate between a cutter and a sloop by the multiple headsails of the former, but in the nineteenth century it was also a matter of hull form, since sloops might also carry a number of jibs.

cutwater. The leading edge of the bow, sometimes a separate structural member, that cleaves the water when the craft is under way.

damloper, damschuit. Ferries operating around the Amsterdam area in the seventeenth and eighteenth centuries, the principal characteristic of the *damloper* ('dam-walker'), and the smaller but otherwise similar *damschuit*, was the ability to be hauled over dams at specially constructed *overtoom* (*qv*) points, to move from one canal system to another with a different water level.

deadeye. Used in tensioning the shrouds (*qv*), these discs of wood were set up in pairs, one attached to the shroud itself and the other, via chains to the hull. Tensioning was achieved by a lanyard rove through three holes in each deadeye and bowsed tight.

deadrise. The angle of the floors in the midship section of a ship; one measure of the relative 'sharpness' of the hull lines, a vessel with a V-shaped section having much deadrise whereas one with a flat bottom had none.

Denmark sloop. A small, relatively fast-sailing Danish coaster developed during the Napoleonic Wars; rigged like a cutter, they rarley exceeded 10 tons.

defence ships. Government-subsidised armed merchant ships built by Denmark and Sweden with a view to their employment by their navies in wartime.

displacement. The mass of the volume of water occupied by the ship when afloat.

dolphin striker. Short spar beneath the bowsprit, perpendicular to its end, over which the martingale (*qv*) ran to guy the jibboom from below.

driver. A sail set on the mizzen that was originally a fine weather addition (initially a square sail but later a fore and aft extension of the mizzen) and finally a temporary replacement for a smaller gaff mizzen. Finally replaced by the spanker (*qv*) with which it is often confused.

Dorstense-aak. A large Rhine sailing barge, a member of the *aak* (*qv*) family and the nineteenth-century successor to the *samoreus* (*qv*).

dowel. Round rod of wood, usually driven into holes drilled into timber as a fastening or filling.

East Indiaman. The major passenger/cargo ship of the European East India Companies; the largest and most prestigious merchant ships of their day. The Dutch and English East India Companies are the best known, but France, Denmark and Sweden had equivalent companies, and very similar ships.

entrance. The fore part of the underwater hull; usually refers to its shape and the fineness of the lines in this area. *See also* run.

fay. To fit together closely.

felucca. Originally a small, fast galley-type Mediterranean craft that developed into a smaller version of the *chébec* (*qv*). The hull form featured a *sperone* (*qv*) and a long overhanging poop deck, rigged with two or three lateen masts. Widely used in Greek and Italian waters.

feluccone. A version of the *felucca* (*qv*) but with a higher stern and more pronounced sheer; essentially Genoese, but used elsewhere around Italy.

flat. Local name for various types of British sailing barge (*qv*), in the Mersey area for example.

floor. In shipbuilding, transverse timbers across the keel and bottom planking.

fluit, fluyt, flute, etc. Characteristically Dutch merchantman, ship rigged and of large carrying capacity, with extreme tumblehome and a narrow 'flute' stern. They were usually austere in decoration, with a plain stemhead, few if any guns, and a small crew relative to tonnage; there were, however, more conventional versions, with more powerful armament, for trading in dangerous waters. They were essentially a product of the late sixteenth century, but dominated the Dutch carrying trade in the seventeenth. Known as 'flyboats' to the English.

flush deck. One without a break or step; later applied to ships with an open weather deck, lacking substantial quarterdeck and forecastle structures above.

flyboat. English term for the Dutch *fluit* (*qv*).

fore and aft sails. Those carried on gaffs, sprits or stays that at rest hung in the fore and aft axis of the ship; opposite of square sails which were set from transverse yards. A vessel whose principal mode of propulsion came from such sails was said to be fore-and-aft rigged, as opposed to square rigged (*qv*).

forecastle. A structure over the forward part of the upper deck; in medieval times, a castle-like addition, but by 1650 a relatively lightweight platform useful for handling the headsails. When forecastle and quarterdeck (*qv*) were combined into a spar deck, the forward portion was still known as the forecastle.

forefoot. The forward extremity of the keel; extended beyond the line of the stem in a ram bow.

frame. The structural ribs of a wooden ship, comprising floor timber, a number of tiers of futtocks, and toptimbers.

frame-first. A term used by modern historians for ship- and boatbuilding in which the hull strakes are fastened to a pre-erected framework, as opposed to shell-first construction like clinker. In many contexts it is synonymous with carvel (*qv*), but is preferred as being a more precise definition than the old dichotomy between carvel and clinker, since there are methods of building hulls shell-first other than clinker.

freccia. A triangular topsail carried above the lateen main by the Italian *tartana* (*qv*).

freeboard. The height of the top edge of the hull amidships, or the bottom edge of an opening in the ship's side, above the water when the ship is afloat.

frigate. English usage generally confined the term to a naval cruiser, but 'frigate-built' was sometimes used of flush-decked ships with a similar layout. Elsewhere in Europe, the term was more widely applied to ship rigged merchantmen that possessed something of the appearance, the arrangements, and above all the speed, of a warship.

futtock. Portion of a ship's frame, between the lowest (floor) and highest (top-) timbers. By the eighteenth century there were four or five futtocks in overlapping pairs contributing to a 'framed bend', or rib.

gaff. A short spar to extend the head of a fore and aft sail; usually hoisted with the sail, for

which purpose it was equipped with jaws that fitted around the mast. A larger permanent (standing) gaff was sometimes called a half-sprit.

galeas (plural **galeaser**). Applied to various types of coastal traders in and around the Baltic, characteristics depending on country of origin and date: for example, the Swedish and Finnish version was a two-masted ketch in the eighteenth century, and a schooner for most of the nineteenth century, but a three-master developed towards the end of that period.

galleot. A small galley or 'half-galley'.

galjoot, galliot. A round-sterned ketch rigged vessel of Dutch origin. Usage varied from country to country: the Swedish galliot, for example, would probably be called a Dutch hoy or dogger in England. Dutch examples came to be employed as naval auxiliaries, and in the eighteenth century a three-masted version evolved. In the Baltic it was replaced by the *galeas* (*qv*), which retained the rig but adopted a flat stern.

garboard. The strake of planking nearest the keel, into which it is usually fitted by means of a 'rabbet' (rebate). It is thought to be derived, via Dutch, from 'gathering board' –presumably because it was where loose water would fetch up before being funnelled to the pumps.

gaskets. A securing for a furled sail, made from rope or canvas.

germa. See *jerma*.

glass shallop. Dutch horse-drawn passenger barge, with large glazed windows in the cabin sides; usually privately owned yachts.

Gozo boat. A lateen rigged coaster developed after 1870 from the Maltese *speronara* (*qv*).

guerre de course. French term for the strategy of commerce-raiding; the war against merchant shipping.

gudgeon. The part of the rudder hinge that was attached to the ship, containing a ring into which the pintle (*qv*) of the rudder itself fitted.

hagboat. See *hekboot*.

hagenaar. Small inland *aak* (*qv*) type vessel developed in the nineteenth century to carry bricks to The Hague, which necessitated passing low and narrow bridges. It had a lowering rig and a water ballast system to reduce 'air draught'.

hakkebord. An ornamental stern board or taffrail in some seventeenth- and eighteenth-century Dutch sailing craft.

halyard. Rope or tackle used to hoist sail or yard; sometimes spelt haliard or halliard.

hanging knee. L-shaped bracket fastening beam end to the ship's side; originally of naturally grown timber, iron knees were introduced in the late eighteenth century and became increasingly common in the nineteenth.

the Hanse. A trading confederation originally based on north German towns but coming to dominate the trade of most of northern

Europe and the Baltic. The Hanseatic League dates its foundation to Lubeck in 1159 and by the first half of the thirteenth century it included Hamburg, but eventually it was to unite the merchants of over thirty German towns into 'hansas' or chambers of commerce; it also set up outstations in important foreign entrepots like Bristol and London, Bergen in Norway, Visby in Sweden, and Novgorod in Russia. The Hanse aimed at commercial monopolies, and was particularly powerful in shipping and fishing, the characteristic ship-type being the cog (*qv*), a very cost-effective carrier in its day. The League declined in importance from the late fifteenth century, as trade patterns changed, new methods of business organisation were introduced, and a more competitive spirit was fostered, but its influence was still felt in the seventeenth century.

Harener punt. A scow-like peat-barge from the German state of Ostfriesland; sprit rigged.

heel. Of a ship, angle of inclination from the upright.

hekboot. Dutch merchant ship, sometimes called a hagboat in other northern European languages. A three-masted full rigged ship, the *hekboot* had a more conventional hull with less tumblehome–and consequently wider decks–than the *fluit* (*qv*).

herna. Inland craft of the Meuse, an *aak* (*qv*) type vessel up to 150ft long.

heude. An early type of Dutch vessel whose exact characteristics are uncertain, but was probably carvel built with a rounded hull and a single sprit mast (to which a small mizzen was later added); employed as both a coaster and an inland craft in the southern Netherlands in the fifteenth and sixteenth centuries.

Hinterhänge. Medium-sized barges of 40-50 tons used on the Weser in northwest Germany in the seventeenth century; up to 100ft long.

hoeker. A very seaworthy Dutch fishing craft characterised by a rig designed to give the maximum working area on the fore deck: a long bowsprit, a tall square rigged main mast stepped amidships, and a small gaff mizzen far aft. In the Baltic the term was applied to a three-masted vessel like a galliot (*qv*) but with a head, as well as a two-master with the Dutch rig.

hogging. Bending or shearing of a ship's hull so that its ends drop relative to the middle; caused by wave action in a seaway. Because of its fine lines fore and aft, a ship had more buoyancy amidships, which could cause the ship to arch upwards, distorting the structure and breaking the sheer, as it was described. This propensity to hog was enhanced in longer and more lightly constructed ships and was a major problem until structural improvements like the employment of iron strapping in the early nineteenth century gradually reduced hogging to manageable proportions.

hulk. Rather mysterious ship type of North Sea origins whose working career paralleled, and eventually outlasted, that of the cog (*qv*). What small iconographical evidence there is suggests a banana-shaped hull of very rounded form. As a regular type-name the word declined in the fifteenth century, and

eventually changed its meaning to indicate a dismasted vessel or one laid up and unfit for sea; if there is any connection between the two usages scholars have been unable to make a convincing case for it.

Humber keels. Barge-like riverine craft of the English east coast powered by a single square sail. This may be a survivor, in usage if not in form, of the medieval ship type the keel. The Humber sloop was similar but set a single gaff main and jib.

interloper. British trade with the East was technically the monopoly of the Honourable East India Company, but there were always unlicensed traders, who were known as 'interlopers'. The term was applied to the ships as well as the merchants.

jacht. The original Dutch type, whose name is derived from the verb *jagen* (to chase), was a fast, fine-lined vessel, rather like a reduced version of contemporary warships or East Indiamen; although etymologically related to the English 'yacht', it was only later that the word came to have connotations of pleasure. See also *pinnas*.

jekt. Family of Norwegian coastal vessels with a single square sail that represent a survival of Viking boat design and construction down to the early twentieth century when the last of the type were still in use.

jerma or *germa.* Ottoman cargo carrier, probably originating in Egypt. Not a lot is known about early examples but later they had a single lateen rigged pole mast and a long steeply steeved bowsprit on a hull of low freeboard and square counter.

jibboom. An extension of the bowprit (in effect its topmast); from the end of the eighteenth century, a further extension, called the flying jibboom, was added.

jigger. Nineteenth-century term for a fourth mast; also applied in earlier times to temporary canvas carried on an ensign staff, for example.

kaag. A common Dutch inland type much used as a ferry; single-masted, initially sprit rigged but later gaff. The vessel became more seaworthy as time went on and by the eighteenth century the characteristic straight stem had become curved.

Kaffekahn. See *kahn*.

kahn. German inland sailing barge of the Oder region; the type could be divided into the *Kaffekahn* with an *aak*-like swim bow, and the *Stevenkahn* with a stem. The original single-masted sprit rig was gradually cut down as steam towage and fixed bridges came to German waterways.

kalite. Turkish version of *galleot*.

kalyon. Turkish form of 'galleon', presumably referring to similar ships. The largest types were called *mogarbinas*.

karamürsal. A large Turkish merchantman of the seventeenth century, usually measuring 100-150 tons, rigged with single fore and main square sails and a lateen mizzen.

katschip. A Dutch merchant ship; in effect a smaller and simpler version of the *fluit* (*qv*), with flat bottom, pole masts, no topsails and a gaff mizzen.

kast. Nineteenth-century iron lighters used on the Rhine and related waterways.

keel.
(i) Lowermost structural member of a ship's hull; in a frame-built vessel effectively the backbone, the frames forming the ribs.
(ii) In many areas of England the term applied to a type of barge for river use, usually propelled by one large square sail, the best known survivor being the Humber keel (qv).

keelson. Longitudinal member laid over and secured to floors inside a ship above the keel.

keen. A sailing barge of the Rhine and related waterways, but smaller than the samoreus (qv); featured an aak (qv) hull form with a two-masted gaff rig.

ketch. A two-masted rig characterised by a main and mizzen (often said to be a ship rig without a fore mast); originally square rigged, but fore and aft versions became common later.

Keulenaar or *Keulsche aak*. *See samoreus*.

knot. Nautical measure of speed, 1 knot being one sea, or nautical, mile per hour. This equals 1 minute of latitude per hour or 1852 metres.

koftjalk. Dutch sailing coaster, a version of the tjalk (qv); called a galliot in Britain.

kray. A Baltic coaster, sometimes called a craier, crayer or cryer in English, ship rigged but with pole masts and nothing above the topsails.

kromstevens. Generic term for a class of Dutch craft with curved stemposts, including the wijdschip (qv) and smalschip (qv) and other predecessors of the tjalk (qv).

Kurische Reisekahn. A large (up to 250 tons) coastal and riverine vessel of the lower Vistula and the Baltic coast; gaff ketch rigged and relatively fine lined although flat-bottomed.

lanyard. Short piece of rope or line used to secure an item or act as a handle, such as the lanyard to a gunlock which allowed it to be triggered from a safe distance; lanyards between the deadeyes (qv) were used to tauten the shrouds.

lap-strake. Another term for clinker (qv).

lasts. An old Scandinavian measure of weight and bulk; of differing value in specific trades. Ships were also measured in lasts of about 2 tons.

lateen. Sail or rig characterised by triangular canvas set from a long yard attached to the mast at an angle of about 45 degrees from the horizontal, the forward end being the lower. It was a fore-and-rig rig dating from at least late Antiquity and was the usual form of sail for most types of Mediterranean craft thereafter, including galleys. In the late Middle Ages it was also added to square rigged vessels, usually as a small after sail to help balance the rig and aid going about, and retained this role with the development of the three-masted ship rig.

lautello. Two-masted coaster largely to be found in Sicily but also elsewhere in the Kingdom of Naples. The masts, which raked

forward for the main and aft for the mizzen, carried boom-footed lug sails; two jibs were set from a form of jibboom. The hull was notable for the reverse rake of the stem.

lee. The side or direction away from the wind or downwind (leeward); hence 'lee shore' is one onto which the wind is blowing.

leeboard. A plate of timber attached to the side of shallow draught vessels to reduce their leeway (drift downwind) when sailing close-hauled, on the same principle as the centre-board of a modern yacht. They were pivoted from the top so that the lee-side board could be let down below the level of the ship's bottom; the windward board was then hauled up out of the water. They are strongly associated with Dutch inshore craft, but the leeboard was widely applied wherever shallow waters restricted draught. The leeboard shape tended to be short and wide for smooth-water craft, and narrower and deeper for vessels intended for more open waters.

Letter of Marque. The formal commission that licensed privateers (qv) to act against their country's enemies. It could also be granted to merchant ships so they could legitimately capture weaker enemy ships if the opportunity should arise. By extension the term came to mean a merchant ship armed with such a licence, as opposed to a privateer proper: the latter went to sea specifically to attack the enemy whereas a Letter of Marque was employed as a trader that could do so if a suitable target should present itself.

liuto. A small cargo carrier from the Ligurian coast of Italy, averaging about 20 tons and mostly used in the wine trade. The rig was two-masted, usually lateen, but a smaller version of the navicello (qv) also developed.

llaut or *llagut*. Small fishing craft of the Catalan coast, usually of no more than 10 tons. They grew in size over time and also became coastal traders.

lodja. Trading and fishing craft of eastern Baltic rivers and the Russian White Sea coast, the term covered a variety of types which also developed over time; early examples were quite crude barge-like craft with a single square sail, built using a sewn plank technique, but nineteenth-century Russian survivors were more ship-like in form and carried a three-masted rig with square fore and main sails and a gaff mizzen.

londra. Turkish ship type about which little firm information exists. They seem to have been medium-sized sail-and-oar vessels in the seventeenth century, but the oars were abandoned in merchant versions before 1700.

lug. A rig characterised by a four-sided sail with a head about two-thirds the length of the foot; hoisted on an angled yard with about a quarter of its length ahead of the mast.

lugger. A lug rigged coastal craft, two- and sometimes three-masted which could also set lug topsails; fast and weatherly, they were popular with smugglers and privateers on both sides of the English Channel, but also with fishermen and legitimate traders.

mahona. A large Turkish sail-and-oar craft used in the Egypt-Istanbul trade; hull form with very pronounced sheer and overhanging stern. Usually powered by two or three large lateen sails.

martigos. *See martingana*.

martingale. The stay tensioning the jibboom from below, set up over the dolphin striker (qv).

martingana. A moderate-sized coaster from the Gulf of Naples and Sicily, ranging between 20 and 100 tons although 60 tons was about the norm. A felucca-like hull carried a form of ketch rig, with square main and topsails and a lateen mizzen. Its use spread to Malta and the Greek islands (where it was known as the martigos) before dying out around 1880.

measured tonnage. British calculation of the size of ships, used when building or buying vessels. From 1695 to 1773 it was calculated by the formula: $\frac{1}{94}$th the sum of length x breadth x $\frac{1}{2}$ breadth; in 1773 it was changed to $\frac{1}{94}$th the sum of (length–$\frac{3}{5}$ breadth) x breadth x $\frac{1}{2}$ breadth. From 1786 this latter calculation was used for the vessel's registered tonnage (qv). It survived until 1836, when it became known as Builder's Old Measurement, a revised calculation being introduced as New Measurement.

mercantilism. Name given to a theory of economics which predicated that the success of one state could only be at the expense of another, leading to protectionist legislation, like the British Navigation Acts (qv), and the use of taxation and customs duties to promote home trade and deter those of foreign rivals. Largely replaced by more liberal Free Trade ideas in the nineteenth century.

metacentre. The point, usually designated M, in the middle plane of the ship through which the buoyancy force passes when the ship is inclined from the upright by a small angle.

metacentric height. The height of the metacentre (qv) above the ship's centre of gravity (usually designated G); it is, therefore, often designated GM.

mignole. Smaller version of the herna (qv).

mistico. A version of the chébec (qv) with similar hull but square rig; other sources treat them simply as small chébecs.

mizzen. The aftermost mast of a ship–or in a two-masted vessel the after mast if the forward one is larger–and the yards, sails and rigging pertaining to it.

moedernegotie. The 'mother trade', the Dutch term for their all-important Baltic business.

mortise. In carpentry a recess cut to receive a tenon (qv).

mot. A German peat barge from Ostfriesland.

navicello. Coastal craft of the Ligurian coast of Italy, in which a tartana-like hull was combined with an unusual two-masted rig–a main with a fidded topmast carried a lateen (later replaced with a loose-footed gaff sail), combined with a short forward-raking fore mast, between which two staysails were set, plus a small jib forward. They flourished from about 1600 to the late nineteenth century.

Navigation Acts. A system of British restrictive legislation dating back to the seventeenth century (although there were even earlier

precedents) which aimed at retaining British trade in British ships. Repealed in 1849 as part of Britain's new commitment to Free Trade.

NHM. Initials of the Nederlandsche Handel Maatschappij, the Netherlands Trading Company, founded in 1824 that dominated trade with Java and the other Dutch Far East colonies.

Noortsvaerder. Dutch term for a vessel in the Norway timber trade; they were usually fitted with special timber loading ports in the bow or stern which were sealed before sailing.

occulus. A device in the form of an eye, sometimes highly stylised, painted on the bows of ships since antiquity for reasons of religion or superstition.

Oostervaerder. Dutch term for vessel trading with the 'East' (ie the Baltic); optimised for the shallow harbours of the region.

overtoom. Seventeenth-century Dutch waterways were often operated at different water levels, requiring expensive locks for large craft, but smaller vessels were simply hauled over dams and dykes by a specially constructed ramp called an overtoom. See also damloper.

packet or **pacquet**. Fast mail-carrying craft; usually government sponsored like British Post Office packets.

pailebot. A Mallorcan schooner type, the name being derived from 'pilot boat', although they did not closely resemble the Anglo-American pattern, being rather more capacious. A nineteenth-century development, some survived with cut-down rig into the 1930s. Also called a paquetbot.

parral, parrel. An assemblage of beads called trucks and wooden dividers called ribs strung onto a series of horizontal ropes. Forming a collar between yards and their masts, and designed to allow the yard to be raised and lowered easily, the parrel vaguely resembled a flexible abacus, with revolving beads intended to reduce friction while the ribs stopped them moving from side to side.

pavillion, *paviljoen*. The cabin on various Dutch craft, in terminology often used to differentiate them from more open craft of similar type: for example, a pavillion-tjalk.

petaccio or *petachio*. A medium-sized vessel of 100-200 tons and 6-18 guns used by the Barbary corsairs for both privateering and trade. Probably derived from the earlier patache, a small pinnace-like vessel (usually less than 100 tons), they were used on duties where speed and manoeuvrability were at a premium.

pinas. *See pinnas*.

pinco, pinque. Probably originating in Genoa, although found throughout the western Mediterranean, this three-masted lateen rigged merchantman somewhat resembled the chébec (qv), but the hull was more capacious; the fore and main lateens could be replaced with square yards and sails when the wind was from astern.

pink. In northern waters the term was usually applied to a vessel with a narrow 'pinched' stern, although the word also described a small Dutch fishing craft.

pinnace. In the sixteenth century, an English version of the Dutch *pinnas* (*qv*) but confined to smaller vessels; they were usually fast warships, used for scouting and dispatch duties–what a later age would call a frigate. By the late seventeenth century the term was confined to a boat type.

pinnas or **pinas** (plural **pinnassen**). A Dutch fine-lined, galleon-type vessel of the sixteenth and seventeenth centuries, usually employed as a warship or armed trading vessel; in some contexts synonymous with *jacht* (*qv*).

pintle. The part of the rudder hinge fixed to the rudder itself, consisting of a downward-facing pin engaging the gudgeon (*qv*) on the sternpost.

pleit. A Flemish inland sailing barge to be found on the Schelde and its tributaries and the Zeeland estuary; single- or two-masted depending on size, which might reach 180 tons for the largest.

polacca, **polacre**. Mediterranean trading vessel, originally lateen rigged; later examples acquired square topsails but set on single-piece masts (*ie* no separate upper masts) and thereafter the term came to denote pole-masted.

polaccone. The single large, spinnaker-like headsail carried by a number of Mediterranean traditional craft.

pole-masted. In conventional sailing ships the masts were usually set up in sections–lower mast, topmast, topgallant, etc– but pole-masted vessels (usually small craft) had single-piece masts without the extra weight of doublings, crosstrees, and so forth associated with fidded masts. *See also polacca*.

poon. Very seaworthy Dutch inland craft, characterised by a curved stem, steep sheer, and exaggerated tumblehome; single-masted sprit or gaff rig. Mostly to be found in the southeastern provinces of the Netherlands.

poop. Deck above the quarterdeck (*qv*); often no more than the roof of the cabins below. On merchant ships with a flush weather deck, the after superstructure which might have been called the quarterdeck on a warship, was usually known as the poop.

praam, prame, pråm. A shallow-draught, barge-like vessel, often with a flat stem–this aspect of the type survives in English in the familiar pram dinghy.

privateer. A privately owned and manned warship, fitted out primarily to profit from capturing the merchant shipping of the enemy. It was controlled by a system of government licence. *See also* Letter of Marque.

quarterdeck. After deck, above the main or weather deck and beneath any poop; the usual position of the ship's wheel and the station of the officer(s) conning the ship.

registered tonnage. In Britain the ship's official tonnage carried in the ship's register; based on carrying capacity and smaller than the calculated 'measured tonnage' (*qv*) figure. From 1786, however, the measured tonnage was used for registration purposes so the two became synonymous.

retourschepen. Ships of the Dutch East India Company, designed to make the long round trip to the Far East, bringing back the rare,

and consequently very valuable, goods that made the trade so profitable. As a result, the ships were large, well armed for self-defence, and costly both to build and to operate; they were regularly employed as auxiliary warships in wartime.

Rhineclipper. Large ketch rigged sailing ships developed in the 1860s and '70s for use on the Rhine; noted for their speed, they were steel hulled and anything up to 300 tons. Some were later tried in coastal trades, but were not well suited to this employment.

river-clipper. See *Rhineclipper*.

round tuck stern. A hull form in which the after planking is curved in to the sternpost, rather than meeting a flat transom as in the square tuck stern (*qv*).

run. The after part of the underwater hull; the opposite of entrance (*qv*).

saëte or **sagete**. In earlier centuries a fast Genoese oar-and-sail craft, rigged with a single lateen mast and ranging in size from 14 oars to 80 oars, but later applied to a large ship rigged Turkish merchantman, although not much is known about its specific characteristics.

sageties. See *saëte*.

sagging. The opposite of hogging (*qv*).

saïka or **saique**. Cargo vessel of moderate size widely used in the Ottoman empire; rigged with a form of ketch sail plan–a square rigged main and lateen mizzen.

sakoleva. A medium-sized Greek coastal trader with a distinctive rig of sprit main with square topsails, a lateen mizzen (and sometimes a jigger as well), and triangular jib headsails. The term occurs from at least 1600 and survived in numbers down to the end of the nineteenth century.

salme. Turkish unit of weight, approximately ¹⁄₁₁th of a ton.

samoreus. Large sailing barge (100-300 tons) operating on the Lower Rhine between the seventeenth century and about 1850 when it was replaced by more modern types; ketch rig with sprit sails plus a square main for running before the wind. Often Cologne was the destination so the type was also known as the *Keulenaar* or *Keulsche aak* to Dutch crews.

sandal. A ship type of various characteristics: a Tunisian small coaster, like a single-masted *tartana*; an open boat used in the Bosporus; a small Spanish two-masted coaster.

schiabecco. See *chébec*.

schifazzo. A Sicilian coaster of capacious hull form; mostly owned in Trapani, but traded as far as Tunis.

schooner. Gaff rigged vessel with two or more masts, originating around 1700; later examples had square topsails. *See also* topsail schooner.

scoote. A variation of *skuta* (*qv*).

Seamen's Sixpences. A form of national insurance raised from British seamen to support the Greenwich Hospital, a home for retired sailors.

shallop. In the early seventeenth century, a large seaworthy boat, possibly the ancestor of

the sloop (*qv*); the term continued to denote a boat type, although a rather lighter and more decorative craft, down to the nineteenth century.

sheer. In the profile of a ship the upward curve towards the ends of the hull.

sheerstrake. The uppermost strake of the hull proper below the gunwale.

shell-first. A term used by modern historians for ship- and boatbuilding in which the hull strakes are fastened together to form the hull shape without the benefit of a pre-erected framework (although strengthening frames may be added later). Overlapping clinker (*qv*) and the ancient Mediterranean method of securing strakes with internal mortise and tenon joints are examples.

ship rig. In the age of sail the ship, or full, rig was defined as the principal driving sails on all three masts being square (in the nineteenth century a few four- and one five-masted full-riggers were built, but the vast majority carried three masts; two square rigged masts made the vessel a brig). The lower sail on the mizzen usually comprised fore and aft canvas but as long as square sail was carried above it the rig was still rated as a ship.

shroud. Heavy rope supporting a mast from behind and transversely.

sixty-fourth share. The ownership of British vessels was conventionally divided in 64 parts, the joint owners taking any number of ¹⁄₆₄th shares.

skuta (*plural* **skutor**). Scandinavian coastal trader; early Swedish versions had one or two masts, each with a single square sail, but there are later examples with three masts.

sloop. Originally a boat designation, in the merchant marine the term came to denote a rig: a single-masted gaff vessel with fixed bowsprit and jib headsails, and usually no square topsails.

smack. Small inshore fishing craft, usually cutter (*qv*) rigged.

smakship. Medium sized Dutch inland craft, but seaworthy enough for operations on the Wadden and Zuyder seas; ketch rigged, in the seventeenth century usually with sprit main and gaff mizzen, but later examples had a gaff main plus square topsails.

smalschip. A Dutch canal craft of the *krom-steven* (*qv*) type; literally translated as 'narrow ship', in contrast to the *wijdschip* (*qv*).

snow. Two-masted square rigged vessel, with gaff-headed main course; in later eighteenth century definitions, this gaff sail had to be hoisted on a rope horse or separate trysail mast (to distinguish the snow from the brig, which hoisted its gaff course directly on the main mast), the sail itself being loose-footed–not being extended by a boom. *See also* brig.

Spanienfarare. Swedish 'Spanish Trader', a vessel in the Iberian and Mediterranean trades, notable for a relatively powerful armament for defence against Barbary corsairs.

spanker. Large gaff-and-boom sail; the main course of a brig and mizzen course of ships and barques.

sperone. The bow extension common on many Mediterranean ship types; a hangover from medieval galley design, which featured an above-water spur, in later types it often served the function of a fixed bowsprit, to secure the fore stays and related headsails. *See also* beak.

speronara. Usually associated with Malta, although this small coaster was also built in Sicily; seaworthy double-enders, sometimes undecked, and rarely more than 25 tons, the rig varied over time, examples including sprit and lateen sail plans carried on one or two masts. Called *xprunara* in Maltese.

spitsbek. Smaller version of the *herna* (*qv*).

sprit topmast. The small mast carried by large seventeenth-century ships at the end of the bowsprit from which a small square sail called the sprit topsail was set; it tended to die out in the early 1700s, being replaced by triangular jib headsails.

square rig. Any sail plan in which the principal power was derived from canvas set from yards which crossed the centreline of the ship (the yards were 'square'–at right angles–to the centreline when the wind was directly aft).

square sails. Canvas set from yards that at rest were carried at right angles to the centreline of the ship; as opposed to fore-and-aft canvas set from stays or yards on the centreline, or nearly so.

square tuck stern. Hull design in which the stern at the waterline is formed of a flat transom, as opposed to the round tuck (*qv*).

staatsie. The high stern, usually enclosing a steering platform, in some seventeenth- and eighteenth-century Dutch sailing craft.

stability. The strength of a ship's tendency to return to the upright, *ie* to right herself. The righting moment in tonne-metres = displacement in tonnes x metacentric height in metres x sine of the angle of heel.

standing rigging. The permanently set up support for the masts and tops–stays, shrouds etc.

stapelmarkt. The Dutch term for the entre-pôt market that grew up in the Netherlands in the seventeenth century and helped to make the country the centre of world trade.

steeve. The angle of the bowsprit relative to the waterline; the larger the angle, the more steeply steeved the bowsprit was said to be.

Stevenkahn. See *kahn*.

stiff. Having a good reserve of stability and hence able to carry sufficient sail in all weathers; the opposite of crank (*qv*).

storebåt. Literally, the 'big boat', the craft owned by many Scandinavian coastal farms that was used to take produce and people to the markets of larger towns.

Straetsvaerder. Dutch term for ship trading through the 'Straits' (of Gibraltar) into the Mediterranean. They tended to be more strongly built and much more heavily armed than *fluits* (*qv*), and were more galleon-like in appearance, with a full head and quarter galleries.

top hamper. General term for masts, spars and rigging.

studding sails. Additional fair weather square sails set on each side of the principal sails with removeable yards and booms; pronounced stuns'ls and often written as stunsails.

sump. A Swedish wet-well fishing craft.

tack. When sailing with the wind anywhere but aft, a rope used to extend to windward the lower corners of courses (*qv*) and staysails as sheets confined them to leeward; by extension it also applied to the parts of the sail to which it was attached. When so sailing, either the port or starboard tacks were said to be on board, from whence came the phrase port tack or starboard tack and the term tacking for the manoeuvre of changing course from one oblique angle to the wind to the other.

tartana, tartane. Another Mediterranean ship-type term whose meaning varied according to time and context. Italian examples tended to have a clipper bow, and set a single-masted lateen rig, although it might include up to three headsails and a triangular topsail, called the *freccia*; and a fair-weather kite called a *pallone*; the term was also applied to three-masted versions, rather like a *felucca* (*qv*). The larger French *tartanes* often carried two lateen masts, and their size grew from around 20 tons in 1680 to 100 tons at the end of the next century, before they began to be replaced by *chébecs* (*qv*) and *barques* (*qv*).

tenon. Rectangular block of hard wood, each half-length being fitted into opposing mortises (*qv*) to join two timbers side by side. Tenons may be locked into place by being drilled through and pegged.

tjalk. Something of a generic term for Dutch inland craft of the *kromsteven* (*qv*) hull form developed from the mid nineteenth century onwards; a related type was the coastal *koftjalk* (*qv*).

tjotter. Originally a small single-masted wet-well fishing boat from Friesland, somewhat like a *boeier* and like the latter later widely adopted as a pleasure yacht in the Netherlands.

topgallant. The mast, yard, sail and rigging above the topmast (*qv*).

top hamper. General term for masts, spars and rigging.

topmast. The portion of a mast (and its rigging) above the top, usually separate from the lower section; its sail was called the topsail, which gave its name to the yard and running rigging.

topsail schooner. A schooner (*qv*) with square canvas on at least one topmast.

trabaccolo. Two-masted lug rigged coaster of the Adriatic region.

trailboard. The timbers (usually decorated) between the cheeks and the knee of the head, below the headrails.

treenails, trenails, trennels, etc. Wooden dowels used as fastenings in shipbuilding; preferable in some situations to nails or bolts since they do not corrode.

trim. The fore and aft attitude of the ship; if the ship draws more water aft than forward, for example, she is said to 'trim by the stern'.

trow. British local type of sailing barge, like those associated with the river Severn.

trysail. A gaff-and-boom sail set from an auxiliary (trysail) mast or rope horse; the trysails that replaced staysails were called spencers in nineteenth century navies. Trysail was also used of the reduced storm canvas employed by small craft in place of the regular main.

tumblehome. The curving-in of the ship's side above the waterline; this feature was abandoned in the nineteenth century, the resulting ships being described as wall-sided.

vangs. Braces from the peak of a gaff, sprit or lateen yard; led to the deck.

velaccière. A nineteenth-century Mediterranean form of barquentine (*qv*) setting square canvas on the fore mast but lateens on the main and mizzen. They were principally associated with Naples but were also to be found in the south of Spain.

VOC. Initials of the Vereenigde Oostindische Compagnie, the Dutch East India Company, founded in 1604 and whose independence was effectively ended when the company was taken over by the state in 1795.

votive ship or **ex-voto.** Usually a model dedicated to a church or saint as a thank offering or a mark of piety by seafarers.

wale. Thickened strakes of external hull planking acting as longitudinal strength members.

weather helm. A well balanced sailing vessel will usually have a tendency to gripe or come up into the wind, which is considered far safer in emergencies because if control is lost the ship will end up head to wind and more or less stationary. However, under sail it is necessary to offset this tendency by use of the steering, holding the helm or tiller up to windward; for this reason a vessel with this most desirable characteristic is said to carry weather helm.

West Indiaman. Any vessel trading with the West Indies, but usually confined to those built specially for the trade.

westlander. A late nineteenth-century replacement for the *bok* (*qv*).

wherry.
(i) A light fine-lined pulling boat mostly used on rivers for the transportation of small numbers of passengers.
(ii) A barge-like inland craft used on the Norfolk Broads; rigged with a single large loose-footed gaff sail.

whipstaff. A vertical lever attached to the end of the tiller to allow the helmsman to stand at least one deck higher and possibly in sight of the sails.

WIC. Initials of the West-Indische Compagnie, the Dutch West India Company, set up in 1621. The original company was dissolved in 1674 and the reorganised company was retitled the GWC, or Geoctroyeerde Westindische Compagnie ('Chartered West India Company'), and survived until the early 1790s.

wijdschip. A Dutch inland craft of the *kromsteven* (*qv*) type; literally translated as 'wide ship', in contrast to the *smalschip* (*qv*), this type was more seaworthy and so was suitable for use on estuaries and inland seas.

windward. Towards or on the side from which the wind blows; the weather side. The opposite of leeward or lee side.

xprunara. See *speronara*.

yard. Spar from which sail was set, irrespective of whether the vessel be square or fore-and-aft rigged (*qv*).

yawl. A two-masted fore and aft rig in which the mizzen was very much smaller than that of a ketch (*qv*) and usually stepped abaft the sternpost.

Zille. A Bohemian river craft that enjoyed a remarkable three-stage existence: initially a crude raft that was floated down the river Moldau to Bodenbach; there it was reconstructed into a a more ship-like craft called a *Markt Zille* and, loaded with coal or basalt, went down the Elbe to Magdeburg or other German cities; on arrival it was usually broken up for the timber, but sometimes traded for a few more years.

Index